The Savory Way

The Savory Way

by

Deborah Madison

Illustrations by Patricia Curtan

BROADWAY BOOKS / NEW YORK

BROADWAY

A hardcover edition of this book was originally published in 1990 by Bantam Books, a division of Bantam Doubleday Dell Publishing Group, Inc.

Broadway Books titles may be purchased for business or promotional use or for special sales. For information, please write to: Special Markets Department, Bantam Doubleday Dell Publishing Group, Inc., 1540 Broadway, New York, NY 10036.

BROADWAY BOOKS and its logo, a letter B bisected on the diagonal, are trademarks of Broadway Books, a division of Bantam Doubleday Dell Publishing Group, Inc.

First Broadway Books trade paperback edition published 1998.

Designed by David Bullen.
Illustrations by Patricia Curtan.

Library of Congress Cataloging-in-Publication Data
Madison, Deborah.
The savory way / by Deborah Madison.
p.   cm.
Originally published: New York : Bantam Books, c1990.
Includes bibliographical references (p.   ) and index.
ISBN 0-7679-0166-5 (pbk.)
1. Cookery.   I. Title
TX714.M335   1998
641.5—dc21   97-45596
CIP

98 99 00 01 02 10 9 8 7 6 5 4 3 2 1

For my sister, Jamie

Table of Contents

SOUPS AND STEWS: *A Meal in a Bowl*

EIGHTEEN QUICK PASTA DISHES AND FIVE FOR COMPANY

STOVETOP VEGETABLES: *Simple Sautés and Braises*

BAKED AND ROASTED VEGETABLES

GRILLED VEGETABLES AND THEIR SAUCES

FINISHING TOUCHES: *Sauces, Salsas, and Condiments*

SWEETMEATS: *The Final Flourish*

APPENDIX

Acknowledgments

Many people have participated in this book, some unknowingly and others very directly. I wish to thank them all.

A book about food and cooking could not come about in a vacuum. Friends who have shared their warmth and support as well as many meals are what have made this book possible. Without them, the joy of cooking would indeed be faint. I particularly wish to thank my new community of friends in Flagstaff—especially the Lamberson family, Dottie House, Jon Shulman, Dena Dierker, Bill Burke, Phyllis Hogan, Dave Edwards, Pat Stein, Ann and Arnold Johnson, and Betty Hoyt, not only for their friendship but for sharing their know-how and the bounty of their gardens. My heartfelt thanks also to James Turrell and the Roden Crater Project for the inspiration to come here and stay; to Craig Baumhofer for rebuilding this old house with phenomenal patience and skill; to Ernie Macy for teaching me to ride; to Shirley and Dimitrios for their Greek dinners and genuine hospitality.

The willing and patient participation of my editor, Fran McCullough, has been utterly essential to the making of this book, and working with her has been truly a pleasure—sharing meals, thinking about food, writing and rewriting. I would also like to thank Coleen O'Shea, my other editor at Bantam Books, for her steadfast support and faith in this project. Michael Katz has been much more than an agent; he has also been a wonderful friend, critic, and voice of encouragement at all times. Jane Hirshfield has been on hand from the beginning, enduring the first rough drafts, always asking the right questions and helping me to shape this book. I am also thankful for the skillful eyes and hands of David Bullen, the designer of this book, and Pat Curtan, the artist, whose visions have helped express my own.

The subject of food is so essential and common to us all that everyone we meet has something to offer. Some people I'd particularly like to acknowledge and thank are Dan Welch, the baddest cook and best of friends I know, who shared many of these meals; Rosanna Migliarino, who cooked the good, simple food for her family that so touched me, and who graciously taught me the ropes in Rome, how to hunt for wild plants, how to shop and so much more; Lindsey Shere, whose wonderfully subtle sensibilities in the realm of desserts have long inspired me; Marion Cunningham, whose forthright manner in life and in the kitchen has given much joy; my father for his sensibility in the garden and appreciation of plants, which he has always shared with me; and my mother for the painterly eye she brings to her cooking, which is also part of my own way of seeing things. I would also like to thank all those people I don't know but whose efforts have somehow touched me—farmers everywhere who work so hard to bring forth the essential elements; the anonymous cooks in restaurants of all kinds who have made something wonderful and sustaining, whether plain or fancy; the women in the markets of Oaxaca with their charcoal braziers and green herb *moles;* the fruit-man in some other foreign market who once encouraged me to try something new . . . this list is truly endless, and so is my gratitude.

Introduction

The word *savory* isn't one we use very often, but to me it suggests the place where flavor and fragrance meet, in foods with deep, full tastes that are exciting to the palate. The savory way takes into account the nature of the food itself, its promise as well as its limitations. It considers how best to bring to the table dishes that are alive and sparkling with colors, shapes and fragrance. This food has character and even elegance; but at heart it's simple home cooking, nourishing food set forth in a climate of happy anticipation.

In my own cooking history simple home food is a relatively recent phenomenon. Although my strong interest in food was established when I was quite young, somehow I was always cooking for crowds of people in other people's kitchens—for a community, for a summer resort, or just running a restaurant. When I was involved in other projects, I sometimes didn't cook at all for a year at a stretch. It's only in the past few years that I've come to see what it really means to cook for oneself every day at home—and I admit that there are days when I'm happy to eat just one simple dish and call it supper. As I've watched my friends add children to their already busy lives, I've begun to see the enormous effort required just to get dinner on the table. I well understand the appeal of the microwave oven in these pressured circumstances. On the other hand, I still have the same standards for what I want to eat as I did in my restaurant days, and the microwave just can't produce the same results (which is not to say that microwave aficionados won't be able to speed up some of the processes here, especially steaming and stewing). Besides, I'd miss the touching, smelling, watching, and listening that are central to traditional cooking and also its joy.

My solution to these dilemmas is to look for dishes that are uncomplicated and quickly made, even if they take a bit longer to develop flavor while they roast or bake or simmer on the stove unattended. The tastes are clearly discernible, either as distinct elements in simple sautés or as more complex combinations that slowly yield their flavors to the whole dish and fill the kitchen with their good aromas as they cook. There are also a number of recipes that are more involving, for those occasions when we want to take some extra time to cook something special.

The recipes are designed to be flexible. Many can be used as a one-dish meal or fit easily into a larger menu. Some will immediately quell an urgent appetite; others require leisurely cooking to prepare pantry items that will brighten ordinary foods. Some dishes are made with very little or even no fat at all while others make use of more traditional amounts of butter and cream for those luxurious foods we like to eat on special occasions. In the absence of the perfect ingredient, there are suggestions that acknowledge the usefulness of frozen or canned alternatives.

Because produce itself, along with herbs and flowers, has always been my surest inspiration in the kitchen, fresh produce is emphasized throughout the book. Our efforts to seek out really good produce are always repaid by the pleasure it gives us. When I lived in California, the quality of produce was never at issue. But this book was written in northern Arizona, in a small town far removed from farms and the urban passion for sophisticated ingredients. At first this seemed like a great limitation, but in the end it inspired me. Even in an ordinary supermarket there is a surprising amount to work with, and of course many American cooks have little else to choose from. While I've had to forget about juicy ripe figs and superlative tomatoes, there is a reliable supply of unusual vegetables, Asian foods, special vinegars, good oils, Mexican chilies and spices, and other pleasant surprises. And I've found some unexpected sources of good ingredients that weren't apparent at first—the chili man from New Mexico who sets up his stand and roaster in the fall, the local arboretum for herbs, a network of women who bring down wonderful fruit from Utah in the summer, the generosity of avid gardeners who grow enough to share, a local Mexican grocery, to name but a few.

These recipes come from many sources, most of them written down in an old notebook. Some are foods I grew up with and have a special affection for, like Concord Grape Pie. Some come from a particular passion for foods like figs and quinces, lovage, or aromatic oils. Others are inspired by people I've had the pleasure to work and cook with, especially Alice Waters, Lindsey Shere, and my other friends at Chez Panisse. I'm always surprised to see how the way someone habitually does some simple thing, like cutting a vegetable in a particular way, can change the entire look and feel of a dish and how much it may differ from my own. Students in my classes have taught me, through their questions, what details to pay attention to and what they mean—the sudden presence of an aroma or sound that alerts you to change the heat or add an ingredient; the essential sign that tells you a dish is done. I've tried to bring this information, which is about the process of cooking itself, to the recipes so that they can serve as points to depart from as well as interesting approaches in themselves. It's my hope that each of us, in our own way, will continue to find in real cooking the pleasure, relaxation, and vitality that are so important to our happiness and health.

Quick Bites

Sandwiches and Toasts

Spreads

Special Breads

This collection of recipes is for all the times you want a quick and tasty bite—sandwiches for light meals or to nibble on while dinner is cooking, snacks to quell a vigorous appetite, savory toasts and flaky pan breads to serve with drinks. They can be used in lots of different ways. An assortment of colorful and tasty open-faced sandwiches can be offered as an hors d'oeuvre to friends before going out to dinner, for instance. Even if the rest of the meal is brought in from elsewhere, one or two of these little bites will bring a more personal touch to your table. If you're serving leftovers or a very light dish, these nibbles will perk up the familiar food or round out a modest meal.

Here are recipes for succulent sandwiches and crisp toasts; fresh herb cheeses, spreads, olive and artichoke pastes to have on hand for impromptu appetizers. Combined with some of the preserves, pickles, and sauces from "Finishing Touches" and kitchen staples like canned chick-peas, tortillas, or frozen loaves of special breads, there are many possibilities for quick bites to make on the spur of the moment.

Good, substantial bread is fundamental; it's the essential foundation of a sandwich and nourishing enough to complete an otherwise light meal. Local bakeries can be a good source for basic breads—white breads, whole wheat, mixed grain, and sourdough, but I've included some recipes that are particularly unusual: two Italian breads filled with cheese or olives, a pine nut bread washed with a red chili glaze, and "Moroccan pizzas" filled with savory butters. These densely flavorful breads can be sliced and served alone or as part of a collection of tidbits on a plate—olives and roasted peppers, walnut sauce with crisp sticks of fennel or jicama.

Of course breads are not in themselves quick to make, but fresh homemade bread always provides a special pleasure to those who partake. Once you're baking, it's not really any more trouble to double a recipe, so plan on making enough to enjoy one loaf fresh and freeze the rest. The finished bread can be frozen whole or sliced, so you can remove just what you need. Or the dough can be shaped and frozen, transferred to the refrigerator to defrost before you leave for work, and then baked in the evening. If your household is small, make little loaves and freeze the extras. They'll be there to use when you want them, and they'll easily become part of your repertoire of quick bites.

Alan Chadwick and a Lovage Sandwich

Alan Chadwick, the noted gardener who introduced the French Intensive Method of gardening to this country, had strong opinions about many things, including food. His memory and appreciation for the old ways of doing things were clear and deep, and he could speak wisely and hypnotically about food, from Turkish delight (clouds of sugar rising) to stuffed marrows. When he described a dish, he began with the plant in the garden—its precise condition and age—and then went on to give equally exacting instruction about the cooking. He used to say that cooking is done in the garden, and when that's not complete, the gardening has to take place in the kitchen.

He once suggested this sandwich for a Scottish breakfast. Lovage is a handsome perennial herb with leaves that look and taste like parsley and celery combined. In fact, in the absence of lovage you can substitute a mixture of parsley and celery leaves. If an herb sandwich seems a bit earthy for breakfast, try it for lunch. Use the lovage butter on page 310 or make a sandwich with the following ingredients.

Makes 1 sandwich

> 1 or 2 slices whole grain bread
> unsalted butter
> chopped lovage leaves and young shoots or a
>   mixture of parsley and celery leaves
> salt
> freshly ground pepper

Spread fresh bread with butter, cover with chopped herbs, salt lightly and season with pepper. Eat as an open-faced sandwich or top with a second slice of bread.

Suggestion: Mix together a few tablespoons of unsalted butter with a generous quantity of lovage leaves or a mixture of parsley and celery leaves. Season with salt and pepper. Spread on sturdy slices of white or whole wheat bread and cover with thinly sliced cucumbers. Dust with additional pepper and serve.

Nasturtium Sandwich

If you think of nasturtiums and watercress as close relatives, which they are, then using nasturtium leaves and flowers in a sandwich might seem almost traditional. The peppery taste of the nasturtium leaves and flowers has a clear similarity to watercress. Be sure the flowers you use are unsprayed.

Makes 1 sandwich

> *nasturtium or watercress leaves*
> *olive oil*
> *lemon juice*
> *salt*
> *unsalted butter*
> *white or whole wheat bread*
> *nasturtium flowers, the petals separated from the calyxes*

Nasturtium plants are prolific, so choose the smallest, most tender leaves. Wash and dry them, remove the stems, and lightly chop the leaves. Dress them with a little oil and lemon juice. Salt lightly. Spread a thin layer of butter over the bread, cover with the dressed nasturtium leaves and several petals, and cover with another slice of bread. Cut the sandwiches into triangles and serve.

Sabzee—Green Herb Sandwich

Sabzee is a wholesome, simple, and vigorous dish from Afghanistan that is eaten in the spring when new herbs have sprouted. Here it's tucked inside whole wheat pita bread spread with a little cayenne-seasoned yogurt. The tastes are very distinct—the tart, cool yogurt, the firm presence of wheat in the bread, and the complexity of flavors in the herbs. The mixture comes completely alive in the mouth.

These are approximate measures—exactness isn't so important, and you can use herbs other than those mentioned below. Arugula, watercress and field cress, and a small amount of lovage or mint would also contribute strong, wild flavors, as would tender turnip, mustard or beet greens.

Makes 2 sandwiches

> *a large handful of tender spinach leaves, stems removed*
> *½ bunch of cilantro*
> *10 large parsley branches*
> *10 large dill branches*
> *2 scallions, including the firm greens, finely diced*
> *olive oil or sunflower seed oil*
> *salt*
> *2 pita breads, sliced in half*
> *½ cup plain yogurt seasoned with a pinch of cayenne pepper*

Clean the spinach and the herbs, dry them, and remove the larger stems. Gather them together and chop them roughly. (At this point you can store them in a plastic bag or damp towel until needed.) Toss them with a little salt and just enough oil to barely coat the leaves.

Line each half of the pita bread with the seasoned yogurt; then stuff in the greens. Nothing more is needed, though you could serve some additional yogurt in a bowl and dip your sandwich in it as you eat.

Toast or Crackers with Artichoke Paste

Artichoke paste makes an unusual and delicate spread for crisp toast or crackers. If the paste is already made, it can be used to make an impromptu hors d'oeuvre. The flavor of the paste is delicate, so the flavorings should be fairly mild.

> *bread or crackers*
> *extra-virgin olive oil*
> *artichoke paste (page 20)*
> *finely chopped chervil or parsley*
> *finely ground pepper*

Broil or toast the bread, if you're using it, on both sides; then brush with olive oil. Spread the paste over the top and garnish with the chopped herbs and pepper.

Another way: Artichokes are often found in combination with hazelnuts, and they do go well together. You could flavor the artichoke paste with a little hazelnut oil and then garnish these toasts with chopped roasted hazelnuts.

Olive Paste with Hard-Cooked Eggs on Toast

A zestier version of the chopped egg and olive sandwiches of our childhoods. The olive paste, a mixture of pungent olives with onion, capers, and herbs, can be bought in tubes or jars; it's also easy to make, and it keeps more or less indefinitely. If you have the olive paste on hand, this can be put together in a moment. Nice to serve with a glass of wine while dinner is cooking.

Makes 2 open-faced sandwiches

> *2 slices sourdough or whole wheat bread*
> *olive paste (page 22) or commercial olive paste*
> *1 or more hard-cooked eggs*
> *chopped parsley*
> *freshly ground pepper*

Slice the bread thinly and toast it on both sides. Spread with a generous layer of olive paste. Finely chop the hard-cooked egg and season it with some chopped parsley and fresh pepper. Cover the olive paste with the egg mixture. If you've used large slices of country bread, cut the finished toasts into quarters or finger-sized strips.

Olive Paste, Mozzarella, and Onion Sandwich

There's so much visual drama in this sandwich that it really should be served open-faced. The mild vinegary pickled onions are suggested, but if you like raw onions, use them instead. This sandwich makes a fine lunch as well as an appetizing bite before dinner.

Makes 1 sandwich

> *a slice of sturdy bread*
> *olive paste (page 22) or commercial olive paste*
> *parsley (Italian, if possible), roughly chopped*
> *fresh mozzarella cheese, sliced into half rounds*
> *pickled red onion rings (page 332) or a fresh onion, sliced in thin rounds*
> *olive oil*
> *freshly ground pepper*

Spread the bread with a layer of olive paste and sprinkle half the parsley on top. Slice the cheese in half-rounds and loosely layer them over the paste, alternating with the red onions. Allow some of the olive paste to show through. Drizzle a little olive oil over all and garnish with the rest of the parsley. Finish with a grinding of pepper.

For a toasted sandwich, pre-heat the oven to broil. Spread the bread with olive paste and cover with the onion rings then the cheese. Set under the broiler until the cheese is melted and bubbling, then garnish with the parsley and finish with pepper, but omit the drizzled oil.

Tomato Sandwich with Mustard Oil

Mustard oil has a hot, pungent taste with overtones of horseradish. It's warm and lively—wonderful on slices of big, juicy tomatoes. Try this unusual sandwich of tomatoes, pickled onion rings, and mustard oil with shallots and Champagne vinegar. Settle the tomatoes into a thin swipe of mayonnaise.

Makes 2 large open-faced sandwiches

> *2 tablespoons mustard oil*
> *1 small shallot, finely diced*
> *2 to 3 teaspoons Champagne vinegar*
> *pinch of salt*
> *2 large slices of whole wheat or country bread*
> *mayonnaise*
> *2 perfectly ripe tomatoes, sliced*
> *pickled red onion rings (page 332)*

Combine the oil, shallot, vinegar, and salt in a bowl. Taste and adjust the amount of vinegar if necessary.

Spread the bread with a film of mayonnaise. Slice the tomatoes and layer them over the bread. Cover the tomatoes with the onion rings. Drizzle the sauce over the top and serve.

If wild mustard blossoms or brassica plants (cabbage, broccoli, etc.) are in bloom, scatter some of the bright yellow flowers over the top and serve the sandwiches open-faced. Rocket (arugula) leaves and their blossoms would also make a lively-tasting, pretty garnish.

Pita Sandwich with Eggplant and Walnut Sauce

This sandwich is substantial—a meal in itself. The small, slender Japanese variety of eggplant are ideal here; they needn't be salted, and when sliced diagonally, they just fit into the pita bread. One eggplant is just enough for one person. Both the walnut and the pine nut sauces are perfect with the eggplant.

Makes 1 sandwich

> *2 tablespoons light olive or peanut oil*
> *1 Japanese eggplant, sliced diagonally just less than ½ inch thick*
> *salt*
> *freshly ground pepper*
> *1 pita bread*
> *walnut sauce (page 322) or pine nut sauce (page 324)*
> *1 medium-sized tomato, sliced*
> *roasted red peppers (page 329) or a few thin slices raw pepper*
> *6 slices of cucumber*

Heat the oil in a skillet just large enough to hold the eggplant, add the slices, and quickly turn them over so that both sides absorb the oil. Fry over medium heat until the eggplant has begun to color, then turn the slices over and cook until the second side is nicely browned and the eggplant is tender. If necessary, add a little more oil to cook the second side. When done, remove the eggplant to a towel and season lightly with salt and pepper.

Cut a pita bread in half, open up the pockets, and spread both halves generously with the sauce. Slide in the eggplant, tomatoes, peppers, and cucumbers and serve.

Open-Faced Sandwich with Gorgonzola and Pears

Blue cheeses, particularly the Italian *Gorgonzola dolcelatte*, have a special affinity for pears and apples. If Gorgonzola is too strong for your taste, try a milder blue cheese or thin it with a larger amount of cream cheese than suggested below.

Juicy, buttery-fleshed pears such as Bartlett or Comice are wonderful here, but an Asian pear, which is at once both juicy and crisp, would be quite good too. The flesh is more granular and less buttery but would certainly add textural contrast

to the soft cheese. If the skins are firm and smooth, leave the pears unpeeled. On an open-faced sandwich the red, russet, and golden skins make a beautiful garnish in themselves.

Though lemon juice will keep pears from browning, it will also add its tart and assertive flavor. Try to assemble these sandwiches just before you serve them so that you don't have to use lemon juice at all. Just omit the chervil if it isn't available.

Makes 2 sandwiches

> *3 ounces Gorgonzola cheese, preferably* dolcelatte
> *2 ounces cream cheese*
> *milk or cream*
> *chopped chervil leaves and additional sprigs, if available*
> *freshly ground pepper*
> *2 large slices country bread*
> *1 firm, ripe pear, sliced*

Combine the Gorgonzola and cream cheese, adding enough milk or cream to make a soft paste that's easy to spread. Add the chopped chervil and season with pepper. Lightly toast the bread, or leave it untoasted, as you prefer. Spread the cheese neatly over the top, then cover the cheese with overlapping slices of pear. Garnish with additional sprigs of chervil.

■ To make thin slices that are easy to overlap, stand the pear on end, slice off a piece, then work your way around the pear, taking away thin slices as you go.

Fresh Bread with Cream Cheese and Berries

This is one of those simple and obvious ideas that pass by unnoticed until someone kindly points them out. In this case it was a waitress at Chez Panisse who used to make this snack before starting work. She made it with fresh *baguettes* or *pain au levain*, but any good-quality bread would be fine. The fresh fruit, unlike jam, is sweet but not cloying. The tart edge of the berries is refreshing and nicely cuts the creaminess of the cheese. Ripe figs, sliced into rounds and set on top of the cheese with a squeeze of lemon juice, would also be perfect with the cheese. When made with really fresh bread, this simple sandwich is superlative, a delightful treat for children and adults any time of day.

cream cheese or ricotta cream cheese (page 353)
milk or cream
fresh bread
ripe berries—strawberries, blackberries, raspberries—or figs
brown sugar or vanilla sugar (page 407) (optional)

Thin the cream cheese with milk or cream to make it soft and easy to spread. Spread it smoothly over the fresh bread and cover the top with sliced or whole berries. If they're tart, sprinkle a little sugar over the fruit.

Avocados on Sourdough Bread

I think this sandwich was just about all I ate during my last two years of college, and it never became tiresome. When it's made with a fresh loaf of sourdough bread, there's nothing better. It's my idea of a perfect snack to take to the beach just before sundown.
    Makes 2 open-faced sandwiches

2 slices sourdough French bread
unsalted butter
1 ripe avocado
a lime
salt
freshly ground pepper
cilantro or watercress

Cut 2 thick slices of fresh bread, spread them with butter, cover with slices of avocado, and sprinkle with lime juice, salt, and plenty of pepper. Top with fresh, shining leaves of cilantro or watercress. Serve with a glass of chilled *sauvignon blanc*.

Avocado Toasts

This makes a quick lunch or, cut into quarters, an appetizer to serve with something cold to drink.
    Makes 2 to 4 servings

1 large avocado
1 tablespoon finely diced shallot or scallion
1 tablespoon balsamic vinegar
2 tablespoons olive oil
salt
4 slices of whole wheat bread, toasted
freshly ground pepper
1 teaspoon roughly chopped marjoram or parsley, approximately
pickled red onion rings (page 332)

Halve the avocado and peel it or scoop out the flesh with a large spoon, keeping it in one solid piece. Discard the pit and slice the flesh about ⅓ inch thick. Whisk together the shallot, vinegar, olive oil, and salt to taste with a fork to make a sauce. Press the avocado slices lightly onto the toast. Spoon a little of the sauce over the top and finish with lots of freshly ground pepper and the chopped marjoram. Garnish with rounds of the onion, or finely dice it and sprinkle it over the top. The onion will give a pleasing bite as well as bright color and crunchy texture to the creamy avocado.

Mushrooms on Toast, Provençale Style

Most mushroom and toast dishes include a creamy sauce or cheese, but this one, based on a Provençale recipe, uses lots of garlic and olive oil. Serve it over toast for an appetizer or a small meal.

Makes 2 generous servings

½ pound firm white mushrooms
¼ cup olive oil
salt
coarsely ground or crushed peppercorns
1 garlic clove, chopped
lemon juice
2 or 3 slices of bread
2 tablespoons chopped parsley
2 teaspoons chopped marjoram and ½ teaspoon chopped thyme,
    or several pinches of herbes de Provence

Cut the mushrooms into halves or, if very large, quarters. Cut them evenly or, for a more jaunty appearance, at odd angles. Toss them with the olive oil, a light sprinkling of salt, the pepper, garlic, a squeeze of lemon, and the dried herbs, if using. Set aside to marinate for at least 15 minutes.

Just before you're ready to eat, toast the bread. Brush one side of the toast with olive oil if desired. Heat a sauté pan, add the mushrooms, and sauté them briskly. They will release the oil and their juices. Sauté until they have begun to color. Taste and season with more salt and lemon juice. Add the parsley and marjoram, toss, and serve the mushrooms over the toast.

Quesadillas, My Style

This is my "fast food" and one that I have come to rely on when I'm really busy working. There is absolutely no claim to any authentic Mexican culinary history here. What I call a quesadilla is a hot tortilla "sandwich" of soft, melted cheese accompanied by any number of other things I might already have on hand. These quesadillas take a little over a minute to make, quick enough to satisfy the most urgent appetite.

Use either wheat or corn tortillas, as you prefer. The wheat ones are softer and easier to fold, as well as larger, but the corn tortillas have the good corn flavor.

THE BASIC INGREDIENTS

tortillas
grated cheese, such as Muenster, Monterey Jack, cheddar or queso fresco
chopped cilantro
salsa, such as Tomatillo-Avocado Salsa (page 319), Smoked Chili
    Salsa (page 320) or Cilantro Salsa (page 318)

AND SOME OTHER POSSIBILITIES

diced tomatoes
chopped onions, either fresh or pickled
roasted green chilies
jalapeño peppers, seeded and finely diced
leftover boiled potatoes
olives
sour cream
scrambled eggs

Lay a tortilla in a nonstick or cast-iron pan set over medium heat. (No oil is necessary.) While it's heating, grate some cheese over the tortilla. Snip some cilantro leaves over the cheese, add a few splashes of salsa, and add any of the items above that appeal to you. When the cheese has begun to melt, fold the tortilla in half or into thirds, cut into wedges, and serve.

If you are mannerly with yourself, you might put it on a plate and sit down somewhere. If not, you can hold it in your hands and begin eating while you're busy starting a second. I've stood around the stove with family and friends and blazed through a big bag of tortillas, bowlfuls of fixings, and some good Mexican beer and found it to be one of the most enjoyable meals ever.

SOME GRILLED CHEESE SANDWICHES

There's a lot to be said for many of the foods we've known more or less forever. Often it's their very familiarity that's nourishing, but some have some good culinary points, and the grilled cheese sandwich is a classic. Even the simplest grilled cheddar cheese on white bread is a great sandwich, with the crisp, golden bread covering the warm melted cheese—clear tastes and good, contrasting textures. Cheese Dreams, the open-faced melted cheese sandwiches of the fifties, also combine the pleasing contrasts of crisp bread with a soft, unctuous covering of cheese. Sometimes the simplicity of a sandwich—just bread and cheese—is refreshing, but if you tend to make lots of grilled cheese sandwiches and crave variety, here are a few new ideas and variations on the theme of toast and cheese.

Toasted Cheese Sandwich with Cumin Seeds

Make these sandwiches on light rye, white or light whole wheat bread. The cumin seeds are just right with the mustard and cheese. They go especially well with tomato soups.

Makes 2 sandwiches

> 2 slices of bread
> ⅔ cup grated Jarlsberg, Swiss or Gruyère cheese
> 2 teaspoons butter
> ½ teaspoon coarse-grained or smooth Dijon mustard
> ½ teaspoon cumin seeds
> freshly ground pepper

Toast the bread on one side in a broiler or toaster oven. Work the cheese, butter, mustard, and cumin seeds together and spread the mixture over the untoasted sides of the bread. Broil until the cheese is bubbly and starting to brown. Grind plenty of pepper on top, cut into halves or finger-sized slices, and serve hot.

Tomatoes, Grilled Onions, and Cheddar on Rye

This is an old favorite standby for me. One cold, rainy summer afternoon in the Adirondacks I found myself in a farm stand/café, shopping for produce and looking for lunch. This sandwich was on the menu, and seeing it there was like finding an old friend. Even better, the proprietors used their excellent aged cheddar and garden tomatoes and served it with freshly pressed apple juice. Superlative.

Makes 1 or 2 sandwiches

safflower or light olive oil
1 yellow onion, halved lengthwise and sliced
salt
Dijon mustard
light rye bread
good-quality aged cheddar cheese, thinly sliced
1 large, firm, ripe tomato, sliced
butter for frying

Heat a teaspoon or 2 of oil in a skillet, add the onions, and sauté them over brisk heat until they begin to color but are still a little crisp. Lightly salt and remove them from the pan. Build the sandwich, starting with a light film of mustard on both slices of bread, some of the cheese, a mass of onions, a couple slices of tomato, and more cheese, ending with bread.

Melt some butter in a cast-iron frying pan, place the sandwich in the pan, and cook over low heat, browning the bread and melting the cheese. When the bread is nicely browned, add a little more butter to the pan, let it sizzle and melt, then carefully turn the sandwich over, settling it into the butter, and cook the other side. Serve it with any remaining onions on the side, a sour pickle, and a glass of cider. Good rain or shine.

Grilled Cheese with Tomatillos and Chipotle Chilies

Tomatillos are almost always cooked, but they can also be eaten raw. Like green tomatoes, tomatillos are tart and crisp, and in fact, green tomatoes would also be delicious here. This sandwich is a hot and spicy mouthful—a beer is just the thing to wash it down.

Makes 1 sandwich

> *2 slices of white or whole wheat bread*
> *puréed* chipotle *chilies or Smoked Chili Salsa (page 320)*
> *cheddar, Muenster or Monterey Jack cheese, thinly sliced*
> *tomatillos or green tomatoes, husked, washed, and sliced*
> *several cilantro branches*
> *butter or vegetable oil for frying*

Spread each slice of bread thinly with puréed *chipotle* chilies or the salsa. Cover one slice of bread with half the cheese and add the tomatillos, cilantro, and the rest of the cheese. Top with the second slice of bread. Melt the butter in a cast-iron pan, add the sandwich, and cook slowly on both sides until the cheese melts and the bread is crisp and golden brown.

Blue Cheese Toasts with Walnuts

This mixture of Roquefort and butter with walnuts, pepper, and a dash of cognac is spread thickly over thin slices of toasted bread (a country-style French or Italian bread or whole wheat bread would be excellent). Then the toast is returned to the oven or broiler, the butter melts into it, and the cheese becomes fragrant and warm. Cut into little squares or wedges, this makes a quick appetizer to serve before a meal or a tasty garnish for a soup.

Makes 6 servings

> *6 ounces Roquefort or other blue cheese*
> *4 to 6 tablespoons unsalted butter*
> *1 tablespoon cognac (optional)*
> *freshly ground pepper*
> *1 to 2 tablespoons finely chopped walnuts*
> *4 thin slices of bread*

Preheat the oven or broiler for the toast. Cream the cheese and butter together. Add the cognac, if using, season with pepper, and stir in the walnuts.

Toast the bread lightly on both sides. Spread the cheese over the toast, then return it to the oven or broiler just long enough for the butter and cheese to melt into the toast a little. It shouldn't melt completely, but just soften. Remove the toasts from the oven, dust them with more pepper, and cut them into smaller pieces. Serve warm. Cool, juicy slices of pears would make a perfect accompaniment to the cheese and walnuts.

Grilled Bread with Olive Oil, Tomato, and Parmesan Cheese

This *bruschetta*, slightly more elaborate than the traditional garlic toast, includes tomato and cheese. If you are grilling outside, toast the bread right over the coals. Otherwise a hot oven will work fine. (If you have a fireplace, consider setting a low grill over the coals and cooking indoors.) A large country loaf, coarse-grained and full of flavor, makes the best toast.

Makes 2–4 servings

> 1 sun-dried tomato for each slice of bread or
>   sun-dried tomato purée (page 326)
> 2 slices country bread, about ⅓ inch thick
> extra-virgin olive oil
> 1 plump garlic clove, cut in half
> a piece of Parmigiano-Reggiano, shaved into
>   enough thin pieces to cover the toast

Preheat the oven to 425°F. If the tomatoes have been preserved in oil, simply mash them into a paste. If not, cover them with a small amount of boiling water and let them sit until they're soft, then pound into a paste or purée. Or use a teaspoon or 2 of the dried tomato purée. Brush the bread with oil and place in the oven (or toast over the coals) until lightly browned and somewhat crisp. Rub the surface with the cut garlic, then spread the sun-dried tomato over the toast. Cover with the shavings of cheese. Cut into wedges or fingers and serve.

Soufflé Cheese Toasts

An hors d'oeuvre that won't ruin your appetite—like any soufflé, it puffs but doesn't wait. Although quite edible once fallen, it's best when you can bite through a thin crisp layer of toast into a fragrant, gossamer froth.

Different cheeses have their own character and go well with different herbs and spices. Try a sharp cheddar cheese with mustard; milder cheeses like Muenster, Monterey Jack, and Gouda with crushed basil or *fines herbes;* a creamy Fontina or even a goat cheese with fresh thyme or rosemary leaves.

Makes 12 small or 4 large toasts

12 slices of baguette or 4 slices of other bread
2 eggs, separated
1 teaspoon Dijon mustard
pinch of cayenne pepper or paprika
¾ cup finely grated cheddar cheese
salt
1 tablespoon freshly grated Parmesan cheese
freshly ground pepper

Preheat the oven to 400°F. Lightly toast the bread, then set it aside. Beat the yolks with the mustard and cayenne or paprika; then stir in the grated cheddar. Whip the whites with a pinch of salt until they form firm peaks; then fold them into the cheese mixture. Divide the cheese mixture among the bread slices, sprinkle them with Parmesan, and set on a cookie sheet. Bake until puffed and golden over the surface, about 5 to 7 minutes. Dust with pepper and serve right away.

Soufflé Cheese Toasts with Tomato Paste

Proceed as above, but after toasting the bread, spread a little tomato concentrate—the Italian paste that comes in a tube or Sun-Dried Tomatoe Purée (page 326)—thinly over the surface. Cover with the cheese mixture and then bake.

Soufflé Cheese Toasts with Chili Paste

Follow the recipe above, using cheddar, Muenster or Monterey Jack cheese. Spread a layer of Red Chili Paste (page 325) thinned with a little olive oil over the toast or use a small amount of the Smoked Chili Salsa (page 320); then pile the cheese on top and bake.

Soufflé Cheese Toasts with Garlic

Follow the recipe above, but after toasting the bread, rub a cut clove of garlic over the surface before adding the cheese mixture. You can also combine the garlic with the tomato.

Toast with Goat Cheese and Herbs

Omit the mustard from the recipe above and use crumbled fresh goat cheese. Spread the cheese on the toast and garnish with chopped thyme leaves, a few pinches of minced rosemary or a sprinkling of *herbes de Provence*.

Cheddar on Rye Toast with Strawberry Jam

Here cheese is paired with jam. It may seem unusual, but think of the jam as a kind of chutney alongside a savory. In fact, Rhubarb Chutney (page 333) or Quince Threads (page 339) would also be quite good with cheese.

Butter a piece of light rye toast, if you like, cover it with thin slices of a good, aged cheddar, and spread it lightly with strawberry jam. The heat of the toast will soften the cheese. The saltiness of the cheese and the sweetness of the jam play against each other. This sandwich is perfect with a pot of dark tea.

Artichoke Paste

Artichoke hearts make a delicate spread with an unusual, mild, nutty flavor. Although some time is needed to prepare and cook the artichokes, this paste keeps for several weeks and is very useful for impromptu hors d'oeuvres—spread on crackers or grilled or toasted bread or sandwiched between paper-thin slices of a delicate white bread with small sprigs of fresh chervil or chopped parsley. It can also be mixed with cream to make a sauce for pasta or spread over warm crêpes.

Cooking the artichokes with oil and herbs brings out the flavors, but you can also make the paste in a little less time by steaming the artichokes (or using leftover cooked artichokes), isolating the hearts, and puréeing them, adding seasonings at that time. Or you can use frozen artichoke hearts and cook them as suggested below, intensifying the seasonings to compensate for the faint taste of the ascorbic acid. Or drain a jar of marinated artichokes and purée them; these will, however, have a rather sharp, acid taste—emphasize it by adding capers, diced shallots, and perhaps some lemon zest. Each method gives slightly different results.

Makes approximately ¾ cup

> *3 cups water*
> *1 large lemon*
> *4 large artichokes*
> *1 tablespoon olive oil*
> *2 garlic cloves, thinly sliced*
> *1 bay leaf*
> *3 thyme sprigs or a pinch of dried*
> *4 parsley sprigs*
> *extra-virgin olive oil, to finish*
> *salt*
> *freshly ground pepper*

Fill a small bowl with the water, remove a few strips of peel from the lemon, and set them aside. Squeeze the lemon juice into the water.

Prepare the artichokes: If the stems are thick and fresh, remove, peel, and cut them into rounds. Break off the outer leaves, leaving behind as much of the meaty base as possible. Slice off the top of the cone of inner leaves close to the choke. Quarter each artichoke, cut away the chokes from each piece with a sharp paring knife, and slice the artichokes into thirds. Put the finished pieces in the acidulated water as soon as you can so that they won't darken.

Use a lidded pan that's large enough to hold the artichokes in a single layer. Heat the olive oil with the lemon peel, garlic, bay leaf, thyme, and parsley; then add the hearts and toss. Cook for a few minutes, turning several times; then add water to cover and season with salt. Bring to a boil, then lower the heat, cover the pan, and simmer until tender and even-colored over the surface—about 45 minutes. The liquid will reduce as the artichokes cook. Add small amounts of water, if needed, until the artichokes are done.

Remove the bay leaf, parsley, and thyme sprigs; then transfer the artichokes to a food processor. Process until you have a smooth purée, adding spoonfuls of cooking liquid if necessary. Some fibrous material will remain, so pass the purée through a fine sieve. Stir in a tablespoon of extra-virgin olive oil for flavor and season the purée to taste with salt and a few twists of the pepper mill.

If you're not going to use the paste immediately, pack it into a jar, spoon a little more olive oil over the surface, cover, and refrigerate. The paste will keep for several weeks.

Suggestion: I suspect I'm not the only person with a can of hazelnut oil that is seldom used. Hazelnuts go nicely with artichokes, and the two are often paired. You can finish the purée with hazelnut rather than olive oil and garnish the toasts or pasta with finely chopped roasted hazelnuts.

If you want to avoid oil altogether, steam the artichokes and use yogurt in place of the oil.

Olive Paste

Pastes made of olives are sure to be strong and robust, good to spread on crackers or bread, good in deviled eggs, lively tossed with pasta or with sturdy vegetables, like broccoli.

Different approaches yield different results, starting with the olives you use, which can be the large kalamatas, the more refined Niçoise or Gaeta olives, or a combination of olives, including some green Sicilians for their tart flavor. Herbs, tomatoes, garlic, capers, wine, or vinegar can be added in varying combinations and the paste can be coarse or smooth, as you like.

Stored in a covered jar and refrigerated, this paste lasts more or less indefinitely.

Makes ½ cup

3 ounces (about ½ cup) olives
1 tablespoon chopped onion
3 tablespoons capers, rinsed
pinch of dried thyme
1 tablespoon olive oil
red wine vinegar or lemon juice

If the olives are salty, rinse them well. Press on them to open them up and remove the stones. Purée the olives, onion, and capers in a food processor with the thyme and oil or pound the mixture in a mortar. Season to taste with the vinegar or lemon juice.

Chick-Pea Spread (Hummus)

I gave a similar recipe in *The Greens Cookbook* starting with dried chick-peas, and although that recipe isn't difficult, you do need to plan ahead to soak the peas. This recipe is ideal when you want a spread immediately. *Hummus* is perfect to spread on crackers or to tuck into pita bread along with the walnut or pine nut sauce (pages 322 and 324) or with seasoned yogurt and an accompaniment of vegetables—tomatoes, green peppers, crisp lettuce leaves, cucumbers.

Makes 1 cup

> 1 15-ounce can chick-peas
> ⅓ cup hot water, approximately
> juice of 1 large lemon
> 2 garlic cloves
> ¼ cup tahini
> olive oil
> salt
> ground red chili

Drain the chick-peas, rinse them well, and put them in the work bowl of a food processor. Begin to process, gradually adding the hot water to make a light, spreadable consistency. Add the lemon juice, garlic, tahini, a tablespoon of oil or more to taste, and season with salt. Process until well blended and smooth. Taste and adjust the seasonings, adding more lemon, oil, or salt, if necessary. Mound the spread into a serving bowl and make a shallow depression in the middle. Drizzle more olive oil over the top and garnish with the ground chili.

Suggestion: Stir 2 tablespoons chopped cilantro into the spread. Instead of olive oil, use an aromatic sesame oil to emphasize the sesame flavor. Season the spread with cumin, finely diced jalapeño pepper, or scallions.

Eggplant Spread with Yogurt and Herbs

Light but creamy textured, this spread can be served with crackers, spread on bread, or tucked into pita bread. The long, slender Japanese eggplants are generally sweeter than the large, round Western types and don't require salting. Ordinary eggplant will work, however, when you take care to choose firm and shiny ones. They don't seem to produce much bitterness, and once baked, they can be handled more quickly and easily than the Japanese variety. If you don't have fresh thyme, just omit it.

Because the eggplant has to bake, this recipe isn't especially quick, but it's simple to put together. Once made, this spread will keep for several days if kept covered and refrigerated.

Begin by seasoning the yogurt so that the flavors can develop while the eggplant bakes.

Makes approximately 1½ cups

THE SEASONED YOGURT

½ cup plain yogurt
1 garlic clove, minced
1 teaspoon finely chopped oregano or ¼ teaspoon dried
½ teaspoon chopped thyme leaves, or a pinch of dried
freshly ground pepper

Combine all the ingredients in a bowl and set them aside until needed.

THE EGGPLANT

1 pound Japanese eggplants or 1 medium-sized, firm, shiny eggplant
1 large garlic clove, thinly sliced
1 bay leaf
several thyme branches, if available
1 tablespoon extra-virgin olive oil, or more to taste
lemon juice or red wine vinegar
salt
coarsely ground pepper
fresh herbs for garnish

Preheat the oven to 400°F. Cut 5 or 6 long slits in the eggplant (fewer if you're using the Japanese eggplants) and put a slice of garlic into each slit. Wrap the eggplant, together with the bay leaf and thyme branches, tightly in foil and bake until completely soft all over—45 minutes to 1½ hours, depending on the size of the eggplant. If you're using the large eggplant, turn it over after 45 minutes and continue baking until soft to the touch and tender at the stem end.

When done, remove eggplant from the oven, open the package, and let sit for 5 minutes or so. Discard any liquid. When the eggplant is cool enough to handle, scrape the flesh away from the skin, put it in a food processor, and add the yogurt mixture and the olive oil. Process until smooth, but leave a little texture. Stir in the lemon juice or vinegar to taste and season with salt. Turn the purée into a serving bowl and season with pepper and fresh herbs, such as thyme leaves and blossoms, marjoram or oregano. If those herbs aren't available, use some chopped parsley or scallions. Serve the spread at room temperature with crackers, pita bread, or bread toasted and brushed with olive oil.

White Cheese with Feta and Walnuts

You can eat this cheese on toast or crackers, lodge it into the hollows of celery branches, or spread it over a warm crêpe, fold the crêpe, and eat it hot and melting. The water thins it out, but after a few hours the cheese will be firm and solid. This spread can be made by hand, with a mortar and pestle, or in a food processor. Feathery bronze fennel leaves would make a beautiful garnish for this cheese.

To make the feta less salty, soak it the day before in a few changes of fresh water.

Makes approximately 1½ cups

> *⅔ cup (about 3 ounces) walnut meats*
> *½ cup boiling water, approximately*
> *¼ pound feta cheese*
> *¼ pound cream cheese*
> *½ cup cottage cheese*
> *1 tablespoon walnut oil*
> *½ teaspoon paprika*
> *pinch of cayenne pepper*
> *lemon juice*
> *freshly ground pepper*
> *finely chopped parsley or walnuts for garnish*

To make the cheese with a mortar and pestle, pound the nuts in the mortar, adding water as needed to make it fairly smooth. In another bowl, work the cheeses together until smooth and well blended; then stir in the nut mixture, oil, paprika, and cayenne. Season to taste with lemon juice and pepper.

To make the cheese in a food processor, begin by processing the nuts, gradually adding the water as needed to loosen the mixture. If the work bowl is too large for these quantities, add all of the water and then the cheeses. Work until smooth; then stir in the walnut oil, paprika, and cayenne. Season to taste with the lemon juice and pepper.

Turn the mixture into a serving bowl and garnish it with paprika and some finely chopped parsley or walnuts. Serve or cover and refrigerate until needed; it will keep approximately a week.

Fresh Cheese with Herbs

This fresh white cheese can be taken in different directions, led by the choice of herb. It makes a fine spread to serve with crackers or bread along with olives, some fresh vegetables or roasted peppers. It can also be used to fill crêpes or ravioli, stirred into scrambled eggs or served alongside boiled or baked potatoes. Oils—olive, walnut, or hazelnut—as well as herbs flavor the cheese and naturally suggest the accompaniment of fresh or toasted nuts.

Chopped flower petals, particularly herb blossoms, like hyssop, rosemary, sage, and thyme or nasturtiums and calendulas make a fragrant and pretty garnish for the green-flecked cheese.

The usual moist-curd cottage cheese will make a creamy, soft cheese that is best heaped into ramekins. If you want to end up with a firm cheese that can be molded and turned out, use a dry-curd cottage cheese or a small portion of ricotta cheese or goat cheese. This spread can be made with all low-fat cheeses or enriched with spoonfuls of sour cream or cream cheese, as you like.

Makes 1½ cups

> 1 cup moist- or dry-curd cottage cheese
> ½ cup ricotta cheese, goat cheese, sour cream or cream cheese or a mixture
> 1 teaspoon herbed vinegar
> 1 tablespoon olive oil
> 1 small shallot, finely diced, or 1 large scallion, diced
> freshly ground pepper
> snipped chives
> 2 tablespoons finely chopped mixed fresh herbs such as parsley,
>   marjoram, dill, lemon thyme, tarragon, and lovage, approximately
> herb blossoms, if available

Combine all the ingredients except the blossoms and mix well. Taste and adjust whatever needs adjusting—a bit more vinegar, a pinch of salt, more pepper. Heap the cheese into a bowl or into small ramekins, if you are using it right away, and garnish with additional herbs and their blossoms, chives, and pepper.

To mold the cheese, use a strainer, a basket, or a mold with holes in the bottom. Line it with several layers of cheesecloth rinsed in cold water and wrung out. Add the cheese, folding the ends of the cloth over the top. Place the mold on an inverted dish inside a bowl so that the liquid can drain out. Refrigerate it for several hours or overnight. When you're ready to serve, unfold the cloth and turn the cheese onto a platter. Garnish it with chopped herbs, their blossoms, and coarsely ground pepper.

Yogurt Cheese

This ancient recipe from the Mediterranean produces a fresh white cheese that's low in fat. Made with whole-milk yogurt, it will be rich and creamy, but you can make it with low fat or nonfat yogurt as well. All have a refreshing tartness and can be variously seasoned with different herbs. There are many uses for this cheese. It can be mixed with grilled eggplant to make a spread, tucked into a pita sandwich, used as a dip, or served with baked vegetables.

Makes 1 pint

1 quart plain yogurt
salt
olive oil
herbal seasonings (below)

Dampen cheesecloth in cold water, wring it out, and line a sieve, folding the cloth into several layers. Put the yogurt into the sieve, tie the ends of the cloth together, and hang the bag on the handle of a wooden spoon set over a bowl. Put it in the refrigerator and allow it to stand all day or overnight, or even longer. The whey will drip out (this can be used for the liquid in bread baking) leaving the yogurt thick, with the texture of a soft, creamy cheese. The longer the yogurt hangs, the thicker the cheese will be. To serve, scrape the cheese away from the cloth, put it in a bowl, and season it with salt. Serve it plain or with olive oil drizzled over the top and a scattering of any of the herbal seasonings suggested below.

Store it covered in the refrigerator. The yogurt cheese will keep for at least 2 weeks.

HERBAL SEASONINGS FOR YOGURT CHEESE

- finely minced garlic, mint, parsley, and scallions or chives
- coarsely ground black pepper and chopped mint leaves
- paprika, ground cumin, toasted cumin seeds, and chopped cilantro
- finely chopped lovage or parsley and celery leaves
- finely chopped herbs, such as a mixture of thyme, marjoram or basil, and parsley

Stuffed Pan Breads

This recipe is a variation on Paula Wolfert's Marrakesh "pizza," with several additional fillings inspired by the original. The basic idea of these tasty breads is akin to puff pastry: dough is wrapped around butter—in this case butters that are full of herbs and spices—then rolled out, re-formed, and rolled again. On a hot cast-iron griddle the butter melts, the dough cooks and crisps in the butter, and steam lifts the layers of dough. The finished bread is cut into strips and served. These breads are perfect with drinks before a meal. They smell wonderful while cooking and emerge from the pan crisp and golden on the outside, tender and aromatic inside.

Even though this recipe involves making a yeast dough, don't think of it as necessarily time-consuming or particularly difficult. Small amounts of dough are easy to handle and take very little rising time. I find this fairly simple to throw together, even at the last minute.

Often I use just half the dough and freeze the rest, uncooked. Or I form all the dough into pan breads and freeze those I don't want to cook just then. Since they're flat, it takes little time for them to thaw and then rise. If you know you'll need them in the evening, you can transfer the frozen breads to the refrigerator before leaving for work, then let them sit at room temperature for at least a half hour, or longer if possible, before cooking.

Makes 4 breads, or about 16 pieces, serving 6 to 8

MAKING THE DOUGH

> *1 ¼-ounce package active dry yeast*
> *¼ cup warm water*
> *1½ cups unbleached white flour*
> *½ cup whole wheat flour*
> *1 teaspoon salt*
> *½ cup water*

Sprinkle the yeast over the warm water and set it in a warm place until foamy—about 10 minutes. Meanwhile, combine the flours and the salt in a bowl and make a well in the middle. Pour in the yeast when it's ready and add the ½ cup water. Stir everything together, then turn the dough out onto a counter and knead it until smooth—about 5 minutes. Set the dough aside to rise and rest for 20 minutes—longer if you wish. Recipes for various fillings follow.

FILLING THE BREADS

Cut the dough into 4 equal pieces. Press each piece into a rectangle, shaping it with your hands, then roll it out into a thin, even rectangle, approximately 8 by 12 inches. Spread a quarter of the butter in the center third of the dough and fold the 2 ends over, envelope style.

Turn the dough a quarter turn, then carefully and slowly roll it out again into a large, thin rectangle. (If the filling is soft and oozing out, set the dough in the refrigerator to harden for 10 minutes or so and then proceed. You can let it harden while rolling out the other 3 pieces.) Roll and turn the dough once more. If you want an even lighter, flakier pastry, add another 3 turns.

After the last turn, prick the package on both sides with a fork in 6 to 8 places; then set it aside to rise for 30 minutes. When you're ready, slowly heat a large cast-iron griddle or skillet, add the dough, and cook it on both sides until it's nicely crisped and brown. The heat needs to be fairly low so that the insides have a chance to rise and cook while the outer surfaces are browning.

When the bread is cooked, cut it into wedges or strips, pile the pieces on a plate log-cabin fashion, and serve them warm.

PISTACHIO BUTTER FILLING

1 bunch (about 1½ cups) of cilantro leaves
½ jalapeño pepper, seeds removed
½ cup shelled unsalted pistachios, peeled
½ cup unsalted butter, at room temperature
zest and juice of 1 lime
salt

Wash and dry the cilantro. By hand or in a food processor, chop the leaves with the jalapeño and the pistachios until fine; then add the butter, lime zest, and juice. Work the mixture until you have a smooth paste. Season it with salt to taste.

GREEN HERB BUTTER

½ cup unsalted butter, at room temperature
1 cup chopped mixed fresh herbs such as parsley, chervil,
*   thyme, marjoram, lovage, chives, nasturtium blossoms*
*   or leaves, and watercress*
1 small garlic clove
1 teaspoon grated lemon zest
1 teaspoon Dijon mustard
salt
lemon juice
freshly ground pepper

Combine the butter, herbs, garlic, lemon zest, and mustard in a food processor and process until fairly well blended so that there is still a little texture in the herbs. Season to taste with salt, lemon juice, and pepper.

SPICY BUTTER, MOROCCAN STYLE

½ cup unsalted butter, at room temperature
2 tablespoons finely chopped parsley
1 tablespoon finely chopped cilantro
2 to 3 pinches of ground cumin
½ teaspoon ground red chili
salt

Combine all the ingredients and work until well blended, either by hand or in a food processor.

BLUE CHEESE BUTTER

6 ounces blue cheese (Gorgonzola, Maytag, Roquefort, etc.)
2 tablespoons unsalted butter
freshly ground pepper

Combine the cheese and butter and season with several twists of the pepper mill.

Piñon Bread

There's a generous cupful of toasted, ground pine nuts in this bread, enough so that their unusual pine flavor is clearly present. This bread makes a delicate, nutty-flavored toast, and the dough can also be shaped into rolls and glazed. I sometimes add a little wild sage, which is very aromatic and right with the pine nuts, but if you decide to add sage that is unfamiliar to you, test it out first in a piece of extra dough. Some sages can be intensely bitter as well as aromatic.

Pure red chili mixed with water and brushed over the dough before baking gives a beautiful warm reddish color to the bread. Where vent lines have been cut, the dough bakes golden brown, and the whole thing looks like a big gourd or pumpkin. I prefer to bake this round bread on a baking stone, allowing it to rise on a wooden peel dusted with cornmeal. But if you choose to use a bread pan, use one suitable for a loaf weighing 1½ pounds.

Served with the Anasazi Beans with Juniper (page 267) and the Wild Green Salad (page 44), this makes a simple southwestern meal filled with strong, clean tastes.

Makes 1 large loaf or a dozen 2-ounce rolls

> 1 cup pine nuts
> 1 ¼-ounce package active dry yeast
> ½ teaspoon sugar
> 1 cup warm water
> 1 teaspoon salt
> 1 cup whole wheat flour
> 2 or more cups unbleached white flour
> cornmeal for the peel
> 1 teaspoon ground red chili, preferably New Mexican

Toast the pine nuts in a dry skillet until they begin to color, shaking the pan occasionally so that they don't burn. Remove them from the heat and set aside to cool; then chop them finely by hand or in a food processor to make a fine meal. (Be careful not to overwork them, or the pine nuts will form a nut butter.)

Stir the yeast and sugar into the warm water and set the mixture aside for 10 minutes or until the surface is covered with bubbles. Stir in the salt, ground nuts, whole wheat flour, and as much white flour as you can, using a spoon. Turn the dough out onto the counter and knead it until it's smooth and silky, about 8 minutes, incorporating extra flour as needed.

Brush a film of oil in a bowl and set the dough in to rise for approximately 45 minutes, covered with a damp towel or a piece of plastic wrap. Let it double in bulk, then turn it out on a counter and knead it briefly. Shape the dough into a round ball and set it aside to rise again on a peel or counter dusted with cornmeal or flour. While it is rising, preheat the oven to 375°F. If you're using a baking stone, heat it at the same time.

When the bread has risen again, after 30 minutes or so, cut 4 or 5 deep slashes across the top. Mix the ground chili with a few spoonfuls of water and paint it over the surface of the bread. Slide the risen bread onto the baking stone and bake it until it's firm on top and lightly browned on the unglazed parts, about 40 minutes. Set the bread on a rack to cool.

Piñon Rolls

After the dough has risen the first time, knead it briefly and then cut it into 12 2-ounce pieces. Form each piece into a ball and set them aside to rise on a peel or baking pan dusted with flour or cornmeal. Cut several vent lines into each roll and brush the rolls with chili water as above. When risen, bake the rolls until lightly browned and firm to the touch, about 25 minutes.

Cheese Bread

This recipe was inspired by an extraordinary bread my neighbor in Rome made one Easter morning. The dough, rich and tender like a brioche, is studded with small cubes of provolone cheese and coarsely grated Parmigiano-Reggiano. The warm bread is fragrant with the scent of melted cheese.

Rosanna also included small bits of sausage in the bread, and it was served warm, with hard-cooked eggs. She said this was the only day of the year her family ate eggs for breakfast, and while we were eating, all the bells in Rome were ringing. The combination of the eggs, cheese, and bread—on this particular morning—felt deeply nourishing.

This is a festive bread that can make an otherwise simple meal quite special, particularly when served warm from the oven. It's also wonderful served before a meal, warm or toasted. Leftover bread can be used to make the Savory Bread Pudding, which follows.

This recipe makes a pound of dough or one long flat loaf that will serve eight or more. I usually make two loaves and freeze one to have on hand.

Makes 1 pound of dough, enough bread to serve 8

1 ¼-ounce package active dry yeast
⅓ cup warm water
2 cups unbleached white flour
1½ teaspoons salt
2 large eggs, at room temperature
5 tablespoons unsalted butter, at room temperature, or crème fraîche
¼ pound provolone cheese, preferably imported, cut in small cubes
1 cup (about 4 ounces) coarsely grated Parmigiano-Reggiano

Sprinkle the yeast over the warm water and set it aside in a warm place to rise until it is bubbly all over the surface, about 10 minutes.

Mix the flour and salt together. (If the eggs are cold when you remove them from the refrigerator, cover them with hot tap water for several minutes to bring them up to room temperature.) Lightly beat the eggs together with a fork and set aside a few tablespoons in a small bowl to use later.

Make a well in the flour and pour in the yeast, the beaten eggs, and the soft butter or crème fraîche. Gradually mix everything together, either by hand or in a mixer, using a dough hook. Knead until the dough is satiny and smooth, about 10 minutes, sprinkling on more flour if needed. Set the dough in a lightly oiled

bowl, cover it with a towel or plastic wrap, and set it aside to rise until doubled in bulk, about 45 minutes.

Preheat the oven to 375°F. When the dough has risen, turn it out onto a lightly floured counter and roll it into a rectangle approximately 12 by 18 inches. Scatter the cheeses over the surface to within about ½ inch of the edges, then roll it up from the long side to make a long jelly roll shape. Transfer the roll to a baking pan, placing it on the diagonal if necessary. Using a spatula, gently press down on the loaf to flatten it slightly, then brush the remaining beaten egg over the surface.

Put the bread into the oven without allowing it to rise again. This will make a loaf that's a bit denser than the usual twice-risen one, but the cheese will be more concentrated throughout the dough. Check the bread after 10 minutes or so and again gently press it down, flattening it slightly. Bake the bread until it's firm and golden brown all over, about 1 hour. Serve it warm. Leftover bread can be re-warmed in the oven, and it also makes an excellent savory toast. Well wrapped, this bread can be frozen. You could make 2 smaller breads and freeze one.

Savory Bread Pudding

Leftover Cheese Bread can be used to make a savory bread pudding to serve with a salad for a quick, homey meal. The shape of the loaf and its golden crust make slices of bread that are beautiful when layered, with alternating arcs of crust visible just above the custard.

Makes 4 servings

> *butter for the baking dish*
> *1 whole egg*
> *1 egg yolk*
> *1 cup milk*
> *salt*
> *freshly ground pepper*
> *10 slices cheese bread (above)*

Preheat the oven to 325°F and butter a baking dish, such as a glass pie plate or a small baking dish about 6 by 9 inches. Lightly beat the egg and egg yolk together; then gradually add the milk. Season with a pinch of salt and a few grinds of pepper. Arrange the slices of bread in overlapping layers and pour the custard over them. Bake until the custard is set and lightly browned on top, about 40 minutes.

Olive Bread

There's a wonderful shop on the via Ripetta in the Centro Historico of Rome called Pan e Formaggio (bread and cheese). This small shop produces a good number of breads and pastries and carries an excellent selection of cheeses. You can sit at the long marble counter and refresh yourself with a sandwich made with the shop's delicious, nutty whole wheat breads or a slice from one of the enormous pizza rusticas that sit impressively in their large, black pans.

One of the shop's special breads is an olive bread, woven to resemble a basket, filled and studded with olives. Dense and aromatic with the unmistakable fragrance of olive, this is a loaf of substance and real character as well as charm. Once olives cook, their flavor changes and becomes more like the essence of olives—like olive oil, but more vegetal.

This would make a very special bread to take on a picnic or to offer at a festive meal. I like to eat it as an hors d'oeuvre with thin slices of ricotta salata or a mild feta cheese. And it's good toasted, too. This isn't Pan e Formaggio's recipe, but it tastes quite similar.

Bake this bread on either a cookie sheet or a ceramic baking stone.

Makes a 10-inch braided round, enough to serve 8 to 12

> ½ cup milk
> ½ cup water
> 1½ teaspoons active dry yeast
> 10 ounces green Sicilian olives, approximately
> ¼ cup olive oil
> ½ teaspoon salt
> 1 cup whole wheat pastry flour
> approximately 3 cups unbleached white flour
> 1 egg or egg yolk, beaten

Warm the milk and water to body temperature, stir in the yeast, and leave it for 10 minutes or until it is foamy. Set aside 8 or so olives. Remove the pits from the rest by pressing down hard with the heel of your palm. For stubborn ones, you may have to use a paring knife and cut away the flesh. Chop the pitted olives, but don't make them any smaller than the size of a large pea. You should have about 1 cup.

Once the yeast is foamy, stir in the chopped olives, olive oil, salt, and whole wheat flour. Stir the mixture to make a smooth batter, then begin adding the white flour until the dough is too stiff to handle. Turn the dough out onto a floured counter and knead it for 5 minutes, adding more flour when the dough sticks. You won't be able to get the dough silky smooth because of the olives, but work it until it has a nice, even consistency.

Film a bowl with olive oil and put in the dough. Rub a little oil on the top as well, then cover the bowl with plastic wrap and set it aside to rise in a warm place.

Once it has doubled in bulk, after an hour or so, punch it down; then turn it out onto the counter. Divide the dough into 3 pieces of equal weight; then roll each piece into a rope about 22 inches long and ¾ inch wide. Make a tight braid, then form the braid into a spiral, the edges of the dough just touching. (The dough is going to rise upward rather than just outward.) Set the dough aside to rise on a peel dusted with cornmeal, if you're using a baking stone, or shape the dough directly on a cookie sheet. Cover the bread lightly with a towel and set aside to rise for about an hour.

Preheat the oven to 400°F, with the baking stone, if you're using one.

After the dough has risen, brush the bread with some of the beaten egg (reserve the rest) and firmly lodge the reserved olives here and there, wherever they look best. Slide the bread onto the hot baking stone or place the cookie sheet in the oven. After 15 minutes, brush a little more egg over the newly exposed surfaces. Continue baking until the bread is nicely colored all over, about 45 minutes. Set the bread on a rack to cool. Serve it warm or at room temperature. This bread keeps well, staying moist because of the oil in the dough.

Saffron Crêpes

Whenever I've been in a kitchen where crêpes are being made, it seems like everyone is hoping for a discard. When they get one, they spread it with butter or wrap it around a piece of cheese and eat it with obvious pleasure. Why not just serve a stack of warm crêpes with fresh ricotta cheese or the olive or artichoke paste (pages 22 and 20) for an appetizer? The crêpes stay warm if they're stacked; if made ahead of time, an entire stack can be wrapped in foil and heated in the oven.

These crêpes are especially pretty, flecked with basil leaves and stained with the rich yellow hue of saffron.

Makes 12 8-inch or 16 6-inch crêpes

> *2 pinches of saffron threads*
> *3 medium or 2 large eggs*
> *¾ cup milk*
> *½ cup water*
> *½ teaspoon salt*
> *2 to 3 tablespoons melted butter or light olive oil*
> *1 cup unbleached white flour*
> *3 to 4 basil leaves, finely sliced*
> *butter for the pan*

To make the batter in a blender, cover the saffron threads with a spoonful of hot water and set aside. Put the rest of the ingredients, except the basil and butter for the pan, into a blender jar and blend briefly. Stop and scrape down the sides of the jar, then blend for another 10 seconds or so. Pour the batter into a bowl, stir in the saffron and basil, cover, and let it rest for at least an hour before using it, so that the gluten can relax and the batter becomes supple.

To make the batter by hand, cover the saffron threads with a spoonful of hot water and set aside. Lightly beat the eggs; then add the milk, water, salt, and melted butter. Whisk in the flour. Stir just enough to combine the ingredients well, then pour the batter through a strainer to remove any lumps. Stir in the saffron and basil; then set the batter aside to rest for at least 30 minutes before using it.

Cooking the crêpes: it works best if you use an omelet or a crêpe pan, both of which have shallow, sloping sides. Heat a little butter in the pan. When it is hot, pour in enough batter to coat the pan lightly when you give it a swirl with your wrist. Cook the crêpe over medium heat until it is lacy-looking and golden brown on the bottom; then turn it over and briefly cook it on the other side. You don't have to flip it; just pry up an edge with the tip of a knife and then grasp it lightly in your fingers and turn it over. The first crêpe often doesn't come out right. It seems to take the pan a crêpe or two to get adjusted, and it will probably take the same for you, to figure out the right temperature and the right amount of batter. But after one or two tries you shouldn't have any difficulty. If the batter seems too thick, thin it with additional water or milk. If the pan gets too hot during cooking, cool it by swinging it back and forth in the air several times between crêpes. Stack the finished crêpes on top of each other. Wrap them when cooled.

Herb Crêpes

Stir in 1 or 2 tablespoons of finely chopped fresh herbs. Serve the warm crêpes in a stack with unsalted butter, salt, and pepper; or use fresh cheese with herbs (page 27) and let people help themselves.

Cheese Puffs
(Gougère)

Cream puff pastry, or *choux* paste, is a useful and easy thing to know how to make. Not only is it used for cream puffs and éclairs, but also for dumplings, ramekins, and this old-fashioned pastry, which makes a savory warm hors d'oeuvre. The batter is dropped by spoonfuls in a ring. The individual puffs rise and bake into each other, and the whole thing can be lifted off as a piece, golden and crisp on the surface, airy and fragrant inside. The batter takes literally just a few minutes to make, and the cheese puffs require 45 minutes or so in a hot oven.

Makes 4 to 6 servings

3 eggs
½ cup milk or water
¼ cup butter, cut into pieces
¼ teaspoon salt
½ cup unbleached white flour
½ cup Gruyère cheese in small cubes (about 2 ounces)
freshly ground pepper

Preheat the oven to 400°F. Lightly butter an 8-inch circle on a heavy baking pan, or use a piece of parchment paper. Beat one of the eggs with a fork and set it aside.

Put the milk or water, butter, and salt in a small, heavy saucepan and bring to a boil. When the butter has melted, add the flour all at once and mix well to make a smooth paste. Remove from the heat and beat in, one at a time, the 2 remaining eggs. Make sure each one is completely mixed in with the paste. Add all but a couple of tablespoons of the beaten egg and mix well. Stir in the cheese and season the batter with pepper to taste.

Drop the batter by spoonfuls into a ring on the buttered pan, close to each other but not quite touching. The spoonfuls can be big or little—1½ inches across makes a large but manageable pastry.

Brush the remaining beaten egg over the top, making sure that none of it drips onto the pan. (The drips will bake onto the pan and tether the batter, keeping it from rising.) Bake in the lower third of the oven for 40 minutes or until the puffs have risen, colored, and are crisp on top. Serve while still hot.

Suggestion: If you like the flavor of curry, stir ¼ to ½ teaspoon curry powder into the batter. Also mix the beaten egg with a couple of pinches of curry powder and brush that over the surface.

Salads
to Start
or Make
a Meal

In a traditional menu the salad serves as a lively introduction filled with bright flavors, colors, and textures or as a graceful transition between the main course and the dessert to come. When it's the first course, the salad can be almost anything—greens of course, but also a vegetable, sometimes a grain—and it can be warm or chilled. When it provides the respite, it needs to be simple and modest without calling undue attention to itself.

In a less traditional menu, more in keeping with how we're eating today, a salad can make the whole meal. Many of these salads are varied and substantial enough to stand alone, like the Chick-Peas and Peppers with Pine Nut Dressing. A lighter meal might also be a collection of little salads that complement one another, such as two or three simple vegetable salads with some fresh or vinegary accents—radishes, pickled onions, strips of roasted peppers, olives, and hard-cooked eggs. In more modest portions most of these salads can begin or conclude a dinner.

Perhaps more than other foods, fresh green salads benefit enormously from efforts in the garden. Handling the tender, delicate leaves with all their varied colors and shapes is one of the keenest pleasures in the kitchen I know. Herbs and their blossoms make salads sparkle with their colors and bright tastes. Odd greens like purslane, cresses, members of the goosefoot family, rocket (arugula), and others make vibrant additions to salads. Fields and meadows are another source of salad greens—the strong-tasting wild greens like dock and watercress as well as the softer ones, like miner's lettuce. Even the supermarket has some hidden sources in the tender tops of beets, turnips, and radishes, salad savoy or ornamental kale, and some of the Asian greens like nappa cabbage.

What makes a salad? I have a friend who is an excellent cook and very open-minded about food, but he absolutely will not eat salad. After trying to puzzle him out, I have concluded it's the vinegar he doesn't like, the acidic sharpness, maybe even the hint of fermentation in the scent. And it's the presence of acid, whether in the form of vinegar or citrus juice, that is common to all salads. Once you have a vinaigrette, everything can become a salad—not only lettuce but rice, pasta, fruit, vegetables, meats, even cheese. I think that virtually anything qualifies as a salad, as long as it has the refreshing, cleansing bite of acid.

With a bag of washed and carefully dried greens and an eye that sees other foods you might have on hand as salad, salads can be prepared very quickly. What's essential are good quality, fragrant oils, and a variety of vinegars that range from the delicate (Champagne and rice wine vinegar) to the sweet (balsamic) and the robust (aged red wine and sherry vinegars). Take the time to search them out, for these will give your salads character.

Endive, Lemon Balm, and Violet Salad

Not just whimsical and romantic—though this would be *the* salad to serve to a Valentine—new violet leaves have a fresh, green, lettucelike quality and come up well before lettuce seeds have even been ordered. The lemon balm usually appears around the same time as the violets. Its pale, gold leaves with the mingled scent of lemon and mint are tender and aromatic, and its cool, springlike flavors sound an uplifting note. The violet flowers look charming scattered among the pale green endive leaves and golden green lemon balm.

Using flowers in the kitchen seems new today, but violets have been used in salads (as well as soups, vinegars, desserts, and other confections) at least since the 15th century.

Makes 2 servings

> 1 plump head of Belgian endive
> about a dozen small violet leaves
> about a dozen small lemon balm leaves, whole or torn into pieces
> salt
> extra-virgin olive oil
> Champagne vinegar
> a dozen violet blossoms
> freshly ground white pepper (optional)

Separate the endive leaves by cutting off a slice at the base, pulling apart the loosened leaves, and then cutting again as needed. They don't usually need to be washed.

Put the endive leaves in a bowl with the violet leaves and lemon balm. Sprinkle with a pinch or 2 of salt, pour over enough olive oil to coat them lightly—a few teaspoons—and then add a small amount of the vinegar, to taste, and toss again. Keep the violet flowers whole or separate the petals and scatter them over the salad. Finish with finely ground white pepper if desired.

Suggestion: For a different effect, quarter the endive, cut out the core, then slice each quarter on the diagonal, making narrow, pointed spears; then mix with the other ingredients as suggested above.

Wild Green Salad
(Plus a Supermarket Approximation)

A tangle of wild, succulent greens dressed with a pure, fragrant olive oil, this salad is unquestionably strong food with untamed tastes and pleasingly rough textures. Every country and region offers enticing possibilities, whether the greens are gathered from the Tuscan countryside, plucked from a California wayside, or picked in a high-desert meadow. I think the best salad I ever ate was served in Florence, in early spring. The menu listed *radicchio di campo*, or field chicory, and what came to me was a rough bunch of "weeds," a cruet of green Tuscan oil, and a wedge of lemon. Neither salt nor pepper was needed. I had earlier noticed, from the train, older people walking in the fields, poking with long sticks in the clods of earth, uprooting greens. And my neighbor in urban Rome had for weeks been combing the park grounds with her eye peeled for the same sort of greens, showing me which plants were good to eat and which weren't.

Backyards and parks as well as meadows and remote roadsides offer many plants to eat: lamb's-quarters, wild mustards and radishes, corn salad, cresses, curlydock or wild sorrel, wild celery, dandelion, purslane, and the tender leaves of bee plants and delicate miner's lettuce, to name but a few. Combined with wild onions and dressed simply with a fine olive oil, they make one of the most wholesome and satisfying salads I know. These greens are also good with sunflower oil and sunflower seeds, which are closer in spirit to the Southwest, where I live.

While a wild harvest may be possible through early summer, later—when the plants are tough and scraggly, covered with dust, and too bitter to eat in a salad—I make an approximate version drawing from more widely available resources, such as my local supermarket.

Many flavorful leaves qualify for inclusion. Start with a base of heart leaves from escarole or curly endive, perhaps tender spinach or small leaves of chard, and add stronger-tasting leaves from there. Mustard greens, watercress, and turnip greens lend real liveliness and character to a salad. And don't overlook beet greens and radish leaves if they're fresh-looking. Also thinnings from your herb or vegetable garden—a handful of rocket (arugula) leaves, some chives, a branch of hyssop leaves and flowers, parsley thinnings, violet leaves, tender leeks or scallions, lettuce thinnings, lovage leaves, mint, lemon balm—any lively, strong-flavored green adds unexpected dimensions of taste and texture to a salad. While these may not have the rough nature of wild greens, they have character and the potential to surprise and delight. Here's a basic recipe to work from.

Makes 4 servings

> 4 cups escarole or curly endive leaves (the inner white ones),
>   small spinach leaves, hearts of romaine or a mixture
> 4 cups mixed greens such as tender mustard greens; radish
>   leaves; rocket (arugula) leaves; watercress, rock cress or
>   field cress; nasturtium leaves; tender dandelion leaves;
>   dill or fennel greens; and hyssop leaves and blossoms
> 20 mint leaves
> 12 sorrel leaves, torn or sliced
> 4 scallions, both white and firm green parts, chopped or
>   newly pulled onions, sliced
> ¼ cup sunflower seeds, toasted
> the dressing (below)

Wash and dry all the greens, tear or cut them into whatever size you like, and put them in a large bowl with the scallions and toasted sunflower seeds. Pour over the dressing below and toss well.

THE DRESSING

> 2 tablespoons plain or herbal vinegar, such as tarragon vinegar
> salt
> 4 to 5 tablespoons sunflower seed oil, extra-virgin olive oil, or walnut oil

Whisk everything together, taste, and adjust with more vinegar or oil as needed.

Refined Green Salad with Herbs and Vegetables

One of the first foods that impressed me as a 17-year-old was a salad of butter lettuce with finely slivered vegetables and strips of peeled tomatoes. It had an easy look, although obvious care had been taken with the preparation of the vegetables, giving them a jewellike appearance. It was the combination of these two elements—ease and care—that was so appealing. Just last year my editor and I were served the same type of salad in a small French restaurant, and it provided the same pleasure. The ingredients were common and obvious, but their assembly was careful and refreshing. Although I am very partial to rather rough foods, there's also a time and place for this kind of refinement. It makes the world of time seem a little less crowded and full.

Makes 2 or 3 first-course salads

> *1 head of butter lettuce or a combination of butter, Bibb, and limestone*
> *1 small carrot, peeled and cut into fine matchsticks*
> *1 medium-sized tomato*
> *2 firm white mushrooms, thinly sliced*
> *1 small avocado, halved and sliced*
> *herb dressing (recipe follows)*
> *freshly ground white or black pepper*

Separate the leaves of lettuce by gently pulling them apart at the base. Discard the outer leaves, which are usually bruised and scarred; wash and dry the rest. Leave them whole, if small, or tear or cut them in halves and quarters.

Bring several cups of water to a boil and blanch the carrot for about 10 seconds. Submerge the tomato for 10 seconds; remove it and then peel it. Cut the tomato in half crosswise and gently pull out the seeds and juice with your fingers. Slice down the walls of the tomato and then cut them into neat sections. Reserve the center core for another use. Slice the mushrooms and the avocado.

Toss the lettuce with most of the dressing and heap it lightly onto serving plates. Add the vegetables, spoon the rest of the dressing over them, garnish with the fresh herbs below, and season with pepper.

HERB DRESSING

1 tablespoon Champagne vinegar
1 shallot, finely diced
salt
2 tablespoons extra-virgin olive oil
1 tablespoon sour cream or crème fraîche
1½ teaspoons chopped fresh tarragon, chervil or other favorite herb
1 teaspoon snipped or finely sliced chives, plus their blossoms if available

Combine the vinegar, shallot, and salt in a bowl; then whisk in the oil, cream, and most of the herbs, setting aside some of them to sprinkle over the salad. Taste and adjust the seasonings as needed.

Nappa Cabbage Salad

Like our hard, round-headed cabbages, nappa cabbage is a member of the *Brassica* genus. But unlike the sturdy Western varieties, this Asian cabbage has tender, crinkly leaves that make a fine, delicate salad. The solid base of the leaves is also crisp and tender and can be eaten right along with the leaves. Nappa cabbage is easy to find in Asian markets and almost any big supermarket. These cabbages are heftier than their pale appearance would suggest, and unlike most salad greens they are very easy to work with, requiring almost nothing by way of sorting through leaves, discarding stems, and so forth.

The dressing uses aromatic Sichuan peppercorns, which can be found in Asian markets. If you can't get them, just leave them out. There are lots of other strong flavors to enjoy: the fresh ginger, orange peel, and aromatic sesame and peanut oils. Using good-quality oils with pure, rich flavors makes this salad really wonderful.

I once served this salad to a Chinese friend who liked it very much but was rather taken aback by the notion of eating nappa raw rather than cooked—in China vegetables may be lightly cooked, but they aren't eaten raw.

Makes 4 to 6 servings

THE VEGETABLES

1 head of nappa cabbage, weighing about a pound or a little more
1 tablespoon finely slivered orange zest
1 tablespoon black sesame seeds
1 tablespoon white sesame seeds
2 tablespoons finely sliced chives or scallions
2 tablespoons chopped cilantro leaves, or more to taste
cilantro sprigs for garnish

Cut the cabbage into quarters or eighths; then cut each piece into ½-inch strips, cutting them narrower as you get to the solid base. Wash, dry, and then set the cabbage aside in the refrigerator until needed.

Blanch the orange zest in boiling water for about 10 seconds to get rid of any bitterness. Toast the 2 kinds of sesame seeds in the same pan until the white ones begin to color.

Combine the nappa, chives or scallions, and cilantro; then toss with the dressing below, the orange peel, and the sesame seeds. Garnish with cilantro sprigs and serve.

THE DRESSING

1 scant teaspoon Sichuan peppercorns or
  ½ teaspoon roasted Sichuan pepper salt (page 330)
4 teaspoons finely chopped fresh ginger
1 tablespoon light soy sauce
1 tablespoon rice wine vinegar
1 teaspoon red chili oil
2 tablespoons dark sesame oil
2 tablespoons roasted peanut oil
2 tablespoons orange juice

Lightly toast the Sichuan peppercorns in a dry skillet until their aroma is released, about 10 or 20 seconds; then grind them in an electric spice mill. Combine them with the rest of the ingredients and whisk together. Be sure to taste and adjust the flavors if necessary, as different brands of soy sauce and oils can vary greatly.

Suggestions: Add small cubes of fresh silken-firm tofu. Or include the flesh of the orange, either sectioned or cut into pieces. For another variation in taste, use mandarin oranges or tangerines in place of the regular orange.

Asian Cobb Salad

This is my version of an East-West dish. The finely sliced and carefully arranged mixture of greens, vegetables, and tofu is reminiscent of a Cobb salad. But the aromatic dressing is more Asian, based on sesame and peanut oils. If you have it, use some cinnamon basil. With its minty-cinnamon tones it would be quite delicious here.

Arrange the salad in small heaps of contrasting colors in a large shallow bowl; then toss with the dressing just before serving. The same dressing, by the way, is also good with cooked asparagus, tofu, and buckwheat noodles.

Makes 2 to 4 servings

THE VEGETABLES

> 2 cups spinach leaves cut in fine, narrow strips
> 2 cups nappa cabbage cut in fine, narrow strips
> 2 cups sliced red cabbage, as thin as possible
> ½ large cucumber, peeled, seeded, and cut into small, even dice
> 4 slender scallions, thinly sliced on the diagonal
> 1 small black radish or turnip, cut into fine matchsticks
> ½ block (approximately 5 ounces) of silken-firm tofu, cut into small cubes
> 1 tablespoon black sesame seeds

Arrange all the vegetables and the tofu lightly in separate heaps in a wide, shallow bowl. You might divide the greens into 2 piles each and place like kinds opposite each other, with smaller piles of cucumbers, radish, tofu, and scallions in the middle. Heat the sesame seeds in a dry pan until they begin to smell toasted, then let them cool. Just before serving, sprinkle the seeds over the salad; then toss with dressing below.

THE DRESSING

> 1 garlic clove
> 2 tablespoons peanut oil
> 2 tablespoons dark sesame oil
> 2½ tablespoons rice vinegar
> 1 tablespoon soy sauce
> ½ jalapeño pepper, seeded and finely minced
> 1 tablespoon tahini
> 6 finely chopped mint leaves
> 2 tablespoons chopped cilantro
> 1 tablespoon chopped cinnamon basil, if available

Mash the garlic in a mortar; then gradually add the rest of the ingredients and work them together to make a thick, homogenous sauce. This can also be done in a blender or food processor.

Suggestions: If you prefer peanuts to sesame seeds, replace the tahini with peanut butter and use chopped roasted peanuts in the salad. Slowly fry ½ cup of raw peanuts in 1 tablespoon peanut oil and remove from the heat when they start to color. Stir frequently until they are nicely browned; then turn them out onto a paper towel to drain.

If you crave a chewier bite, use fried tofu (*aburaage*) or other prepared tofus, usually available in health food stores or the Asian section of supermarkets.

Nasturtium Salad

Nasturtium flowers, leaves, and seeds have been used for centuries by many cultures in dishes ranging from pickles to punch, soups to sandwiches and sweets. The generic word *nasturtium*, which is also the botanical name for watercress, derives from the Latin words that indicate an excitement or convulsion of the nose. In other words, both nasturtiums and watercress are spicy, peppery greens that stimulate the nose and the palate. The tastes are not dissimilar, and both make a lively beginning to a meal.

Here are two old recipes and a third contemporary one that are more or less in tune with today's fashion.

From *The Concise Encyclopedia of Gastronomy*, published in England in 1941:

Shred a lettuce finely; mingle with it a quantity of nasturtium leaves and two hard-boiled eggs cut in quarters. Place in a salad bowl, dress with oil and vinegar, salt and pepper, and decorate with nasturtium flowers.

And here's another, from a Turkish cookbook published in 1862:

Put a plate of flowers of the nasturtium in a salad-bowl, with a tablespoon of chopped chervil; sprinkle over with your fingers half a teaspoon of salt, two or three tablespoons of olive oil, and the juice of a lemon; turn the salad in the bowl with a spoon and fork until well mixed, and serve.

I can't quite imagine eating a whole salad of blossoms. To me the flowers have a rather strange, almost furry texture, especially when dressed with oil. But mixing in a quantity of the leaves and even some of the tender buds would solve the textural problem.

Here's what I like to do with nasturtiums:

Makes 4 first-course salads

> 2 handfuls of small nasturtium leaves
> 1 or 2 bunches of watercress, trimmed
> a handful of field cress, if available
> the inner leaves of butter lettuce, finely cut into strips
> extra-virgin olive oil or walnut oil
> Champagne vinegar
> salt
> nasturtium flowers, the petals separated
> 1 hard-cooked egg, the yolk and white separated
> a few whole flowers for garnish

Carefully wash and dry the greens. Using a large, flat bowl, lay out the greens in easy, overlapping layers. Toss with enough oil just to lightly coat the greens; add vinegar to taste and a light sprinkling of salt.

Cut the petals into strips and scatter them over the greens. Chop the egg whites into very fine dice, scatter them over the salad, and force the yolk through a sieve over the greens. Garnish the plate with a few perfect whole flowers.

Parsley Salad

Parsley makes one of the most invigorating salads you can eat, and certainly it deserves to be more than decoration on a plate. Its flavor is strong and cleansing, and although discussions of vitamins can detract from the charm of an herb or vegetable, parsley is full of vitamins (A, B, and C) as well as calcium and iron.

Regular curly parsley makes a high, fluffy salad. The tightly crimped leaves catch on each other and stand up nicely. However, the same ridges and flourishes sometimes catch in the throat, which doesn't always make for pleasant eating. Italian or flat-leaf parsley is better. Though it's not as commonly available in some parts of the country, your grocer can get it if you ask.

You can take lots of liberties with the general idea of this salad. Limit your green to parsley alone or mix it with other herbs. Certain strong, dry cheeses stand up well to this herb, such as feta, Romano, or Parmesan, thinly shaved. A fine julienne of radish, each white piece tipped with red, looks very cheerful and tastes good with the parsley. Parsley salads are lovely to make in early spring when the first new leaves of mint, marjoram, and chives have emerged from the melted snow. You won't need as much of this as you would a lettuce salad, but allow at least ½ cup per person.

Makes 4 servings

> *2 to 3 cups Italian parsley leaves, snipped or pulled from the stems*
> *several sprigs of mint leaves, chopped or torn*
> *several small marjoram sprigs, separated and torn*
> *1 tablespoon finely snipped chives or 1 scallion, minced*
> *1 or 2 radishes*
> *salt*
> *1 tablespoon extra-virgin olive oil*
> *lemon juice, to taste*
> *1 to 2 ounces feta, Romano, or Parmesan cheese, thinly sliced (optional)*

Wash and dry the parsley, mint, marjoram, and chives. Slice the radish into thin rounds; then cut the rounds into narrow strips. Combine the parsley, herbs, and radishes in a bowl, sprinkle with salt, pour over the olive oil, and toss. Add more oil if desired. Season to taste with lemon juice, add the cheese, if you're using it, and toss again.

Serve a parsley salad in a meal that has been heavily seasoned with garlic or with rich dishes, such as Pasta with Gorgonzola. A simpler version also goes well with a meal full of aromatic and complex flavors, such as Couscous with Winter Vegetables or Stewed Artichokes with Olives and Moroccan Spices.

Cooked Greens and Herbs with Garlic and Oil

An assortment of assertive greens is steamed then cooked in the dressing—olive oil and an amalgam of cilantro, garlic, and parsley with lots of cumin. A squeeze of lemon juice finishes the dish. This salad has big, bold, robust flavors and can be eaten tepid or hot from the pan or at room temperature. You could also serve it as a vegetable with a pilaf or mix it with yogurt and fill a pita bread.

Makes 4 to 6 servings

> 12 cups mixed greens such as mustard, rocket (arugula), watercress,
>   dandelion, kale, spinach, chard, escarole, collard greens, etc.
> 4 large garlic cloves
> salt
> 2 good handfuls of parsley leaves
> 1 or 2 good handfuls of cilantro leaves
> 2 to 3 tablespoons olive oil
> 2 teaspoons paprika
> 2 teaspoons ground cumin
> 1 lemon, cut into wedges

Make a mixture of greens using those suggested above. If you like greens with a pronounced edge, use mostly the stronger ones, like mustard, collard greens, and dandelion. If you prefer a sweeter dish, include plenty of spinach or chard—a third or more. Wash the greens well and cut away any tough stems and stalks.

Set the greens in a steamer, with the tough ones on the bottom. Cover and steam until they are tender, 8 to 10 minutes. Or bring a large pot of water to boil, add salt, and cook the greens in separate batches, separating tough from tender, until they are done. The times will vary according to the type of green, so check by tasting them. Set the cooked greens in a colander to drain, squeeze out the excess liquid, and chop them roughly.

To make the herb paste in a food processor, put the garlic, a little salt, and the fresh herbs in the work bowl and process until everything is finely chopped.

To make the herb paste by hand, pound or chop the garlic and salt together until finely broken down; then add the herbs and continue working until you have a rough paste.

Gradually warm the olive oil with the paprika and cumin. When it begins to smell good, add the paste and mix it in with the oil. Next add the greens and cook everything together for a minute or so until excess moisture has evaporated from the pan. Pile into a serving dish and garnish with the lemon wedges.

Asparagus with Salsa Verde and Pickled Onions

The scarlet-colored onions and fine slivers of orange peel in the green sauce look and taste like spring. Since the pickled onions take only a minute or two to make, you can start with them if you don't have any on hand. They will have colored up by the time you're ready for them.

This salad makes a beautiful opening to a meal. The sauce can be made ahead of time, the orange juice and vinegar added at the very end so that the greens remain bright and snappy. This sauce is also good over grilled asparagus. Serve at room temperature or slightly chilled.

Makes 2 to 4 servings

THE ASPARAGUS

1½ pounds asparagus
salt

Trim the asparagus by snapping off the woody, tough ends. If the asparagus is thick, peel it. Bring several quarts of water to a boil, add salt to taste and the asparagus, and cook until it is tender and bright green, about 3 minutes for thin asparagus, 5 minutes if it's fat. Or, if you prefer, steam it. Set the cooked asparagus on a towel to drain while you make the sauce.

THE SAUCE

¼ cup chopped parsley
1 tablespoon capers, rinsed
1 wide band of orange zest, cut into fine slivers and blanched for 10 seconds
several tablespoons pickled red onion rings (page 332), neatly chopped
4 to 5 tablespoons extra-virgin olive oil
¼ teaspoon Dijon mustard
1 tablespoon orange juice
tarragon vinegar
salt
freshly ground pepper

Combine the parsley and capers in a bowl. Finely dice half the slivered orange zest and add it to the bowl along with half of the onion. Stir in the oil, mustard, orange juice, and vinegar to taste. Season with salt and pepper.

Lay the asparagus on a platter or individual serving plates. Ladle the sauce over the stems and garnish with the remaining slivers of orange peel and pickled onion.

Suggestion: You can vary the taste by using aromatic sesame or peanut oils in place of the olive oil or in combination with a light olive oil. Both flavors go well with asparagus and also harmonize with orange. Keep the parsley or use cilantro instead.

Celebration Salad with Blossom Confetti

At Greens I always used to serve a big, colorful, festive salad to parties celebrating graduations, weddings, birthdays, or any other occasion special to someone. But actually this salad mainly celebrates summer and the generosity of the garden, especially the lettuces, herbs, and blossoms.

Although a garden is the best source of an interesting harvest of salad plants, a supermarket can provide some good choices, too. The variegated purple or green and white leaves of ornamental or savoy kale leaves provide a lively, decorative element to work with. (They're a little tough, so they should be torn into small pieces.) Make a salad that is entirely purples and reds, using the red-tipped leaves of prize head or red-leaf lettuce and the purple kale, garnished with the red blossoms of pineapple sage and purple Johnny-jump-ups. Or make one that is soft and delicate, using the green and white kale, the creamy leaves of butter lettuce, and pale spears of endive, garnished perhaps with white onion blossoms. Or leave all boundaries behind and make an outrageous salad that includes all the shapes, colors, and textures you can find.

Look around for edible leaves of all kinds, either in the store or in your garden, including herbs as well as lettuces. Handle them carefully when washing and drying; then lay them out attractively in a large, flat bowl with gently sloping sides. Dress them simply with olive oil and lemon juice or make a more robust dressing that includes capers, pounded garlic, shallots, herbs, and other lively elements.

Take blossoms—rose petals, calendulas, nasturtiums, mustard blooms, all the herb flowers—and slice them cleanly to make a confetti of color. Scatter them over the greens for the final flourish. All these pretty, tasty leaves and petals will make everyone feel like celebrating!

Beet and Fresh Onion Salad

Perhaps because they're roots, we tend to think of beets as a winter vegetable. But you can tell when you see fresh leaves on bunched beets that they are newly harvested, and that can be almost any time of year. Onions are fresh in summer and can often be found in farmers' markets, with a portion of their long green tops still attached. Inside they are juicy and sweet, perfect with the earthy flavors of the beets. The combination of beets and onions is delicious and classic.

This salad calls for red beets, but if they're available, Chioggia and golden beets can be used as well. Some greens that go especially well with these sweet vegetables are rocket (arugula), thick-leaved rosettes of lamb's lettuce (also known as *mâche* or corn salad), watercress or land cresses, and the tender beet greens themselves.

Makes 4 servings

THE VEGETABLES

4 to 5 (about 1¼ pounds) beets
2 handfuls of rocket (arugula), mâche, or beet greens or a mixture
2 small fresh red or yellow onions
2 hard-cooked eggs
1 tablespoon finely chopped parsley
freshly ground pepper

Preheat the oven to 375°F. Trim the beets, leaving an inch of the stems and tails, and rinse off any loose soil. Put them in a pan with ¼ inch water, cover with foil, and bake until they are tender when pierced with a knife—about 35 minutes, depending on their size. Let them cool; then slip off the skins and slice into ¼-inch rounds or quarters.

Wash and dry the greens and slice the onions into thin rounds. Quarter the eggs. Make the vinaigrette below.

Gently toss the sliced beets and onions together with all but a tablespoon of the vinaigrette. In another bowl, dress the greens with the remaining vinaigrette. Lay the beets on a platter and set the greens around them. Garnish with the eggs and the chopped parsley and finish with a grinding of pepper.

THE VINAIGRETTE

1½ tablespoons strong red wine vinegar
2 teaspoons balsamic vinegar
1 teaspoon Dijon mustard
salt
3 tablespoons olive oil
2 tablespoons walnut oil

Combine the vinegars with the mustard and salt; then whisk in the oils. Taste and adjust the seasonings if necessary.

Fall Salad of Chicories, Pears, Walnuts, and Cheese

Made with the blanched creamy hearts of escarole and yellow-skinned pears, this salad has a tender and delicate appearance; red chicories (radicchio) and red-skinned pears make a salad with quite a lot of drama. Both combinations, however, bring together the slightly bitter taste of the greens and the sweetness of fruit. Newly harvested walnuts with their flawless, unspoiled flavor are perfect with the pears and the cheese.

Makes 4 to 6 servings

THE SALAD

2 heads of escarole
2 or 3 Bartlett or Comice pears
8 walnuts
3 ounces blue cheese such as Gorgonzola, Danish blue,
*   Maytag, or Roquefort*
10 chervil or parsley branches, stems removed
freshly ground pepper

Separate the leaves of the escarole and use only the innermost pale heart leaves. (The remaining tougher leaves can be used in a soup or chopped up and sautéed; see page 198.) Wash and dry them and set them aside.

To cut the pears, stand them upright and slice off a round from the side. Then work your way around the pear, slicing it thinly into crescent-shaped pieces. Or quarter the pears, remove the cores, and cut in thin slices.

Crack the walnuts and break them into pieces, none smaller than an eighth. If they are really fresh, leave them as they are. Otherwise toast them first for 5 minutes in a preheated 350°F oven.

Prepare the vinaigrette below and dress the leaves with about half of it. Lay them on salad plates. Dress the pears with the remaining vinaigrette, turning them gently with your fingers. Settle the pears into the leaves. Scatter the walnuts over the salad along with the cheese, broken into pieces. Garnish the salad with the chervil or parsley leaves and season with freshly ground pepper.

THE VINAIGRETTE

1 tablespoon pear or Champagne vinegar
salt
2 tablespoons extra-virgin olive oil
3 tablespoons walnut oil

Combine the vinegar and salt to dissolve the salt; then whisk in the oils. Taste and add more vinegar if necessary.

■ A new walnut oil on the market (under the Loriva label) is lighter than the French oils but full of the flavor of walnuts. You could use it as the only oil in the dressing (the full 5 tablespoons).

Fig and Rocket Salad

I love this combination—the honey-sweet figs with peppery greens, the mild cheese and the acid surprise of vinegar. Figs have two brief moments, one in June and another in the fall. In the fall you might include a few of the new crop of milky-fleshed walnuts tucked among the greens.

Ripe figs don't travel, so in some ways this is a regional kind of salad. For me it evokes the feeling of the Central Valley of California, which is home—the heavy summer heat that brings on the figs, the flat expanse of sky, and the smell of dust and crops.

Makes 2 servings

6 perfectly ripe figs, beginning to show milky seams in their skins
2 large handfuls of rocket (arugula) or garden lettuces, such as red oak leaf
2 ounces creamy goat cheese or the mildest feta, approximately
rocket (arugula) blossoms, if available
freshly ground pepper

Quarter the figs or slice them into rounds. Wash and dry the rocket or lettuce leaves. Make the vinaigrette below and dress the greens with enough vinaigrette to coat them lightly. Arrange them loosely on 2 plates, lay the figs among them with the sliced or crumbled cheese, and spoon the remaining sauce on top. Garnish with some rocket blossoms and dust with pepper.

THE VINAIGRETTE

1 shallot, finely diced
1 tablespoon balsamic vinegar
salt
2 to 3 tablespoons extra-virgin olive oil

Combine the shallot, vinegar, and a pinch of salt in a bowl; then whisk in the olive oil. Taste and adjust the seasonings if necessary.

Celery-Apple Salad with Currants and Walnuts

This is a sophisticated cousin to the familiar Waldorf salad, but the creamy dressing is replaced with a walnut oil vinaigrette. Crisp and refreshing in taste and appearance, celery salad travels well and is put together easily. The pale green celery and golden apples are very pretty dotted with currants, and the salad contains nothing you can't buy in a supermarket. However, if you have garden thinnings of rocket (arugula), mustard greens, cress, or nasturtium leaves, you can strew them over the top and then toss them in just before serving.

Use a dark-colored walnut oil with the rich flavor of nuts or try using a hazelnut oil and hazelnuts in place of the walnuts. If neither of these oils is available, use a sunflower seed or light olive oil mixed with a little dark sesame oil.

Makes 6 to 8 servings

> ½ *cup dried currants*
> *1 large head of celery*
> *2 Golden Delicious apples*
> *5 or 6 pale green celery leaves*
> *4 parsley branches*
> *10 walnuts, cracked and left in large pieces*
> *1 to 2 tablespoons walnut oil*
> *lemon juice or Champagne vinegar*
> *salt*
> *freshly ground pepper*

If the currants are hard, cover them with warm water and set them aside to soften while you cut the celery and apples. When they're soft, after 10 minutes or so, drain them and squeeze out the water.

Separate the stalks of celery and peel the tougher outer stalks. Slice the celery into thin pieces, straight across or at an angle. Cut the apples into quarters or sixths if they're large and thinly slice them crosswise. Finely chop the celery leaves and the parsley and crack the nuts.

Combine the celery, apples, currants, celery leaves, parsley, and walnuts in a bowl. Toss them with just enough walnut oil to coat everything lightly. Add the lemon juice or vinegar to taste, salt lightly, season with pepper, and toss again.

Oranges with Pickled Onions and Pomegranates

This salad brings any rich or spicy meal to a perfect conclusion. The clean, sweet taste of the orange refreshes the mouth, and the mild acidity of both the orange and the pickle wakes it up. The brilliant colors—orange, pink, and red, with green flecks of pistachio nuts—especially served on a bright blue plate, brighten the eye as well as the tongue.

Start the pickled onions first. They'll need at least 20 minutes in the refrigerator to begin to color and cure.

Makes 4 to 6 servings

> *pomegranate seeds from part of 1 pomegranate*
> *4 large or 6 small navel oranges*
> *a handful of pickled red onion rings (page 332)*
> *10 unsalted pistachio nuts, peeled and lightly chopped*
> *2 to 3 teaspoons olive oil (optional)*
> *balsamic vinegar or juice of the pomegranate*

Cut the pomegranates into quarters with a sharp knife then separate the seeds. (Pomegranate juice stains, so work carefully.)

Slice off even pieces from both ends of each orange, then set each orange securely on the counter and using a downward, sawing motion, slice away the peel, cutting right to the flesh. A good, sharp knife makes this a very easy job. Slice the oranges into thin rounds and arrange them on a platter. Scatter the onions over the top and garnish with pomegranate seeds and the chopped pistachios. Just before serving, dribble the oil, if you're using it, over the surface and add a teaspoon or so of vinegar or the tart juice of the pomegranate.

Suggestions:
- If blood oranges are available, use them in place of or mixed with the navels. Or include a few thin slices of lime or lemon among the oranges for a tart surprise. Some people really enjoy eating the tart citrus fruits.
- Sprinkle orange flower water over the oranges to intensify their perfume.
- Include a green, especially one that contrasts with the sweetness of the fruit, like watercress or curly endive. Dress it lightly or not at all and use it around the edge of the platter.
- To make a more substantial first-course salad, include some thinly sliced fennel, sliced radishes, or celery.
- For more complex flavors, include herbs or spices—for example, cumin and paprika, cilantro or parsley, lemon balm or verbena, or a scented basil.

Avocado and Papaya Salad with Mango Vinaigrette

Mango and raspberries go into the dressing, which is a little tart and fruity, with the color of a sunrise. A peppery green, like watercress, makes a good contrast to the sweet, smooth fruit, and the glossy dark green leaves set off the fruit and sauce beautifully. With each salad arranged on its own plate, this makes a rather special beginning to a meal.

Makes 4 salads

> 2 shallots, finely diced
> zest and juice of 2 limes (about ¼ cup juice in all)
> ¼ cup light olive oil
> salt
> 1 mango
> ½ cup raspberries
> balsamic vinegar
> 2 small or 1 large ripe but firm avocado
> 1 papaya
> 3 to 4 handfuls of watercress, field cress or rocket (arugula) leaves

Put the shallots, lime zest and juice, and olive oil into a bowl with a few pinches of salt; whisk together.

Peel the mango over a bowl to catch the juice; then slice it into pieces. Purée enough mango, with the juice, to measure ½ cup and add it to the lime juice and oil. The remaining mango, if any, can be sliced and arranged with the avocado and papaya. Crush the berries with the back of a spoon against a strainer, forcing the juice into the bowl with the dressing. Whisk again to bring everything together. Add balsamic vinegar to taste.

Peel and slice the avocado and papaya attractively. Arrange them on salad plates and ladle most of the sauce over and around them. Toss the greens with the remaining sauce and set them around the fruit. If you're using a delicate green like field cress, don't toss it—the dressing is too heavy—but just settle it lightly around the fruit.

Potato Salad with Tomatillo Sauce

Tomatillos, garlic, chilies, and cilantro make a lively, light, and unusual dressing for a potato salad. There's little oil to make it shine and slide, so the potatoes will look best if you dress them just before serving. This particular salad is very simple, but you could include any of the vegetables that usually go into potato salads—celery, green peppers, sliced raw or pickled onions, or small cubes of cucumber.

Makes 4 or more servings

> 1½ *pounds new red-skinned or yellow-fleshed potatoes*
> 1 *or 2 jalapeño peppers*
> ½ *onion*
> 6 *plump tomatillos, husks removed*
> 3 *garlic cloves, peeled*
> 1 *cup cilantro leaves*
> 1 *to 2 tablespoons peanut, sunflower, or other light oil, optional*
> *grated zest and juice of 1 lime*
> *salt*
> 2 *hard-cooked eggs*
> 6 *radishes for garnish*
> *fresh cilantro sprigs for garnish*

If the skins on the potatoes look fresh, leave them on. Otherwise, peel the potatoes and then slice them into rounds about ¼ inch thick. Steam them in a vegetable steamer until they are tender but still firm, about 25 minutes.

While they are steaming, make the sauce. Slice the jalapeños in half and take out the seeds. Cut the onion into several large pieces. Bring a few cups of water to a boil and add the tomatillos, jalapeños, onion, and garlic. Simmer until the tomatillos turn from bright green to dull, 10 to 15 minutes; then drain. Transfer them to a food processor or blender, add the cilantro, and purée. Stir in the oil, if you're using it, and the lime zest and juice. Season with salt to taste.

Arrange the potatoes on a platter or in a shallow bowl. Slice the eggs and intersperse them with the potatoes. Ladle the sauce over all. Garnish with the radishes and fresh sprigs of cilantro and serve.

Suggestions: For a hotter sauce, reserve half the garlic and jalapeños; then add them, uncooked, to the tomatillos as they're being puréed. For a creamy tomatillo sauce, add ¼ cup sour cream or plain yogurt.

Wild Rice and Asparagus Salad

Wild rice, whether cultivated or actually harvested from the wild, has a vigorous, earthy taste, and in a salad it would be well matched with thin stalks of wild asparagus. Lacking that, here is a recipe using cultivated asparagus. This particular rice salad is seasoned with both light and dark sesame oil, orange peel, and ginger; the asparagus stalks are cut into small rounds and dispersed among the grains of rice.

Rice salads are best when the dressing is mixed with warm grains; the heat releases the fragrant oils from the herbs and spices, and the oil is absorbed by the grain. But there's no reason why an impromptu salad can't be fashioned out of leftover rice. The aromatic explosion won't be as great, but it will still taste good. Wild rice can also be mixed with long-grain brown rice or white rice or both. (If you're using different types of rice, be sure to cook them separately, as they have different cooking times.) Serve this as a first-course salad or include it on a buffet table. It's good warm, chilled or at room temperature.

Begin with the rice. While it is cooking, blanch the asparagus and make the vinaigrette.

Makes 4 to 8 servings

THE RICE AND GARNISHES

1 cup wild rice
1 quart water
salt
1 to 1½ pounds asparagus
2 tablespoons sesame seeds
3 or 4 handfuls of nappa cabbage, cut into
*   squares, or watercress leaves*
whole cilantro leaves

Rinse the rice and put it in a pot with the water and salt. Bring it to a boil; then lower the heat and simmer until the grains have expanded and the rice is cooked, about 40 minutes. Drain it well.

Snap off the tough ends of the asparagus and discard them. Slice off the tips, leaving them 2 to 3 inches long, and cut the tender remaining portion of the stems into short pieces, using a zigzag motion so that they'll have an irregular shape. Or cut them into rounds. Drop them into boiling salted water and cook

them until they're bright green and tender but still a little firm—the exact time depends on the size of the asparagus, but not more than a few minutes. When done, refresh them under cold water and set them aside on a towel to drain.

Make the vinaigrette below and toast the sesame seeds. Combine the asparagus, rice, and sesame seeds and toss with about two thirds of the dressing. Use the other third to dress the greens. Heap the rice on a platter and encircle it with the nappa or watercress. Garnish with whole cilantro leaves.

THE VINAIGRETTE

2 scallions, finely chopped
1 tablespoon finely sliced orange zest
5 tablespoons orange juice
3 tablespoons light sesame oil
2 tablespoons dark sesame oil
1 tablespoon soy sauce
1 tablespoon balsamic vinegar
1 tablespoon grated ginger
2 teaspoons minced garlic
pinch of sugar
2 to 3 tablespoons roughly chopped cilantro

To make the dressing, combine all the vinaigrette ingredients. Be sure to taste and adjust the seasonings if necessary as various brands of oil and soy sauce differ in strength.

Quinoa Salad with Dried Fruits and Pine Nuts

Quinoa is an ancient grain from the Andes that has recently been introduced as the "superfood"—it has more protein, and higher-quality protein, than any other grain. The tiny seeds are very light and digestible. Here they are mixed with dried apricots, currants, golden peppers, chives, and roasted pine nuts, all finely cut to match the diminutive size of the quinoa. This makes a lovely salad to cup in a leaf of lettuce, and leftover salad can be used to fill a grape leaf or a leaf of blanched chard. The salad tastes best when first made and served warm or tepid, but it also keeps well, refrigerated. If you're making it in advance, add the pine nuts just before serving so that they will remain crisp.

Quinoa must be rinsed well before cooking, or there will be a bitter edge to the otherwise delicate flavor. While the quinoa is cooking, the rest of the ingredients can be prepared.

The viscous cooking liquid can be used in place of all or some of the oil to make this salad virtually fat-free. Although it won't have the flavor of the oil, it has a somewhat unctuous quality that will coat the grains and act as a vehicle for the herbs and spices.

Makes 4 generous servings

THE QUINOA

    1 cup quinoa
    2 cups water
    salt
    6 dried apricots, finely diced
    2 tablespoons snipped chives or 3 small scallions, cut into narrow rounds
    ¼ cup dried currants, softened in hot water and squeezed dry
    3 tablespoons finely and evenly diced yellow or green bell peppers
    3 tablespoons pine nuts

Rinse the quinoa thoroughly in a bowl of cold water; then pour it into a fine-meshed strainer and rinse it again under running tap water. Bring the water to a boil, add salt to taste, and stir in the quinoa. Lower the heat, cover the pan, and cook for 15 minutes. Taste the grain—there should be just a little resistance, and the opaque spiraled ring of germ should show. If necessary, continue cooking until done, then pour into a strainer and set it to drain over a bowl. (Save the liquid, which can replace the oil in the dressing or be used in soups.)

While the quinoa is cooking, cut the apricots and vegetables as suggested, keeping everything as fine and even as possible. Toast the pine nuts in a dry pan until they are golden brown; then turn them into a bowl.

Make the vinaigrette below. Then toss the warm quinoa with the fruits, vegetables, pine nuts, and dressing. Serve the salad nestled in rounded lettuce leaves.

THE VINAIGRETTE

grated zest of 1 lemon
1 tablespoon lemon juice
2 teaspoons finely chopped cilantro or parsley
¼ teaspoon paprika
¼ teaspoon ground cumin
¼ teaspoon ground coriander
salt
2 tablespoons light olive oil
2 tablespoons extra-virgin olive oil

Combine the lemon zest, juice, spices, herbs, and salt together in a bowl. Stir to combine; then whisk in the olive oils. Taste and adjust the balance of flavors, adding lemon juice if necessary.

Summer Vegetables, Butter Beans, and Basil

This can easily be a main-course salad for a summer lunch or dinner. The summer produce is bright and colorful, and there's a pleasing range of textures, from the crisp peppers to the soft butter beans. Anything that comes fresh from a garden would make it that much better—a few bush beans, some radishes or peas, a fresh red onion. The small leaves of purple salad savoy (ornamental kale), shredded radicchio, or small leaves of red lettuces all make beautiful garnishes.

The salad can be dressed with the oil mixture an hour before serving; the vinegar should be added at the last moment.

Makes 4 to 6 servings

THE VEGETABLES

½ cucumber
1 small red bell pepper
1 small yellow bell pepper
1 small green bell pepper
1 small onion or ½ bunch scallions
2 ripe but firm tomatoes or a handful of small tomatoes, like
   yellow pear tomatoes or Sweet 100s
12 black Greek or Italian olives, stoned and halved
12 basil leaves, mixed varieties or whatever kind is available,
   cut into ribbons
1 15-ounce can (1½ cups) butter beans or chick-peas, rinsed
2 hard-cooked eggs, sliced
12 small leaves of salad savoy, radicchio, or red oak leaf lettuce

Peel the cucumber and cut it lengthwise into quarters or sixths if it's large. Scoop out the seeds and dice the pieces into cubes about ½ inch wide. Halve the peppers, remove the seeds and membranes, and slice them into strips a little less than ½ inch wide. Slice the onion or scallions, plus an inch or so of the greens, into thin rounds. If the tomatoes are large, cut them into wedges. If using a smaller variety, cut them in half.

Make the vinaigrette below. Put the vegetables in a large, shallow bowl with the olives, basil, and beans. Pour over all but a tablespoon of the dressing and

gently mix everything with your fingers. Tuck in the egg slices here and there. Cover well and refrigerate for an hour. Just before serving, toss the greens with the remaining vinaigrette. Sprinkle 2 to 3 teaspoons vinegar over the vegetables and toss gently. Garnish with the dressed leaves and serve.

THE VINAIGRETTE

1 garlic clove, roughly chopped
12 peppercorns
salt
1 tablespoon capers, rinsed
3 to 4 tablespoons extra-virgin olive oil
2 to 3 teaspoons red wine vinegar

Pound the garlic with the peppercorns and salt in a mortar until they are well broken up. Add the capers, break them up a little with the pestle, and stir in the oil. Use this to dress the vegetables; then add the vinegar just before serving.

Hot White Beans with Condiments

Serve this as an appetizer or a light, inexpensive spring or summer lunch. A heap of tender, warm beans—plump limas or cannellini beans—is surrounded by smaller piles of diced vegetables and herbs and served with a cruet of fine olive oil and wedges of lemon. Each person drizzles oil over the beans and tosses them with the condiments. The oil is warmed by the heat of the beans, and the flavors explode and rise in the steam. Very simple, but a delight.

Exact amounts aren't really needed, but below are some suggestions. A cup of dried beans yields about 2 cups, plus a little, cooked. A half cup per person is more than adequate for an appetizer and about right for a small meal.

Makes 4 to 6 servings

THE BEANS

1⅓ cups dried white beans, soaked 6 hours or overnight
2 garlic cloves
2 bay leaves
2 fresh sage leaves or a pinch of dried
1 tablespoon olive oil
salt

Pick through the beans, rinse them, and then cover them generously with water. Set them aside to soak for at least 6 hours or overnight. Drain and cover them with fresh water, bring to a boil, and boil vigorously for about 5 minutes. Remove any scum that rises to the surface and lower the heat. Add the garlic, bay leaves, sage, and oil. Cook slowly for 45 minutes, add salt to taste, and continue cooking until the beans are tender but still hold their shape, another 30 minutes or so, depending on the type of bean used. Lima beans cook more quickly than other varieties, so add the salt after 30 minutes and check soon afterward to see if they're done. While the beans are cooking, prepare the following condiments.

THE CONDIMENTS

You'll need a cup or so of each condiment.

> *1 small onion, finely diced, or 1 bunch of scallions, thinly sliced*
> *several celery stalks, finely diced*
> *bell peppers, any color or a mixture of colors, cut into small squares*
> *2 ripe tomatoes, peeled, seeded, and finely chopped*
> *3 large white mushrooms, diced into small squares and tossed with*
> *   lemon juice*
> *1½ cups chopped mixed herbs such as parsley, thyme, dill or basil,*
> *   and rocket (arugula) leaves*
> *¼ cup capers, rinsed*
> *extra-virgin olive oil*
> *wedges of lemon*
> *a pepper mill*

When the beans are done, drain them. Heap them in the middle of 4 individual plates. Surround the beans with mounds of the condiments and serve with a cruet of olive oil, lemon wedges, and a pepper mill. Let each person pour the oil over the hot beans and toss his or her own wonderfully aromatic salad.

Chick-Peas and Peppers with Pine Nut Dressing

In this salad sautéed peppers and onions, seasoned with cumin and paprika, are mixed with chick-peas and dressed with a pine nut sauce. It's a substantial and full-flavored salad, suitable in small portions for an appetizer or as a side dish for grilled brochettes of vegetables or meats. It also makes a filling one-dish meal.

To speed things along when you haven't any cooked chick-peas, this salad can be made with rinsed canned chick-peas. White beans are also delicious treated this way, but canned varieties tend to be a little too mushy. Serve this salad warm or at room temperature.

Makes 4 or more servings

THE BEANS AND VEGETABLES

1 cup dried chick-peas or white beans, soaked 6 hours or overnight
  or 2 15-ounce cans chick-peas
salt
1 onion, quartered and thinly sliced crosswise
1 small green bell pepper, thinly sliced into pieces 2 inches long
1 garlic clove, finely chopped
1 tablespoon olive oil
1 teaspoon ground cumin
½ teaspoon paprika
1 teaspoon tomato paste
juice of ½ lemon
12 Niçoise olives, pitted or 6 Kalamata olives, pitted and cut into large pieces
additional paprika for garnish
cilantro or parsley branches for garnish

Drain the beans after they've soaked, cover them with cold fresh water, and bring to a boil. Boil vigorously for 5 minutes and remove any foam that rises to the surface. Lower the heat and simmer for 30 minutes. Add salt and continue cooking until the beans are soft but still hold their shape, about an hour. Drain the beans, but reserve the liquid for the dressing. Prepare the vegetables while the beans are cooking.

Warm the olive oil in a skillet and add the onion, bell pepper, garlic, cumin, paprika, and lightly salt. Cook over medium heat, stirring frequently, until the

onions and peppers are just slightly softened, for about 3 minutes. Stir in the tomato paste and lemon juice and cook for another 30 seconds or so.

Make the pine nut dressing below and toss it with the beans. Add the vegetables and the olives and lightly toss again. Set the salad in a serving bowl, dust with paprika, and garnish with leaves and branches of cilantro or parsley.

THE PINE NUT DRESSING

¼ cup bean broth or (if using canned chick-peas) milk or water
⅓ cup pine nuts
1 garlic clove
¼ cup extra-virgin olive oil
juice of ½ large lemon
salt
freshly ground pepper
2 tablespoons chopped parsley
1 to 2 tablespoons chopped cilantro

Heat the bean broth, milk or water. Put the pine nuts in the work bowl of a food processor and process, gradually adding the heated bean broth, making as fine a purée as possible. Next add the garlic, olive oil, lemon juice, and a little salt and continue to process until smooth. Season to taste with pepper and stir in the parsley and cilantro.

Salad of Roasted and Pickled Vegetables

There's an extravagant range of tastes, colors, and textures in this salad. It's one I've made for years, probably never the same way twice, but it has some fairly constant elements—roasted beets and peppers, pickled onions, briefly blanched or steamed beans, and, when possible, bronze-leaved garden lettuces. All the parts are dressed with an herb vinaigrette and arranged haphazardly on a colorful platter.

This salad can be pleasantly complicated with ingredients (see the variations at the end of the recipe), and it can also be simple, with just a few elements. If pickled onions and roasted peppers are already on hand, all you need to do is roast the beets, steam some beans, and wash a few leaves of lettuce. I prefer golden beets, but red ones will do fine, too. Just be sure to place them right where you want them, or their color will stain everything else.

Makes 4 servings

THE VEGETABLES

8 small red or golden beets
½ pound fresh beans, such as yellow wax, Blue Lake, haricot vert, etc.
1 roasted red, yellow or orange bell pepper (page 329)
a handful of pickled red onion rings (page 332)
8 tiny new potatoes or 3 small red potatoes
2 handfuls of red lettuce
herb blossoms for garnish, if available

Preheat the oven to 375°F. Trim the beets, leaving an inch of the tops and the tails, rinse them well, and put them in a pan with enough water just to cover the bottom. Cover with foil and bake until tender but still a little firm, about 30 minutes. The exact baking time will depend on the size of the beets. When they are cool enough to handle, slip off the skins and cut them into quarters or sixths.

Steam the beans or blanch them in boiling salted water until just tender; then remove and rinse them under cold water to stop the cooking. Prepare the peppers and onions according to the recipes. Steam or roast the potatoes until tender and slice them into wedges or rounds. Wash and dry the lettuce.

Make the vinaigrette below. Use some of it to dress the lettuce leaves lightly

and arrange them in a shallow bowl or platter. Dress the beets, beans, and potatoes separately and arrange them loosely. Add the strips of roasted peppers and the pickled onions and garnish with a scattering of herb blossoms, if any are available. Deep purple hyssop flowers, lavender, chive, or rosemary blossoms would all be particularly pretty.

THE VINAIGRETTE

1 tablespoon Champagne vinegar
1 teaspoon balsamic vinegar
salt
1 shallot, finely diced
1 tablespoon lightly chopped basil leaves
1 tablespoon finely chopped parsley
¼ cup extra-virgin olive oil
1 tablespoon large capers, rinsed

Combine the vinegars, salt to taste, shallot, and herbs. Gently whisk in the oil and stir in the capers. Taste and adjust the seasonings if necessary.

Suggestions:

Here are some other vegetables you might include:

- new potatoes, roasted and then sliced or left whole if very small
- broad, flat Romano beans
- tiny currant tomatoes
- roasted onions

Tomato Aspic with Saffron Cream

The tomato base of this gel is seasoned with lemon zest and *herbes de Provence* and then poured into a flat dish to set. It is served in the dish, covered with a layer of saffron-flavored sour cream flecked with the purple bracts and leaves of basil, chives, and their blossoms. Actually, the sour cream covering serves as a blank piece of paper. There is no end to the fanciful designs and decorations that can be made with thinly sliced vegetables and delicate blossoms.

In my experience a little aspic is cool and refreshing—more than that is suddenly tiresome. But small portions, combined with crisp and lively things like radishes, olives, and the inner leaves of romaine, can make a bright start to a summer meal. This aspic can be cut into squares, triangles, and diamonds with ease.

Agar-agar, a flavorless substance derived from seaweed, is used to set the aspic rather than gelatin. It comes in different forms, but the flakes are easiest to use. They can be found in natural foods stores.

Makes 8 or 10 servings

THE ASPIC

1 teaspoon herbes de Provence *or 2 tablespoons chopped
 fresh herbs such as parsley, marjoram, and thyme*
2½ cups tomato juice
3 level tablespoons agar-agar
grated zest and juice of 1 lemon
sugar
1 tablespoon finely sliced chives
2 tablespoons finely chopped parsley or chervil
2 shallots, finely diced

Crush the dried herbs a little with a pestle or chop them with a knife. Heat the tomato juice with the herbs, slowly bringing it to a boil. Stir in the agar-agar, lower the heat, and simmer for 10 minutes, stirring frequently. Remove the pan from the heat, stir in the lemon zest, and add the lemon juice, sugar to taste, and the fresh herbs.

Pour the aspic into a small, flat serving dish measuring approximately 6 by 9 inches and put it in the refrigerator to set, about 2 hours. Make the cream below. When the gel is cold and set, spread it over the top of the aspic and garnish it.

THE SAFFRON CREAM

6 tablespoons sour cream or a mixture of plain yogurt and sour cream
⅛ teaspoon crumbled saffron threads, dissolved in 2 teaspoons hot water
milk or cream, if needed
garnishes, as available: small leaves and flower bracts of opal
or cinnamon basil; small leaves and blossoms of flowering thyme
or hyssop; a few chives, sliced into narrow rounds; and chive blossoms

Whisk the sour cream with the saffron until creamy and smooth. If it is too thick to spread easily, stir in a little milk or cream to make it spreadable but not runny. Pour it onto the set aspic and spread it evenly over the surface. Scatter the herbs over the top and refrigerate until needed.

Cucumber Mousse with Mustard Oil Vinaigrette

All the coolness we associate with cucumbers is present in this frothy mousse. In contrast to its delicacy, I like to serve it with a mustard oil vinaigrette. Mustard oil is a little hot and very aromatic, smelling exactly like mustard and tasting slightly like horseradish. Mixed with shallots, Champagne vinegar, and fresh dill, it makes the whole dish come alive.

Chill the mousse in a single attractive mold and serve it as the centerpiece of a salad plate that includes thin slices of sturdy dark rye bread and something crisp—a garden radish and a few heart leaves of romaine. Or mold it in individual ramekins and serve one to each person.

Makes 6 to 8 servings

THE MOUSSE

> *3 large cucumbers*
> *½ cup plain yogurt or sour cream*
> *1 teaspoon Worcestershire sauce*
> *1½ tablespoons finely chopped dill*
> *2 to 3 tablespoons finely chopped parsley*
> *3 small scallions, including a little of the green, finely sliced*
> *finely grated zest of ½ lemon*
> *salt*
> *freshly ground white or black pepper*
> *1 teaspoon lemon juice or Champagne vinegar, approximately*
> *3 tablespoons agar-agar*
> *⅓ cup water*
> *½ cup cream*
> *1 hard-cooked egg for garnish (optional)*

Peel the cucumbers, cut them in half lengthwise, and scoop out the seeds. Chop them roughly into ½-inch pieces. Bring a quart of water to boil, add the cucumbers, boil for 3 minutes, and drain. Put them in a food processor and work until smooth, about 1 minute; then transfer them to a bowl. Stir in the yogurt or sour cream, Worcestershire sauce, herbs, scallions, and lemon zest. Season to taste with salt, pepper, and lemon juice or vinegar. Make sure everything is highly seasoned.

Combine the agar-agar and water in a small saucepan and bring to a boil. Lower the heat and cook gently until the agar-agar is dissolved, about 10 minutes. If there isn't enough liquid for the size of the pan, add a little of the cucumber mixture. While the agar-agar is heating, whip the cream with a pinch of salt until stiff. Stir the dissolved agar-agar into the cucumber mixture and then fold in the cream. Pour the mixture into a 6-cup mold or into individual ramekins. Refrigerate until completely cold and firm, at least 2 hours.

To serve, run a knife around the edge, set the mold in hot water briefly to loosen the bottom, and turn the mousse out onto a platter or individual plates. Make the vinaigrette below and serve the mousse with a spoonful ladled over each serving. Garnish with the egg yolk, if you're using the egg, pushed through a sieve directly over the mousse, and the egg whites, very finely diced.

THE MUSTARD OIL VINAIGRETTE

If mustard oil isn't available, make the dressing with a combination of a strong, virgin olive oil mixed with light olive oil and stir about ½ teaspoon dried mustard, *wasabi* or preserved horseradish to taste into the vinaigrette.

> *2 shallots or 2 tablespoons pickled red onion rings (page 332), finely diced*
> *2 tablespoons finely chopped dill*
> *2½ tablespoons Champagne vinegar or white wine vinegar seasoned with dill*
> *salt*
> *¼ cup mustard oil*

Combine all the ingredients except the oil and stir to dissolve the salt. Then whisk in the mustard oil. Taste and adjust the seasonings if necessary.

Variation: In place of the mustard oil, make a hazelnut oil vinaigrette and garnish the top of the mousse with chopped roasted hazelnuts.

Fresh Mozzarella with Herbs

Fresh mozzarella makes a cheese salad that is light, tender, a little chewy, but not at all rubbery. All in all this salad is the work of a moment. It can be made either hours ahead of serving, giving the herbs a chance to penetrate the cheese and merge with one another, or at the last moment, leaving the flavors fresher and more distinct.

Use a single favorite or mix several together, such as marjoram and Italian parsley with a bit of thyme and hyssop, or peppery nasturtium leaves and their flowers, or lemon thyme and chives. Different varieties of basil are heady and strong, while salad burnet and young borage leaves suggest the taste of cucumbers.

The rest of the ingredients add liveliness to the mixture. Grinding the peppercorns in a mortar and leaving them coarse contributes warmth on the tongue. As this salad is mainly white and green, this is a perfect occasion to use flowering herbs as a garnish.

Makes 6 to 8 servings

> 1 1-pound whole fresh mozzarella cheese
> 25 black peppercorns
> 4 to 5 tablespoons extra-virgin olive oil
> 5 tablespoons finely chopped mixed herbs (see note above)
> 2 tablespoons small capers, rinsed
> 6 green olives, stoned and finely chopped
> 1 tablespoon finely diced green bell pepper
> 1 teaspoon lemon zest, grated or cut into narrow slivers
> lemon juice
> butter lettuce or red oak leaf lettuce, the leaves separated but left whole
> finely sliced or snipped nasturtium petals, if available

Slice the cheese into rounds about ⅓ inch thick; then slice the rounds into strips about the same thickness or whatever shape you like. Set in a colander to drain while preparing the rest of the ingredients.

Crush the peppercorns in a mortar or grind them under a heavy bowl if you haven't a mortar, leaving them rather coarse. Put the drained cheese in a wide bowl. Add the olive oil, herbs, crushed pepper, capers, olives, green pepper, and lemon zest and gently toss together. Taste and add lemon juice if you wish more tartness. Refrigerate until ready to serve.

Pile the salad on a bed of perfect lettuce leaves and garnish with the nasturtium petals.

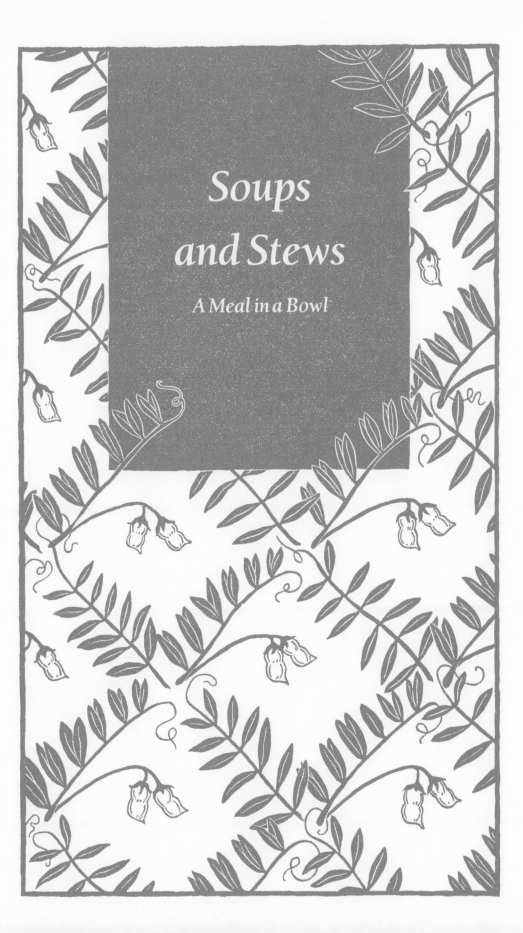

Soups
and Stews

A Meal in a Bowl

A light soup can begin a meal, but a heftier one can become the mainstay, warming when it's cold, cooling when it's hot, and always nourishing. A little time is needed for the flavors to develop—once made, soups keep, and the flavors generally improve with time. Most of these recipes make about 6 cups of soup, enough to serve a family or sustain one or two people for a couple of meals. Soups are among the most flexible and easiest foods to multiply; they also freeze fairly well, so extra amounts can be put away for future meals.

Stocks usually provide the background flavor for the soup vegetables. The subject of vegetable stocks—different kinds of stocks and their uses as well as the effects of particular ingredients in stocks—was thoroughly explored in *The Greens Cookbook*. The soups in this book have been chosen in part because they taste good made with water or a very simple stock made from the vegetable trimmings, assembled at the same time you're making the soup. Of course stock can be used if desired, but these soups have plenty of flavor without taking this extra step—and often stocks obscure the delicate flavors of vegetables.

For those concerned about their intake of fat, these soups use very little and sometimes none at all. Sautéing the vegetables in a little oil at the beginning helps develop flavors, but that step can be modified, or even omitted, if necessary. The same is true for swirling in a spoonful of herb butter or olive oil to finish the soup; a little goes far, but if necessary, it can be omitted.

Stews are slowly and gently cooked mixtures of vegetables that create their own aromatic sauces. They are the opposite of tender-crisp vegetables, which retain their own separate identities; rather, they are cooked until their flavors merge and blend and the sum is larger than its parts. Some of these stews are rustic, while others are more elegant, served with delicate toast points or squares of puff pastry, either as the first or main course. The merging of the fragrant sauces with the pastry is quite wonderful. There are more points to watch in making a stew than a soup, but once you get the hang of it, you may find that a vegetable stew is something you make frequently and with ease. To me, a tender mélange of seasonal vegetables makes one of the most satisfying and interesting meals.

One of the joys of cooking soups and stews is working with the produce itself. When the vegetables first begin to cook, their colors are astonishingly pure and brilliant; then this luminescent beauty fades as its vitality is transformed into broth and sustenance. Each time I see this phenomenon I think that it's one of the privileges of cooking.

Fennel Soup with Watercress Purée

Fennel bulb stewed with leeks makes a sweet-tasting soup, while the watercress finishes it with a lively, peppery flourish. Fennel is so flavorful that there's no need to make a stock or even use the ubiquitous and trusted aromatics—bay leaf, parsley, and thyme. In fact, using water for the liquid allows the full taste of the vegetables to come forward completely unmasked.

Serve this soup with just the swirl of watercress or enrich it with a spoonful of butter. A handful of little croutons, fried in butter, always adds a nice crunchy touch to puréed soups.

Wash and slice all the vegetables first. If the inner core of the fennel is tough and stringy, remove it with a paring knife, but usually even a well-developed core will be tender.

Makes 4 to 6 servings

> 1 tablespoon butter
> 1 large leek, white part only, chopped (about 1½ cups)
> 2 large fennel bulbs, quartered and sliced
> 2 tablespoons chopped fennel greens
> 1 medium-sized red potato, sliced or chopped
> salt
> 6½ cups cold water
> additional water, milk or cream for thinning
> ½ bunch of watercress

Melt the butter in a heavy soup pot; add the vegetables, salt, and ½ cup of the water. Sweat them over low heat for about 12 to 15 minutes, then add the remaining 6 cups cold water and bring it to a boil. Lower the heat and simmer until the vegetables are tender, about 20 minutes.

Purée the soup in a food processor or blender until smooth and return it to the pot. If the soup needs thinning, add enough water, milk, or cream to get the right consistency. Season to taste with salt if necessary.

Sort through the watercress and discard the large stems and any yellow or damaged leaves. Purée in a food processor or blender until fine, adding enough water to loosen the leaves from the blades. Stir in half the purée and taste it before adding the rest. Sometimes watercress can be very strong, with an extra-bitter edge that will completely take over. I've ruined this very soup by puréeing a whole bunch of cress and blindly adding it without tasting it first. Although I'm a fan of bitter greens, this was overwhelming.

If you're making the soup in advance, wait until the last minute to purée the watercress to enjoy its bright, green freshness.

Spring Tonic Soup

Before modern growing and shipping methods began to erode our relation to the seasons, the appearance of the first greens in spring must have been anticipated with longing and welcomed with enthusiasm. After a long season of eating dried foods, the fresh, strong flavors of wild mustards, lamb's-quarters, sorrel, green herbs, and chicories would taste extremely good and restorative. This soup is for anyone who still feels a deep craving for masses of greens in early spring.

Sorrel is especially distinctive for its clean, tart taste, so include it if it's available. If not, you can use a stalk of rhubarb in its place or sharpen the flavors at the end with lemon juice or vinegar.

Various combinations of greens can be used in this soup, reflecting what's on hand or your own preference for sweet or bitter tastes. With lettuce and escarole, use the outer leaves and save the tender hearts for salads. And if you've any broth that remains from cooking lentils and beans, use it in place of water for its flavor and the body that it gives to soups.

One of the most vigorous-tasting spring plants is the stinging nettle, which is traditionally used in restorative soups and broths. Although it's a wild plant, it frequently volunteers in the garden. Anyone who has unknowingly brushed against a nettle plant understands its name; tiny needles cover the undersides of the leaves and give a fast, sharp prick to the skin. The burn dissipates after a few minutes, and the stingers disappear when the nettles are cooked. Always use gloves when handling nettles.

Makes 8 to 9 cups serving 4 to 6

> *1 or 2 tablespoons olive oil*
> *2 medium-sized red potatoes, scrubbed and diced*
> *2 to 3 medium-sized leeks, white parts only, sliced into rounds*
> *2 medium-sized carrots, peeled and diced*
> *5 garlic cloves, peeled*
> *2 good pinches of dried thyme*
> *a handful of parsley leaves*
> *salt*
> *a handful of watercress*
> *2 cups chopped chard leaves, spinach or tender beet greens*

4 cups roughly chopped nettles, if available
2 cups sorrel leaves or 1 stalk rhubarb, chopped
2 cups chopped mustard greens, turnip greens, or broccoli rabe
2 cups chopped escarole
2 cups chopped lettuce leaves
1 or 2 handfuls of rocket (arugula) leaves
2 quarts water, stock or bean broth
tarragon or white wine vinegar
extra-virgin olive oil, butter or cream
rice or croutons, to finish the soup
coarsely cracked pepper
wild mustard or radish flowers for garnish, if available

Warm the oil in a wide soup pot; add the potatoes, leeks, carrots, garlic, thyme, parsley leaves, and salt. Stir to coat with the oil, cover, and cook over medium heat for about 5 minutes. Add the greens and allow them to gradually wilt down, stirring them every few minutes.

When they have wilted, add the water or stock, bring to a boil, and lower the heat to a simmer. Cook until the potatoes are soft, about 25 minutes. Let the soup cool a bit; then blend it. Leave the texture a little coarse if you like; for a finer texture, pass it through a food mill.

To finish the soup, taste for salt and a little vinegar to bring up the flavors. Stir in a spoonful of olive oil, cream, or some butter, to enrich the soup, add plenty of coarsely cracked pepper, and serve. If you like a little more texture in the soup, add some cooked rice or a scattering of croutons to each bowl. Wild mustard or radish flowers floating on top would make a pretty and appropriate springtime garnish.

Asparagus and Pea Velouté

This rather refined soup makes the most of new spring vegetables and herbs when they are still a little scarce and not yet old hat. A couple of handfuls of sorrel, melted with the leeks, taste wonderful with the rest of the vegetables, though the sorrel will give the soup a slightly dull color.

Flour gives this soup its creamy texture, though the velvet-smooth texture of this style of soup is traditionally further ensured with cream and egg yolks. The soup then must be reheated carefully so that the yolks don't curdle. I usually omit this addition as the soup seems already sufficiently rich and smooth, but if you want to include it, directions are given.

To bring out the flavors of the vegetables I use the trimmings (the leek greens, asparagus stems, and pea pods) to make a stock. The stock is cooked for only 20 minutes to retain the fresh taste of the vegetables. If you're using frozen peas, use some in the stock in place of pea pods.

Makes about 1½ quarts serving 4 to 6

> 1 pound thin asparagus
> 4 small leeks (about ½ pound when trimmed)
> 1 pound fresh peas or 1⅓ cups frozen peas
> 1 quart water
> salt
> 5 parsley branches, roughly chopped
> 3 tablespoons butter
> 3 tablespoons flour
> 2 cups milk
> ½ to 1 cup half-and-half or cream (optional)
> freshly ground white pepper
> herbs for garnish: several fresh basil or sorrel leaves,
>   finely sliced; thinly sliced rounds of chives and their blossoms,
>   if available; or chopped chervil
> 1 egg yolk (optional)

Preparing the vegetables and stock: Trim the asparagus. Slice the top third of the asparagus on the diagonal, leaving the tips whole. (For thick asparagus, cut the tips in half lengthwise.) Set aside and roughly chop the rest of the stems for the stock. Cut off the green part of the leeks. Use just the 3 or 4 inches closest to the

base, chop them roughly, and rinse well. Discard the rest of the greens. If you're using fresh peas, shell them, reserving the pods. Select a couple of handfuls of the best-looking pods and chop them.

Bring the water to a boil and add salt to taste. Blanch the asparagus tips and sliced stems until they are nearly tender, after 3 minutes or so, and remove. If the peas are really small, fresh, and tender, it shouldn't be necessary to precook them. But if they are not so fresh or a little tough, boil them until nearly done and remove. Rinse both the peas and the asparagus in cold water and set aside.

Using the same water, add the asparagus stems, leek greens, pea pods, and parsley. If you're using frozen peas, add ⅓ cup of them to the stock. Lower the heat and simmer for 20 minutes; then strain.

Making the soup: Thinly slice or chop the white part of the leeks and rinse well. Melt the butter in a wide soup pot and add the leeks, along with any water clinging to them, and ½ teaspoon salt. Cook gently until they have begun to soften, about 10 minutes; then stir in the flour. When it is well mixed, whisk in the strained stock. Bring to a boil, then simmer for 20 minutes, stirring occasionally to make sure the flour doesn't stick to the bottom. Remove the soup to a blender and purée until smooth.

Return the soup to the stove and add the milk and the partially cooked asparagus and peas. Cook until the soup is warmed and the vegetables are tender. Taste and check for salt. If necessary, thin the soup with additional stock or water or, if you wish to enrich it, stir in the cream. Season with pepper and serve with the fresh herbs scattered over the top.

If you are using the egg yolk, instead of adding cream to the soup, beat it with the yolk, gradually adding a cup of the hot soup. Make sure that the rest of the soup isn't boiling; then pour the yolk-cream mixture into it, stirring constantly. Cook for another 2 minutes and serve. Don't let the soup boil or the egg will curdle.

If you have soup left over or are making it in advance, set a piece of plastic wrap directly on top, gently pressing it against the surface so that a skin won't form. Refrigerate until needed.

Leek and Artichoke Soup

This soup is light and thin, the greens muted, but it masks a much bigger flavor than appearances suggest. Serve it with a spoonful of fine olive oil laced into each bowl, freshly ground pepper, and a generous dusting of Parmigiano-Reggiano. Fresh chervil, finely chopped and added just before serving, is an excellent herbal garnish with these spring vegetables.

If you prefer creamy-textured soups, blend the mixture until smooth or leave it with some texture, as you like. Or blend just a portion of the vegetables and stir them back into the soup to give it a more substantial background, at the same time keeping the different textures and shapes of the vegetables intact.

Makes 4 servings

THE SOUP

1 large or 2 medium-sized artichokes
1 cup water acidulated with the juice of 1 lemon
1 tablespoon olive oil
1 large or 2 medium-sized leeks, white part only, washed and sliced
2 garlic cloves
1 small new potato, quartered and thinly sliced
6 leaves butter lettuce sliced into ¼-inch strips or a handful of
  sorrel leaves, sliced
1 tablespoon chopped parsley
2 mint leaves, chopped
salt
5½ cups water
1 pound fresh peas, shucked or 1 cup frozen peas

THE GARNISHES

freshly ground pepper
chopped chervil, if available, or chopped parsley
extra-virgin olive oil
freshly grated Parmigiano-Reggiano

Trim the artichokes. Break off the tough outer leaves and slice off the top two-thirds of the remaining inner leaves. Trim the outsides, cut the artichokes in quarters and remove the chokes. Dice the trimmed hearts into small pieces. Put them in the acidulated water as you work. Keep the garlic cloves whole.

Warm the olive oil and add the leeks, artichokes, garlic, potato, lettuce or sorrel, parsley, and mint. Season with the salt, add ½ cup water, and stew gently until the vegetables are wilted, about 5 minutes. Add the peas and the rest of the water. Bring to a boil, then lower the heat and simmer, partially covered, for 20 minutes or until the artichokes are cooked. Taste for salt.

Blend the soup or leave it as is and serve with the freshly ground pepper, a few good pinches of chervil or parsley, a spoonful of olive oil drizzled into each soup plate, and a dusting of cheese.

Celery Soup with Lovage and Rice

It's the herb, lovage, that gives this soup its strong personality and particular edge of flavor, but even without it—and it's not easy to find—this soup is unusual and fortifying, with a clean, bracing taste. Everyone uses diced raw celery for its nice crunchy texture, but it's also delicious as a cooked vegetable.

Lovage isn't something you can find in a supermarket, at least in mine. But it might be someday, or you might be able to find it at farmers' markets; if you garden, you can certainly grow it. The plant is a tall, handsome perennial with large leaves that look like parsley or celery. In fact the leaves taste something like celery, but more wild and rich, and the whole thing looks like a somewhat disorganized celery plant.

Stock for this soup consists simply of briefly simmering the vegetable trimmings.

Makes 4 to 6 servings

THE STOCK

2 cups chopped leek greens and the root
2 to 3 celery stalks, chopped, plus a handful of celery leaves
2 bay leaves
5 parsley branches
salt
1½ quarts water

Wash the leek greens and celery, put all the stock ingredients in a pot, cover with water, and bring to a boil. Simmer for 25 minutes and strain.

THE SOUP

2 medium-sized or 1 large leek, white part only, cut into small squares
1 small red or yellow onion, finely diced
2 tablespoons chopped parsley
2 cups diced celery, in small, even pieces
1 tablespoon chopped lovage
2 tablespoons butter
salt
1 cup milk or light cream

THE GARNISH

½ cup cooked white rice
2 teaspoons finely chopped lovage leaves or lovage butter (page 310)
freshly ground pepper

While the stock is cooking, wash and chop the vegetables for the soup. Melt the butter in a soup pot, add the vegetables and salt, and cook gently for 10 minutes. Add the stock, bring to a boil, and simmer until the celery is tender, about 25 minutes.

To give the soup a creamy background texture, purée 1 or 2 cups; then return it to the pot. Stir in the milk or cream. Season to taste with salt. Serve the soup in warmed soup plates with a couple of spoonfuls of rice in each plate. Garnish with fresh lovage and pepper or stir in a spoonful of lovage butter.

Garlic Soup

Garlic soup—essentially a broth of water, herbs, and garlic flavored with olive oil—appears all over the world. Sometimes it's made with chicken broth, sometimes with water. Eggs are often included, either in a liaison, added at the end for thickening, or stirred into the broth, forming "rags." Or a poached egg might be slipped into the bowl and covered with soup. Sometimes the garlic cloves are visible; other times they are strained. Whatever the particularities of culture or household, garlic soup is rustic and simple and considered to be restorative and healing, which in my experience it is. I've known it to prevent an otherwise deserved hangover, and it's helped me to shorten a flu and turn the course of a cold.

Not only is garlic soup one of the most straightforward, uncomplicated soups there is; it is also one of the only clear and strongly flavored meatless broths I know of. As such it is very useful to have in one's repertoire.

Light and invigorating, garlic soup is appropriate as a first course to a larger meal, and it lends itself to adornments and additions, such as croutons, a spoonful of cooked rice, tiny stellar *pastini*, or small pieces of boiled potatoes. It can be poured over grilled bread, covered with grated Parmesan or Gruyère cheese, and garnished with parsley and pepper. It can also serve as a broth for floating a few plump ravioli filled with ricotta cheese seasoned with herbs, saffron, or nutmeg.

The saffron gives the soup a subtle flavor and a rich-looking, golden hue, as convincing in color as chicken broth.

Makes 1½ quarts, serving 4

> 1 large head of garlic or 2 small heads, broken apart
> 2 quarts water
> 8 parsley branches
> 1 bay leaf
> 10 large fresh sage leaves or ½ teaspoon dried
> 6 fresh thyme branches or ¼ teaspoon dried
> 2 cloves
> salt
> 1 tablespoon virgin olive oil
> pinch of saffron
> freshly grated Parmesan cheese
> finely chopped chervil or parsley

Break the garlic head or heads apart and rub off most of the paper. Rap the cloves firmly with the flat side of a knife to break the paper; then remove it. Put all the ingredients except the cheese and chervil or parsley in a soup pot, bring to a boil, then reduce the heat and boil slowly for 30 minutes, partially covered. Strain, correct the seasoning, and serve with the cheese and chervil or parsley.

Suggestions:

If you're using *pastini*, the tiny star-shaped pasta, cook ½ cup or so right in the soup after it has been strained.

Large pasta shapes, potatoes, or anything else starchy should be cooked separately and then added to the soup so that the starch doesn't absorb all the liquid. Conversely, leftover soup can be used as the cooking liquid for rice, potatoes, or pasta; they will be particularly delicious.

Garden Garlic and New Potato Soup

The cooking for this summer soup is really done in the garden and merely finished in the kitchen. Fresh heads of garlic are pulled after the heads have matured but before the leaves have had a chance to dry. New garlic occasionally can be found in supermarkets, particularly in May and June. The cloves of the newly formed heads are moist, milky white, and unblemished, and the flavor is delicate and sweet, a pure essence of garlic. New potatoes, with their papery skins and creamy flesh, have a pure, earthy taste. Although this soup is really extraordinary when made with new garlic and potatoes, more mature produce will make a robust and delicious soup. All you need to do is a little slicing and chopping and then boil the garlic and potatoes in water with sweet butter and parsley. Serve the soup garnished with fresh basil leaves or other garden herbs such as dill or lovage. The same ingredients, cooked with just a cup of water, make a heavenly potato purée (see page 196).

Makes 4 servings

> *2 heads of newly pulled garlic*
> *1 pound new potatoes*
> *2 to 3 tablespoons unsalted butter*
> *2 tablespoons chopped parsley*
> *1 bay leaf*
> *2 thyme branches*
> *salt*
> *1½ quarts water*
> *chopped basil, dill or lovage for garnish*
> *freshly ground pepper*

Remove the damp, papery husk that surrounds the garlic cloves. Separate the cloves and slice them thinly. Wash the potatoes, cut them into quarters, and then slice them about ¼ inch thick. Combine all the ingredients except the basil and the pepper in a soup pot. Bring to a boil; then lower the heat and simmer, partially covered, until the potatoes are cooked, about 45 minutes. Break up a few of them with the back of a spoon, if desired, to give the soup a thicker background consistency. Serve with the fresh herbs and plenty of pepper.

Barley-Buttermilk Soup

A cold soup for hot weather. Once the barley is cooked, you need only about a minute to put it together. The herbs gain strength with time, so this is a fine soup to make a day or two before serving. In fact, it tastes best after two days, when the flavors have strengthened and merged.

I like the chewiness of the barley mixed with the creamy, tart buttermilk. Whole kernels of cooked wheat or cracked wheat would also taste good and could be used in place of the barley. Many cold soups are made with yogurt, but I prefer buttermilk—its pleasant edge is refreshing. It has a smooth, creamy texture, and the quality is generally quite consistent. Different brands of yogurt, on the other hand, vary a great deal; some are overstabilized with gelatin, while others are runny; some are mild, and some are sour.

Makes 1 quart, serving 4

> *½ cup barley*
> *1 quart water*
> *salt*
> *¼ cup finely diced red onion*
> *3 cups buttermilk*
> *½ teaspoon turmeric*
> *¼ cup finely chopped parsley*
> *2 tablespoons finely chopped dill or ½ teaspoon dried*
> *1 tablespoon finely chopped cilantro*
> *1 tablespoon snipped chives*
> *freshly ground pepper*
> *dash of paprika or herb blossoms, if available, for garnish*

Rinse the barley and put it in a pot with the water and salt to taste. Bring to a boil, lower the heat, and simmer until the barley is tender, about 45 minutes. Drain the barley. (The liquid can be reserved to use in a soup.) Toss the onions into the warm barley to wilt them slightly; then put the mixture in a soup bowl with the buttermilk. Stir in the turmeric and herbs and season to taste with additional salt. Cover and refrigerate until chilled. Serve with freshly ground pepper and paprika or with a garnish of blossoms, such as chive blossoms, cilantro flowers, or mustard petals.

Green Pepper and Tomato Soup

This soup calls for truly ripe tomatoes, the kind that are sweet and fragrant and not ripe in appearance only. Those wrinkled tomatoes that are left on the vine to ripen at the very end of the summer would be the best. The sugars are concentrated, and they give the soup sweetness, body, and density of flavor. In contrast, the mild, tart edge of the green peppers is just right. This green pepper soup is even better the second day.

Makes approximately 1½ quarts, serving 4

> 2 large garlic cloves, peeled
> salt
> 1 tablespoon chopped basil or ½ teaspoon dried
> 2 tablespoons chopped parsley
> ¼ teaspoon dried thyme
> 2 teaspoons sweet paprika
> 1 tablespoon tomato paste
> 2 tablespoons virgin olive oil
> 2 bay leaves
> 1 large red onion, cut into sixths and thinly sliced crosswise
> generous pinch of saffron threads
> 2 medium-sized green bell peppers, chopped into small squares
> 3 large ripe tomatoes, peeled, seeded, chopped, the juice reserved
> 5 cups water
> sugar
> ⅓ cup white rice
> freshly ground pepper
> chopped basil or parsley for garnish
> freshly grated Parmesan cheese

Pound the garlic in a mortar with salt until it has broken down to a paste; then gradually add the basil, parsley, thyme, paprika, and tomato paste. Work until well combined.

Gently warm the olive oil in a soup pot, add the garlic-herb paste, and mix together. As soon as the oil is hot, add the bay leaves and the onion. Sprinkle the saffron directly over the onion, stir everything together, and cook for several minutes or until the onion begins to soften.

When the onion is soft, add the green pepper, tomatoes, and water. Bring to a boil; then immediately lower the heat and cook over very low heat for 25 min-

utes. Taste after about 15 minutes; if the soup is tart, add sugar as needed to balance the acidity.

While the soup is cooking, bring a few cups of water to a boil; add salt to taste and the rice. Boil until the rice is tender, about 15 minutes; then drain. Stir the rice into the finished soup, season to taste with salt and pepper, garnish with fresh herbs and cheese, and serve.

Cold Tomato Soup with Avocado and Lime

A fresh tomato soup can be used as the base for this cold soup, but canned tomato juice also is a good place to start. This is one of the quickest soups you can make, and except for the avocado, it hasn't any fat. It's the perfect fast food to make on a hot day.

Makes 1 quart, serving 4

> *1 quart tomato juice*
> *½ bunch (about ½ cup leaves) cilantro*
> *1 small garlic clove*
> *2 scallions*
> *½ jalapeño pepper, or more to taste*
> *¼ teaspoon ground cumin*
> *juice of 1 large lime*
> *1 avocado*
> *salt*
> *1 thin slice of lime for each bowl*
> *whole cilantro leaves for garnish*
> *virgin olive oil or sour cream, to finish the soup*

Pour the juice into a tureen and chill. Finely chop the cilantro, garlic, scallions, and jalapeño together. Add the cumin and lime juice and stir into the cold juice. Halve the avocado, cut it into slices or cubes, and add them to the mixture. Taste and season with salt if necessary or add more lime juice to sharpen the flavors. Serve very cold, garnished with thin slices of lime and cilantro leaves. If you like, stir a spoonful of olive oil or sour cream into each bowl of soup.

Corn and Summer Squash Chowder

The flavors in this chowder are similar to those used in the Summer Squash and Corn Stew (page 120), but milk forms the base instead of cream. Puréeing the corn first gives it a rich, creamy texture. This chowder is good cold as well as hot.

If yellow tomatoes are available, use some mixed with the red. The exotic flavor of cinnamon basil would also be delicious with the other spices. The deep red flower bracts as well as the leaves and flowers make a beautiful garnish.

Makes 5 cups, serving 3 or 4

1 quart milk
1½ cups fresh corn kernels or frozen corn, defrosted
4 teaspoons flour
1 2-inch piece of cinnamon stick
5 cilantro sprigs, finely chopped
1 mint sprig, finely chopped
3 large basil leaves
4 cloves
6 peppercorns
6 coriander seeds
½ jalapeño pepper, seeded and finely diced
½ teaspoon dried safflowers, if available
salt
½ small onion, finely chopped
2 medium-sized ripe tomatoes
½ pound summer squash such as green or gold zucchini or patty pan
lime juice
chopped cilantro and mint leaves or cinnamon basil, if available, for garnish

Put half the milk in a blender with 1 cup of the corn and the flour. Blend for 2 minutes or until the texture is smooth. If the corn is very tough, you could strain it after blending. Put the corn-milk mixture in a soup pot with the remaining milk, all of the seasonings, and the onion. (If you don't like finding whole spices

in the soup, tie them loosely in cheesecloth and then remove them at the end.) Set the pot over medium-low heat and slowly bring it to a boil.

While the milk mixture is warming, submerge the tomatoes in boiling water for 10 seconds to loosen the skins; then peel them and cut them in half. Slice away the walls or sides of the tomatoes, then dice them into even pieces. Finely mince the remaining cores. Cut the squash into small cubes, about ¼ inch square.

Add half the tomatoes, the squash, and the remaining corn to the heating milk. Simmer until the squash is cooked, about 15 minutes. Taste for salt. Stir in the remaining tomatoes, season to taste with lime juice, and garnish with fresh herbs.

Bean, Corn, and Barley Soup

In older times this kind of sustaining soup would have been eaten when little or no fresh foods were available. It's extremely simple—beans, barley, and corn boiled in water, served with parsley, pepper, and oil pounded in a mortar. Without the presence of other strong tastes, the soft and subtle flavor of the grains is clearly noticeable. This soup is deeply nourishing—a good one to come home to. Although the grains must be soaked the night or day before, assembling the soup is effortless, and it takes about an hour to cook.

A similar ancient Italian soup, *mis-ciua*, made of chick-peas, white beans, and wheat, is still served in country restaurants around La Spezia. The ingredients are soaked and cooked separately and then mixed together (*mis-ciua* is a dialect word for mixture) and finished with a spoonful of Tuscan olive oil. There's also a soup called *corn*, a biblical term indicating a mixture of lentils, barley, millet, and wheat, all seasoned with cumin. All these soups have a rather prehistoric feel to them.

Dried corn is hard to find and requires many hours of cooking. Although I prefer its taste and texture, frozen corn is easier to come by for most people and requires less fussing. If you can find dried corn, boil it separately until it softens and add it to the cooked beans and barley.

This soup can easily become the mainstay of a winter diet. You could make a big pot on the weekend and eat it several times during the week. A salad of cooked herbs or fresh bitter greens and a piece of cheese, like ricotta salata, would make a complete meal.

Makes 2½ quarts, serving 6 to 8

THE SOUP

1 cup Romano or red kidney beans, soaked 6 hours or overnight
1 cup barley, soaked 6 hours or overnight
2½ quarts water
1 tablespoon olive oil
1 garlic clove, minced
salt
2 cups fresh or frozen corn kernels or 1 cup dried, cooked until tender,
*   about 3 hours*

Drain the beans and barley. Put them in a soup pot with the water, olive oil, and garlic and bring to a boil. Skim off any foam that rises to the surface. Lower the heat and simmer, partially covered, for 30 minutes. Add salt to taste and continue cooking until the beans and barley are tender. Add the corn and cook for 10 more minutes. Make the parsley sauce below and stir it into the soup just before serving.

THE PARSLEY SAUCE

1 garlic clove
½ teaspoon peppercorns
¼ cup chopped parsley leaves
1 tablespoon extra-virgin olive oil

Pound the garlic and peppercorns together in a mortar. When they are well broken up, add the parsley and the oil. Work together into a rough paste.

Winter Squash Soup with Cinnamon, Cloves, and Mint

The winter squash in this soup is seasoned with the same herbs and spices used in the Summer Squash and Corn Stew—coriander, cinnamon, mint, and clove. Chili is added to give piquancy to the naturally sweet squash. Unusual seasonings for a squash soup, but utterly appropriate and very tasty.

Hard-skinned squash often has dense, convoluted surfaces that are difficult to work with. Halving the squash first and baking it in the oven provides an easy way to get at the delicious meat inside. While the squash is baking, you can prepare the rest of the soup—even the rest of the meal.

Cooked with the same seasonings but less liquid, this squash makes a delicious purée.

Makes approximately 1½ quarts

> *2 pounds dense winter squash such as buttercup, perfection,*
> *   kabocha or butternut*
> *light olive or vegetable oil*
> *12 coriander seeds*
> *12 peppercorns*
> *2 cups milk or light cream*
> *1 3-inch cinnamon stick, broken into pieces*
> *8 cloves*
> *a small handful of mint leaves, roughly chopped*
> *1 jalapeño pepper or 2 small dried red chilies, seeds removed*
> *2 tablespoons butter*
> *1 onion, finely diced*
> *salt*
> *2 teaspoons each finely chopped mint and cilantro for garnish*

Preheat the oven to 375°F. Cut the squash in half using a cleaver or a heavy chef's knife; scoop out the seeds. Brush the surfaces lightly with oil, place them face down on a cookie sheet, and bake them until they're soft and tender, 30 to 45 minutes, depending on the type of squash used. (Some squash will give off a wa-

tery, sweet liquid that can also be used in the soup. If the cooked squash sits for a while, it will reabsorb the liquid.) When the squash is cooked and cool enough to handle, scoop out the flesh.

While the squash is baking, make an infusion with the herbs and milk: First lightly crush the coriander seeds and peppercorns; then put them in a saucepan with the milk or cream, cinnamon, cloves, mint leaves, and chilies. Heat the mixture slowly, but turn off the heat just before the milk comes to a boil. Let it stand until needed.

Melt the butter in a soup pot and add the onion and salt lightly. Gently cook the onions until they begin to soften, about 5 minutes. Add the squash and 1 quart water. Bring to a boil; then lower the heat and simmer until the squash is broken up, about 25 minutes.

Pass the soup through a food mill or blend it briefly, leaving as much texture as you like. Return the soup to the stove and add the milk, pouring it through a strainer. Taste for salt. Gently reheat the soup, but do not allow it to boil. Serve garnished with the chopped mint and cilantro.

■ Squash soups tend to thicken as they sit. If this happens, just thin with additional milk or water.

Variation: A Squash Purée

Bake the squash as above and make an infusion with the spices and 1⅓ cups milk, half-and-half or cream. Let the milk sit for at least 30 minutes and then strain it and reheat. Scoop out the cooked squash and beat it with 2 tablespoons of butter and the seasoned milk or cream. Add salt to taste and serve.

■ Two pounds of squash will yield about 2 cups cooked.

Winter Vegetable Soup

It's always tempting to make creamy-textured puréed soups. The method is easy, and all vegetables, especially winter vegetables, taste good this way. But it's also nice to see the forms and colors of the various vegetables—here the pure white and pale yellow turnips and rutabagas, the red skins on the potatoes, and the pale green leeks. The distinctly separate vegetables are served with toasted whole grain bread and Gruyère cheese in a milky broth perfumed with herbs. The soup makes a light winter supper that might be followed by a salad and a substantial dessert, like a slice of the Orange-Currant-Walnut Cake (page 376).

Whenever I use turnips and rutabagas in classes, students talk about how much they dislike them. It's true that these humble roots are often overgrown and unpleasantly strong-tasting. If they're blanched first, though, any bitterness will usually be eliminated. Even better, if you've grown them yourself, you can pull them before they get old and tough to capture their delicate sweetness. People are always surprised at how good they are.

Makes 4 servings

THE BROTH

> *3 cups milk*
> *2 bay leaves*
> *several thyme branches or 2 pinches of dried*
> *several of the inner leaves from the leeks (see below), chopped*
> *1 small onion, roughly chopped*
> *5 parsley branches, roughly chopped*
> *5 peppercorns, crushed*
> *¼ teaspoon celery seeds, crushed*
> *salt*

Put everything in a saucepan, bring it gradually just to a boil, and then turn off the heat. Set it aside, covered, to steep for at least 30 minutes.

THE SOUP

1 large leek, white part only
½ small onion
1 medium-sized rutabaga
1 medium-sized turnip
1 medium-sized red potato
1 small celery root
juice of 1 lemon
salt
1 to 2 tablespoons butter
3 thyme branches or 2 pinches of dried
½ cup half-and-half or cream
*   (optional)*

THE GARNISHES

2 or 3 slices of whole wheat bread
½ cup grated Gruyère or Fontina cheese
finely chopped parsley or chervil
freshly ground pepper

First wash and cut all the vegetables. Slice the leek into thin rounds and the onion into ¼-inch dice. Peel the rutabaga and cut it into sixths. Peel the turnip and cut it into large chunks. Scrub, quarter, and slice the potato; the potato can be cut rather irregularly as the smaller pieces will disintegrate and give the soup body. Peel the celery root, cut it into ½-inch cubes, and put it into water that has been acidulated with the juice of a lemon to keep it from discoloring.

Bring several quarts of water to a boil in a large pot, add salt to taste, and boil the turnips and rutabagas for about 1 minute. Remove them and set aside. If the vegetables are small and sweet, this step isn't necessary.

Melt the butter in a soup pot. Add the leek, onion, potato, celery root, and thyme, lightly salt, and add enough water to cover the bottom amply. Cook over low heat for 5 minutes. Pour the steeped milk through a strainer and add the milk and the cream or half-and-half, if you're using it, to the pot. Bring it to a boil; then lower the heat and simmer for 10 minutes. Add the turnips and rutabagas and continue simmering until everything is tender but still retains a little texture, about 15–20 minutes. Taste for salt.

Toast the whole wheat bread and cut it into squares or fingers. Divide the bread among 4 warmed soup plates, sprinkle the cheese over it, and ladle the soup over all. Garnish with the fresh parsley or chervil and plenty of pepper.

Black Bean Soup for a Crowd
(and Black Bean Soup for Six)

At some point almost everyone has to cook a large quantity of something good, hearty, and cheap. It might be for a benefit, a work party, or a large family gathering. All kinds of occasions present themselves, and with this recipe you will be prepared. This soup is untaxing to make; it's certainly hearty and good; and it's inexpensive. Sour cream and cheese are delicious additions to the soup, but it also tastes fine with just some chopped cilantro leaves scattered on top along with some small dried red chilies *pequins*, which float on top of the purple-black soup looking dangerous. Puréed *chipotle* chilies give it a warm, smoky taste.

Once made, the soup can be allowed to cool to room temperature and then refrigerated for one or two days until needed; the flavors will be even better. Outside of the long simmering time, it takes only about 25 minutes to put the soup together. However, allow for as long as an hour or more for it to come to a boil. This recipe can be divided with no problem, and a scaled-down recipe to feed six follows.

Makes 4 gallons, serving 40 to 50

THE SOUP

5 pounds black beans
5 medium onions, diced into small squares
4 large garlic cloves, chopped fairly fine
2 32-ounce cans peeled tomatoes, chopped, the juice reserved
3 chipotle chilies, minced or puréed, or ¼–½ cup
    smoked chili salsa (page 320)
2 large bunches of cilantro
2 tablespoons salt

THE GARNISHES

grated Muenster or Monterey Jack Cheese
sour cream
chilies pequins *or other small dried red chilies*

Sort through the beans, remove any pebbles, and rinse the beans well in cold water. Put them in a 4-gallon pot, cover with cold water to about 4 inches from the top, and bring to a boil. (Setting the pot on a Flame-Tamer will allow the

beans to cook slowly without sticking to the bottom.) When the beans finally come to a full boil, they will give off some foam. Skim it off; then add the onions and garlic.

Lower the heat and cook until the onions have softened, about 15 minutes; then add the tomatoes and their juices, the *chipotle* chilies, to taste, and half the cilantro. Occasionally give the beans a stir. Cook for 1 hour; then add the salt and continue cooking until the beans are soft, another 30 minutes or possibly longer, depending on the beans. Once they're cooked, stir in the remaining cilantro, taste for salt, and garnish as desired.

Black Bean Soup for Six

THE SOUP

1½ cups black beans, rinsed and soaked 6 hours or overnight
1 small onion, diced into small squares
1 garlic clove, finely chopped
½ chipotle chile, minced or 1 tablespoon smoked chili salsa (page 320)
1 16-ounce can peeled tomatoes, chopped, juice reserved
½ bunch of cilantro

THE GARNISHES

sour cream
grated Muenster or Monterey Jack cheese
chili pequins or other small dried red chilies

Drain the beans and put them in a soup pot with enough cold water to cover them by a couple of inches. Bring to a boil and skim off the foam that rises to the surface; then add the onions and the garlic. Lower the heat and cook until the onions are soft, about 15 minutes; then add the tomatoes and their juice, the puréed chilies, half the cilantro, and lightly salt. Simmer until the beans are tender, an hour or so. Occasionally give them a stir while they're cooking. When done, taste for salt, stir in the remaining cilantro, and garnish as desired.

Chestnut and Lentil Soup

Late autumn is the season for chestnuts and for this special soup, which is invigorating and warming. The chestnuts are roasted, finely chopped, and then cooked with wine and a bit of tomato, which gives them a lively edge. They go wonderfully with the lentils. Serve this soup with a spoonful of your best olive oil floating over the surface and grilled bread or croutons.

The chestnuts require a half hour or so to bake, so begin with them. While they're baking, you can cook the lentils.

Makes 4 to 6 servings

THE CHESTNUTS

¾ pound chestnuts
safflower or light olive oil

Preheat the oven to 350°F. Score the chestnuts on their rounded sides, toss in just enough oil to coat them lightly, and bake them on a cookie sheet until the skins have opened and the meat is tender, about 20 minutes. When they're cool enough to handle, peel them and cut into small pieces.

THE LENTILS

1 cup lentils
2 quarts water
1 medium-sized carrot, peeled and finely diced
1 celery stalk, finely diced
½ small onion, cut into small squares
1 large garlic clove, finely chopped
1 bay leaf
salt
5 parsley sprigs

Rinse the lentils; then put them in a soup pot with the water and bring to a boil. Cook for a few minutes at a gentle boil and remove any foam that forms on the surface. Add the remaining ingredients, lower the heat, and cook slowly until the lentils are tender, about 35 minutes. When done, remove the parsley sprigs and the bay leaf.

FINISHING THE SOUP

2 to 3 tablespoons olive oil
1 teaspoon chopped fresh marjoram or
   ½ teaspoon dried
¼ teaspoon fennel seeds, crushed or ground
several thyme branches or generous pinch of dried
½ cup dry white wine
1 tablespoon tomato paste
salt
freshly ground pepper
extra-virgin olive oil, to finish the soup
fried or toasted croutons
chopped parsley

Warm the olive oil in a pot large enough to hold the soup; then add the roasted chestnuts and herbs. Stir frequently over medium heat for several minutes; then add the wine and tomato paste. Stir to dissolve the paste and let the wine reduce for a minute. Set the pot aside.

Purée half the lentils until they're smooth. Pour them into the pot with the chestnuts and the wine and add the remaining lentils. If the soup is too thick, thin it with vegetable stock or water. Heat the soup and season with salt and plenty of pepper. Serve as suggested above, with a spoonful of fine olive oil ladled into the soup, a little fresh parsley, and croutons.

Sorrel-Lentil Soup

It's difficult to imagine how a recipe as simple as this one can also be so good. This recipe is derived from one of Elizabeth David's, which calls for only lentils, sorrel, and cream. I have never been able to resist adding some red onion and bay leaf, and sometimes a *mirepoix* of celery and carrots. But even with these additions this is the simplest of soups. There is no browning of onions or sautéing of vegetables; just a few ingredients boiled together and blended. Although leguminous soups usually improve after a few days, I find this one is best when served right away.

This plain-looking soup—neither lentils nor sorrel boasts stunning color—is light, nourishing, and surprisingly delicious. It is one of my favorites.

Makes 1 quart

> *½ cup lentils*
> *½ small red onion, finely diced*
> *1 bay leaf*
> *salt*
> *1½ quarts water*
> *3 handfuls sorrel leaves, shredded*
> *1 to 2 tablespoons cream or* crème fraîche
> *freshly ground pepper*

Rinse the lentils and combine them in a soup pot with the onion, bay leaf, ½ teaspoon salt, and water. Bring to a boil; then simmer, partially covered, for 30 minutes or until the lentils are completely soft.

Purée half the cooked lentils in a blender until smooth; then return them to the pot. Add the sorrel and cook for another 10 minutes; the sorrel will turn olive green. Stir in the cream, taste for salt and serve with freshly ground pepper.

Pinto Bean Soup with Mexican Cream and Pine Nuts

Beans have a delicious and subtle flavor of their own that is brought out by slow, careful cooking. Sometimes it's nice to enjoy the pure taste of the beans and their broth alone. However, there are several condiments that go wonderfully with beans, one of which is the thick Mexican cream, *natas*, which can be found in Mexican markets. Thick and silky, like Devon cream, *natas* are usually sold in plastic jars, but in larger markets, like the Grand Central Market in Los Angeles, you can find them mounded in trays in glossy, shimmering heaps. If you can't find *natas*, use *crème fraîche* or sour cream thinned with milk.

This thick, smooth soup would go well with Mustard Greens with Tomatoes, Onions, and Chilies (page 199), the Wild Green Salad (page 44) or a salad of bitter greens.

Makes 4 servings

> 1½ *cups pinto beans, soaked 6 hours or overnight*
> 2½ *quarts water*
> ¼ *cup finely diced onion*
> *salt*
> ½ *to 1 cup* natas, *crème fraîche or sour cream*
> ¼ *cup pine nuts*
> *finely sliced chives or scallions for garnish*
> *several mint leaves, finely chopped*

Drain the beans, put them in a soup pot with the water, and gradually bring to a boil. Skim off any foam that rises to the surface; then lower the heat, add the onion, and simmer gently for 30 minutes. Add salt and continue cooking over low heat until the beans are soft, another 30 minutes or so.

Once the beans are cooked, put them through a food mill or purée them in a blender. Return them to the pot and stir in the cream, adding as much as you like. Taste for salt.

Toast the pine nuts in a dry pan until they are lightly colored; then chop them finely. Serve the soup garnished with the chopped nuts, the chives or scallions, and the mint.

Suggestions: Ground red chili is perfect with beans. Use pure New Mexican chili if possible. Stir in 2 or 3 teaspoons or enough to suit your own taste. Don't forget that the heat of the chili will gain in strength as it sits.

White Bean Soup with Pasta and Potatoes

This soup always reminds me of a trip I made with some friends to Carrara to see the marble mines. It was winter, the sky was white and gray with fog and clouds, and the mountains of exposed marble were also white. None of us felt thrilled by all this cold and damp paleness; we were chilled and hungry, and there didn't seem to be a place to eat. Finally we found a restaurant where some men were eating. There were no lights on, which should have told us it wasn't open to the public, but we went in. In fact it wasn't open, except to the mine workers, but we were graciously taken care of and served bowls of soup something like this one. Green Tuscan oil and crusty bread were placed on the table, as well as a bottle of Chianti, and it was one of those meals for which you are grateful from the bottom of your heart. It was exactly what we needed—warmth and nourishment, served with kindness and without pretension. When we returned to the street, we all suddenly became excited by the layers of whites and grays and the immense presence of the marble mountains.

The beans in this soup remain whole, the potatoes thicken the broth, and the herbs and vegetables contribute a splash of color. The vegetables can be prepared while the beans are cooking. This is the kind of soup that tastes better as it ages, and a bowlful can make a meal.

Makes 6 servings

> 1 cup cannellini or other dried white beans, soaked 6 hours or overnight
> 2 quarts cold water
> 2 medium-sized white or red potatoes
> 8 large sage leaves or 1 teaspoon dried
> 2 teaspoons rosemary leaves or 1 teaspoon dried
> 3 garlic cloves
> 2 celery stalks
> 2 medium-sized carrots
> 1 small onion
> 2 tablespoons olive oil
> 1 cup dried pasta, a short tubular variety
> salt
> freshly ground pepper
> extra-virgin olive oil, to finish the soup

Drain the beans, put them in a soup pot, and cover them with the water. Slowly bring to a boil; then boil vigorously for 5 minutes. Skim off any foam that rises to the surface; then lower the heat to a simmer.

While the beans are cooking, scrub the potatoes and cut them into cubes. They needn't all be the same size—smaller pieces will break down to provide a creamy background, while large ones, say ½ inch square, will hold their shape. Chop the sage, rosemary, and garlic together. Dice the celery, carrots, and onion into small squares, no larger than ¼ inch.

Warm the olive oil in a small skillet and add the herbs, and vegetables, then salt lightly. Cook them over gentle heat for 3 or 4 minutes. After the beans have cooked for 30 minutes, add the herb-vegetable mixture to the pot. As the soup cooks, add more water in small amounts to keep it as thick or thin as you like.

Bring some water to boil for the pasta. Add salt and the pasta and cook until the pasta is barely done. Drain and set aside. When the beans are tender, stir in the pasta. Serve the soup with a cruet of extra-virgin olive oil to stir into each bowl and, if you like, a piece of hard cheese, such as Parmigiano-Reggiano, to grate over the top.

Spring Vegetable Stew

This little stew of spring vegetables is cooked at a leisurely pace, taking enough time for the different flavors to merge but not so long that they become murky. I've made this many times, trying to find what works—what member of the onion family to begin with, which vegetables to use, what kind of butter to finish with. What I like best is rather thickly sliced leeks stewed with the artichokes. Their flavor is mild and sweet, and even after cooking they still hold their shape. If lots of other things are happening in the kitchen, I briefly blanch the asparagus and other hard vegetables, such as new turnips and carrots, and add them together during the last five minutes of cooking. Otherwise I try to time how long they will take, without blanching, and add them at the appropriate moment.

To finish, I often add a few spoonfuls of olive oil or butter and a handful of fresh herbs, or I make a little herb butter with the same ingredients, adding shallot and lemon zest. I have also served this on puff pastry with a *beurre blanc*, making a much fancier—and richer—dish.

No matter how many times I make a spring stew, it's never the same twice. Ingredients change, their qualities change, and each time you have to feel your way as you go, taking everything into account.

Makes 4 servings

THE VEGETABLES

> *2 large leeks, white parts only, sliced into rounds about ⅓ inch thick*
> *2 large artichokes*
> *juice of 2 lemons*
> *¾ pound fava beans, shelled, if available*
> *1 pound thick asparagus*
> *1 tablespoon unsalted butter*
> *1 tablespoon olive oil*
> *4 to 5 small garlic cloves, unpeeled*
> *salt*
> *1½ cups water*
> *6 small turnips, peeled and halved*
> *6 small carrots, peeled and cut in half lengthwise*
> *1 pound fresh peas, shelled, or 1 cup frozen peas*
> *lemon juice or Champagne vinegar*

Thoroughly wash the leeks. Trim the artichokes: break off the tough outer leaves and slice off the inner cone of remaining leaves. Trim the outside, slice the hearts

into sixths or eighths, and remove the choke from each piece. As you work, keep the pieces in a bowl of water acidulated with the juice of 1 lemon.

Bring a large pot of water to a boil, add the fava beans, and cook for about a minute; then scoop them out and put them in a bowl of cold water, reserving the cooking water. Slip each bean out of its skin and set aside.

Cut the top 3 inches off the asparagus. Set the stalks aside for another use. If the tips are very thick, slice them in half lengthwise. Warm the butter and olive oil in a wide skillet. Add the leeks, artichokes, and garlic, then salt lightly. Toss everything immediately to coat with the oil and squeeze the juice of the second lemon over all. Cook gently for several minutes, without frying; then add the water. Simmer, partially covered, for about 15 minutes or until the artichokes are tender but still a little firm. Make sure there is some liquid. If the liquid has boiled away, add more water as needed, in small increments, and lower the heat.

Return the water used for the fava beans to a boil and blanch the turnips for 2 minutes and the carrots and asparagus for 1. Add these to the artichokes along with the fava beans and the fresh peas. Remove the lid and continue to cook gently until the vegetables are tender and the liquid has reduced to a syrup. If you're using frozen peas, add them during the last 2 minutes or so. Taste for salt.

While the vegetables are cooking, combine the herb butter ingredients below. Put half the butter in the pan and gently stir it into the vegetables. Taste, and if you want more butter, add the rest. Taste again, and if you feel a little "something" is needed, add a splash of lemon juice or Champagne vinegar to pick up the flavors. Serve the stew in warm soup plates with grilled bread or croutons and thin shavings of a good dry cheese, such as Parmigiano-Reggiano, a dry Monterey Jack, or aged goat cheese.

THE HERB BUTTER

¼ cup unsalted butter, at room temperature
½ cup chopped mixed fresh herbs such as chervil,
    tarragon or parsley, basil or marjoram or savory
1 shallot, finely diced
½ teaspoon grated lemon zest
pinch of salt

■ In his book *Simple French Food*, Richard Olney has an inspired section on vegetable stews. If this recipe appeals to you, by all means read what he has to say. One of the things he says, which makes perfect sense, is to limit yourself to 5 or so vegetables so that the dish stays clear and "readable." It is sometimes tempting to use more, because so many spring vegetables would be perfect. The only recourse is to make stews often and vary the ingredients. He also suggests using leafy greens, such as sorrel and tender new chard leaves, all of which are excellent.

Summer Vegetable Stew

Summertime offers a generous profusion of colorful vegetables: pole beans, broad beans, yellow wax, and shell beans; tomatoes in all colors, sizes, and shapes; green and golden scallop squash and zucchini; tender new carrots and onions. Herbs as well are in fragrant abundance. It's always a temptation to put all this color and taste into one dish, but the clarity of forms and flavor will be sharper if you can limit yourself to 5 or 6 vegetables. The recipe below is basically a suggestion, a framework to depart from. Vary the vegetables as the season progresses.

Serve the stew in soup bowls with toast fingers or on puff pastry for a more formal presentation. The same dish also goes wonderfully with pasta, especially wide noodles, such as inch-wide lasagne noodles.

This makes a good first course or even a light meal. It also works as a side dish to accompany something more uniform in texture, like the Cottage Cheese and Cheese Pie (page 286).

Makes 4 servings

> 6 ounces green beans or yellow wax beans
> salt
> 2 medium-sized tomatoes
> 2 garlic cloves
> 1 to 2 tablespoons mixed fresh herbs such as marjoram, basil,
>   thyme, and savory
> a narrow scrap of lemon zest
> 1 small red or yellow onion, quartered and thinly sliced crosswise
> 2 small red and yellow bell peppers, thinly sliced
> 2 green or golden patty pan squash, quartered and thinly sliced
> 2 zucchini or crookneck squash, halved, cut into 2-inch lengths,
>   and sliced
> 5 to 6 mushrooms, thinly sliced or quartered
> 2 to 3 tablespoons olive oil
> approximately ½ cup water
> 3 tablespoons unsalted butter
> juice of ½ lemon, or more to taste
> freshly ground pepper

Use tender, small beans and leave them whole or, if you're using longer ones, cut them into pieces about 3 inches long. Bring a generous amount of water to a boil, add salt, the beans, and cook until just tender. Remove them with a scoop, rinse them briefly, and set them aside.

Plunge the tomatoes into the pot for 10 seconds. Peel, cut them in half, and gently squeeze out the seeds. Cut into nice-looking pieces.

Chop the garlic with half the herbs and the lemon zest and prepare all the other vegetables.

In a large, wide pan gently warm the olive oil and add the onion and half the garlic-herb mixture. Cook slowly over medium-low heat, stirring frequently, for about 3 minutes. Add the peppers, squash, and mushrooms. Add half the water, season lightly with salt, and cook until the vegetables have begun to soften, about 5 minutes. If the liquid evaporates, add more water in small increments just to cover the bottom of the pan.

Add the green beans and tomatoes and continue cooking until they are warm; then stir in the butter, the remaining herbs, and lemon juice. Raise the heat a little to help melt the butter and shake the pan back and forth to combine all the juices. Taste for salt. Add more lemon juice, if desired, and pepper to taste. There should be an herbaceous sauce at the end, the tender (but not overly so) vegetables, and a soft perfume of garlic and herbs.

Summer Squash and Corn Stew

For years my favorite recipe for summer squash has been one of Diana Kennedy's, a stove-top stew of zucchini cooked with cream, peppercorns, coriander, mint, cinnamon, and clove. In her own words it has an exotic flavor, and I, for one, never tire of it. In fact, I've used this particular blend of herbs and spices in other recipes, such as the Winter Squash Soup with Cinnamon, Cloves, and Mint and Corn and Summer Squash Chowder.

In the original recipe everything cooks together in the pan until the vegetables are soft and the cream has reduced. Once, needing a slightly spiffier presentation, I decided to steep the spices in the cream and sauté the vegetables, adding scented cream at the end to make a more sophisticated-looking plate. Both methods produce a wonderful dish.

With black bean and some tortillas, this stew makes a quick summer supper. It would also be a good accompaniment to a simple grilled meat platter.

The vegetables can be cut while the cream is steeping.

Makes 2 main course servings or 4 servings as a side dish

> 4 cloves
> 6 peppercorns
> 6 coriander seeds
> 1 cup half-and-half or a mixture of cream and milk
> ½ teaspoon dried safflower stamens (optional)
> 1 2- to 3-inch piece of cinnamon stick
> 5 cilantro sprigs, roughly chopped
> 5 mint leaves, roughly chopped
> 6 cinnamon basil leaves, if available
> 1 jalapeño pepper, seeded and sliced into sixths
> 1¼ pounds summer squash—zucchini, crookneck,
>   patty pan or a mixture
> kernels from 2 ears of yellow corn or 1 cup frozen corn
> 1 large tomato, peeled, seeded, and chopped
> ½ onion, chopped into small squares
> 1 tablespoon peanut or safflower oil
> salt
> 2 tablespoons roughly chopped cilantro leaves

Bruise the hard spices with a pestle and add them to the half-and-half or cream with the safflowers, cinnamon, herbs, and half the jalapēno. Gradually bring to a boil; then turn off the heat and let the mixture steep while you cut the vegetables.

Cut the squash into pieces about ½ inch thick. Quarter the zucchini lengthwise and then cut the quarters into chunks. Do the same for the crookneck, or cut it into rounds. Quarter the patty pan and slice the quarters. Cut the corn kernels off the cobs if you're using fresh corn.

Heat the oil in a wide skillet or sauté pan and add the onion. Sauté briskly for a minute or so; then add the zucchini, corn, remaining jalapeño, and lightly salt. Continue to sauté over fairly high heat for about 5 minutes. The zucchini and onion may color slightly.

Pour the cream directly into the pan through a strainer and add the tomato. Simmer for several minutes, until the sauce has reduced a little and the squash are done. Season to taste with salt and garnish with the remaining cilantro leaves.

Squash, Pepper, and Hominy Stew

Hominy is corn that has been treated with slaked lime or ash. Its flavor is unusual, nutty, and nice. While many people are familiar with hominy grits, whole hominy is not that well known. In the Southwest you can buy it dried, usually called *posole*, and treat it as you would beans, but for most people it's easier to find it canned in supermarkets or Hispanic markets.

The flavors in this stew are strong, simple, and sufficient. The chili is warm and rich, the hominy nutty, and the squash sweet. Although no garnishes are needed, if you find yourself making this dish often you can easily vary it, adding tomatoes, using spices like cumin, cinnamon, and clove, or garnishing it with cheese. You could also expand the vegetables to include fresh corn and summer squash or even fresh shell beans.

Pure red chili, such as the New Mexican chili, has the richest flavor. Two tablespoons of mild chili will make a fairly spicy dish, but the sour cream will soften the heat considerably. So will using thick tortillas to mop up the sauce. If you want something milder, use just half the amount of chili powder with a tablespoon of sweet paprika.

I've suggested banana squash because it's so easy to work with, but any winter squash will do. (You'll find banana squash in your market cut into pieces weighing a pound or so and wrapped in plastic—whole, they are too big for most people to handle.)

This takes little time to prepare, and it freezes well.

Makes 4 servings

> 1 29-ounce can hominy
> ¾ pound banana squash, approximately
> 2 to 3 tablespoons light olive, safflower, or peanut oil
> 1 medium onion, diced into ½-inch squares
> 1 teaspoon dried Greek oregano
> salt
> 1 large garlic clove, finely chopped
> 2 tablespoons ground red chili, preferably New Mexican
> 1 tablespoon flour
> 3½ cups water
> 1 green bell pepper, diced into ½-inch squares
> ½ cup or more sour cream or plain yogurt, at room temperature
> chopped cilantro for garnish

Drain the hominy, rinse it briefly, and set it aside. Peel the banana squash, cut it into ½-inch strips, and cut each strip into pieces about ½ inch wide.

Warm the oil in a 12-inch skillet or cast-iron pot and add the onion, squash, and oregano, then season lightly with salt. Cook over medium-high heat for about 4 minutes. Add the garlic, ground chili, and flour, and stir well to distribute the flour. Add the hominy and the water, lower the heat, and simmer for about 45 minutes. Add the green pepper and continue to cook until the squash is completely tender and the pepper is cooked, another 15 minutes or so. Taste for salt. Just before serving, stir in the sour cream or yogurt and garnish with the cilantro.

Tomato, Fennel, and Potato Stew with Saffron

You could call this a failed fisherman's soup; it has all the elements of *bouillabaisse* except, of course, the fish. It was Joseph Wechsberg's chapter on *bouillabaisse* from his delightful gastronomic memoir, *Blue Trout and Black Truffles*, that prompted this recipe. His listing of ingredients before you get to the fish—fennel, potatoes, saffron, orange, and tomato—sounded absolutely delicious on their own, strong and aromatic. And they are. The classic accompaniment to fish soups, the bold *rouille* (a garlic mayonnaise with the fiery addition of crushed cayenne) is equally good here.

This stew can be cooked entirely on top of the stove, or it can be started on the stove and finished in the oven. This is the kind of food that cooks beautifully in earthenware and looks wonderful served directly from the baking dish. Make this just before dinner or hours before. The flavors will merge as the stew sits, but it's delicious both ways.

Makes 2 or 3 servings as a main course

THE STEW

1½ pounds red or yellow-fleshed potatoes
2 fennel bulbs
1 pound ripe tomatoes, peeled and seeded, juice reserved
    or 2 cups whole canned tomatoes
salt
3 to 4 tablespoons olive oil
1 large leek, white part only, finely diced
1 large yellow onion, cut into wedges ½ inch thick
2 garlic cloves, finely chopped
1 teaspoon herbes de Provence
2 to 3 pinches of saffron threads
a large strip of orange zest, about 2 inches long
2 bay leaves
1 cup dry white wine
2 tablespoons chopped parsley
12 Niçoise, Gaeta or oil-cured black olives, pitted

Peel the potatoes and slice them lengthwise into quarters or, if large, into sixths. Trim the fennel, remove the outer leaves if they're scarred, and cut into wedges ½ inch thick or a little wider. Leave some of the core so that the pieces stay intact. Cut the tomatoes into large, neat pieces.

Bring a pot of water to a boil, add salt to taste and the potatoes, and boil for 5 minutes. Remove the potatoes, but save the water.

While the potatoes are cooking, warm the olive oil in a wide pan. When hot, add the leek, onion, garlic, herbs, a little salt, saffron, orange zest, and bay leaves. Cook slowly over medium heat until the onions have begun to soften, after 6 or 7 minutes; then add the wine. Let it reduce by approximately half, then add the tomatoes and their juices, the potatoes, fennel, half the parsley, and the olives. Pour in enough of the reserved potato water to cover, bring to a boil, and lower the heat.

At this point you can set the stew aside and finish it later, either in the oven or on top of the stove. If cooking on top of the stove, cover the pan and cook slowly until the vegetables are tender, about 35 minutes. If cooking in the oven, preheat it to 375°F, cover loosely, and bake for about 1 hour or until done. Garnish with the remaining parsley and serve with a bowl of garlic mayonnaise (page 314) or the *rouille* below.

THE ROUILLE

3 to 5 garlic cloves
½ teaspoon coarse salt
1 to 2 teaspoons ground red chili or cayenne pepper
1 egg yolk, at room temperature
½ cup olive oil
extra-virgin olive oil

Pound the garlic in a mortar with salt until it is broken down into a smooth paste; then work in the ground chili and egg yolk. Gradually add the light olive oil, drop by drop at first and eventually in a small stream. Stir in the virgin olive oil to taste and add a few spoonfuls of hot water to thin the sauce to the consistency of thick cream.

Eggplant and Potato Stewed with Cumin Seeds and Fresh Ginger

This stew has a marvelous fragrance and pleasing textures, with the firm potato and the completely softened eggplant. The eggplant and potatoes are both roasted in the oven first, giving them a faintly smoky flavor. The vegetables take an hour to roast, leaving the cook free to prepare the rest of the meal or do something else altogether. The rest of the preparation for this dish is easy and takes but a few minutes.

This dish was shown to me years ago by a friend from India. I'm sure he used at least ½ cup of oil for cooking the onions, which made the whole dish very unctuous and rich. I've used about half that much. Those on a stricter diet could easily halve that amount again.

Serve the stew with rice and a refreshing salad of oranges and pomegranates or chilled melons with lime.

Makes 4 servings

1 large, firm eggplant (weighing about 1½ pounds)
4 large garlic cloves, thinly sliced
3 small russet or red potatoes
2 teaspoons cumin seeds or 1 teaspoon seeds and 1 teaspoon ground cumin
4 to 5 tablespoons peanut or safflower oil
1 bay leaf
1 large yellow onion, cut into ½-inch squares
1 tablespoon grated fresh ginger
4 medium-sized tomatoes, fresh or canned, peeled, seeded,
    and chopped (about 1 cup)
½ cup water or juice from the tomatoes
salt
½ cup plain yogurt, approximately, at room temperature
2 tablespoons chopped cilantro
whole cilantro leaves for garnish

Preheat the oven to 375°F. Cut several slits in the eggplant and stuff them with the sliced garlic. Bake the eggplant and the potatoes on a cookie sheet until the eggplant has shriveled and the potatoes are done, about 1 hour. The eggplant will

be a little firm at the stem end. When the vegetables are cool enough to handle, peel the eggplant and chop the flesh into large pieces. Cut the potatoes, with their skins on, into ½-inch chunks.

Roast the cumin seeds in a dry skillet until you can smell them, 10 seconds or so. Grind half of them into a powder and set the whole seeds aside for a garnish.

In a large, heavy pan, heat the oil with the bay leaf. When it is hot, add the onion, ground cumin, and ginger. Cook, stirring frequently, until the onions are lightly colored, 12 to 15 minutes. Add the eggplant, potato, tomato, and liquid and gently combine with the onions. Season with salt. Cook over medium heat until the whole stew is thoroughly warmed and cooked. Stir in the yogurt and chopped cilantro, leaving marbled streaks throughout, and garnish with the whole cumin seeds and the cilantro leaves.

Mushrooms Flagstaff

One recipe that many people have mentioned to me recently is Mushrooms Berkeley from Anna Thomas's book *The Vegetarian Epicure*. Having missed it in the seventies, I gave it a try recently. The mushrooms looked dark and evil, as the author had promised, and had an enticing aroma. They were a little richer and sweeter than anyone remembered, but they were very tasty, and the recipe was straightforward.

Here's my version, which includes dried *shiitake* mushrooms, red peppers, tofu, and less butter and sugar. Serve this stew with white or brown rice. It takes about 40 minutes to cook, but only a few minutes to assemble.

Makes 4 servings

THE SAUCE

2 tablespoons Dijon mustard
2 tablespoons Worcestershire sauce
2 tablespoons brown sugar
¾ cup dry red wine
1 tablespoon soy sauce
plenty of freshly ground pepper

Combine all the ingredients in a bowl and set aside.

THE VEGETABLES

1 to 2 ounces dried shiitake *mushrooms*
½ cup boiling water
1 pound large, firm white mushrooms
2 tablespoons butter
1 onion, diced into ¼-inch squares
salt
1 large red bell pepper, diced into ½-inch squares
¼ pound tofu, cut into ½-inch cubes
chopped cilantro or parsley for garnish

Cover the dried mushrooms with the boiling water and set them aside until they soften, after 10 minutes or so. Reserve the soaking liquid and cut the mushrooms into strips. Discard the hard stems. If necessary, clean the fresh mushrooms. Cut them into halves or quarters if they are very large and leave smaller ones whole. Or, if you prefer, slice them all into pieces at least ¼ inch thick.

Melt the butter in a large, heavy-bottomed pan, add the onion, salt lightly, and cook over medium heat for 3 or 4 minutes or until the onions are transparent. Add the fresh and dried mushrooms and the peppers and cook for a few minutes, stirring often, until the mushrooms begin to color; then add the sauce and the soaking liquid from the mushrooms. Add the tofu and simmer slowly until the sauce has reduced and thickened, about 40 minutes. Serve in soup plates with rice or noodles and garnish with cilantro or parsley.

Stewed Artichokes with Olives and Moroccan Spices

Artichokes are often cooked with lamb in Moroccan dishes, but here I've left out the lamb and used just the thick wedges of artichoke hearts, which are meaty and substantial. In the spring, when artichokes are inexpensive, you can use the hearts by themselves. When artichokes are less plentiful, use fewer of them and include large pieces of carrots, nicely cut, and a cup or so of cooked chick-peas.

Serve this with rice or couscous and follow it with the Oranges with Pickled Onions and Pomegranates and, for dessert, Cardamom-Orange Oeufs à la Neige.

Makes 4 servings

> *4 large artichokes*
> *juice of 2 lemons*
> *2 to 3 tablespoons olive oil*
> *1½ cups finely diced onion*
> *¼ teaspoon turmeric*
> *1 teaspoon hot paprika*
> *¼ teaspoon ground cumin*
> *½ teaspoon freshly ground pepper*
> *good pinch of saffron, soaked in a few tablespoons hot water*
> *salt*
> *4 cilantro branches*
> *4 parsley branches*
> *½ cup Kalamata olives, rinsed and pitted*
> *1 lemon, quartered*
> *cilantro leaves for garnish*

Trim the artichokes: break off the tough outer leaves and slice off the inner cone of remaining leaves. Trim the outside with a paring knife, slice the hearts into quarters or eighths, as you like, and remove the chokes. As you work, put the finished pieces in a bowl of water with the lemon juice.

Warm the olive oil in a sauté pan or wide skillet with a tight-fitting lid, and add the onion, turmeric, paprika, cumin, and pepper. Cook together for 3 or 4 minutes; then add the saffron with its soaking liquid. Add the artichokes, salt lightly, and add the fresh herbs. Cook for another 3 or 4 minutes, turning the artichokes occasionally. Pour 1½ cups water over all, cover, and cook over low heat until the artichokes are tender, about 30 minutes. Add the olives during the last 10 minutes of cooking. Taste and season with salt, if needed. Serve with the lemon wedges and a garnish of cilantro leaves.

Couscous with Winter Vegetables

This dish of golden vegetables served with two sauces over a mound of delicate couscous is more of a production than most of the recipes in this book, but not impossible if you're organized. It takes about 15 minutes to prepare the vegetables and get them started; the sauces can be made while they are cooking, and the instant variety of couscous can be cooked just before you're ready to eat. It's a dish for a special occasion or a party. Peas aren't winter vegetables, of course, but they lend a bright note to the stew, and I always include them.

I like to serve this with both the traditional spicy red *harissa* sauce and a green sauce of cilantro and chili. The green sauce has a fresh, sharp taste and makes a lively contrast to the rich subtleties and sweetness of the vegetables. The red sauce can be made from a commercial *harissa* or the red chili paste on page 325.

I have called for the quick-cooking variety of couscous because it's less complicated to cook and because it's what's most readily available. If you wish to cook couscous the traditional way, by steaming it, look at Paula Wolfert's definitive book on Moroccan cooking, *Couscous and Other Good Food from Morocco*, for detailed instructions.

Before you begin to cook, gather all the spices together and cut the vegetables as suggested. Cut the thick ends of the carrots and parsnips in halves or quarters so all of the pieces are approximately the same size. Very small carrots can be left whole. If you are using canned chick-peas, drain off the liquid and give the peas a quick rinse.

Makes 4 generous servings

THE SPICES

2 large pinches of saffron threads
½ teaspoon turmeric
¼ teaspoon cayenne pepper
1 3-inch piece of cinnamon stick
½ teaspoon ground cinnamon
1 teaspoon ground ginger
½ teaspoon freshly ground black pepper
salt

THE VEGETABLES

2 to 4 tablespoons unsalted or clarified butter (page 416)
1 large yellow onion, cut into ½-inch wedges and then halved
2 (½ pound) small turnips, peeled and cut into ½-inch wedges
6 medium-sized or 12 small (½ pound) carrots, cut into 3-inch pieces
3 medium-sized parsnips, peeled and cut into 2-inch lengths
½ pound winter squash such as banana or butternut, cut into chunks
*   or cubes about 1½ inches long*
1 to 1½ cups cooked chick-peas
⅓ cup black raisins
1 jalapeño pepper, seeded, and finely diced
2 tablespoons chopped cilantro
2 tablespoons chopped parsley
2 cups water or broth from the chick-peas (unless canned)
1 cup fresh peas, shelled, or frozen

Warm the butter in a wide, heavy pot or casserole, add the onion, and cook over medium heat for 1 or 2 minutes. Add the saffron, ground spices, and cinnamon stick. Lightly salt and cook for another 3 minutes or until the onions have begun to soften, stirring occasionally. The onions should be exceedingly aromatic and golden.

Add the turnips, carrots, parsnips, squash, chick-peas, raisins, jalapeño, cilantro, and parsley. Give the mixture another stir to combine; then add the broth (or water if beans were canned). Bring to a boil, lower the heat, and simmer, covered, for 25 minutes or until the vegetables are nearly tender. Add the peas and cook until everything is done, another 5 minutes or so. Taste for salt. (You can cook the vegetables ahead of time, up to the point of adding the peas, and then finish them just before serving.)

Make the cilantro salsa (page 318) and the red sauce below and cook the couscous.

THE RED SAUCE

1 teaspoon harissa, *or more to taste, or the red chili paste (page 325)*
1 cup broth from the vegetables
1 tablespoon olive oil
1 tablespoon lemon juice
1 tablespoon chopped cilantro

Combine all the ingredients in a small saucepan. Break up the paste with a spoon or whisk, boil vigorously for a minute, and remove from the heat.

THE COUSCOUS

2½ cups water
½ teaspoon salt
1½ cups instant couscous

Bring the water to a boil, add the salt, and stir in the couscous. Remove from the heat, cover, and set aside until all the liquid is absorbed, about 10 minutes. Lightly fluff the grains with a fork and pile them into a mound in the middle of a shallow, round platter. Serve the vegetables over the top and serve the sauces on the side.

Winter Vegetable Stew Baked in a Clay Pot

The clay pot, or Romertopf, is good for vegetables; the flavors are intensified by slow cooking in a near-hermetic atmosphere, and moisture is drawn out but not lost. Although the microwave oven may be a tempting time-saver, the quick cooking doesn't allow sufficient time for the flavors to merge, which is one of the pleasures of stews—the complexity of mingled tastes.

When you're making a vegetable stew, it's a good idea to cut the pieces rather large and use different shapes to make it visually appealing on the plate. Otherwise some elements overcook and create a confusing appearance. The different colors and distinct shapes are part of what's nice about a mixture of vegetables.

Begin by making the sauce. While the onions are browning and the broth is reducing, you can prepare the vegetables. Vary the vegetables as you wish, but be sure to include lots of carrots for their bright color and sweet taste.

Makes 4 generous servings

THE SAUCE

1½ tablespoons light olive or sunflower seed oil
1 large yellow onion, chopped into large squares
6 juniper berries
5 sage leaves or ½ teaspoon dried
2 bay leaves
3 thyme branches or 2 pinches dried
3 parsley branches
1 teaspoon rosemary leaves or ½ teaspoon dried
½ cup dry red wine
½ to 1 ounce dried cèpes (porcini) or shiitake mushrooms,
    rinsed briefly in cold water
2 tablespoons mushroom soy or other soy sauce
3 cups water
salt

Heat the oil in a saucepan, add the onion and herbs, and cook over medium-high heat, stirring occasionally, for about 12 to 15 minutes or until the onions begin to brown. They can get as dark as you have time for—caramelizing them enriches the flavor.

Add the wine, bring it to a boil, and reduce for a couple of minutes. Add the mushrooms, soy sauce, water, and any juice from the tomatoes below. Bring to a boil; then lower the heat and simmer for 25 minutes while you prepare the vegetables. The amount should reduce by a third, or to about 2 cups. Taste for salt.

THE VEGETABLES

4 large parsnips
5 medium-sized carrots
6 celery stalks
2 or 3 leeks, white parts only
¼ to ½ pound firm white mushrooms
½ pound potatoes (small White Rose potatoes are a good choice)
2 medium-sized rutabagas
1 medium-sized turnip
4 garlic cloves
6 whole canned tomatoes
salt
chopped fresh parsley

Preheat the oven to 350°F and soak both halves of the clay pot in cold water. Prepare all the vegetables. Scrape the parsnips and carrots and cut both into 2-inch lengths, halving the thicker pieces so that they are roughly the same size as the rest. The parsnip cores can remain unless they are extremely woody. Cut the celery into 2-inch lengths. Halve the leeks lengthwise, cut them into 1-inch pieces, and wash them well. Clean the mushrooms and halve the potatoes lengthwise, leaving the skins on if they look fresh. Peel the rutabagas and the turnip and cut both into ½-inch wedges. Leave the garlic cloves unpeeled and whole. Cut the tomatoes into quarters. There should be about 12 cups of vegetables in all.

Drain the clay pot, put the vegetables in the pot, and toss them together with salt to taste. Remove the mushrooms from the sauce, cut them into smaller pieces if necessary, and add them to the clay pot. Strain the sauce and pour it over the vegetables. Cover and bake until the vegetables are tender, about 1½ hours.

Serve the stew in soup plates with the sauce and garnish with parsley. Or use the sauce to make the gravy below and serve it with the vegetables.

THE GRAVY

the sauce from the stew (there should be at least 2 cups)
2 tablespoons flour
1 tablespoon butter
2 to 3 teaspoons Dijon mustard
soy sauce, to taste
freshly ground pepper

Pour the sauce from the vegetables into a saucepan. Work the flour into the butter, add it to the sauce, and heat. Stir constantly. After a few minutes it will begin to thicken. Add the mustard and soy sauce to taste and season with pepper.

Eighteen Quick Pasta Dishes and Five for Company

It's hard to remember what we did for quick and satisfying meals before pasta. Of course there was always pasta—macaroni with cheese and ravioli in a can—but nothing like the vastly extended variety we enjoy today. Because it's quick to cook, inexpensive, wholesome, and delicious, pasta has become one of our most important foods. Pasta makes a satisfying meal in itself, and for some people there's pasta for dinner night after night, without monotony. For the sake of variety and their good, hearty textures there are three baked pasta dishes that can, at least in part, be assembled a little ahead of time or multiplied to serve a crowd. But for the most part these dishes are substantial enough to make a meal and simple enough to do so with ease, often in the time it takes a large pot of water to boil and the pasta to cook.

With two exceptions, all the pasta recipes are especially suited to the firm bite and varied shapes of dried pasta, reflecting the reality that our concerns are practical and dried pasta is very good. The exceptions are two special recipes for those occasions when you want to take a little extra time with a dish—the Saffron Butterflies with Basil and Peas and the Wonton Ravioli which actually make use of prepared squares of pasta.

There are many varieties of dried pasta on the market. My favorite brand is De Cecco. It seems to be everywhere and its quality is excellent. A few small companies make some exotically flavored noodles that are very beautiful and tasty; they're fun to use on a special occasion. Occasionally I enjoy the tender feel of fresh pasta and then I take the effort to make it or buy it. For many people, fresh linguine and fettucine are easy to buy in their supermarkets or delis, and they can be used instead of dried pasta. If you want to make your own pasta from scratch, extensive directions for different kinds of pasta are given in *The Greens Cookbook*.

Here are a few tips for cooking pasta:

Cook pasta in plenty of boiling water, at least 4 quarts to a pound of noodles. The pasta needs room to roll around and the water needs to stay boiling. The more water there is, the easier this is to accomplish.

Just before adding the pasta to the pot, salt the boiling water to suit your taste. If the water isn't salted, the pasta will taste flat.

When the pasta is finished cooking, don't rinse it unless you're going to use it for a salad or it's going to be baked later. There's no reason to cool off the pasta before saucing it. Just lift it out of the water and transfer it directly to the sauce. It's fine to let some of the water drip into the sauce. An oval shaped pasta scoop works well for this; you can usually get all the noodles at one swipe. A pair of tongs can be useful too for lifting out spaghetti and other long shapes.

As for cooking time, that depends on how much water, the altitude, the shape, and how you like your pasta. Pasta that is still a little chewy, or *al dente*, is more interesting to eat than a noodle that's too soft. But some people like it cooked a little softer. Many packages will have cooking instructions, but it's best to taste as you go and decide for yourself when the pasta is done.

Pasta waits for no one so before you begin cooking, make sure your table is set and your serving bowl or pasta plates are warm. Pasta cools down quickly so we must do all we can to keep it warm. Not only does it taste better hot, but warm plates keep sauces, particularly those with cream or cheese, nice and fluid.

Saffron Butterflies with Basil and Peas

The beautiful yellow-orange color of the saffron butterflies is cheery and spring-like, perfect with early peas and the first hot-house basil. This is a dish to make for a special occasion, and it's the only recipe for fresh pasta in this book. For other times, when peas aren't available or you aren't inclined to make pasta, the same exciting combination of flavors and colors can be more simply achieved by using dried pasta and frozen peas.

Makes 100 butterflies, serving 2 to 4

THE PASTA

⅛ teaspoon saffron threads
1 tablespoon hot water
1 cup unbleached white flour
¼ teaspoon salt
1 egg

Cover the saffron threads with the hot water and let stand until cooled. Mix the flour and salt in the food processor; then add the egg and saffron. Process for 10 seconds or so, until the liquid is completely distributed throughout; then turn it out onto a board. Knead it into a fairly smooth lump, press it out with your hand to flatten, then wrap in plastic and set aside for 1 hour.

Roll the pasta out to the thinnest setting on your machine and cut it crosswise into ½-inch strips using a fluted pastry wheel. Cut each strip into 3 pieces. Pinch each piece in the middle to make a butterfly or bow tie shape and set them on a tray while you make the others. You can use them right away or let them dry and store them for use another time.

THE PEAS

¼ cup unsalted butter
1 large or 3 small leeks, white parts only, sliced into thin rounds
salt
a splash of dry white wine or water
1½ pounds fresh peas, shelled (about 1½ cups)
freshly ground pepper
6 to 8 basil leaves, torn or sliced
freshly grated Parmigiano-Reggiano

Have a large pot of boiling, salted water ready for the pasta.

Melt half the butter in a sauté pan; add the leeks. Turn them in the butter and, when it begins to get hot, add a splash of white wine or water. Cook the leeks over medium heat until they're tender, about 8 to 10 minutes. Season with salt. Keep some liquid in the pan so that you will have a sauce later.

When the leeks are tender, add the peas. At the same time, you can start cooking the pasta. Add ½ cup of the water from the pasta pot to the vegetables, along with the rest of the butter, and let it melt, occasionally shaking the pan back and forth. Season with salt and pepper to taste and add the basil. As soon as the noodles are done, lift them out of the water and add them to the peas. Toss together gently with tongs and serve with a fine, light dusting of cheese.

Suggestions: Add cream to the vegetables and reduce it to make a creamy sauce. Or cook additional peas, purée them, add them to a little light cream or half-and-half, and reduce to make a pale green, pea-flavored sauce. Both variations make more substantial dishes than the recipe given.

If making this dish with dried egg noodles, introduce the saffron by making a saffron butter. Soak a pinch of saffron threads in a tiny spoonful of hot water for a few minutes then work it into 3 or 4 tablespoons of butter, along with a finely diced shallot. Use this flavored butter, along with a spoonful of extra-virgin olive oil, to cook the peas and leeks, as above. The color and the flavor will permeate the entire dish.

Capellini with Lemon and Basil

Brightened with the zest and juice of lemon, this is a lively and delicate pasta, perfect to begin a meal. It's best made with a very narrow noodle, such as *capellini*, and served in small portions; 3 ounces of noodles is fine for two people. This is an easy dish to multiply.

You can play with the sauce, varying the amount of butter or oil. Sometimes I've made it with only extra-virgin olive oil, other times with a mixture of butter and oil, as given here. It can also be finished with heated cream or crème fraîche for a rich, creamy pasta. A light dusting of freshly grated Parmigiano-Reggiano enriches the flavors, but it's also nice to taste just the lemon, basil, and the pasta without any embellishment.

Use a peeler or citrus zester to remove long, thin strips of lemon zest, making sure not to take up any of the white part that lies below. Either opal basil or the aromatic Italian green basil would be good here; don't use lemon basil, which is so close to the actual flavor of lemon it would only confuse the flavors.

Assemble the lemon and herbs before dropping the pasta into boiling water—thin noodles, whether fresh or dried, take only 2 to 3 minutes to cook.

Makes 2 servings

> zest of 1 lemon, cut into narrow strips
> juice of 1 lemon
> 1½ tablespoons unsalted butter
> 1½ tablespoons extra-virgin olive oil
> 8 fresh basil leaves, finely sliced
> 2 teaspoons finely chopped parsley
> 3 ounces capellini
> salt
> freshly ground pepper
> freshly grated Parmigiano-Reggiano (optional)

Put the lemon zest, juice, butter, oil, and herbs in a bowl large enough to hold the cooked pasta comfortably. Also have ready 2 heated pasta bowls or plates.

Bring several quarts of water to a boil, salt to taste and add the pasta, and cook until *al dente*. Lift out the noodles with a pasta scoop and add them immediately to the large bowl. Repeatedly lift the noodles with a pair of tongs, mixing them with the other ingredients as you do so. Divide the pasta between the 2 bowls and add a little pepper. Serve with cheese, if desired.

Shells with Spinach and Chick-Peas

This dish is hearty, substantial, and delicious—a well-balanced one-bowl meal. If you have chick-peas already cooked or are using canned peas, it can be ready in the length of time it takes to boil the pasta. If you're using chick-peas that you've cooked yourself, be sure to use the broth for the liquid.

The purée made from dried tomatoes lends depth to the flavor of the dish, but if you haven't any, use canned tomato paste in its place; fresh tomatoes are a little too sweet.

Makes 3 large servings

>2 tablespoons olive oil
>1 small onion, finely chopped
>1 large garlic clove, minced
>pinch red pepper flakes
>1 carrot, finely diced
>2 tablespoons finely chopped parsley
>salt
>1 tablespoon sun-dried tomato purée (page 326)
>   or 2 teaspoons tomato paste
>1 15-ounce can chick-peas, drained, or 1½ cups
>   cooked chick-peas and their liquid
>1 bunch of spinach leaves, chopped and washed
>½ pound medium-sized pasta shells
>freshly ground pepper
>additional olive oil to finish
>freshly grated Parmesan cheese

Heat the olive oil in a large skillet and add the onion, garlic, pepper flakes, carrot, and parsley; sauté for 2 minutes. Season with salt and add the tomato purée, chick-peas, spinach, and a cup of water or cooking liquid from the chick-peas. Lower the heat and simmer while the pasta is cooking.

Bring a large pot of water to boil for the pasta. Salt to taste and add the pasta, give it a stir, and then boil until *al dente.* (If the vegetables require more liquid, use some of the pasta water.) Drain the pasta and add it to the pan. Toss everything together and season generously with pepper. Serve in hot soup plates with olive oil drizzled over the top and freshly grated cheese.

Suggestion: Use a large quantity of cooking liquid from the chick-peas, if available, to make the dish more like a thick bean and pasta soup. This is delicious, too.

Spaghetti with Handfuls of Herbs

A pasta for summer, when herbs are most prolific. Handfuls of herbs, at least a couple from fairly small hands, are what it takes. Rather than pounding them into a paste or *pesto*, here they are simply chopped and left separate. When you bite into this dish, there will be many explosions of different tastes rather than one big mysterious one. Your tongue will be continually surprised by the celery-like lovage leaves, the familiar parsley, the acid bite of the sorrel, the summery flavor of marjoram. There's no need for cheese on this pasta, but crisp golden bread crumbs provide both color and texture for contrast.

If you grow herbs, you can make this pasta easily and frequently, varying it each time according to fancy or to what is coming into leaf or flower. If you don't, you can make a simpler version drawing on the herbs that supermarkets carry, basing the mixture perhaps on parsley and adding basil, marjoram, thyme, and a shallot or scallion. A few narrow slivers of lemon zest will provide the tang that the sorrel does.

You'll need about a cup of chopped leaves in all. Here are some suggestions. Vary amounts according to your tastes and what's available.

Makes 4 servings

> 6 long marjoram branches
> 12 regular or lemon thyme branches or a mixture
> 12 large parsley branches
> 8 sorrel leaves
> 3 lovage leaves
> 4 summer savory branches
> 2 small shallots or 1 small freshly pulled onion, finely diced
> 2 to 3 tablespoons extra-virgin olive oil
> 2 to 3 tablespoons unsalted butter
> 1 tablespoon light olive oil
> ½ cup fresh bread crumbs
> salt
> freshly ground pepper
> 8 to 10 ounces spaghetti or linguine

Run your fingers down the branches of the herbs to remove the leaves. If there are any flowers, set them aside for a garnish. Cut off the sorrel stems and slice the leaves in narrow ribbons. Chop the rest of the herbs fairly fine, but leave some texture. Put the herbs and shallots into a bowl with the extra-virgin olive oil and the butter and set aside.

Bring a large pot of water to a boil for the pasta. While it is heating, heat the

light olive oil in a frying pan, add the bread crumbs, and fry them until they are golden and crisp. Set aside.

When the water boils, salt to taste and add the pasta. Cook until *al dente*. Drain or scoop it out of the pot and add it to the bowl with the herbs, oil, and butter. Season generously with pepper and toss well. Serve with the bread crumbs strewn over the top and garnish with herb blossoms, if there are any.

Whole Wheat Noodles with Rocket, Garlic, and Chili

A favorite restaurant of mine in Rome serves this pasta as one of its first courses. Unlike many first courses, this one is very uncomplicated and simple, but the strong-tasting rocket (arugula) greens and warm bite of red pepper flakes do their job to stimulate the appetite. This recipe also makes a good, fast supper dish when you don't feel like doing a lot of cooking. It's a great way to use rocket leaves when the plants are ready to bolt. They are often too spicy and hot when used raw in a salad, but are fine when cooked.

Use a thin, flat whole wheat noodle; De Cecco makes a good one.

Makes 2 servings

> salt
> ¼ *pound whole wheat pasta*
> 2 *tablespoons olive oil*
> 2 *garlic cloves, thinly sliced*
> 1 *or 2 pinches red pepper flakes*
> 5 *to 6 large handfuls of rocket (arugula) leaves, roughly chopped*
> *freshly grated Romano or Parmesan cheese*
> *extra-virgin olive oil to finish*

Bring a large pot of water to boil, add salt to taste, and drop in the pasta. While it is cooking, slowly warm the olive oil in a skillet with the garlic and red pepper and cook for about 2 minutes. Next add the rocket greens and let them wilt. Scoop out a little water from the pasta pot and add it to the pan—let the greens, garlic, and red pepper stew gently.

When the pasta is *al dente*, scoop it out and put it in the pan with the greens. Let some of the water drip into the pan. Toss everything together with a pair of tongs. Serve the pasta with a dusting of cheese and the extra-virgin olive oil dribbled over the top.

Penne with Roasted Peppers, Saffron, and Basil Cream

This colorful pasta is filled with the smoky, rich flavors of grilled peppers and saffron. *Penne*, or any other hollow or twisted pasta shape, is right for this sauce. If you have roasted peppers on hand, this pasta can be assembled in just a few moments.

Makes 4 servings

> *1 large red bell pepper*
> *1 large yellow bell pepper*
> *⅛ teaspoon saffron threads*
> *½ cup hot water*
> *2 large tomatoes*
> *1 tablespoon olive oil*
> *1 medium-sized red onion, finely diced*
> *3 garlic cloves, pounded to a paste or finely chopped*
> *a handful of basil leaves, finely sliced*
> *1 cup half-and-half*
> *salt*
> *¾ pound* penne *or other dried pasta*
> *freshly ground pepper*
> *freshly grated Romano or Parmesan cheese*

Roast the peppers according to the directions on page 329. Cut them into small squares and set aside.

Cover the saffron threads with the hot water. Bring a small pan of water to a boil, submerge the tomatoes for 15 seconds, and remove them. Take off the skins, slice the tomatoes in half, gently squeeze out the juices, and cut the flesh into small squares.

Warm the oil in a wide skillet and add the onion. Cook over medium-high heat until the onion is just starting to color; then add the garlic, a few tablespoons water, and half the basil. Continue cooking until the onions have softened; then add the peppers, tomatoes, saffron threads and the liquid, and half-and-half; simmer until the sauce has thickened as much as you like.

Bring a large pot of water to a boil, add salt to taste and the pasta, and cook until it is *al dente*. Drain and add it to the sauce. Gently toss to combine and season with plenty of pepper. Serve garnished with the remaining basil and a light dusting of cheese.

Rigatoni with Peppers, Zucchini, and Garlic Mayonnaise

Garlic mayonnaise is good on virtually everything—vegetables, chick-peas and white beans, grilled bread, fish. . . . When it's stirred into warm pasta, it melts and makes an unctuous, garlicky sauce. This is robust, full of summer tastes, and fairly filling. You may not want to use an entire recipe of the mayonnaise, but what's left will keep for several days in the refrigerator.

Make the mayonnaise first so that the flavors have a chance to mellow.

Makes 4 servings

> 1 red bell pepper
> 1 yellow bell pepper
> cooking oil
> 2 tablespoons olive oil
> 1 small red onion, quartered and thinly sliced crosswise
> 2 medium-sized zucchini, cut in ½ inch squares
> salt
> handful of basil leaves, lightly chopped or cut into strips
> ¾ pound rigatoni, penne, or other tubular pasta
> 1 large or 2 medium-sized tomatoes, peeled, seeded, and chopped
> garlic mayonnaise (page 314)
> freshly ground pepper

Preheat the oven to 400°F. Slice the peppers in half, brush them on both sides with oil, and set them, cut side down, on a cookie sheet. Bake them until the skins have become wrinkled and loose, about 25 minutes. Remove them from the oven, let them cool, and pull off the skins. Cut the peppers into small squares. While the peppers are roasting, put a large pot of water on to boil for the pasta.

Heat the olive oil in a large frying pan or sauté pan; add the onion and zucchini, and salt lightly. Cook over medium heat until the onion is soft and the zucchini has started to color, about 5 minutes. Shake the pan every so often to keep things from sticking. Add the peppers and half the basil.

When the water boils, add salt to taste and the pasta and cook until it is *al dente*. Ladle a little of the water into a serving bowl to warm it; then drain the pasta. Combine the pasta with the vegetables, stir in the mayonnaise, and gently mix everything together. Season with plenty of pepper and garnish with the remaining basil. Or serve the vegetables and pasta on individual plates with a spoonful of the sauce in the middle and let each person mix his or her own.

Spaghetti with Broccoli and Tomato

The strong flavor of broccoli requires some other assertive flavors—in this case red pepper flakes and olives. The tomato is cooked briefly in a bath of olive oil and garlic, and the dish is tossed with a good handful of parsley.

Makes 3 to 4 servings

> 1 pound broccoli
> salt
> 2 large ripe tomatoes
> ½ pound spaghetti
> ¼ cup olive oil
> 2 garlic cloves, chopped
> ½ teaspoon red pepper flakes
> 12 Niçoise or Gaeta olives, stones removed, or 6
>   Kalamata olives, stoned and cut into quarters
> ½ cup coarsely chopped parsley, preferably Italian
> freshly ground pepper
> freshly grated Romano cheese

Cut the broccoli into small flowerets with about an inch of stem. Peel the remaining stems and dice them into small pieces.

Bring a large pot of water to boil. Add salt to taste then submerge the tomatoes for about 10 seconds and remove them. Peel, seed, and cut them roughly into large pieces. Next add the broccoli and cook it for several minutes, until it is just tender; then scoop it out, rinse it with cold water, and set it aside. Add the pasta to the boiling water and give it a stir.

While the pasta is cooking, warm the oil in a skillet with the garlic and the red pepper flakes. When it is hot, add the tomatoes. Give them a stir and cook gently for several minutes. When the pasta is just about done, return the broccoli to the pot just to warm it, then pour the noodles and the broccoli into a colander. Transfer the mixture to a warm serving bowl, add the tomatoes, olives, parsley, and pepper to taste, and toss together. Serve with the cheese on the side or lightly grated over the top.

Pasta with Gorgonzola

Here is another dish taught to me by my Roman friend and neighbor, Rosanna Migliarino. What I especially enjoy about it, in addition to the incredible taste and fragrance of the melting cheese, is the clever economy of space and fuel—of warming the cheese over the pot of pasta water. This is, without a doubt, the easiest dish to put together that I know. And for those who love blue cheeses, it will undoubtedly become a favorite. This pasta, a salad of crisp greens, and a glass of red wine makes a perfect meal.

You can be fairly flexible with the quantities. If the cheese is especially strong, increase the amount of butter in proportion to it. You can also add light or heavy cream if you want more of a sauce or if you haven't much cheese and want to extend it. Tubular or shell-shaped pasta works best in this dish—the shapes nicely capture the unctuous sauce.

Makes 2 to 4 servings

> *½ pound dried pasta*
> *1 garlic clove, thinly sliced*
> *6 ounces Gorgonzola cheese, more or less*
> *2 tablespoons unsalted butter*
> *salt*
> *freshly ground pepper*

Bring a large pot of water to boil for the pasta. Set a bowl large enough to hold the cooked pasta over the pot of heating water and add the sliced garlic, the cheese, broken into pieces, and the butter. As the water heats, everything will begin to soften and melt.

When the water comes to a boil, remove the bowl, and add salt to taste. Add the pasta, and give it a stir to separate the pieces. Cook until the pasta is as done as you like it; then scoop it out and add it directly to the bowl with the melted cheese. (Don't worry if all of the cheese hasn't melted—the heat of the pasta will do the rest.) Toss everything together, season with pepper to taste, and serve right away in heated soup plates.

Macaroni and Cheese

When I bit into my first expensive plate of *pasta e quattro formaggi*, I was surprised that it immediately struck a homey and familiar note. This is not macaroni and cheese out of a box; it isn't cheap; it isn't slimming; and while not particularly complicated, it also isn't an instantly made dish. But it *is* resoundingly delicious and always pleases people. As one friend said upon digging in, "You *can* go home again!"

For the pasta you can use any substantial pierced pasta. Shops that sell loose pasta often have macaroni or the larger *ziti*, about 18 inches long. The long pieces look wonderful curled around in the dish, but you need a very large pot to cook them in. If your pot isn't big enough, just break the noodles into halves, thirds, or whatever will fit comfortably.

This will make eight generous servings. It's the kind of dish that those who are clearly untroubled by thoughts of calories confess to enjoy eating the next day, fried in butter.

The most efficient way to organize your work is first to put the water on to boil for the pasta and then, while it's heating, make the white sauce and grate the cheese. Once the noodles are cooked, toss them with the sauce and cheese and cover them with a layer of bread crumbs. The dish can either be baked right away or held and baked hours later.

Makes 8 servings

THE WHITE SAUCE

3 cups milk
½ small onion, sliced
1 bay leaf
4 parsley sprigs
10 peppercorns
2 branches thyme or 2 pinches dried
a couple of gratings of nutmeg
2 tablespoons butter
2 tablespoons flour
salt
freshly ground pepper

Slowly bring the milk to a boil in a saucepan with the onion, bay leaf, parsley, peppercorns, thyme, and nutmeg, then strain. Mix the butter and flour together; then whisk it into the hot milk. Lower the heat and simmer, partially covered, for 25 minutes. Season to taste with salt and pepper.

THE PASTA AND THE CHEESES

salt
1 pound macaroni or ziti, in short or long pieces
2½ cups fresh bread crumbs
¼ cup melted butter
6 ounces (about 2 cups) Gruyère, Fontina, or Swiss cheese, grated
2 ounces (about ⅔ cup) smoked cheese such as Swiss, Gouda,
*   or mozzarella, grated*
½ pound mozzarella cheese, fresh if possible, sliced or grated
freshly ground pepper

Bring to a boil a pot of water large enough to hold the long pasta easily, if you're using it. If your pot isn't large enough to allow the noodles to become quickly submerged, break them into smaller pieces. When the water boils, salt to taste and add the pasta. Cook until slightly underdone since it is going to cook again. With tubular noodles this will take less time than you might guess since, being pierced, they cook from both the inside and the outside. Check frequently—they may be done after only 4 or 5 minutes. Drain and rinse in cold water to stop the cooking; set the pasta aside.

Toss the bread crumbs with the melted butter. Preheat the oven to 375°F. Lightly butter a large gratin or baking dish. Toss the pasta with the first 2 cheeses and the white sauce. Put a third of it into the dish, make a layer of sliced mozzarella, season with pepper to taste, and repeat with the rest of the pasta and cheese.

Cover the dish with a blanket of the buttered bread crumbs and bake until the crumbs have browned and the dish is hot, about 30 minutes. If you are going to bake the macaroni later, set aside the bread crumbs until you put the dish in the oven. If the dish goes directly from the refrigerator to the oven, it will take about 45 minutes to heat.

If you're serving macaroni and cheese as a main dish, serve it with something fresh, simple, and a little tart, such as a tomato and onion salad or a salad of endive or crisp romaine lettuce with fresh herbs and a lemon vinaigrette.

Baked Rigatoni with Eggplant and Garlic Sauce

Eggplant is not often combined with milk or cream sauces, but the combination is quite good—the flavors deep and rich. Like the Macaroni and Cheese, this baked dish has three parts—the pasta, the sauce, and the eggplant. The eggplant can be cut and salted first; then the sauce, which includes a half-head of pounded garlic, should be started as it needs time for the garlic to cook. The pasta can be cooked and drained at any point. When everything is finally combined, the casserole can be baked either right away, or hours later.

This recipe multiplies easily—twice the amount will feed eight to ten people.

Makes 4 servings

> *1 large or 2 small eggplants, weighing about 2 pounds*
> *salt*
> *½ head of garlic*
> *2 cups milk*
> *pinch of freshly grated nutmeg*
> *3 branches thyme or 2 pinches of dried*
> *2 tablespoons chopped basil or 1 teaspoon dried*
> *1 bay leaf*
> *3 tablespoons butter*
> *2 tablespoons flour*
> *2 tablespoons olive oil*
> *freshly ground pepper*
> *1 cup freshly grated Romano or Parmesan cheese*
> *8 ounces rigatoni*

Wash the eggplant, slice it into ½-inch rounds, slice the rounds into strips, then slice the strips into ½-inch cubes. Put them in a colander, toss them with salt, and set them aside for 30 minutes while you begin the sauce.

Peel the garlic; then mash the cloves until broken into a rough purée. Alternatively, chop the garlic very finely. Combine it with the milk, nutmeg, and herbs in a small pan and set over low heat. In another pan, melt the butter and stir in the flour to make a roux. Cook it for several minutes over a low flame, then pour

in the milk mixture all at once and whisk together. Add ½ teaspoon salt and cook, stirring frequently, over the lowest possible heat, for 30 minutes. The taste of the garlic should soften and permeate the sauce. Stir in half the cheese.

While the sauce is cooking, boil the pasta in plenty of salted water until it is *al dente*. Pour it into a colander and immediately rinse it with cold water to stop the cooking, and set aside.

Rinse the eggplant briefly then pat it dry with a towel. Heat the oil in a wide skillet, add the eggplant, and toss it to distribute the oil. Cook over medium heat, frequently tossing the cubes until they are lightly browned and soft, about 15 to 20 minutes. Season with salt and pepper. Preheat the oven to 375°F and lightly butter or oil an 8- by 10-inch baking dish. Toss the pasta with two thirds of the sauce and the eggplant. Pile the mixture into the dish, cover with the rest of the sauce and sprinkle the remaining cheese over the top. Bake for twenty-five minutes or until the surface is bubbly and lightly browned. Let settle for a few minutes then serve.

Pasta Soufflé with Mushroom Filling

This pasta dish takes a little more effort than most of the pasta recipes in this book, but the separate elements are not at all difficult and can, in part, be made well before baking and assembled at the last minute. A pasta soufflé won't rise quite like a cheese soufflé, but it looks impressive and is a good dish for a special family meal or company. Both spinach linguine and egg pasta, fresh or dried, are delicious here.

There are three parts to this dish—the noodles, the white sauce, and the mushrooms. The sauce will need 25 minutes to cook, so start it first.

Makes 6 servings

THE SAUCE

2 cups milk
1 branch thyme or a pinch dried
1 bay leaf
1 slice of onion, minced
¼ cup butter
3 tablespoons flour
½ cup freshly grated Asiago or Parmesan cheese
salt
freshly ground pepper
a few gratings of nutmeg
3 eggs, separated

Heat the milk with the thyme, bay leaf, and onion. While it is warming, melt the butter in a small saucepan and stir in the flour. Stir over low heat for 2 to 3 minutes. Pour in the warm milk all at once; then whisk with the roux until smooth. Set the sauce on a Flame-Tamer and cook over low heat for 30 minutes. Occasionally give it a stir to prevent it from sticking to the bottom and forming a skin. When the sauce is finished, remove the bay leaf, stir in the cheese, and season with salt, pepper, and nutmeg to taste. The seasonings should be fairly strong.

Beat the egg yolks with a little of the sauce to warm them; then whisk them into the sauce. If the soufflé won't be assembled right away, set a piece of plastic wrap directly over the surface of the sauce and refrigerate it until needed. If the soufflé is going to be made immediately, mix the sauce into the pasta as soon as it is cooked.

THE PASTA

½ pound egg or spinach linguine, or fettuccine
salt

While the sauce is cooking, bring a large pot of water to a boil, salt to taste and add the pasta. Cook the pasta, but remove it just before it is done; then immediately drain it and rinse it with cold water to stop the cooking. The pasta can be held in a little cold water, or if the sauce is ready, the two can be combined.

THE MUSHROOMS

½ pound fresh mushrooms
1 tablespoon olive oil
2 teaspoons butter
salt
1 teaspoon chopped marjoram or several pinches of dried
1 tablespoon chopped parsley
1 garlic clove, finely chopped
freshly ground pepper

Roughly chop the mushrooms either by hand or in a food processor. The pieces needn't all be the same size.

Heat the oil and butter in a wide pan, add the mushrooms, lightly salt, and sauté over a high heat. The mushrooms will immediately absorb the fat, but after a few minutes they will begin to release their juices. As soon as that starts to happen, add the marjoram, parsley, and garlic and sauté a few more minutes or until the liquid is mostly evaporated. When done, taste to make sure there's enough salt and season with plenty of pepper.

Assembling the soufflé: Preheat the oven to 400°F and lightly butter a 2-quart soufflé dish. If the sauce has been made earlier, warm it over a double boiler or, very carefully, directly on the stove, stirring constantly so that the eggs don't cook. When warm, combine the sauce with the pasta.

Whip the egg whites until they form stiff peaks; then fold them into the sauce and pasta. You may find it easiest to use your hands and gently lift the pasta over the whites. This operation is slightly awkward because of the bulk of the noodles, but work quickly and don't worry about getting everything perfectly mixed. Put three quarters of the noodles into the dish. Spoon the mushroom mixture into the middle and cover with the remaining noodles. Bake until the soufflé has risen and the top is firm and golden brown, about 40 minutes. Serve right away, before it falls.

Fettuccine with Mushrooms and Dried Tomatoes

The smoky, dark flavors of dried tomatoes and mushrooms give a wintry feel to this dish. Sun-dried tomatoes that haven't been packed in oil work very well in the sauce, but oil-packed tomatoes can be used too. They needn't, of course, be soaked in hot water first.

The dried mushrooms and tomatoes need to soak for 30 minutes, during which everything else can be chopped, the water put on to boil, and the table set. Other than the soaking time required, this is a fast and easy dish with big, strong flavors.

Makes 4 to 6 servings

> *½ ounce dried porcini*
> *1 cup boiling water*
> *3 sun-dried tomatoes or dried tomatoes packed in oil*
> *2 teaspoons fresh rosemary or ½ teaspoon dried*
> *2 garlic cloves*
> *1 tablespoon chopped parsley*
> *1 tablespoon butter*
> *2 to 3 tablespoons olive oil*
> *1 small onion, finely diced*
> *½ pound fresh mushrooms, roughly chopped into irregular pieces*
> *salt*
> *freshly ground pepper*
> *10 to 12 ounces narrow lasagne noodles, fettuccine or spaghetti*

Put the dried mushrooms in a bowl and pour the boiling water over them. If the tomatoes are dry (not packed in oil), combine them with the mushrooms. Set them aside to soak for 30 minutes; then rub the mushrooms through your fingers to dislodge any sand. Squeeze both the mushrooms and tomatoes dry and chop them into small pieces. Reserve the soaking liquid. If the tomatoes are oil-packed, chop them into small pieces and set them aside. Finely chop the rosemary, garlic, and half the parsley together.

Heat the butter and oil in a wide skillet. When hot, add the mushrooms and tomatoes, onion, and garlic-herb mixture. Sauté for about a minute; then add the fresh mushrooms. Add salt, a generous amount of pepper, and cook over medium-high heat until the mushrooms begin to give up their liquid, after 3 or 4 minutes. Carefully pour the soaking liquid from the dried mushrooms into the pan. Bring to a boil; then lower the heat and simmer for 15 minutes. Taste for salt and pepper.

Bring a large pot of water to boil for the pasta, add salt to taste and the noodles. Cook until they are done; then drain the noodles and put them in a heated serving dish. Pour the mushroom sauce over them and garnish with the remaining parsley.

Suggestion: For a juicier dish, make this with the Tomato Sauce with Rosemary, on page 328.

Buckwheat Noodles with Brown Butter and Cabbages

The earthy flavor of buckwheat is perfect with the nutty taste of brown butter, Brussels sprouts, and nappa cabbage. Many people find the flavor of Brussels sprouts too strong, but here the leaves are separated and scattered among the noodles and nappa. This way they make a much more delicate impression.

Japanese buckwheat noodles can be found in Asian markets and in natural foods stores, but if you can't find them where you live, use whole wheat noodles instead. The large, pale green heads of nappa cabbage can be found in Asian markets and in most supermarkets. They are delicious in salads or cooked, as they are here.

Makes 4 servings

> 6 tablespoons brown butter (page 416)
> 2 garlic cloves, minced
> ½ pound Brussels sprouts, the leaves separated
> ¼ cup water
> salt
> 1 pound nappa cabbage, thinly sliced
> 10 to 12 ounces buckwheat noodles
> 3 tablespoons finely chopped parsley
> 1 bunch of scallions, including some of the firm greens, sliced into rounds
> ¼ cup grated Gruyère or Fontina cheese
> 1 tablespoon toasted black sesame seeds, if available, or white sesame seeds
> freshly ground pepper

Bring a large pot of water to a boil for the pasta and prepare the vegetables while it is heating.

Heat 2 tablespoons of the butter in a wide skillet, add the garlic and Brussels sprouts leaves, and cook over medium heat, turning the leaves frequently until they begin to shine, after a minute or 2. Add the water and a little salt and cook until the leaves are sweet and tender, about 3 or 4 minutes more. Add water, if needed, in small increments. Once the Brussels sprouts are cooked, add the cabbage, and cook until the cabbage is wilted. Season with salt and set aside.

Add salt to the pasta water; then add the pasta. Unless the package has any special cooking instructions, just cook as you would other pasta and remove as soon as it is done. Scoop it out and add it directly to the vegetables. Add the remaining butter, parsley, scallions, cheese, and sesame seeds, and combine gently. Season with pepper and serve.

Spaghetti with Cauliflower and Sun-Dried Tomato Sauce

Use large spaghetti or *bucatini*, (spaghetti with a hole in it) or another dried pasta such as *penne* or shells. This is a hearty, substantial sauce that needs a strong, firm noodle.

The tomato purée is made from sun-dried tomatoes, the kind sold loose rather than packed in oil. They have a deep, rich, almost smoky flavor. If you haven't any of the purée on hand, it's simple to make. The tomatoes need only a soak in hot water before being puréed. If sun-dried tomatoes aren't available, use 2 cups chopped fresh or canned tomatoes, fortified with several teaspoons tomato paste.

Makes 4 servings

> 1 medium-sized head (a little over 1 pound) of cauliflower
> salt
> 2 to 3 tablespoons olive oil
> 2 garlic cloves, sliced
> ½ small onion, diced into ¼-inch squares
> 2 tablespoons sun-dried tomato purée (page 326)
> ¼ cup finely chopped parsley
> ¾ pound spaghetti
> freshly ground pepper
> freshly grated Parmesan or Romano cheese

Bring a large pot of water to a boil for the cauliflower and the pasta. While the water is heating, break the cauliflower into little flowerets. When the water boils, add salt to taste and the cauliflower. Return the water to a boil and cook until the cauliflower is tender but still a little firm, about 2 minutes. Scoop out the cauliflower and set it aside. Keep the water on the stove for the pasta.

Warm the olive oil in a wide skillet with the garlic. When the garlic browns, discard it and add the diced onion. Cook over medium heat for 1 or 2 minutes; then add the drained cauliflower and cook together until the onion has softened and is beginning to color, another 3 minutes or so. Add the tomato purée or the canned tomatoes, another cup or so of water, and half the parsley; cook over medium-low heat while you cook the pasta. Season with salt.

Drop the pasta into the same water used for the cauliflower and cook until it is *al dente*. Scoop it out with a strainer and add it to the cauliflower. Toss well, garnish with the remaining parsley, and serve with plenty of pepper and grated cheese.

Pasta with Cranberry Beans and Greens

Although various types of dried beans are familiar to us, the same beans, fresh and tender in their pods, are something of a novelty. In late summer and autumn, shell beans, as they are called, can be found in some markets, particularly farmers' markets. Basically any bean can be treated as a shell bean by allowing it to mature, but cranberry and *borlotti* beans are the most common. They're undeniably curious-looking; their drying pods are twisted and shriveled, but inside, the beans are moist and plump, vermilion-colored with black and purple stripes. Unfortunately the gorgeous colorations disappear under heat and fade to a single dull rose color. Cooking with shell beans is one of the possibilities that makes growing vegetables such a pleasure. If fresh shelling beans aren't available, use dried beans, soaked and cooked until tender, in their place.

The earthy, soft flavor of the beans is brightened by the bite of the mustard. Although a bunch of mustard greens weighing about a pound looks like a lot, it cooks down. You could easily use two bunches, for they really enliven the dish.

Makes 4 to 6 servings

> 1 pound cranberry beans in their pods (1 cup, shelled, or ⅓ cup dried)
> 1 quart water
> 1 bay leaf
> 6 sage leaves or ½ teaspoon dried
> 3 to 5 tablespoons olive oil
> 4 garlic cloves
> 1 medium carrot, finely diced
> salt
> 1 or 2 bunches of mustard greens, kale, collards, or turnip greens
> 1 medium-sized red onion, finely diced
> ¼ teaspoon red pepper flakes
> 8 to 10 ounces penne, ziti, butterflies or little shells
> freshly ground pepper
> freshly grated Parmesan or Romano cheese

If you're using dried beans, soak them first for 6 hours or cover them with boiling water and soak them for an hour; then treat them like the fresh beans, as follows. Shell the beans; then put them in a sauté pan with the water, bay leaf, 3 of the sage leaves or half the dried sage, and 1 tablespoon of the olive oil. Slice 1 of the garlic cloves and add it to the pan along with the carrot. Salt lightly and simmer gently until the beans are tender, about 30 minutes or possibly longer, depending on the maturity of the beans. Should they absorb all the water, add more as needed, including enough to leave some broth. When the beans are done, set them aside with their cooking liquid.

Remove the tough stems of the greens and chop the leaves. Heat 2 tablespoons of the oil in a skillet and gently wilt the onion. Finely chop the remaining garlic, chop the remaining sage leaves, and add them to the onion with the pepper flakes. Cook for a minute or 2; then add the greens. Lightly salt and add a little cooking water from the beans and cook until the greens are tender. Add the beans and enough liquid to make a nice sauce. Bring a large pot of water to a boil. Add salt to taste and the pasta and cook until the pasta is *al dente*. Drain and toss with the greens and the beans. Season to taste and serve with plenty of ground pepper, the remaining olive oil laced over the top, and freshly grated cheese.

Twisted Noodles with Olive Sauce

The twisted pasta called *fusilli* picks up the pungent flecks of olives, capers, chilies, and herbs, making a dish with lots of strong, assertive flavors. There's nothing mild or dainty about this pasta. And the sturdy sauce is one of those staples that will keep well, refrigerated, and can be made either weeks in advance or at the last moment.

Makes 6 servings

6 ounces (1½ cups) Kalamata olives
5 sun-dried tomatoes, either oil-packed or loose, or 1 tablespoon
    sun-dried tomato purée (page 326)
4 to 6 tablespoons olive oil
½ medium-sized onion, finely chopped
2 garlic cloves, minced
¼ teaspoon red pepper flakes
1 teaspoon chopped rosemary leaves or several pinches dried
1 tablespoon chopped marjoram or 1 teaspoon dried
¼ cup chopped parsley
½ cup dry red wine or water
1 to 2 tablespoons capers, rinsed
salt
1 pound fusilli
freshly grated hard cheese such as Parmesan, Asiago or dried Monterey Jack

If the olives are very salty, give them a brief rinse under the tap. Press on the olives to open them, remove the pits, and chop them finely, either by hand or in a food processor. Don't let the olives turn to mush—they should have some texture. Chop the sun-dried tomatoes into small pieces. If using dried tomatoes that are not preserved in oil, plump them up by covering them with boiling water and letting them stand for 10 minutes or until they are soft; then chop them.

Gradually heat ¼ cup of the olive oil and add the onion, garlic, red pepper flakes, rosemary, marjoram, half the parsley, and the olives. Cook gently for several minutes; then add the wine and capers. Continue cooking until the wine is fairly well reduced.

While the sauce is cooking, bring a large pot of water to a boil; salt to taste and add the pasta. Cook until it is *al dente;* then drain and transfer it to a warm serving bowl. Add the sauce, the remaining olive oil, and the remaining parsley. Toss together and serve with the cheese.

Spinach Pasta with Ricotta and Walnuts

This delicate pasta dish is easy to put together. If you're inspired to make your own ricotta, be sure to try it with pasta—its texture is much finer and less granular than that of most commercial brands. Both whole wheat and spinach noodles are particularly good with the mixture of ricotta and walnuts.

The amounts given here are flexible. If you prefer a richer pasta, use cream. For a lighter one, use milk or the pasta water for the liquid. It's best to have everything at room temperature as the sauce is cooked mainly by the heat of the pasta.

Makes 2 to 4 servings

> salt
> ½ pound spinach or whole wheat pasta
> 1 cup ricotta cheese, at room temperature
> 2 to 4 tablespoons butter, at room temperature
> 1 tablespoon walnut oil
> ⅓ cup finely chopped walnuts
> ¼ cup freshly grated Parmesan or Romano cheese
> ½ to 1 cup cream, milk or pasta water
> 1 tablespoon snipped chives
> 1 tablespoon chopped parsley
> salt
> freshly ground pepper
> additional Parmesan or Romano cheese for garnish

Bring a large pot of water to a boil for the pasta and add salt to taste. If the pasta is dried, add it at this time. If it's fresh, wait until you've put together the sauce ingredients. Have a heated serving bowl or pasta plates ready.

Mix together the ricotta, butter, walnut oil, ¼ cup of the walnuts, and the ¼ cup grated cheese. Thin with liquid until it's the texture of thick cream; then stir in the herbs and season with salt and pepper. Transfer the mixture to a skillet and set over a very low flame.

When the pasta is finished cooking, lift it out with a pasta scoop and put it directly into the pan with the ricotta. Mix together using a pair of tongs; then place in the heated bowl or pasta plates. Garnish with the remaining walnuts and additional cheese and grind plenty of pepper over the top.

Suggestion: Make the same dish with fresh cheese with herbs (page 27) in place of the ricotta. It will have a more lively, less subtle presence with all the herbal additions.

Cold Noodles with Peanut Sauce

Everyone loves Chinese noodles, with their spicy, pungent sauces. This particular sauce is based on ground peanuts brightened with ginger, lots of garlic, cilantro, and chili. It's wonderful on cold Chinese noodles and perfect with grilled foods. Because the sauce tends to thicken as it sits, it's best tossed with the noodles just before serving.

The peanut sauce is very useful to have on hand. Try it spread on grilled or fried tofu, with grilled eggplant or as a dipping sauce for cubes of fresh tofu or sticks of cucumber or jicama. Tossed with a bowl of rice and topped with some chopped roasted peanuts, scallions, and cilantro, you have a more or less instant, one-bowl meal. Covered and refrigerated, it will keep for months.

Although I love using fresh Chinese egg noodles for this salad, they aren't always available. However, I've had consistently good luck using dried linguine and spaghettini, as well as Japanese *somen*.

Makes 8 to 10 servings

> salt
> 1 pound Chinese egg noodles or linguine
> 2 tablespoons roasted peanut oil or dark sesame oil
> ½ cup chopped cilantro leaves
> 6 scallions, thinly sliced on the diagonal
> 1 ½-pound package silken-firm tofu, cut into small cubes
> peanut sauce (recipe follows)
> chopped roasted peanuts or toasted black sesame seeds
> fresh cilantro sprigs for garnish

Bring a large pot of water to boil for the noodles. Have a colander ready in the sink. When the water boils, add salt to taste and the noodles. Cook until the noodles are just done, about 3 minutes. Immediately dump them into the colander and rinse them with cold water to stop the cooking. Shake off the excess water; then toss the noodles with the oil, cilantro, scallions, and tofu. Cover and refrigerate until ready to use; then toss with the peanut sauce. Garnish with the roasted peanuts or sesame seeds and fresh cilantro sprigs.

■ If you prefer to have the noodles hot, shake off the excess water when they're finished cooking, but don't rinse them. Warm the sauce over a double boiler and toss it with the noodles.

THE PEANUT SAUCE

Using commercially prepared peanut butter instead of frying and grinding peanuts shortens the number of steps, but be sure to use a pure, unsweetened variety, usually found in natural foods stores. Arrowhead Mills makes a good peanut butter, and Loriva makes an excellent blend of peanut and sesame butter.

Makes approximately 2 cups

> 6 large garlic cloves
> 1 large bunch of cilantro, leaves and upper stems only
> 1½-ounce piece fresh ginger, peeled and roughly
>   chopped (about 2 tablespoons)
> 1 tablespoon peanut oil
> 1 tablespoon dark sesame oil
> 1 tablespoon hot chili oil
> ½ cup peanut butter or sesame-peanut butter
> ½ to ⅔ cup soy sauce
> 3 tablespoons sugar
> 3 tablespoons rice wine vinegar or to taste
> hot water, if necessary

Put the garlic, cilantro, and ginger in the work bowl of a food processor and work until they are finely chopped. Add the oils, peanut butter, ½ cup soy sauce, and sugar; process again until well combined with the seasonings. Stop and scrape down the sides once or twice. Add the vinegar and season to taste with the additional soy sauce, if necessary. If the sauce is thicker than you wish, thin it with hot water. Store the sauce in an airtight jar and keep it refrigerated. Thin it again with hot water as needed before using. This sauce will keep for months.

Wonton Ravioli

When I worked in a restaurant and had the time—and the crew—to make fresh pasta, that's what I used for ravioli. But now, as a home cook, I don't always have the time, and the discovery of wonton skins has been a boon. The precut squares of egg dough can usually be found in the produce section of the supermarket, near the tofu. If well wrapped once opened, they'll keep for at least a week in the refrigerator or several months in the freezer. The finished ravioli can also be frozen, but their texture is better when eaten fresh.

These ravioli make a tender, refined plate of pasta. Because the textures are so soft, they work best as a first course, with only three or, at the most, four ravioli per serving. The Aromatic White Sauce (page 321), fragrant with herbs and onions, is creamy and smooth but made with milk. The Garlic Soup (page 94) is also delicious—and light—with the ravioli.

When using wonton skins (or if cutting rolled pasta into squares approximately 3 by 3 inches), you'll need just less than a tablespoon of filling per ravioli. A cup of filling will provide enough for four or five servings. A ravioli crimper is very helpful—practically necessary—for getting a good tight seal on the pasta, and it leaves the edges nicely crimped.

In addition to the recipes that follow, you could fill the wonton skins with other vegetable purées, such as a winter squash purée, vegetable mixtures with more texture, or an herb-flavored cheese filling. Instead of topping each square with another piece of pasta, use less filling on just one square, fold it in half diagonally, and bring the ends together, or use the skins to make more traditional Chinese shaped wontons. There are many ways you can use the combination of fillings and wonton skins.

Ravioli with Potato-Garlic Purée

Stuffing pasta with potato may sound odd, but it's delicious and utterly tender. The ravioli are particularly good when made with the new summer crop of garlic, and they are excellent served in any of the suggested sauces.

Makes 16 to 18 ravioli, serving 4 to 6

> *½ recipe potato and garlic purée (page 196)*
> *36 wonton skins*
> *2 cups garlic soup (page 94), mushroom sauce (page 169) or*
>   *aromatic white sauce (page 321)*
> *freshly ground pepper*
> *snipped chives, chopped basil or other chopped herbs for garnish*
> *freshly grated Parmigiano-Reggiano*

Make the potato purée and whichever sauce you want to use. Set half the wonton skins on the counter and fill them with 2 or 3 teaspoons of the potato purée. Brush the edges with water and cover with the second skin, gently stretching it over the filling. Press the 2 skins tightly with your fingers; then run a ravioli crimper around the edges to seal. Set them on a lightly floured surface when finished.

Warm the sauce and cook the ravioli. Slip them into a pan of gently boiling salted water and cook until they float to the surface, about 3 to 5 minutes. Transfer them to the pan with the sauce and slide the pan back and forth to cover the pasta. Season with pepper, the fresh herbs, and a dusting of cheese.

Mushroom Ravioli with Mushroom Sauce

Mushrooms have a distinctive, woodsy, earthy flavor, and the tart green olives give it an exciting edge. The richly flavored sauce is based on red wine and dried wild mushrooms. Using wonton skins instead of your own pasta makes a reasonable job of what would otherwise be a fairly complicated procedure.

Makes 16 ravioli, serving 4

> ½ *pound mushrooms*
> 8 *large green olives*
> 1 *tablespoon butter*
> 2 *tablespoons olive oil*
> 2 *tablespoons finely chopped onion*
> ¼ *teaspoon Greek oregano*
> 1 *tablespoon finely chopped parsley*
> *salt*
> 1 *large garlic clove, minced*
> *freshly ground pepper*
> 32 *wonton skins*
> *mushroom sauce (recipe follows)*
> *freshly grated Parmigiano-Reggiano*

Chop the mushrooms finely, either by hand or in a food processor, so that they end up in coarse fragments rather than fine pieces, ⅛ inch or so long. Press down on the olives to break out the pits or, if this doesn't seem to work (this is a little harder with green olives than with black), slice away the flesh with a paring knife and chop them slightly finer than the mushrooms.

Heat the butter and oil in a skillet and add the onion, oregano, parsley, and mushrooms. Salt lightly and cook over brisk heat, stirring constantly, for 5 or 6 minutes. The mushrooms should start to color a little and the onions soften. Add the garlic during the last few minutes of cooking so that it doesn't burn. Season with pepper and set aside to cool before filling the ravioli.

Lay out 16 wonton skins. Heap 2 to 3 teaspoons of filling neatly into the center of the squares, then paint the edges with water and cover securely with the top pieces of dough. Firmly press the sides together, squeeze out any air, and cut with a ravioli crimper to secure. Set the ravioli aside on a tray dusted with flour, cover, and refrigerate until ready to use. Make the sauce below.

To cook the ravioli, slip them into gently boiling salted water and simmer until

the edges of the squares are done and they rise to the surface, about 3 to 5 minutes. Serve in warm pasta plates with the sauce and a grating of Parmigiano-Reggiano.

MUSHROOM SAUCE

8 dried porcini (cèpes) *(about ½ ounce)*
3½ cups hot water
2 teaspoons butter
2 teaspoons virgin olive oil
1 cup diced onion
2 pinches of dried oregano
1 pinch of dried thyme
1 bay leaf
2 tablespoons roughly chopped parsley
4 fresh mushrooms, roughly chopped
2 garlic cloves, roughly chopped
salt
2 teaspoons butter
1 tablespoon flour
1 cup dry red wine
1 teaspoon Dijon mustard
1 teaspoon tomato paste or sun-dried tomato purée (page 326)
freshly ground pepper

Cover the dried mushrooms with the hot water and set them aside to soak while you prepare all the other ingredients. When you're ready to use them, run your fingers over the mushrooms to loosen any hidden sand, then pour the soaking water through a paper towel.

Heat the butter and oil in a wide skillet or a saucepan and add the onion, dried herbs, parsley, fresh mushrooms, and garlic. Cook over medium-high heat, stirring frequently, for about 5 minutes. Add salt to taste and continue cooking until the onions begin to color a little, another few minutes.

Add another 2 teaspoons butter to the pan. Stir in the flour, working it into the vegetables as well as you can; the whole mass will be quite thick, and the pan will become very dry. Next pour in the red wine, bring it to a boil, and let it reduce for a few minutes. Stir in the mustard and tomato paste and pour in the mushrooms and their soaking water. Bring to a boil and cover the pan; then lower the heat and simmer slowly for 25 minutes. Strain and season to taste with salt and pepper.

■ This sauce would also be good with other pasta or rice.

Ravioli with Spring Vegetable Purée

Asparagus, artichokes, and peas are the spring vegetables in this purée. To give the finished dish some texture, you might include some blanched peas or asparagus tips and stir them in at the last minute.

The creamy-textured milk-based white sauce can be made ahead of time and reheated before serving. Fresh basil, finely cut into strips and added to the sauce at the last minute, would be delicious with these vegetables.

Makes 1 cup purée, enough for 18 ravioli, serving 6

> *aromatic white sauce (page 321)*
> *10 large asparagus spears*
> *1 large artichoke*
> *1 bunch of scallions or 1 small leek, white part only, chopped*
> *1 small (3 ounces) red potato, peeled and chopped*
> *1 tablespoon unsalted butter*
> *salt*
> *1 tablespoon chopped parsley or chervil*
> *1 thyme branch or pinch of dried*
> *½ cup water*
> *½ cup shelled fresh or frozen peas*
> *additional unsalted butter*
> *32 wonton skins*
> *freshly ground pepper*
> *basil leaves, cut into fine strips, for garnish*
> *finely grated Parmesan cheese*

Make the sauce and set it aside until needed.

Snap the asparagus stems and discard the tough bottoms. Roughly chop the remaining tips and stalks. Trim the artichoke: Break off the outer leaves, slice off the top two thirds of the remaining leaves, and trim around the edges. Quarter the artichokes, cut away the choke with a paring knife, and roughly chop them.

Put the asparagus, artichokes, scallions, potato, 1 tablespoon butter, a little salt, herbs, and water in a saucepan. Bring to a boil; then simmer, partially covered, until all the vegetables are tender, about 25 minutes. Add the peas and cook

until they are done. The water should be evaporated by the time the vegetables are done, but if necessary, add more in small increments.

Transfer the vegetables to a food processor and purée them until smooth. Or pass them through the fine screen of a food mill. Stir in additional butter to taste and season with salt and pepper. The purée should not be watery. If it is, return it to the stove and cook it gently while stirring until the excess moisture has cooked away. Let it cool before filling the ravioli.

Lay out 18 of the wonton skins. Pile 2 teaspoons of filling in the middle of each of the squares. Dip a pastry brush in water and paint a thin film of water around the edge of each filled square. Lay a second square on top and gently stretch it over the filling. Press the edges together tightly, forcing out all the air, then run a ravioli crimper around the edges to seal them tightly. Set the finished ravioli on a cookie sheet lightly dusted with flour. If they are to be held for more than an hour, cover them with plastic wrap and refrigerate until they are to be cooked.

When you're ready to cook the ravioli, first make sure the serving dishes are warm and have the sauce heating in a wide sauté pan. Fill another wide pan with water and bring it to a boil. Add salt to taste and adjust the heat so that the boil is gentle; slip in the ravioli. Cook until the dough tastes done around the edges and they float, 3 to 5 minutes. Gently lift out the cooked ravioli and put them in the pan with the sauce. Slide the pan back and forth to coat the ravioli; then serve them in the heated soup plates. Season with pepper, add the fresh basil, and dust lightly with the cheese.

Ravioli with Fresh Herbed Cheese

The herb-flavored fresh cheese is delicious in ravioli. The creamy texture can be repeated in the sauce by using aromatic white sauce, or the ravioli can be served with something more brothy, such as mushroom sauce or the garlic soup. If you're using the cream sauce, garnish the ravioli with finely chopped roasted pine nuts or walnuts or golden fried bread crumbs for textural contrast.

Makes 16 ravioli, serving 4

> *32 wonton skins*
> *1 cup fresh cheese with herbs (page 27)*
> *aromatic white sauce (page 321), mushroom sauce*
> *   (page 169) or garlic soup (page 94)*
> *freshly ground pepper*
> *finely grated Parmigiano-Reggiano*

Lay half the wonton skins on a counter and heap 2 to 3 teaspoons of the filling in the middle of each one. Brush a film of water around the edge, lay a second wonton skin on top, and press the edges firmly together. Run a ravioli crimper around the edges to secure them. Set them on a lightly floured tray and cover them with a towel or plastic wrap until needed. Make the sauce and keep it hot in a second pan.

Cook the ravioli in a pan of gently boiling salted water until they float to the surface and are done around the edges, 3 to 5 minutes. Slip them into the second pan with the sauce and slide the pan back and forth to cover the pasta. Serve on heated plates and dust with pepper and cheese.

Stove-Top Vegetables

Simple Sautés

and Braises

Cooking on top of the stove is immediately effective. The directness of the heat and the fact that you can see and smell the transformation taking place tell you exactly what's happening, when the food will be cooked, how crisp or how tender it will be. When the heat is high, vegetables can be sautéed quickly and finished with aromatic herbs and oils. The colors are bright, the flavors clean and pure. This is one of the best ways to appreciate the character of a particular vegetable. When the heat is low and liquid is included, the vegetables cook gently and are bathed in their own juices. The flavors and colors are softened and transformed by time and heat.

For the most part these are simple dishes that feature just a single vegetable. They are intended to accompany other dishes, but some make a light meal in themselves. There are also a few vegetables that are dusted lightly with flour or coated with bread crumbs and fried in a shallow film of oil. Their crisp and chewy textures are especially delightful, a change from blanched and sautéed foods; served with a splash of vinegar or sauce, they make a lively start to a meal.

The quality of each ingredient in a dish always matters, but in simple dishes like these that's especially true. The vegetables should of course be as fresh as possible, but the choice of cooking oil is also very important. The unique flavors of aromatic oils—olive, mustard, sesame, peanut—are especially effective and clearly convey their characteristics to the vegetable. The same is true of butter; brown butter is robust and toasty, while plain butter is complementary but much more delicate. The choice of butter or oil will do a great deal to determine the end result of the dish, so be sure that whatever you use is of good quality and fresh. And try using different oils and vegetables in combination; this is one instance where a single departure is very effective.

Asparagus with Peanut Oil, Shallots, and Parsley

The success of such a simple dish depends entirely on the quality of the ingredients, especially the oil, which should be one of the fragrant peanut oils that smell of freshly roasted peanuts. They are as sublime as the best olive oils. And because the flavor is so pure and the taste so big, you'll find you need to use only a small amount of oil. (See glossary for information on specific brands.)

Makes 2 to 4 servings

1½ to 2 pounds asparagus
salt
2 to 3 teaspoons roasted peanut oil
2 shallots, finely diced
finely chopped parsley

Snap off the tough ends of the asparagus and trim them. If you're using thick asparagus, peel the bottoms. If you're using thin asparagus, leave it unpeeled.

Bring a large pot of water to a boil; add salt to taste and the asparagus. Boil gently until the asparagus is sufficiently cooked—bright green and tender, but still a little firm. When cooked, remove the asparagus to a clean towel to drain it briefly; then put it in a large bowl and toss with two or three teaspoons of peanut oil, to taste, the shallots, and the parsley. Salt lightly, set on a platter, and serve.

Asparagus with Brown Butter and Parmesan

Once the asparagus season has gone on for a while, we can feel comfortable venturing into stronger seasonings, such as brown butter with its toasted, nutty taste. The asparagus can either be dressed while hot and served with thin shavings of cheese or cooked first and later heated in the oven with the butter and a covering of cheese.

The strong, slightly unusual flavors make this a fine dish to serve for a first course, followed with Capellini with Lemon and Basil (page 142), which is light and summery, or an omelet for a casual, easy supper.

Makes 4 servings

> *2 pounds asparagus*
> *salt*
> *4 to 5 tablespoons unsalted butter*
> *thinly shaved or grated Parmigiano-Reggiano*
> *freshly ground pepper*

Snap off the tough ends of the asparagus and trim them neatly. If the stalks are thick, peel the lower few inches; if they're thin, leave them as they are.

Bring several quarts of water to a boil and add salt to taste. While it is heating, prepare the butter. Melt it in a small pan or skillet and cook until it begins to color and take on a nice, nutty aroma. Skim off the foam that collects on the surface, carefully pour off the liquid, and set aside.

Add the asparagus to the boiling water and cook until it is tender but still bright green and a little firm. Remove it to a clean towel to drain it briefly; then set it on a serving platter, all the ends pointing one way. Drizzle the butter over the asparagus and lay the sliced cheese on top. Dust lightly with pepper and serve. The heat of the asparagus will soften the cheese.

If you're cooking the asparagus ahead of time, set the boiled stalks in an ovenproof serving dish. When you're ready to eat, drizzle the butter and grated cheese over the top. Heat the asparagus under a broiler until the cheese is melted and lightly colored. Lightly pepper and serve while hot.

Artichokes with Cilantro Salsa and Cumin

This green sauce of chilies, garlic, and cilantro seasoned with cumin is very good with steamed artichokes and a refreshing change from the usual mayonnaise or melted butter. The ingredients can be put together hours in advance, with the vinegar added at the last minute so the colors stay bright and green.

Makes 4 servings

4 large artichokes
¼ teaspoon ground cumin or to taste
cilantro salsa (page 318)

Set a steaming basket over a pan of water wide enough to hold the artichokes. Cut off the top third of each artichoke and slice off the stem to make a firm base. Trim the remaining outer leaves with a pair of scissors, cutting off the sharp tips. Set the artichokes in the steaming basket, cover, and steam until a leaf will come out when tugged firmly, about 30 minutes. When done, set them upside down on a rack briefly to drain.

While the artichokes are steaming, make the salsa and stir in the cumin. Divide it among ramekins or pour it into a communal bowl for everyone to dip into. Serve the artichokes hot or cold.

Artichokes and Peas with Sage

Sage is perhaps unexpected here, but it goes well with both the peas and the artichokes and lends a kind of sobering note to the dish, something like a spring day that has threatened to revert to winter. Fresh basil leaves in place of the sage would completely transform this dish, giving it a summery taste and feel.

About a half hour of slow, gentle cooking is needed for this dish. Water is added in small amounts at several points; it reduces and combines with the sugars from the onions to form a syrupy glaze.

Makes 2 to 4 servings

> 2 large artichokes
> juice of 1 lemon
> 2 tablespoons olive oil
> 6 to 8 sage leaves or ½ teaspoon dried
> 1 large white or yellow onion, sliced ¼ inch thick
> salt
> ¾ cup water
> 1 pound fresh pod peas, shelled, or 1 cup frozen
> freshly ground pepper
> finely chopped parsley
> 1 tablespoon unsalted butter or extra-virgin olive oil (optional)
> lemon juice or Champagne vinegar

Slice the upper two thirds of the leaves off the artichokes; then break off the remaining leaves, snapping them off at the base. Trim off the dark green stubs, going around the artichoke with a paring knife. Cut them into quarters, remove the fuzzy choke, and slice each quarter into pieces between ¼ and ½ inch thick. As you work, rub the cut surfaces with lemon and put them in a bowl with the lemon juice and water to cover.

Gently warm the olive oil with the sage leaves. When it is fairly hot, but not sizzling, add the onions and the sliced artichokes. Salt lightly and give them a stir to coat them with the oil; then add the water and cook over medium-low heat. As the water cooks off, add more, in ½-cup increments, until the artichokes are cooked, about 25 minutes.

Add the peas and continue cooking until they are done. Let any liquids reduce until they are syrupy. Taste and season with salt and pepper. Add the parsley and the butter or olive oil, if using. To brighten the flavors, stir in a little lemon juice or Champagne vinegar to taste.

Carrots, Roman Style

Although this dish derives from chronicles of Ancient Rome, it is rather contemporary in feeling. Its method is straightforward, the herbal flavorings are clear yet surprising, and the vinegar both sharpens the flavor and leaves the carrots with a firm texture. I have omitted the fermented fish paste that was so frequently used by the Ancient Romans, but one could include an anchovy, finely chopped or pounded and added to the liquids at the beginning.

Makes 2 servings

> ½ pound carrots
> 8 small mint leaves
> 1 lovage leaf, if available or several pale inner leaves of celery
> 2 teaspoons olive oil
> ½ teaspoon cumin seeds
> salt
> 2½ cups water
> 1 tablespoon Champagne or white wine vinegar
> freshly ground pepper
> finely chopped mint or lovage leaves, for garnish

Scrape the carrots and slice them into pieces 2 to 3 inches long. Cut each piece lengthwise into quarters or, if the carrots are very large, into sixths or eighths. All the pieces should be approximately the same size. Tear or chop the herbs.

Warm the oil with the cumin seeds and green herbs for a few moments to bring out their fragrances; then add the carrots and toss them in the oil. Add a few pinches of salt, the water, and the vinegar; bring to a boil, lower the heat, and simmer until tender, about 40 minutes. By this time the liquid should have reduced to almost nothing, leaving the carrots nicely glazed. If the pan becomes dry before the carrots are done, add more water in ¼- or ½-cup increments until they are sufficiently tender. When done, season with pepper and serve with a garnish of fresh herbs.

■ Leftover carrots are good eaten cold, as a vegetable condiment or salad.

Garden Peas, New Onions, and Basil

If one could use peas, onions, and basil plucked from the garden, this dish would make indifferent eaters really excited about food. To eat a bowl of fresh tender peas and new onions is a rare treat. There may be one or two weeks of the year when those who have gardens or access to a farmers' market can have everything so fresh, but the rest of the time frozen peas can be used. They taste fine, especially with fresh basil.

When you're buying fresh peas, check to make sure they're small, bright green, and sweet. The pods should look lively and crisp too, not limp and bruised. If possible, use a freshly pulled onion with the greens still attached—it will be delicate and sweet.

Use either sweet butter or a fine olive oil. The tastes will be different, and both will be excellent; in fact, they can also be used together.

Makes 2 generous servings

> 1 small red onion, freshly pulled if possible
> 1½ to 2 pounds fresh pod peas or 1½ cups frozen
> 6 large basil leaves, thinly sliced
> 1 to 2 tablespoons unsalted butter or extra-virgin olive oil
> salt

Peel the onion, cut it into quarters, and slice it very thinly crosswise. Shuck the peas if they're fresh. If using frozen peas, remove them from the freezer and break them apart.

Gently melt the butter or warm the oil, add the onion and a spoonful of water, and cook for several minutes or until the onion is limp. The onion should just gradually soften, not fry. Add the peas, half the basil, about ½ cup water, and salt lightly. Stew until the peas are cooked and tender, 3 or 4 minutes, depending on the condition of the peas. Add the rest of the basil and taste for salt.

Suggestions: With fresh peas and basil it shouldn't be necessary to add much salt or other seasonings. However, if you have so many fresh peas that you wish to vary the flavors, try them with some of the following seasonings:
- grated Parmigiano-Reggiano and a dusting of freshly ground pepper
- another type of basil, such as lemon basil or cinnamon basil
- a bunch of scallions, or several shallots, or a fresh young leek, stewed in place of the onion
- a garnish of chives and chive blossoms for the color and delicate trace of onion flavor
- combine the dish with tender egg pasta for a lovely spring supper.

Sugar Snap Peas with Sesame Oil

Here the sesame oil is as important as the peas since these are the only two elements in the dish except for a garnish of parsley or cilantro. Use an aromatic oil, either the dark roasted Chinese or Japanese oil or the lighter-colored but equally aromatic American oil made by Loriva.

Sugar snap peas should be plump and bright green. The skins are crisp and tender and are meant to be eaten right along with the peas inside. If they aren't available, use snow peas. Or use a mixture and throw in some shelled peas as well for fun.

Makes 3 to 4 servings

> 1 pound sugar snap or snow peas
> salt
> dark sesame oil
> chopped parsley or cilantro

Cut across the stem end of the peas and pull off the string that runs along the length of the pea. Bring a pot of water to a boil; add salt to taste and the peas. Blanch until the peas turn bright green and are tender-crisp, after a minute or so. Taste to make sure; the time will depend on the type of pea and how mature it is. Scoop them out with a strainer and shake off as much water as possible. Put the peas in a bowl and toss them with just enough oil to coat them lightly, a teaspoon or so. Add the parsley or cilantro and serve.

Suggestion: Make the recipe using peanut oil or a fine virgin olive oil tossed with basil rather than cilantro.

Green Beans Stewed with Onions, Tomatoes, and Dill

This way of cooking green beans is ideal for the kind of beans we find in super-markets, the rather large Blue Lakes or Kentucky Wonders, which require more than a quick dip into boiling water. The beans are cooked over thinly sliced garlic and onions, with chopped tomatoes and herbs on top. They cook slowly and emerge tender, with the sweet taste of the onions and the lively bite of the to-matoes and herbs.

Any kind of onion can be used, but large boiling onions, thinly sliced into rings, are particularly nice. Use fresh tomatoes, if they're ripe, or canned toma-toes. This recipe calls for dill, but basil and marjoram would also be good choices.

Makes 4 servings

> 1 pound green beans or a mixture of green and yellow wax beans
> 8 boiling onions, about an inch and a half wide
> 2 tablespoons olive oil
> 1 large garlic clove, thinly sliced
> pinch of cumin seeds or ground cumin
> salt
> 1 cup canned tomatoes, chopped, or 2 large fresh tomatoes,
>   peeled, seeded, and chopped
> 1 tablespoon chopped fresh dill or ½ teaspoon dried
> 1 tablespoon chopped parsley
> tomato juice or water

Choose beans that are bright green and firm. The smaller ones will be less fi-brous. Top and tail them, then cut into pieces about 1½ inches long and wash them well. Peel the onions and slice them into thin rounds.

Warm the olive oil and add the onion, garlic, and cumin seeds. Cook over a gentle heat for several minutes, until the onions begin to soften. Salt lightly then add the beans; cover them with the chopped tomatoes and herbs. Add several ta-blespoons tomato juice or water, cover the pan tightly, and cook over medium heat until the beans are tender, about 15 minutes.

Green Beans with Mustard Oil
and Black Mustard Seeds

The idea of using mustard in various forms was inspired by Indian recipes. The spicy mustard oil and the popped black mustard seeds might be a little overwhelming for your first crop of *haricots verts*, but it's a perfect treatment for large supermarket beans whose flavor is not quite so delicate. A garnish of yellow mustard flowers, if they can be found, would complete the theme and be quite enchanting with the green beans and black mustard seeds.

Makes 4 servings

> 1 pound green beans
> 1 bunch of scallions, including some of the greens
> salt
> 1 to 2 tablespoons mustard oil
> ½ teaspoon black mustard seeds
> 1 tablespoon chopped cilantro

Choose beans that are bright green and as small and slender as possible. Top and tail them, but leave them long. Slice the scallions into narrow rings. Bring several quarts of water to a boil. Add salt to taste and the beans and cook until they are tender but still a little firm, about 4 minutes. Drain them and set them aside.

In a skillet that is large enough to hold the beans, heat the oil with the mustard seeds. As soon as they start to pop, add the scallions. Sauté rapidly for 20 seconds or so; then add the beans. Toss them in the oil or repeatedly turn them over in the pan with tongs until the oil is evenly distributed. Add the cilantro and toss again. Taste for salt and turn them out onto a serving plate.

Sautéed Tomatoes with Vinegar

Quickly sautéing tomatoes and deglazing the hot pan with vinegar helps give a little character to the bland, firm tomatoes that are most commonly available. They take about two minutes to prepare and can be used as a side dish, especially for creamy or soft-textured foods that want the sparkle of something acidic. Different kinds of vinegars will lend their character to the tomatoes—sherry vinegar is strong and assertive; balsamic is sweet and rich; herb-infused wine vinegars carry the flavor of the herbs. Try different ones.

Makes 2 to 3 servings

1 large, firm tomato
2 teaspoons butter
2 to 3 teaspoons olive oil
salt
1 to 2 tablespoons vinegar (see above)
freshly ground pepper
chopped parsley, basil or marjoram for garnish

Wash the tomato, remove the core, and cut the tomato into eighths. Heat the butter and oil in a sauté pan. When it's hot, add the tomato wedges and salt them lightly. Cook for about a minute on one side; then turn and cook the other side. Slide the pan back and forth several times so that the tomatoes don't stick.

When the tomatoes have cooked on both sides, turn off the heat. Set them in a serving bowl and pour the vinegar into the pan. It will immediately begin to sizzle and evaporate. Shake the pan back and forth to combine the vinegar with the juices; then pour the sauce right over the tomatoes. Grind plenty of pepper on top and garnish with the fresh herbs.

■ A pair of tongs is the perfect tool for handling the tomatoes.

Zucchini with Lemon-Caper Butter

The mixture of butter with lemon, herbs, and capers gives a sparkle to zucchini. It would also be delicious on charcoal-grilled zucchini. Medium-sized squash can be sliced into coins or lengthwise into 3-inch pieces, but smaller squash can simply be halved.

Makes 4 servings

> *1 pound zucchini*
> *2 teaspoons capers*
> *2 to 3 tablespoons butter*
> *grated zest of 1 lemon*
> *1 teaspoon lemon juice*
> *1 shallot, finely diced*
> *1 teaspoon finely chopped parsley*
> *1 teaspoon chopped basil or marjoram*
> *salt*
> *freshly ground pepper*

Slice the zucchini into even-sized pieces of any desired shape. Rinse the capers, squeeze out the excess liquid, and roughly chop them. Work them into the butter with the rest of the ingredients. Season to taste with salt and pepper and set aside. Steam the zucchini until tender, 5 minutes or so; then toss it with the butter and serve.

Zucchini and Peas with Basil

A simple, tasty dish of beautiful green vegetables. The measurements don't really require exactitude. I've made this with a handful of pod peas, a few snow peas, and sugar snap peas mixed in with the zucchini. And I've made it with different basils—lemon basil, cinnamon basil, and the deep plum-colored leaves of opal basil. All combinations are delicious, and each has its own charm. Use an oil with deep, pure flavor, either extra-virgin olive oil or peanut oil, and stew the vegetables slowly in just a little liquid.

Serve this as a side dish or toss with pasta or warm rice to make a more substantial one-bowl meal.

Makes 2 to 4 servings

> 1 pound small, firm zucchini
> 1 pound fresh pod peas or 1 cup frozen, approximately
> snow peas or sugar snap peas, as desired
> 1 tablespoon extra-virgin olive oil
> 1 teaspoon peanut oil
> salt
> 3 to 4 basil leaves, torn or finely sliced
> 2 mint leaves, finely sliced

Cut the zucchini lengthwise into quarters; then cut it into ½-inch pieces. Shuck the peas if you're using fresh ones and remove the strings from the snow peas or sugar snap peas. Warm the oils in a wide sauté pan; add the vegetables and a tablespoon or so of water. Salt lightly, add half the basil leaves, and cook over medium-low heat. Occasionally give the vegetables a stir. When the squash and peas are tender, toss them with the rest of the basil and the mint leaves and serve.

Suggestions: It would be a simple matter to build this into a more complex mélange of vegetables—a seasonal vegetable stew. New spring onions or tiny leeks, sorrel leaves, fava beans, new carrots, and the tender leaves of sweet lettuces, like Bibb, would all taste wonderful with the zucchini and peas.

Shredded Zucchini with Yogurt Sauce

This type of recipe is given as a salad in Turkish cookbooks, but I always find it utterly irresistible while it's warm. Because of the pastalike shape of the cut zucchini and the texture of the yogurt, it's like eating noodles in cream sauce, only much lighter.

With some fresh tomatoes and slices of dark bread, this makes an easy summer lunch for two people. Chilled, it can be served as an hors d'oeuvre with sesame crackers, used as a filling for pita breads, or served as one of the elements on a plate of small salads.

Makes 2 generous servings

> 1 pound medium-sized, firm zucchini
> 2 to 3 tablespoons water
> salt
> ½ cup plain yogurt
> 1 garlic clove, pounded in a mortar or finely minced
> 2 teaspoons chopped dill or several pinches dried
> 1 teaspoon chopped mint leaves or 2 pinches dried
> 1 teaspoon white wine vinegar
> 1 tablespoon extra-virgin olive oil
> freshly ground pepper
> additional fresh herbs, whole or chopped, for garnish

Grate the zucchini coarsely, using the large holes of a 4-sided grater or the shredding disk of the food processor. Heat a few tablespoons of water in a wide non-stick skillet; add the zucchini and lightly salt. Cook gently over medium heat until there is little moisture in the pan and the zucchini is cooked, about 8 minutes. Stir occasionally to make sure that it isn't sticking or browning.

While the zucchini is cooking, mix the yogurt with the garlic, herbs, vinegar, oil, and pepper. Stir it into the cooked zucchini, toss, and heat gently until it is warm throughout. Taste for salt. Serve the zucchini warm or at room temperature with freshly ground pepper and a garnish of fresh herbs.

Broccoli with Roasted Peppers, Olives, and Feta Cheese

Many people I know frequently make a meal of a single vegetable garnished with tasty tidbits, some bread or rice, and a piece of cheese. This is one of those dishes. Two people can polish it off with ease and call it dinner, or it can be part of a larger meal and serve four. With roasted peppers on hand, this can be made very quickly.

The garnishes can all be prepared while the broccoli is steaming.

Makes 2 to 4 servings

1 large bunch of broccoli
1 to 2 tablespoons olive oil
1 garlic clove, thinly sliced
10 Kalamata olives, pits removed, chopped into large pieces
3 tablespoons roasted peppers (page 329), diced
2 teaspoons finely chopped marjoram or ½ teaspoon dried
1 tablespoon finely chopped parsley
2 ounces feta cheese
salt
freshly ground pepper
lemon wedges (optional)

Cut the broccoli into fairly large flowerets. Set aside the stalks for another purpose or thickly peel them, cut into spears or rounds, and include a few of them in the recipe. Steam the broccoli until it has cooked as much as you like. While the broccoli is steaming, prepare the rest of the ingredients.

When the broccoli is cooked, warm the oil in a large pan with the sliced garlic. Remove the garlic when it has browned; then add the steamed broccoli, olives, peppers, marjoram, and parsley. Sauté over lively heat until everything is warmed. Scatter the cheese over the broccoli, season it lightly with salt, and add pepper to taste. Serve the dish warm. The cheese will soften and melt into the vegetables. If you like, serve it with a wedge of lemon and eat it as a warm salad.

Red Cabbage Braised in Red Wine

This is a rather traditional treatment of cabbage and a good one. The finished vegetable emerges coated with the reduced wine, vinegar, and pan juices. This is a darkly colorful dish, best served with something very uncomplicated, like a plump piece of baked winter squash.

Makes 6 servings

> 1 head of red cabbage, about 1½ pounds
> salt
> 2 tablespoons olive oil
> 2 large celery stalks, cut into ¼-inch dice
> 1 large carrot, peeled and cut into ¼-inch dice
> 1 medium-sized red or yellow onion, finely chopped
> 2 garlic cloves, minced
> 2 tablespoons finely chopped parsley
> 1 bay leaf
> pinch of dried thyme
> 10 juniper berries
> freshly ground pepper
> 1 large tart apple, grated
> 1 cup dry red wine
> ½ cup water
> strong red wine vinegar

Blanching the cabbage keeps it sweet-tasting, so begin by bringing a large pot of water to a boil. While it is heating, cut the cabbage into quarters, remove the cores, and cut the cabbage into narrow shreds. When the water comes to a boil, add salt to taste and the cabbage. Boil for 2 minutes; then pour the cabbage into a colander and set it aside to drain.

Warm the oil in a wide pan and add the celery, carrot, onion, garlic, parsley, bay leaf, thyme, and juniper. Season with salt and plenty of pepper and cook over medium heat for 3 or 4 minutes. Add the cabbage and the apple. Stir everything to combine. If the pan is crowded, use a pair of tongs to pick everything up and turn it over.

Pour in the wine and water, cover the pan, and cook over medium heat. Check after 20 minutes or so and turn the vegetables over. Continue cooking until the liquids are reduced to a syrup, about 25 minutes more. Taste for salt, add enough red wine vinegar to give it a lively edge, and serve.

Cauliflower with Paprika and Garlic Sauce

This recipe comes from Joe Colanero, a gardener and writer with a special love for paprika. When he sent me a package of his homegrown paprika and a number of recipes, I was reminded how delicious paprika can be. After years of exploring new herbs and exotic tastes, paprika seems new again and all the more special for its rich, warm flavor and deep color.

The important point in working with paprika, as with other ground peppers, is to have the oil warm but not hot when you add it; otherwise it will burn and the beautiful flavor will be spoiled. Even though paprika is dried and ground, it will be best when it's fresh. Buy it in small enough cans that you can replace it at least once a year if not more frequently.

This is a straightforward procedure, taking in all about 10 or 15 minutes. Potatoes would also be delicious treated exactly the same way. You will need a small mortar and pestle.

Makes 4 servings

> *1 medium-sized head of cauliflower, about 1¼ pounds*
> *3 to 5 tablespoons olive oil*
> *3 medium-sized garlic cloves, peeled*
> *2 tablespoons chopped parsley*
> *salt*
> *1 tablespoon sweet paprika*
> *2 tablespoons strong red wine or sherry vinegar*

Cut the cauliflower into pieces the size you'll want to serve. Steam them over boiling water in a steaming basket until they are fairly tender but not completely cooked, about 5 minutes. Turn off the heat and cover the pan. While the cauliflower is steaming, heat the oil with the garlic in a heavy skillet over medium-low heat. When the garlic has turned light brown, turn off the heat and put the garlic cloves in a mortar. Pound the garlic with half the parsley and several pinches of salt, forming a rough paste. Place the cauliflower on a serving platter, reserving the cooking water.

Return the pan to low heat and add the paprika, vinegar, ¼ cup of the cooking water from the cauliflower, and the garlic-parsley mixture. Stir rapidly; then pour the sauce over the cauliflower and garnish with the remaining parsley. Serve right away.

Fried Fennel Slices

Here's a good knife-and-fork food for those who seldom or never eat meat. Lightly coated in bread crumbs and fried, the fennel is pleasantly chewy and retains its characteristic fresh, clean flavor.

Makes approximately 4 servings

> 2 large or 3 small fennel bulbs
> 2 slices firm white bread
> 1 egg
> 1 heaping tablespoon chopped fennel greens
> salt
> freshly ground pepper
> clarified butter (page 416) or light olive oil

Wash the fennel; then pry off the thick outer leaves if they are tough and scarred. (Save these for soup or peel them with a vegetable peeler, slice them thinly, and use them in a salad.) Slice each fennel bulb lengthwise into pieces about ⅓ inch thick, leaving the core attached. You will end up with a cross section of the bulb.

Remove the crusts from the bread and make bread crumbs from the pieces in a food processor or by hand. Beat the egg, add the fennel greens, and season with salt and pepper. Dip each piece of fennel into the egg and then into the bread crumbs. Use one hand to dip into the egg and the other hand to dip into the bread crumbs. This keeps the egg from becoming filled with soggy crumbs—a good practice whenever you are dipping and coating. Make sure each piece is generously coated.

Heat a generous amount of clarified butter or oil in a cast-iron skillet or other heavy pan. When it is hot enough to sizzle a crumb of bread, add the fennel and lower the heat to medium-low. Cook slowly so that the fennel is done just as the crumbs have turned a beautiful golden brown. Fry on both sides and serve hot, as a first course, with a wedge of lemon or a spoonful of mayonnaise flavored with a few drops of Pernod. This is also delicious with garlic mayonnaise (page 314).

Fried Leeks with Tarragon Vinegar

These leeks are steamed until tender, dipped in beaten egg and flour, and then lightly fried. They emerge crisp and golden on the outside and soft inside and are finished with a splash of vinegar and a sprinkling of tarragon. One or two make a good first course.

Makes 4 servings

> *4 medium-sized leeks, white parts only*
> *1 egg*
> *salt*
> *freshly ground pepper*
> *1 teaspoon finely chopped parsley*
> *1 teaspoon finely chopped tarragon, if available, or parsley*
> *flour*
> *safflower or canola oil for frying*
> *tarragon vinegar*

Trim the leeks. Cut off the root, but leave a little so that the leaves remain joined at the bottom. Slice them in half lengthwise and rinse them well. Set up a steaming rack over boiling water and steam the leeks until they are tender, about 10 minutes. Remove to a towel to drain and cool.

Beat the egg in a flat dish and season with salt and pepper. Add the parsley and half the tarragon. Dip the leeks into the egg and slosh it about so that it covers the leaves. Then dip them in the flour to coat.

Heat enough oil in a heavy pan to cover the bottom generously. When it is hot enough to sizzle a drop of water, add the leeks. Fry them, turning them frequently until they're nicely browned all over. Set them on a towel to drain briefly; then serve them with the remaining tarragon or parsley sprinkled over the top and a cruet of the vinegar on the side.

Fried Winter Squash or Pumpkin Slices

Like zucchini in the summer, hard squashes are plentiful in the winter. They make sweet soups and purées and are also good baked in gratins and fried.

Lightly frying preserves the chewy texture and rich taste. The arcs of golden-colored squash or pumpkin garnished with finely chopped herbs make a beautiful warm appetizer for a fall or winter dinner, followed perhaps by the Chestnut and Lentil Soup and an endive salad with walnuts and Gorgonzola cheese.

Not all pumpkins and squashes are the same. Some will have more moisture, like pumpkins, while others will be flavorful but a little dry. In general, though, banana squash, butternut, baby blue Hubbard squash, and small sugar pumpkins are all good to use.

Makes approximately 4 servings

> 1 to 1½ pounds winter squash or pumpkin
> ½ cup flour
> salt
> freshly ground pepper
> light olive oil, canola oil, or clarified butter (page 416)
> balsamic vinegar
> 6 sage leaves or ½ teaspoon dried
> 1 garlic clove, thinly sliced
> a mixture of chopped parsley and mint for garnish

Slice the squash in half, remove the seeds, and cut into pieces about ¼ inch thick but no thicker—or the squash will burn before it is thoroughly cooked through. Pare away the skins with a small knife. Season the flour with salt and pepper.

Heat enough oil or clarified butter in a wide skillet to cover the bottom of the pan generously. Add the sage leaves and the garlic. When the garlic has browned, remove it along with the sage leaves.

Lightly coat the squash or pumpkin slices with the flour and knock off any excess flour so that it won't burn. Add the pieces to the hot oil in a single layer. Cook them over medium heat for about 3 minutes. Check the bottoms; when they are mottled golden brown, turn them over and cook until the second side is browned and the squash is tender. Blot quickly on paper toweling; then serve with a sprinkling of chopped herbs, pepper to taste, and a cruet of vinegar.

Suggestion: If you have squash leftover, it can be used to make a gratin. Layer it with a little tomato sauce and slices of cheese such as provolone, mozzarella, or Fontina. Bake in a hot oven until the cheese is melting and the squash is hot.

Mushrooms with Wine, Tomato, and Herbs

These mushrooms, with their dark, wine-colored sauce, can be ready to eat in about 10 minutes. Although mushrooms aren't particularly substantial on their own, they make a satisfying accompaniment to a plateful of hot polenta, steamed couscous or millet. And they are always good tucked into an omelet or used to sauce a plate of pasta.

Makes 3 to 4 servings

> 1 pound mushrooms
> 3 tablespoons tomato paste or 2 tablespoons
>   sun-dried tomato purée (page 326)
> ½ cup dry red wine
> 2 small garlic cloves, finely chopped
> 2 tablespoons finely chopped parsley
> 2 teaspoons chopped marjoram or ½ teaspoon dried
> a few mint leaves, finely chopped, if available, or 1 pinch of dried
> 2 to 4 tablespoons light or virgin olive oil
> salt
> freshly ground pepper

Wipe the mushrooms with a damp cloth to clean them, if necessary. If they're small, leave them whole. If they're large, cut the mushrooms into quarters or thick slices. Cutting them at odd angles produces a more interesting effect. Dilute the tomato paste with the wine and set it aside.

Heat the oil in a wide skillet. As soon as it is hot, add the mushrooms, salt lightly, and give them a stir to distribute the oil. They will immediately absorb it, but it's not necessary to add more. Lower the heat a little and cook, shaking the pan occasionally, until the mushrooms begin to give up their juices. Raise the heat and add the garlic, parsley, marjoram, and mint. Add the wine mixture to the pan and cook briskly for a minute or so; then simmer until the mushrooms are done and the sauce is reduced and slightly thickened, 2 to 3 minutes. Finish with a twist of the pepper mill and serve.

Suggestion: Cook exactly as above; then let the mushrooms cool in their juices. Season with a little vinegar or lemon juice to taste and add a tablespoon of pine nuts that have been roasted in a dry skillet until golden. Serve at room temperature as a little salad or hors d'oeuvre.

Blanched Winter Vegetables with Thyme

This delicate dish of springtime colors has humble origins—turnips, rutabagas, and the oft-discarded stems of broccoli. Though it may sound unlikely, it has just the cheery element that's needed in a drab month like January or February.

Many people balk at the thought of eating turnips and rutabagas and will scarcely give them a try. It's unfortunate that these two vegetables are so maligned, for they can be quite sweet and very good, particularly when they are young. Older vegetables will tend to be bitter, but blanching will take the bitterness away.

This makes a really lovely side dish just as it is, but it could also be served with a squeeze of lemon juice as a warm vegetable salad, or it could be tossed with pasta.

Makes 4 servings

>3 small turnips
>2 small rutabagas
>2 or 3 broccoli stalks
>2 medium-sized carrots, peeled
>salt
>2 to 3 teaspoons butter
>finely chopped parsley
>½ teaspoon fresh thyme leaves or two pinches of dried
>freshly ground pepper

Peel the turnips and rutabagas. If you notice an area just below the skin that seems tougher in texture and a slightly different color from the rest of the vegetable, remove it as you peel. Slice the turnips into rounds about ¼ inch thick; then slice the rounds into strips about the same thickness. Peel the broccoli stalks; then slice them ¼ inch thick on the diagonal, then slice them again into narrow strips. Do the same with the carrots. Taste the vegetables to determine if any seem tougher than the others. Often the rutabagas will be tougher and will need to be cooked a little longer.

Bring a large pan of water to a boil. Add salt to taste and then the vegetables, starting with those that are tougher. Boil for about 30 seconds, add the rest, and cook until they are just tender, a minute or so. Scoop out the vegetables and put them in a wide sauté pan set over medium heat. Add the butter, parsley, and thyme and cook gently to melt the butter and evaporate the water, leaving a little sauce. Don't let the vegetables fry. Taste for salt and serve with a dusting of pepper.

Potato and Garlic Purée

If possible, try to make this purée when the new garlic comes out in late spring or early summer. I don't mean the immature bulbs with their greens, although these are also wonderful, but the new, mature bulbs. These can be found even in supermarkets. They will have a fresh, clean look about them, and inside the cloves will be pure white, unblemished, and with no sprouts. When cooked with the potatoes and puréed, they are unbelievably good.

This purée makes an excellent filling for ravioli (page 167).

Makes approximately 2 cups, serving 2 to 4

2 heads of garlic
2 pounds small red potatoes
3 tablespoons chopped parsley
2 tablespoons butter
salt
6 to 8 tablespoons milk or cream
additional butter (optional)
freshly ground pepper

Separate the garlic cloves and remove their papery husks. Slice each clove into halves or, if large, thirds. Peel the potatoes (unless they are newly harvested), quarter them, and slice thinly. Put the garlic, potatoes, parsley, and butter in a small saucepan, add water to cover by 2 inches, and lightly salt. Bring to a boil, lower the heat, and simmer, partially covered, until the potatoes and garlic are soft and the water has cooked away, about 25 minutes.

Pass the potatoes and garlic through a food mill. Don't use a food processor or blender as it will give the purée a gooey, unpleasant texture. If you don't have a food mill, mash the potatoes by hand; then work them through a strainer for a smooth texture or leave it a little rough and irregular. Stir in the milk or cream and additional butter, if desired. Add salt to taste and season with pepper.

Winter Vegetable Purée

The winter root vegetables—big leeks, turnips, and the gnarly celery root—make the most delicious sweet purées. Even without copious amounts of butter or cream, they are full of flavor. Usually vegetables are blanched in large amounts of water so that they will cook as quickly as possible, but here the vegetables are cooked in just enough water to keep them floating in the pot. By the time the vegetables are cooked, the water is thick and flavorful and used, in place of cream, to thin the purée. Cream can, of course, be used if you prefer.

This purée also makes a delicious and unusual filling for ravioli (page 170).

Makes about 2½ cups, serving 4 to 6

> 2 cups White Rose or red potatoes, scrubbed and diced into ½-inch pieces
> 3 cups mixed winter vegetables such as turnips, rutabagas, leeks, celery root, and fennel, diced into ½-inch pieces
> 3 sprigs chopped parsley
> 1 pinch of dried thyme
> 3 garlic cloves, roughly chopped
> salt
> butter or cream (optional)
> Champagne vinegar
> freshly ground white pepper

Put the vegetables in a saucepan with the parsley, thyme, garlic, salt, and enough water to cover. Bring to a boil, lower the heat, and simmer until the vegetables are completely soft, about 20 minutes. Pour them into a colander set over a bowl; reserve the liquid.

Pass the vegetables through a food mill or mash by hand. (The food processor will tend to make them too gummy and glutinous.) Use the cooking water to thin the purée to the proper consistency. Stir in additional butter or cream to taste and season with salt, a dash of vinegar, and pepper.

Escarole with Garlic and Chili

Like most greens, escarole is wonderful stewed in a little oil with garlic and red chili, with vinegar added at the end to sharpen the tastes. The flavor is clean, slightly nutty, and goes very well with richer foods, especially with any of the potato cakes. If you've been using the blanched escarole hearts in salads, this recipe will allow you to make use of the outer leaves, which are usually set aside.

Makes 2 generous servings

> 1 head of escarole
> 1 to 2 tablespoons olive oil
> 2 garlic cloves, sliced
> 1 small dried red chili, broken into pieces or a few pinches red pepper flakes
> salt
> balsamic or red wine vinegar
> freshly ground pepper

Separate the escarole leaves at the base, discarding any that are really tough or bruised. Cut them into large pieces and wash them well. Warm the olive oil with the garlic in a wide pan. When the garlic is golden brown, remove it. Add the pepper flakes and the escarole, with the water still clinging to its leaves. Salt lightly and cook over medium-high heat. A pair of tongs is the easiest thing to use to turn over the leaves while they're cooking. When the leaves are wilted and tender, taste for salt, and add a few dashes of vinegar and plenty of pepper. Turn once more to combine everything; then serve.

Suggestions: Use a red onion, thinly sliced, and stew it with the garlic until it is soft and sweet. Don't discard the garlic. Add a little water to keep it from frying; then add the escarole and cook as above.

Bring out the nuttiness of the greens by adding some walnuts. Toast a few, roughly chopped, in a moderate oven for about 5 minutes. Cook the escarole as above, and when it is done, toss it with the walnuts and a spoonful of walnut oil before serving.

Mustard Greens with Tomatoes, Onions, and Chilies

Mustard greens are available year-round, but they seem to taste best when the weather turns cool. In choosing a bunch, look for bright green leaves and avoid those that are yellow and limp. Collard greens and the mature leaves of red mustard can be treated in the same fashion, or all can be combined and cooked together.

Makes 4 servings

>2 pounds mustard greens
>1 tablespoon safflower, canola or light olive oil
>1 medium-sized onion, cut into ½-inch squares
>3 medium-sized tomatoes, peeled, seeded, and chopped
>2 to 3 garlic cloves, finely chopped
>3 small dried red chilies or several pinches red pepper flakes
>salt
>vinegar
>fried or toasted croutons (optional)

Remove the stems from the greens and discard them. With very large leaves, take out the whole stem, not just the bottom end. Roughly chop the leaves, wash them well, and steam them over boiling water for about 5 minutes or until they are tender. Set them aside.

Heat the oil in a wide skillet, add the onions, and cook them over medium-high heat for about 2 minutes. Add the tomatoes, garlic, and chilies. Salt lightly and cook for another minute, then add the greens. Mix everything together and continue cooking until the greens are thoroughly warmed. Taste for salt and season with a splash of vinegar. Serve alone or with some fried or toasted croutons to soak up the juices.

Suggestion: Use a *poblano* or Anaheim chili, roasted, peeled, and sliced into strips, in place of the dried red chilies.

Winter Greens and Potatoes
(Vegetable Hash)

This dish was taught to me by my Roman neighbor, Rosana Migliarino. It proved to be a comforting and nourishing dish, exactly the thing to eat when it's chilly and damp, which Roman winters are. It makes a good one-dish supper and meets the urge that some people have during the winter to eat greens, particularly the strong, peppery or bitter type.

Here the greens are softened by the potato and brightened with a little tomato, chili, and garlic. The vegetables are well cooked and brought together to make a kind of rustic hodgepodge or hash. This is a forgiving and flexible kind of dish, for you can use whatever proportion of greens to potatoes appeals to you or reflects what you have on hand. For the greens the strong varieties such as mustard, collards, kale, and escarole are best for their flavor and strength. But you can also use sweeter spinach and chard if that's your preference. Beet greens, turnip tops, broccoli rabe, and dandelion would also be good.

This dish can make a satisfying informal meal, accompanied by bread—Cheese Bread (page 34) would be very good—red wine, and a salad of greens or winter fruits.

Makes 2 to 4 servings

> 1 pound mixed greens (see note above), approximately
> salt
> 2 medium-sized potatoes, scrubbed, quartered, and thinly sliced
> 2 tablespoons olive oil
> 1 or 2 small dried red chilies, seeds removed, torn into pieces, or ¼
>   teaspoon red pepper flakes
> 2 medium-sized fresh or canned tomatoes, chopped
> 2 garlic cloves
> freshly ground pepper
> freshly grated or sliced hard cheese such as Parmesan, Asiago or Romano
> extra-virgin olive oil, to finish the dish

Bring several quarts of water to a boil. While it is heating, sort through the greens and remove any leaves that are yellow or tired-looking. If the greens have tough, fibrous stems, discard them. Chop the leaves, rinse them well, and set them aside.

When the water boils, add salt to taste and the potatoes. Cook until they are tender, 5 to 7 minutes; then remove them with a strainer. Add the greens and cook them until they're done. Cook the tougher greens—mustard, turnip, collards, and kale—first. They will take longer than spinach or chard. Check for doneness by tasting; then remove when they are cooked.

Warm the olive oil in a wide pan and add the chilies. When the oil is hot, add the potatoes, stir to coat them well, and cook for a minute or so. Next add the greens, the tomatoes, and the garlic. At this point the dish will be very pretty with its distinctly separate colors—dark green, red, and white. It would look at home in a good restaurant. But continue cooking the vegetables another 5 minutes or so, breaking up the potatoes with a wooden spoon and working everything together. In the end everything should be mixed and the colors somewhat muddied, but it is delicious this way: you can taste everything at once in your mouth instead of several disparate elements. Taste for salt, add freshly ground pepper, the cheese, and serve with a spoonful of extra-virgin olive oil threaded over the top.

Parsnips with Brown Butter and Bread Crumbs

The natural sweetness of parsnips goes well with the nut-flavored brown butter, and the crisp bread crumbs contrast with the softness of the cooked vegetable.

Parsnips have cores, and frequently it is recommended that they be cut out, a practice that does away with about half the vegetable. Most of the time it isn't necessary; unless the parsnip is really big and old, with a fibrous, woody center, I leave the cores in and they seem to cook just fine.

A chicory salad is just the thing to serve with the parsnips. The pungent leaves keep the mouth keen while the parsnip softens it.

For 3 to 4 servings

> 1 pound parsnips, peeled
> 2 to 3 tablespoons brown butter (page 416)
> juice of ½ lemon
> salt
> 2 tablespoons bread crumbs, toasted until crisp and golden
> 1 tablespoon finely chopped parsley or a mixture of fresh
>   tarragon, parsley, and chives

Cut the parsnips into even lengths. Halve or quarter the large ends so that all the pieces are about the same size. Set them in a steaming basket over boiling water, cover, and cook until they are tender but still just a little firm. Heat the brown butter in a sauté pan. Add the cooked parsnips and sauté over medium-high heat. Make sure the parsnips are coated with the butter. Cook for 3 or 4 minutes, stirring occasionally, until the parsnips begin to brown here and there. Squeeze in the lemon juice, lightly salt the parsnips, and add the bread crumbs and the herbs. Toss several times and serve.

Suggestion: Parsnips go well with curry spices, and the two are often combined in soups. You could use curry here, too, adding ¼ teaspoon or more to the butter before adding the parsnips. In that case, don't use tarragon, but consider a garnish of cilantro mixed with the parsley.

Baked and Roasted Vegetables

Baking and roasting vegetables is a more discreet way of cooking than sautéing and blanching. The results are not immediate; the vegetables take longer to cook; you can't see what's happening; and for the first half hour there's no aroma—although later there's plenty. When the dish finally emerges, though, the change is astonishing. The flavors will have deepened and merged, cream or cheese will have been transformed to a golden crust, and the juices of the vegetables will have reduced to a syrup. Cooking vegetables in the oven involves complete transformation, whereas blanching and sautéing keep vegetables truer to their garden state. Both ways of cooking are wonderful, yet they are completely different.

Many of the dishes in this chapter are called gratins and *tians*, referring to the dishes they are baked in. Gratins often include milk or cream, bread crumbs, and cheese—or even all three. They form a crust that captures the flavors and juices beneath. Both summer and winter vegetables respond well to slow baking, and these dishes can be enjoyed either warm or hot. The summer vegetables in particular are also good cold, and they can be eaten as a salad with lemon, capers, and a dash of vinegar or as a sandwich, spread over bread and covered with Garlic Mayonnaise. The juices that come from baked summer vegetables are sweet and filled with sugars. When reduced over a brisk heat, they form an intense, syrupy glaze to spread over the top of the finished dish.

Most vegetable dishes require about an hour to bake. An hour may seem like a long time in the days of 20-minute meals, but look at it like this: it takes only about 15 minutes to put a dish together; then the time it's baking is yours—to relax with a quick bite in hand to hold off appetite or to do something else. The truly satisfying results are worth it—a complex mingling of flavors and textures that can be achieved only with time and gentle cooking.

Zucchini-Tomato Tian with Olives

Layers of zucchini and tomatoes are baked on a bed of onions and herbs—fresh rosemary, sage, and thyme or dried herbs, such as the aromatic *herbes de Provence*. This is easy to assemble and delicious either warm or at room temperature. A few Greek olives, pitted and sliced, punctuate the summer tastes with their pungent, salty flavors. Use a richly flavored olive oil for this *tian*.

Makes 4 servings

> 2 tablespoons olive oil, approximately
> 1 large onion, quartered and thinly sliced
> 2 garlic cloves, thinly sliced
> 1½ teaspoons chopped rosemary or ½ teaspoon of dried
> 2 sage leaves, thinly sliced or a pinch of dried
> 1 teaspoon chopped thyme leaves or 2 pinches of dried
> ½ teaspoon herbes de Provence if fresh herbs aren't available
> salt
> freshly ground pepper
> 1¼ pounds zucchini, sliced into ¼-inch rounds, approximately
> 6 to 8 ounces Roma, plum or large cherry tomatoes, sliced into rounds
> 4 Kalamata olives, pitted and cut into quarters
> lemon wedges or red wine vinegar (optional)

Preheat the oven to 375°F. Warm 2 or 3 teaspoons olive oil in a large pan and add the onion, garlic, half the herbs, and lightly salt. Stew gently for about 5 minutes. Remove the onions to a gratin dish, spread them evenly over the bottom, and season with pepper. Warm another 2 or 3 teaspoons oil in the same skillet, raise the heat to medium-high, and add the zucchini, a little salt, and the rest of the herbs. Sauté, stirring frequently, until they just start to color, about 10 minutes. Distribute the zucchini over the onions; then tuck the slices of tomato here and there along with the olives. Drizzle the remaining oil over the top.

Cover with foil and bake for 25 minutes; then remove the foil and continue to bake for 10 minutes or so to evaporate the juices. Serve warm or tepid, with a wedge of lemon or a cruet of vinegar on the side if desired.

Ratatouille

Although they agree in essence, recipes for ratatouille all have their characteristic quirks and variations—the vegetables are individually sautéed before being combined or not; they are cooked on the stove or baked in the oven; only pure olive oil is used, or it is mixed with peanut; the onions are sliced or finely chopped; and so on. What I like to do is sauté each vegetable separately and then combine them in an earthenware dish and bake them slowly in the oven until they are meltingly soft and the flavors are merged. If there's a lot of juice, pour it off and boil it until it is a sweet amber-colored syrup; then pour it back over the vegetables.

Ratatouille can be served hot from the oven with rice or pasta, but the flavors emerge most fully when it is allowed to cool until tepid. It is also good chilled, served with capers and wedges of lemon or a dash of vinegar—the perfect dish for a hot summer evening, served with grilled bread, garlic mayonnaise, or thin slices of Parmesan cheese, followed by the Fresh Figs with Ricotta and Honey for dessert.

Makes 4 to 6 servings

> *1 large (about 1½ pounds) eggplant or 6 Japanese eggplants*
> *salt*
> *1 red bell pepper*
> *1 yellow bell pepper*
> *1 large red onion*
> *3 medium-sized (about 1 pound) ripe tomatoes*
> *5 medium-sized (about 1 pound) zucchini*
> *2 garlic cloves*
> *7 tablespoons olive oil or a mixture of olive and*
>   *peanut oil, approximately*
> *¼ teaspoon dried thyme or* herbes de Provence
> *1 bay leaf*
> *freshly ground pepper*
> *2 tablespoons torn or chopped basil leaves*

To Finish:

> *1 tablespoon capers, rinsed*
> *chopped basil*
> *extra-virgin olive oil*
> *lemon wedges*

Slice the eggplant into rounds about ½ inch thick. If you're using a large egg-plant, slice the rounds into ½-inch strips and then cut the strips into pieces about 2 inches long. If you're using the smaller Japanese eggplants, leave them in rounds. Place the eggplant in a colander, salt lightly all over, and set aside to drain for 30 minutes. (This is necessary only with the large variety.)

Halve the peppers lengthwise, remove the seeds and veins, and cut them into strips about ½ inch wide and 1½ inches long. Chop the onion into ½-inch squares. Submerge the tomatoes in boiling water for 10 seconds, remove the skins, halve them crosswise, and gently press out the seeds. Chop the flesh into large pieces. Quarter the zucchini lengthwise and cut it into pieces 1 inch or so long. Finely mince the garlic. Preheat the oven to 350°F.

Heat 2 tablespoons of the oil in a wide skillet and add the onions, garlic, and dried herbs. Sauté over medium-high heat for several minutes. Salt lightly, add the tomatoes, and cook for about 7 minutes over medium heat or until the juices of the tomatoes have evaporated and you have a thick sauce. Season with pepper and pour the sauce into a large gratin dish.

Add another tablespoon of the oil to the pan and, when it is hot, add the zuc-chini and salt lightly. Sauté briskly until the zucchini is golden and beginning to soften, about 8 minutes. Add the zucchini to the dish. Wipe out the pan, heat an-other tablespoon of oil, and sauté the peppers for about 5 minutes, letting them color just a little; then add them to the dish.

Pat the eggplant dry with paper towels. Heat the remaining oil in the pan, add the eggplant, and sauté until it is nicely browned and beginning to soften, about 10 minutes. When the eggplant is cooked, season it with salt and pepper to taste.

Add the eggplant to the dish with the rest of the vegetables and the fresh basil, and gently mix everything together. Cover with foil and put in the oven. After 20 minutes, remove the foil and continue cooking the vegetables until they are com-pletely tender, about 1 hour in all. Check them a few times while they are cook-ing and, if they look dry on top, dip a pastry brush into the juices and bathe the tops.

If, once the vegetables are cooked, there is an excessive amount of juice in the dish, not just a rich film on the bottom, carefully pour it into a small saucepan, bring to a boil, and reduce until a syrup is formed. Pour the syrup back onto the vegetables.

Serve the ratatouille warm or at room temperature or set it in the refrigerator, covered, until chilled. Serve with the capers and basil scattered over the top and drizzle the oil in a crisscross pattern over the surface. Serve lemon wedges on the side.

Summer Vegetable Tian

Colorful summer vegetables are sliced and layered into the dish in an easy fashion, drizzled with oil, sprinkled with herbs, and baked. Slices of lemon add tartness and zest. The flavors are best at room temperature, so the *tian* can be baked in the morning, when the day is still cool.

With all the new varieties of summer vegetables on the market you needn't limit yourself to a single type of squash or tomato or to the ingredients in the list. Try whatever comes your way.

With a loaf of bread, like the Olive Bread (page 22), a variety of cheeses, and something fresh and crisp from the garden, this *tian* makes a simple but perfect summer supper.

Makes 4 servings

> *5 Roma or plum tomatoes*
> *1 torpedo onion or red onion, quartered*
> *4 to 5 small summer squash, one variety or a mixture*
> *2 to 3 small Japanese eggplant*
> *2 to 4 tablespoons olive oil*
> *2 large garlic cloves, thinly sliced*
> *1 tablespoon marjoram leaves or ½ teaspoon dried*
> *1 teaspoon fresh thyme leaves or several pinches of dried*
> *1 lemon wedge, very thinly sliced*
> *salt*
> *freshly ground pepper*
> *extra-virgin olive oil (optional)*
> *lemon wedges*

Preheat the oven to 400°F. Slice the vegetables into pieces about ¼ inch thick. The zucchini and eggplant can be sliced on a gentle diagonal (not too extreme, or they will be difficult to place).

Brush 1 or 2 teaspoons of the oil over the bottom of the baking dish and scatter half the garlic slices and half the marjoram or thyme leaves over it. Build the *tian* by overlapping layers of the vegetables. Make a layer of zucchini, followed by a

layer of eggplant, tomatoes, and so forth; or mix them all together in random fashion. Placing a slice of tomato over each piece of eggplant helps give the eggplant some moisture while it's baking. Don't worry about making the rows even: when you get to the end of the dish, push everything together and insert vegetables where gaps appear. Tuck the garlic slices and the lemon slices here and there among the vegetables then brush them all with the remaining olive oil. Be sure to put a little extra oil on the eggplant as it tends to dry out more than the other vegetables. Sprinkle lightly with salt and scatter the rest of the herbs over the top.

Cover the dish and put it in the oven. Check after 25 minutes; the vegetables should be beginning to steam in their own juices. Dip a pastry brush into the juice and brush it over the vegetables; then cover the dish and return it to the oven for 20 minutes more. When they're tender, baste the vegetables again; then cook them, uncovered, for another 7 to 10 minutes. If the vegetables have exuded a great deal of juice by the time they're finished cooking, pour it off into a saucepan and boil until it is reduced to a syrup. Spoon this sauce over the top. Remove the *tian* from the oven and let it cool. Serve it with freshly ground pepper and extra-virgin olive oil drizzled over the top, if you like, and wedges of lemon.

Summer Squash and Spinach Gratin
with Ricotta Custard

This is a handsome gratin, the golden-crusted surface punctuated with flecks of dill, bands of green and yellow squash, and pockets of spinach. The taste is a delicate but complex blend of summer flavors.

The quantities of vegetables given are not absolutes. I work with whatever I have on hand, in more or less these proportions, possibly substituting some tender chard leaves for the spinach or using golden patty pan squash instead of the zucchini. Sometimes a bunch of spinach will come with a bonus of a few nettle branches or lamb's-quarters or a few strands of purslane. Just leave them and cook them along with the spinach.

I've also made this dish using fresh cheese with herbs (page 27) when I had more than I wanted to eat, and another time I used a mixture of ricotta, cottage cheese, and sour cream that had been intended for pancakes. Both worked fine.

Makes 4 servings

THE VEGETABLES

2 large leeks or a combination of leeks and onions, sliced
　　into rounds or chopped
2 garlic cloves, thinly sliced
1¼ pounds summer squash, including zucchini and
　　crookneck, thinly sliced
¼ pound mushrooms, thinly sliced
1 large bunch of spinach, well washed, the stems trimmed
1 to 2 tablespoons olive oil
2 tablespoons chopped dill or 1 teaspoon dried
2 tablespoons chopped parsley
salt

THE CUSTARD

1 cup ricotta cheese
2 eggs
1 cup milk or cream
½ cup freshly grated Parmesan cheese
salt
freshly ground pepper

Wash and cut all the vegetables as suggested. Preheat the oven to 350°F. Warm the oil in a large skillet and add the leeks. Sauté for about 1 minute; then add the squash, mushrooms, half the herbs, and several pinches of salt. Cook over medium-high heat for about 4 or 5 minutes, stirring frequently, until the squash begins to color just a little in places; then transfer the mixture to a gratin dish.

Add the spinach to the same skillet and cook just long enough to wilt it down. Press out as much of the liquid as possible, roughly chop the spinach, and distribute it over the vegetables.

Beat the ricotta with the eggs; then stir in the milk or cream, the cheese, and the remaining herbs. Season with salt and pepper; then pour it over the vegetables. Bake until the custard is set and lightly browned on top, about 40 minutes. Allow the gratin to stand ten minutes before serving. Serve warm.

Red Onion Tian

In August, when the red Spanish or torpedo onions are pulled, you'll always find among the large ones some small onions, which are particularly delectable. Farmers' markets are a likely place to find them. They are wonderful in this dish, bathed with olive oil and baked slowly with sweet red and yellow peppers and tomato. If torpedo onions aren't available, use red onions cut into quarters. The juices that flow out of the vegetables are boiled with vinegar until they've reduced to a syrup, making a naturally sweet and tart sauce.

This colorful *tian* is delicious with slices of grilled polenta. It's also wonderful piled on top of grilled bread that has been spread first with a layer of garlic mayonnaise (page 314). Serve the *tian* hot, tepid, or even chilled, as part of a plate of small salads or with the main part of the meal.

Makes 3 to 4 servings

> *1 pound small torpedo onions or red onions*
> *1 small red bell pepper*
> *1 small yellow bell pepper*
> *2 medium-sized ripe tomatoes*
> *1 to 2 tablespoons olive oil*
> *5 to 6 thyme branches or several pinches of dried*
> *6 small garlic cloves, peeled and left whole*
> *salt*
> *freshly ground pepper*
> *balsamic vinegar*

Preheat the oven to 350°F. Quarter the onions, leaving the base intact, and peel them. Halve the peppers both crosswise and lengthwise, remove the seeds and veins, and cut them into pieces roughly ½ inch wide. Remove the core from the tomatoes and cut them into sixths.

Brush a film of oil over the bottom of a gratin dish, scatter the thyme over it, and add the vegetables, including the garlic, in an attractive (it can't help but be attractive), easy fashion. Brush the remaining oil over the vegetables, being sure to coat the onions and peppers. Season with salt and pepper.

Cover the *tian* with foil and bake it for 1½ hours. The vegetables should be very soft, the tomatoes melting into a jam. Remove it from the oven and carefully pour the liquid that has collected into a small saucepan. Add a teaspoon of vinegar, bring the liquid to a boil, and reduce until it is thick and syrupy. Taste for vinegar and salt; then pour or brush this syrup back over the vegetables.

Tomato Gratin

Tomatoes, a splash of cream, and a few chopped basil leaves are all that's needed for this summery gratin. It takes about a minute to assemble and 12 minutes in a very hot oven. The creamy tomato-scented sauce will be on the thin side (unless you reduce the cream first on top of the stove) but it can be absorbed by dry fingers of toast.

Italian basil always tastes wonderful with tomatoes, but try the cinnamon variety as well, and not just the leaves but also the purple bracts and their blossoms. The flavor is exotic, and the colors are beautiful.

Makes 2 servings

> *3 medium-sized ripe tomatoes*
> *3 to 4 tablespoons cream*
> *several basil leaves, chopped*
> *salt*
> *freshly ground pepper*
> *3 slices of whole wheat bread*
> *freshly grated Parmesan cheese (optional)*

Preheat the oven to 450°F. Slice the tomatoes into rounds about ½ inch thick or slightly thinner. Overlap them in a baking dish so that they aren't too crowded. Pour over the cream, sprinkle the basil over the top, and lightly season with salt and pepper. Bake for 12 to 15 minutes or until the cream has boiled up around the edges. While the tomatoes are baking, toast the bread and cut it into strips. Distribute the strips over 2 serving dishes, serve the tomatoes with their sauce over the toast, and garnish, if desired, with freshly grated Parmesan cheese.

Broiled Tomatoes with Feta Cheese

These can be ready, from start to finish, in about 10 minutes. The feta cheese is sharp and tangy and makes even so-so tomatoes taste pretty good. This would be a fine accompaniment to a lunch or dinner omelet.

Makes 2 servings

> *2 medium-sized or large firm but ripe tomatoes*
> *2 to 3 ounces feta cheese*
> *2 teaspoons chopped oregano or basil leaves or*
> *several pinches of dried Greek oregano*
> *2 teaspoons olive oil*
> *freshly ground pepper*

Preheat the broiler. Slice the tomatoes into rounds, a little less than ½ inch thick, and overlap them in a baking dish. Crumble the cheese over the top, add half the chopped herbs, and drizzle over a teaspoon of the olive oil. Place the dish a few inches below the heat source and broil until the cheese is melted and starting to brown, about 7 minutes. Remove, drizzle the remaining oil over the top, add the rest of the herbs, and serve with a twist of black pepper.

- Feta cheese is salty enough that extra salt probably isn't necessary.

Broiled Eggplant with Walnut Sauce

Walnut sauce goes beautifully with these thick rounds of eggplant. The eggplant can be either broiled or fried. Broiling takes a little less oil, but the skins tend to get a little too crisp. I usually fry them when I'm making just a few and broil them when making a lot. If you serve this as a first course, one slice of eggplant per person should be enough. If available, a garnish of bronze fennel leaves would be ideal, picking up the flavor of the fennel seeds and the rich purple of the skins.

Makes 4 servings

> salt
> 4 round slices of eggplant, about ½ inch thick
> safflower, olive oil or peanut oil
> walnut sauce (page 322 or 323)
> freshly ground pepper
> bronze or green fennel leaves, chopped or left
>   in sprigs or finely minced parsley

Lightly salt the eggplant, let it sit for at least 30 minutes, then blot it with a paper towel to draw off the liquid.

To broil the eggplant, preheat the broiler. Brush the surfaces generously with oil. Place the eggplant about 3 inches from the heat source and broil until golden brown. Turn the rounds over and broil them on the other side until the eggplant is browned and soft. If the eggplant looks dry, brush a little more oil over the surface.

To fry the eggplant, film a nonstick frying pan with oil and, when it's hot, add the eggplant. Immediately turn the pieces to coat both sides with the oil; then fry over medium heat until golden and soft on each side.

Spoon the sauce over the eggplant, season with pepper, and garnish with the fennel leaves or the parsley.

Suggestion: Try this with the Pine Nut Sauce (page 324) in place of the walnut sauce. This dish can also be made with Japanese eggplants: Slice them in half lengthwise and make a few diagonal slashes on the cut surfaces. Brush them generously with oil and broil them until the surfaces are golden brown. If the eggplant is still firm after it has browned, place it in a 400°F oven to bake until it has softened, about 5 to 10 minutes.

Baked Miniature Pumpkins

These diminutive squash have been very popular with window decorators for the past several years, but they also make good eating. Their cavities will hold a few spoonfuls of filling—such as wild rice with sautéed onions and roasted nuts— or they can be baked with just a bit of butter or an aromatic oil, like sesame or peanut, with salt and pepper rubbed into the flesh. My preference is to add a splash of cream, a leaf of sage, and a spoonful of Gruyère or Fontina cheese, making a tiny version of a pumpkin soup baked in the shell.

Miniature pumpkins look exactly like very tiny pumpkins. Sweet Dumpling squash are a bit larger, either bright yellow with orange stripes, when mature, or creamy white with dark green vertical strips. One small squash is perfect for 1 person. The little pumpkins might be especially amusing for children.

Makes 1 serving

> *1 miniature pumpkin or sweet dumpling squash*
> *salt*
> *freshly ground pepper*
> *1 to 2 tablespoons cream, milk or mascarpone cheese*
> *1 fresh or dried sage leaf*
> *grated Fontina or Gruyère cheese*

Preheat the oven to 350°F. Slice off the top ½ inch of the pumpkin, scoop out the seeds, and rub salt and pepper into the cavity. Pour in the cream, add the sage leaf and the cheese, replace the lid, and bake in a pan until tender, 35 to 45 minutes. Take care not to overcook the squash or it might split and collapse in the oven.

Artichokes, Potatoes, and Dried Mushrooms Baked in Clay

One of the benefits of cooking in clay is that flavors do not escape but are concentrated and returned to the vegetables. This method is especially well suited to those who wish to cook with very little fat or even none at all.

There's a generous amount of garlic in this stew, but by the time it's cooked, it will be soft and sweet. Push it out of the skins with a fork and eat it with the potatoes.

Makes 4 servings

> *½ ounce dried* cèpes (porcini)
> *½ cup boiling water*
> *3 large artichokes*
> *juice of 1 large lemon*
> *1¼ pounds red skinned or yellow fleshed potatoes, sliced ⅜ inch thick*
> *12 garlic cloves, unpeeled*
> *salt*
> *coarsely ground pepper*
> *2 bay leaves*
> *several thyme sprigs or ¼ teaspoon dried*
> *2 to 3 tablespoons virgin olive oil (optional)*

Fill both the top and bottom halves of the clay pot with cold water and let them stand while you prepare the vegetables. Preheat the oven to 350°F.

Cover the dried mushrooms with the boiling water and set them aside to soak. Trim the artichokes: Break off the tough outer leaves and slice off the remaining cone of inner leaves. Trim the outside and scoop out the choke with a spoon. As you work, put the cut artichokes in a bowl with lemon juice and water to cover to keep them from browning. Slice the trimmed hearts into pieces about the same width as the potatoes.

Remove the mushrooms from the soaking water and run your fingers over the surfaces to loosen any grit; then squeeze them dry. Cut them into bite-sized pieces. Let the soaking water stand until the particles settle to the bottom.

Empty the clay pots then add the potatoes, artichokes, garlic cloves, and mushrooms. Season with salt and pepper and toss with the oil, if using, and the herbs. Carefully pour in the soaking water from the mushrooms.

Cover the pot with the lid and bake it for 1 hour. Once or twice while cooking, give the vegetables a gentle stir. By the time they're done, most of the liquid will have been absorbed, leaving behind a glossy glaze.

Celery Root Gratin

This celery root gratin is rich with aroma and flavor. With a salad and a thin piece of dry cheese set right on top of the warm gratin, this makes a fine supper.

It takes about 15 minutes to assemble the gratin and another 45 or so to bake it. It can be assembled hours ahead or even the day before it's baked. Leftovers also make a delicious meal served cold with some grilled red peppers, olives, and a splash of vinegar.

Makes 4 servings

> 1 pound red-skinned or yellow-fleshed potatoes
> 1 large celery root
> juice of 1 lemon
> salt
> 1 to 3 tablespoons olive oil
> 1 medium-sized red onion, quartered and sliced crosswise
> 2 garlic cloves, finely chopped
> 2 small celery stalks, finely diced
> 1 tablespoon chopped basil or 1 teaspoon dried
> coarsely ground black pepper
> 1 cup dry white wine, stock or cooking water from the potatoes
> 1 pound ripe tomatoes or 1 15-ounce can whole tomatoes,
>   seeded and cut into large pieces, juice reserved
> thinly shaved Parmesan, dry Monterey Jack or dried goat cheese (optional)

Scrub the potatoes and, if the skins look firm and fresh, leave them on; if not, peel them. Slice the potatoes into rounds just slightly more than ¼ inch thick. Peel the celery root; slice it into quarters and then into pieces the same thickness as the potatoes. As you work, put the celery root in a bowl and cover with cold water and the lemon juice.

Bring several quarts of water to a boil. Add salt to taste and the potatoes and cook until they are tender but not yet done, about 5 minutes. Remove them; then add the celery root and cook until tender but still firm, about 3 or 4 minutes. Remove. Reserve the water.

Warm the oil in a frying pan and add the onion, garlic, celery, basil, and season with salt and pepper. Cook gently over medium heat until the onions have begun to soften, about 5 minutes. If the pan becomes dry, add either a little more oil or a few tablespoons water. When the onions are soft, add the wine, raise the heat, and reduce the wine by about half; then add the tomatoes and their juices plus ½ cup of the cooking water from the potatoes. Simmer for 4 or 5 minutes.

Preheat the oven to 375°F. Lightly film an 8- by 10-inch gratin dish with oil. Ladle half the tomato sauce in the bottom of gratin dish, make a layer of alternating pieces of potato and celery root, and season with pepper. Repeat, using the rest of the potatoes and celery root; then cover with the remaining sauce. Cover and bake until the potatoes and celery root are completely tender, about 45 minutes. Remove the gratin from the oven and let it settle several minutes before serving it. As it cools a little, the flavors will emerge.

Serve this, if you like, with thin shavings of dry cheese on top, such as Parmesan, dry Monterey Jack, or a dried goat cheese.

Suggestion: If you prefer to make a more substantial dish, layer 3 ounces of Gruyère or Gouda cheese, grated, between the sauce and the potatoes.

Baked Celery and Leeks

Celery is delicious as a cooked vegetable. It takes less than 10 minutes to assemble this dish and 25 minutes to bake it. It holds well and can be easily reheated.

Fennel is also wonderful prepared this way. Quarter the bulbs and prepare them exactly the same way.

Makes 3 to 4 servings as a side dish

> 6 celery stalks, cut into 3-inch lengths
> 3 leeks, white parts only, halved lengthwise and cut into 3-inch lengths
> salt
> 1 tablespoon butter, plus a little for the dish
> 2 to 3 tablespoons freshly grated Parmesan cheese
> freshly ground pepper

Preheat the oven to 375°F. Cut the celery and leeks as suggested. Scrape the celery with a vegetable peeler if the stalks are rough and thoroughly wash the leeks. Tie the leeks together in a little bundle. Bring a large pan of water to a boil; add salt to taste and the celery. Parboil for 3 minutes; then add the leeks and boil for another 2 minutes. Remove the celery and leeks from the pan and drain them. Remove the string from the leeks.

Lightly butter a baking dish that will comfortably hold the vegetables. Add the vegetables, dot with the butter, sprinkle with the cheese, and season with pepper. Add a tablespoon or so of the cooking liquid, cover with foil, and bake for 25 minutes. Serve hot or let cool slightly and serve tepid.

Baked Endive with Gorgonzola

This unusual dish is a simplified—and lighter—version of one served in a Roman restaurant in which the endive is charcoal-grilled, then covered with cream and cheese, and baked until bubbling and golden. Grilling before baking is a wonderful technique that adds an elusive quality to any dish, but it is much more easily adapted to restaurant kitchens than home kitchens.

There are pleasing contrasts in this dish—mildly bitter vegetable, which is also slightly firm, against the sweet cheese and creamy sauce. This could be an extravagant dish for a party with the endive beautifully arranged in a large baking dish.

A milk-based sauce is used in place of thick cream. Begin the sauce first; then prepare the endive while it is cooking.

Makes 4 servings

> 1 cup milk or light cream
> 1 tablespoon butter, plus a little for the dish
> 1 tablespoon flour
> salt
> freshly ground pepper
> a few gratings of nutmeg
> 4 plump Belgian endives
> 2 to 3 ounces Gorgonzola cheese
> 3 tablespoons fresh bread crumbs tossed in 2
>   tablespoons melted butter (optional)

Warm the milk in a small pan. While it is heating, melt 1 tablespoon butter in another saucepan and stir in the flour. Cook together for 3 or 4 minutes over low heat; then whisk in the warm milk. Bring it to a boil, lower the heat, and simmer for 25 minutes, stirring occasionally. Season it with salt and pepper and a little freshly grated nutmeg. While the sauce is cooking, cut the endives in half lengthwise, place them in a steaming basket, and cook them until tender but still slightly firm when pierced with a knife, about 12 minutes.

Preheat the oven to 400°F. Lightly butter a gratin dish. Arrange the endives in the dish, season them with salt and pepper, and spoon the sauce over them. Break up the cheese over the sauce and add the buttered bread crumbs. Bake until the sauce and cheese are bubbling and starting to brown, about 10 minutes.

Winter Squash Gratin

Substantial and aromatic with the irresistible smell of melting cheese, this homey gratin can serve as the main part of a meal for four. The squash is settled on a bed of browned onions covered with cheese and then with soaked bread. The bread looks rather unappetizing at first, but it forms a protective crust and keeps the squash from drying out. In the end it turns brown and crisp.

Even when baked in an oven set as low as 300°F, the milk will probably separate, but by the time the gratin is done, it will all have been absorbed into the squash, leaving no traces.

Makes 4 servings

> *butter for the baking dish*
> *1 to 2 tablespoons light olive oil*
> *1 bay leaf*
> *6 sage leaves, torn into pieces or ½ teaspoon dried*
> *2 medium-large yellow onions, thinly sliced*
> *salt*
> *freshly ground pepper*
> *1½ to 2 pounds hard winter squash such as banana, perfection or butternut*
> *4 slices of whole wheat or white bread, crusts removed*
> *3 ounces (1 cup) Swiss, Gruyère or Fontina cheese, grated*
> *1½ cups warm milk*

Lightly butter an 8- by 10-inch gratin dish. Warm the oil in a sauté pan with the bay leaf and sage; then add the onions. Cook gently over medium heat, stirring occasionally, until the onions are limp and colored in places, about 15 minutes. Season with salt and pepper and spread them over the bottom of the gratin dish.

Bring several quarts of water to boil. While it is heating, prepare the squash: Slice the squash in half lengthwise and scoop out the seeds. Then, with the cut surface on the counter, slice it into arcs ¼ to ½ inch thick. Peel each arc with a few quick movements of the paring knife; then cut them into pieces about 1½ inches long. If you're using a smooth-skinned butternut squash, peel it first with a vegetable peeler, then cut it into pieces. When the water has come to a boil, add salt to taste and the squash. Let the water return to a boil, lower the heat, and simmer for 1 minute; drain.

Tear the bread into pieces and cover it with some of the boiling water from the squash pot. When it has been absorbed, after a few minutes, squeeze out the excess water and chop the bread.

Preheat the oven to 325°F. To form the gratin, lay the squash over the onions, season it with salt and pepper, and add the grated cheese, working it into the crevices between the squash with your fingers. Pour in the warm milk and then distribute the bread over the top. Cover with foil and bake for 1 hour; then remove the foil and bake until the squash is tender when pierced with a knife and all the liquid has been absorbed, another 20 minutes or so. Let the gratin settle for a few minutes, then serve.

Potato and Kale Gratin

Bands of dark green kale and yellow-fleshed potatoes are melded with cream and baked until golden and glossy. This is a frankly rich treatment of humble foods and very good. Because of the richness, it makes sense to include this gratin among a number of other dishes in a meal. It's easy to multiply it to feed a crowd.

Makes 4 to 6 modest servings

> 1 pound russet or yellow Finnish potatoes
> salt
> 1 large bunch of kale
> butter for the baking dish
> 1 cup cream
> freshly ground pepper

Scrub the potatoes, leave their skins on if they look firm and fresh, and slice them into rounds about ¼ inch thick. Bring a large pot of water to a boil and add salt to taste and the potatoes. Boil for 5 minutes, then scoop them out and set them aside, reserving the water. Cut the kale leaves away from the stems, which are too tough to use. Chop the leaves into large pieces and rinse them well. Plunge them into the same water the potatoes cooked in, push them down to submerge them, and cook them briefly, about 2 minutes. Pour them into a colander to drain.

Preheat the oven to 325°F and lightly butter a gratin dish. Layer the kale and potatoes in alternating bands, pour the cream over the top, and season with plenty of pepper. Bake until the cream has been absorbed and formed a golden crust around the edges, about 45 minutes.

Leek Gratin

Although the French nicknamed leeks "poor man's asparagus," to us they are something of a luxury—often as expensive as asparagus, not always available, and to me, just as delicious. They're lovely in this baked dish, covered with a light, creamy sauce scented with garlic and finished with Gruyère cheese.

　　Choose large leeks with a long white part, if possible. The sauce needs 25 minutes to cook, so start with that. The leeks can steam while it is cooking. The gratin can be set up ahead of time, refrigerated, and baked just before serving.

Makes 4 servings

> *6 large leeks*
> *butter*
> *salt*
> *freshly ground pepper*
> *white sauce (recipe follows)*
> *1 ounce (⅓ cup) grated Gruyère cheese*

Prepare the leeks: Cut away the root at the base and most of the green leaves, leaving the white of the leeks and a little of the pale green part. Cut the leeks in half lengthwise, rinse them well under running water, and steam them in a steaming basket until tender, about 15 minutes. When done, cut the leeks into pieces about 1½ inches long or leave them whole, if you prefer.

　　Preheat the oven to 400°F and lightly butter a gratin dish. Add the leeks and season them with salt and pepper. Cover them with the sauce, the grated cheese, and grind a little pepper over all. Bake the gratin, uncovered, until brown and bubbly—about 10 minutes if the dish was warm, about 20 if it just came from the refrigerator.

THE WHITE SAUCE

> *1½ cups milk*
> *1 bay leaf*
> *1 garlic clove*
> *1½ tablespoons butter*
> *1½ tablespooons flour*
> *salt*
> *freshly ground pepper*
> *a few gratings of nutmeg*

Warm the milk with the bay leaf and garlic. While it is heating, melt the butter in a small saucepan and stir in the flour. Cook over low heat for several minutes; then add the milk all at once. Whisk together, bring to a boil, lower the heat, and simmer, stirring frequently, for 25 minutes. Remove the bay leaf and garlic and season with salt and pepper and a little nutmeg.

Suggestion: Leeks go so well with other vegetables. Consider making the gratin with half as many leeks mixed with potatoes, cabbage, artichokes, or large pieces of fennel. All vegetables should be parboiled so that they just finish cooking in the oven.

Savoy Cabbage with Brown Butter and Taleggio Cheese

Sometimes when I'm making pasta with vegetables, the vegetables themselves are so enjoyable that I want to eat them without the noodles. One such dish is a gratin of buckwheat noodles with cabbage and potatoes seasoned with brown butter and creamy Taleggio cheese. Though perfectly matched with the earthy buckwheat noodles, the cabbage and potatoes are also absolutely wonderful on their own and are substantial enough to make a hearty one-dish meal, washed down with a glass of Chianti.

Taleggio cheese may be difficult to find. If it isn't available, use another cheese in its place, like Fontina, Bel Paese, mozzarella or a mixture of the three.

This dish can be assembled earlier in the day and then finished in the oven or it can be made completely on the stove, the potatoes added after the cabbage is cooked and the cheese shredded and tossed in at the end.

Makes 4 to 6 servings

> 4 to 6 tablespoons brown butter (page 416)
> 1 pound red-skinned or yellow-fleshed potatoes
> salt
> 6 fresh sage leaves, chopped or ½ teaspoon dried
> 3 large leeks, white parts only, sliced ¼ inch thick
> 2 garlic cloves, minced
> 1 or 2 pinches of red pepper flakes
> 1½ to 2 pounds savoy or regular green cabbage, quartered and
>   shredded into ½-inch strips
> ½ cup freshly grated Parmesan cheese
> ½ pound Taleggio, Bel Paese or fresh mozzarella cheese, sliced

Make the brown butter first if you haven't any already made. If the skins on the potatoes look fresh, scrub them and leave them on. Otherwise peel them and cut them into ½-inch chunks. Bring several quarts of water to a boil; add salt to taste and the potatoes. Lower the heat to a slow boil and cook until they are just tender, about 7 or 8 minutes. Remove them from the water and rinse them briefly to stop the cooking.

Heat half the brown butter in a skillet and add the sage, leeks, garlic, red pepper flakes, and enough water just to cover the bottom of the pan. Stew the mixture over medium-low heat until the leeks have softened; then add the cabbage by handfuls or in whatever size batches the pan will accommodate. When the

cabbage wilts down, add more until all is used; then salt it lightly. Cover the pan and cook until the cabbage is tender.

Preheat the oven to 400°F. Toss the cabbage mixture together with the potatoes, the remaining brown butter, and the Parmesan cheese. Season with salt and plenty of freshly ground pepper. Layer the cabbage in an earthenware dish with the cheese. Cover and bake until the cheese is melted and the vegetables are hot, about 20 minutes.

Baked Winter Squash with Spicy Moroccan Butter

Like zucchini and other summer squash, winter squash are plentiful and economical. The spicy Moroccan butter, inspired by one of Paula Wolfert's recipes, transforms a common enough vegetable into something unexpected and exciting. If you have the butter in your freezer, it takes only a few moments to have the squash ready for the oven.

Banana squash is the large winter squash that is sold precut with the seeds scooped out. It works very nicely if you buy a large piece and cut it crosswise into triangular pieces. Or use any of the smaller winter squash, halved and scooped out, such as butternut, acorn, or the nifty little Sweet Dumplings.

Makes 4 servings

> 2 pounds banana squash or 2 acorn squash or sweet dumplings
> ¼ cup water
> 2 to 4 tablespoons spicy moroccan butter (page 313)
> salt

Preheat the oven to 375°F. Prepare the squash, if they are whole, by halving them and removing the seeds and fibers. If you're using banana squash, cut it into triangular pieces. Pour the water into a baking dish and set the squash on top. Spread 1 or 2 teaspoons of butter over each piece and sprinkle with salt. Cover with foil and bake for 30 minutes.

Remove the squash from the oven, spread the melted butter around with a brush, and poke a few holes into the squash so the butter can seep in. If the squash isn't done, return it to the oven until it is. The exact time will depend on the type of squash used, but the total cooking time shouldn't be much longer than 40 minutes. Serve with a little more butter spread over the top.

Pan-Roasted Vegetables

A number of handsome old roasting pans—cobalt blue, beautifully propor-
tioned, and variously sized according to the bulk of a turkey, a roasting hen, and
something even smaller—inspired this recipe. A variety of vegetables are cut
into large pieces, tossed with olive oil and herbs, and roasted in a hot oven. A few
tablespoons of water in the bottom of the pan turn to steam and get things moving; then the vegetables roast in their own juices. Eventually the juices cook off,
leaving the vegetables lightly glazed, tender, and very flavorful.

Carrots, onions, potatoes, parsnips, and turnips are all good vegetables for
roasting. If you like Brussels sprouts, include them also, but their flavor will tend
to dominate. Chunks of celery root, celery stalks, kohlrabi, winter squash or
yams would also taste good roasted. Use just one or two vegetables or several, in
various combinations. One important factor in the success of this method is to
give the vegetables lots of room so that they'll color nicely and not just steam on
top of each other. In place of a roasting pan with a cover, use a large baking pan
and cover it tightly with foil.

The vegetables need about an hour in the oven, ample time to comfortably
cook some rice and make a salad or just relax with one of the toasts in the "Quick
Bites" chapter and a glass of wine.

Makes 4 servings

> 4 small red potatoes, peeled if desired, and quartered
> ½ pound parsnips, peeled and quartered
> 3 celery stalks, cut into 3-inch lengths
> 4 large carrots, peeled and cut into 2-inch lengths
> 8 large boiling onions, left whole or 4 small yellow onions, peeled
>   and quartered, 1 chopped into large pieces
> 4 garlic cloves, unpeeled
> 2 to 3 tablespoons olive oil
> salt
> freshly ground pepper
> 6 thyme branches or ¼ teaspoon dried
> ¼ teaspoon dill seed
> 2 bay leaves
> 4 parsley sprigs

Preheat the oven to 425°F. Prepare all the vegetables as described above, making
allowances for different sizes—cutting large vegetables into smaller pieces or
leaving small vegetables, such as carrots, whole. Put them in a bowl with the
garlic and toss them with 1 or 2 tablespoons of the oil, season with salt and plenty

of pepper, half the thyme, and half the dill. Put a few tablespoons of water and another tablespoon of oil in the bottom of the roasting pan. Scatter the chopped onion over the bottom with the rest of the thyme and dill, the bay leaves, and the parsley. Settle all the cut vegetables over this bed of onions and herbs and cover.

Bake the vegetables for 30 minutes; then remove the pan and gently turn the vegetables about. Return the pan to the oven and bake for another 20 minutes. Check again to see if they're tender. If not, remove the lid and return them to the oven for 10 minutes or until they are done.

Roasted Onions with Sage

An aromatic dish with few ingredients and minimal preparation, these roasted onions can be used as a side dish but are also delicious to cook with. You could chop them up and toss them into a pasta with cauliflower, lots of parsley, and a smattering of pungent dried tomatoes or lay them on a piece of grilled bread brushed with walnut oil and cover them with thin shavings of Parmesan cheese.

Both red and yellow onions can be used. If you're lucky enough to find a source of small new onions, rather than cut them into rings, just halve them lengthwise, peel, and cook.

Makes 4 to 6 servings as a side dish

> 2 pounds red or yellow onions
> salt
> 2 to 4 tablespoons olive oil
> a dozen fresh sage leaves or 1 teaspoon dried
> 1 teaspoon coarsely ground pepper
> 2 tablespoons balsamic vinegar
> butter or oil for baking dish
> finely chopped parsley

Preheat the oven to 375°F. Peel the onions and slice them into rounds about ½ inch or more thick. Separate the rings; then toss them with salt, olive oil, sage, pepper, and vinegar. Lightly butter or oil a large gratin dish, add the seasoned onions, cover with foil, and bake for 30 minutes. Remove the foil, give the onions a stir, cover, and return the dish to the oven for 15 minutes. They should be starting to brown all over. Stir again and return to the oven, uncovered, fifteen minutes more or until the juices reduce to a syrup and the onions are done. Serve heaped in a bowl with some finely chopped parsley.

Grilled Vegetables and Their Sauces

Cooking over fire is one of the special pleasures of summer. For most people the barbecue is for meat, but vegetables also taste wonderful grilled. The smoke from various woods and herbs bathes the vegetables with mingled scents, and the heat of the grill will leave rustic crosshatched marks over eggplants and onions as well as steaks. Grilled vegetables are delicious hot or at room temperature, served with a splash of vinegar or any number of sauces. They are also useful as ingredients—their smoky essence can completely transform a corn soup or tomato sauce; charcoal-grilled peppers make a most delicious and useful condiment; and there's nothing more delectable than a sandwich of grilled vegetables and garlic mayonnaise or pasta tossed with grilled vegetables.

Here are a few things to keep in mind when you're grilling. For fuel you can use different woods, such as fruit woods, oak, hickory, and grape thinnings (but never scraps of plywood!), and each will impart its own subtle scent. Pieces of bark—hemlock, hickory, oak—and herbs, particularly rosemary and fennel branches, are also very aromatic. It takes only a little of their fragrant smoke to impart their flavors to the food. Charcoals, like mesquite, burn very hot and also impart particular flavors. Briquets are probably the least interesting fuel to use, but they can be enhanced by tossing a few soaked wood chips and herbs over their coals. (Charcoal briquets should not imply the use of lighter fluid, which will make everything smell like an airport.)

Allow the fire to die before you begin to cook. It's time to begin when the coals are coated with ash. If you're planning to grill over several hours, keep a fresh supply of coals over to one side and move them into the cooking area as they become ready. A pair of 14-inch tongs will make grilling much easier; they allow you to work just out of range of searing heat and smoke.

All vegetables need to be brushed with a protective coat of a light, neutral oil before being grilled to keep them from drying out. To get a pattern of crosshatched lines, place the food exactly where you want it and leave it alone—as well as you can—until it's about halfway cooked. (Practice will make it easy to judge this.) Then turn it once, 45 degrees from the original position, and again leave it to finish cooking without moving it. When you turn the vegetable over, you will see the strong lines of the grill. If you keep moving the food and looking to see how it's doing, the lines will never really set well. An alternative to grilling vegetables over the fire is to wrap them in foil and set the packages right over or next to the coals.

In some parts of the country you can grill outdoors all year. But even in cold climates, if you have a fireplace, grilling can continue through the winter—just prop a simple grill over some bricks or stones. Mushrooms, onions, leeks, fennel, and potatoes all taste good cooked over—and in—the coals.

Asparagus

It may seem unusual to grill asparagus, but it's very good cooked this way. Thick stalks work best. Cut off the tough ends and peel the lower part of the stalks. They needn't be parboiled, but they do need to cook slowly. Brush the stalks generously with olive oil, season them with salt, and grill them over a slow fire, turning them frequently. To test for doneness, pierce the stalks with the sharp point of a knife; they should be firm, but the knife should penetrate them easily.

Grilled Asparagus with Salsa Verde

Grill the asparagus and arrange them on a platter. Ladle salsa verde (page 317) over the top and garnish with pickled red onion rings (page 332) and quartered hard-cooked eggs, if desired. Serve as a main-course salad or an elegant side dish.

Grilled Asparagus with Egg and Caper Sauce

Hard-cooked eggs, chopped and mixed with olive oil, vinegar, shallots, and capers, make a sauce with a rich, velvety texture, but one that uses less oil than a mayonnaise.

Makes 6 to 8 servings

> *2 pounds thick asparagus*
> *light olive oil for grilling*
> *salt*
> *2 or 3 hard-cooked eggs*
> *¼ cup extra-virgin olive oil*
> *2 to 3 tablespoons tarragon or Champagne vinegar*
> *2 tablespoons capers, rinsed*
> *1 large shallot, finely diced*
> *freshly ground pepper*
> *finely chopped chervil or parsley*

Prepare the asparagus for grilling. Brush the stalks with oil and lightly salt them.

Separate the whites and yolks of the cooked eggs and finely chop them. Put all the ingredients in a bowl and gently combine them with a rubber scraper. The yolks and oil will gradually emulsify. Season to taste with salt and plenty of pepper and add more vinegar if desired.

Grill the asparagus, lay it on a platter, and ladle the sauce over it.

Corn

Grilling is a very good way to cook corn, especially after the first rush of the season has passed and we've had our fill of basic boiled corn-on-the-cob. The heat caramelizes the sugars and gives it a good, rich taste that is quite different from the delicacy of boiled corn.

To prepare corn for grilling, open up the husks and pull out the silk; then close the husks around the corn again and grill them in this protective covering. If the corn has a chance to soak in cold water before being rewrapped, the moisture that's trapped inside turns to steam, and the corn is effectively steamed and grilled at the same time. If the corn is tough, boil it first and then finish it on the grill. Butter, salt, and pepper are always good with corn in any form, but here are some suggestions for other delicious seasonings.

A soup or *ragoût* made with grilled corn would be good enough to warrant grilling some extra ears to use later. If you're making mixed brochettes of vegetables, try slicing corn into disks and grilling them as well.

Grilled Corn with Lime Juice and Salt

Grilled field corn with a wedge of lime and a packet of salt is sold as a street food in parts of Mexico. It's a delicious combination. Squeeze the lime over the cooked corn and sprinkle on the salt.

Grilled Corn with Roasted Sichuan Pepper Salt

This aromatic salt seasoned with roasted Sichuan peppercorns (page 330) is wonderful with corn. The salt can be used to season butter or just sprinkled over the roasted corn.

Grilled Corn with Chili Butter

The hot chili and sweet corn are quite compatible. Make a chili butter by working a little ground red chili into soft butter. Season with the zest and juice of either lime or orange and salt to taste. Or make a butter with finely diced jalapeños, the lime zest and juice, and some finely chopped cilantro. Remember, the chili gains in strength with time.

For similar flavors without the butter, serve the grilled corn with cilantro salsa (page 318).

Grilled Corn with Herb Butters

Serve the corn with any of the herb butters (pages 309 to 313). Basil is especially good with corn; lovage is too, and even parsley, as common as it is.

Eggplant

Eggplant is the vegetable that's made for grilling. Its size and shape make it easy to handle, and its rather neutral flavor goes well with a wide variety of sauces. Eggplant needs to be brushed with oil and seasoned before grilling.

There are 2 basic types of eggplant and several ways to approach them. The large, round Western variety is usually sliced into rounds or lengthwise into oblong pieces. To ensure that it won't be bitter, it's best to take the time to salt it and let it stand for a half hour for the bitter juices to be drawn out. It can then be blotted with a paper towel, seasoned, and grilled.

The slender Japanese varieties of eggplant can also be sliced, either diagonally or lengthwise, and grilled without salting. If you're slicing it lengthwise, remove 2 narrow pieces on the edges so that you won't have pieces that are mostly skin on one side; then slice the remaining eggplant into 3 or 4 pieces about ⅜ inch thick.

Smaller eggplants can be halved lengthwise, scored across the top so that the oil can penetrate, and grilled on both sides. They can also be grilled whole; each person opens an eggplant to find a creamy white interior ready to be anointed with olive oil and herbs.

Roasted eggplant is also very nice to cook with; the smoky flavor of the fire manages to penetrate the skin. If there's extra room on the grill, add an eggplant, or wrap one in heavy foil and set it in the coals until it's shriveled and soft. Grilled or roasted eggplant provides an exotic foundation for spreads and soups.

Grilled Eggplant with Garlic Mayonnaise

Serve the grilled eggplant with garlic mayonnaise (page 314) or cut it into smaller pieces and pile it on a piece of grilled bread that has been spread first with the mayonnaise and some chopped parsley. Squeeze a little lemon over the top to cut the richness and add a generous grinding of pepper.

Grilled Eggplant with Salsa Verde or Cilantro Salsa

Grill the eggplant, season it with salt and pepper, and spoon either salsa verde (page 317) or cilantro salsa (page 318) on top. Since the eggplant has already been oiled, you might make the sauce with a little less oil than the recipe calls for or with more herbs in proportion to oil.

Grilled Eggplant with Olive Oil, Lemon, and Herbs

Combine finely chopped herbs—parsley, basil, or lemon thyme—with extra-virgin olive oil and lemon zest. Grill the eggplant, brush the herbs and oil on top, and season with salt and pepper to taste.

Grilled Eggplant with Peanut Sauce or Peanut Oil

Combine diced shallots with roasted peanut oil and lots of finely chopped parsley. Spread it over the grilled eggplant and season with salt and pepper. Or make the peanut sauce for the pasta dish on page 164 and serve it with the eggplant.

Grilled Eggplant with Nut Sauces

The walnut sauces (pages 322 and 323) and pine nut sauce (page 324) all go wonderfully with the grilled eggplant. They are especially nice mixed into halved grilled eggplants with a spoonful of yogurt for tartness, or they can be spooned over grilled rounds.

Grilled Eggplant with Balsamic Vinegar, Garlic, and Basil

Combine garlic, balsamic vinegar, and lots of fresh basil and purée in a blender. Moisten with a little oil if desired. Brush over grilled eggplant and season with pepper. Or layer the grilled eggplant with slices of garlic, torn or shredded basil leaves, a sprinkling of vinegar, and salt and pepper. If you want to, add a few drops olive or peanut oil as well. Keep layering the eggplant in this fashion until done; then serve. This is very delicious, and the flavors will be just as good, if not better, the second day.

Whole Grilled Eggplants

Nothing could be simpler than this dish. Medium-sized eggplants are grilled until soft and tender. The flesh inside is soft and pale-colored. Eat it with salt and pepper, a spoonful of your most delicious olive oil, an herb-infused salsa, or yogurt seasoned with garlic and mint.

Makes 4 servings

> *8 Japanese eggplants*
> *salt*
> *freshly ground pepper*
> *extra-virgin olive oil or salsa verde (page 317)*

Choose eggplants that are firm and shiny. Grill the vegetables close to the coals. Turn them every 5 minutes or so to cook them on all sides. When the eggplants are wrinkled and feel soft when prodded with a finger, remove them. Slice them in half lengthwise and season the flesh with salt, plenty of freshly ground pepper, and a spoonful of oil or green sauce.

You could also spread the seasoned eggplant on crisp slices of grilled bread. Any leftovers can be served cold as part of a plate of hors d'oeuvres or tucked inside pita bread with the walnut sauce with fennel seeds (page 322).

In lieu of grilling, bake the eggplants in a moderate oven until wrinkled and soft and serve them the same way.

Fennel

The clean anise flavor of bulb fennel is rounded and softened by grilling while the texture remains firm and juicy. The dried stalks of wild fennel are often thrown on the fire to make an aromatic anise flavoring for grilled fish. The combination of fennel, fire, and smoke seems especially harmonious.

It's easiest to work with large bulbs. Pull off the outer leaves if they're scarred or damaged and remove the tall stalks. Reserve a few of the greens for garnish. The fennel needs to cook slowly over the coals to be done properly in the end.

Stand the bulb firmly on its bottom and slice it into pieces about ⅜-inch thick. Each piece needs to be attached at the bottom. (Save those end pieces that fall away to use in a salad or soup.) Handle them carefully so that they don't fall apart. Set them in a pan, brush them lightly with light olive oil on both sides, and season them with salt to taste. Grill them slowly over the coals, turning each side once 45 degrees to mark them.

Grilled Fennel with Olive Oil, Fennel Greens, and Lemon

Finely chop some of the fennel greens and mix them with some good olive oil. Brush the mixture over the grilled fennel, season with salt and pepper, and serve with lemon wedges.

Grilled Fennel with Garlic Mayonnaise

Grill the fennel and serve it with a spoonful of garlic mayonnaise (page 314) spread over the top or on the side.

Grilled Fennel with Mayonnaise and Pernod

The Pernod echoes the anise taste of the vegetable. Season plain mayonnaise with a few drops, stir in snipped fennel greens, and serve alongside the grilled fennel.

Grilled Fennel with Mustard Cream Vinaigrette

Mustard cream vinaigrette (page 315) also goes particularly well with fennel. Serve it alongside the grilled fennel and garnish with fennel greens or snipped fresh chives. You could also make a delicious composed salad with the fennel, chick-peas and roasted peppers, all dressed with the mustard cream vinaigrette.

Grilled Fennel with Herb Butters

Spread any herb butter (pages 309 to 313) over the warm fennel, season with freshly ground pepper to taste, and serve.

Leeks

Unless they're very small and tender, leeks need to be cooked before they're grilled. The cooking can be done hours in advance and the leeks set aside until needed.

To prepare the leeks, cut off most of the greens, leaving the white parts of the

leeks plus an inch or 2 of the pale green part. Trim the roots, but leave the bottoms intact. Slice the leeks in half lengthwise; then wash them carefully.

Put the leeks in a steaming basket or tray and cook over boiling water until they're tender, about 15 minutes. Remove and set them on a plate, cut side down, until you're ready to grill. Before grilling, brush the leeks lightly on both sides with light olive oil. Grill the leeks far enough above the coals to give them a chance to warm thoroughly before they color. Grill them on both sides, turning the cut side once at a 45-degree angle to get a crosshatched effect.

Grilled Leeks with Parsley and Olive Oil

This is a very pretty and simple way to finish grilled leeks. Combine some finely minced parsley in a bowl with extra-virgin olive oil. Set them cut side up on a platter and spoon a little of the parsley oil over them. Season with salt and freshly ground pepper and serve. The addition of some finely chopped hard-cooked egg and a few olives makes a lovely dish.

Grilled Leeks with Mustard Cream Vinaigrette

Grill the leeks and serve them cut side up with a spoonful of mustard cream vinaigrette (page 315) ladled over the top. Garnish with snipped fresh chives.

Grilled Leeks with Herb Butters

When the butter melts against the hot leeks, the aroma of the herbs suddenly emerges. Spread any of the herb butters (pages 309 to 313), softened, over the leeks as soon as they are off the grill. Finish with salt and freshly ground pepper to taste and serve.

Mushrooms

Many varieties of mushrooms are excellent for grilling not only because of their good taste but also because they are sturdy and large—like *cèpes*, *shiitake*, and imported Italian field mushrooms. These varieties aren't always available, but the regular supermarket mushrooms will work fine. They shrink as they cook, so choose those nice, large, firm caps for best results. Cut off the stems at the base so that they will lie flat on the grill.

Mushrooms on Skewers

First toss the mushrooms in light olive oil and lemon juice, season with salt and freshly ground pepper, and let them stand for at least 15 minutes. Then carefully thread them on a skewer and grill. This makes it easier to handle several at once. Serve with a wedge of lemon and plenty of coarsely ground pepper.

Grilled Mushrooms with Herb Butter

Carefully remove the entire stem at its base. Season the mushrooms with light olive oil, lemon juice, and salt and freshly ground pepper. Place them on the grill cut side down first. Turn them over and, as they are grilling on the other side, slip a teaspoon of any herb butter (pages 309 to 313) into the cavity. It will melt and become the sauce for the mushroom.

Grilled Mushrooms with Salsa Verde

Grill the mushrooms the same way as above, but fill the cavity with an herb-rich salsa verde (page 317) instead of the herb butter. Or set them on a platter and spoon the sauce over them. Make the sauce a little more tart than usual with an extra splash of Champagne vinegar since the mushrooms have already been marinated in oil before being grilled.

Onions

Onions are one of the best vegetables for grilling. They emerge sweet, tender, and a little smoky. Freshly ground pepper and a dash of vinegar make a perfectly delicious dressing requiring no oil or butter. A particularly wonderful way to finish grilled onions, though, is with the cinnamon-flavored butter below or the pungent rosemary butter with sage and juniper (page 311).

When you're grilling onions, choose large ones, red or yellow, and slice them into rounds a little less than ½ inch thick. Skewer them with a few toothpicks to keep them from falling apart on the grill. Brush them with a light oil, season them with salt, and grill them until they're nicely colored. Gently loosen them with a spatula, turn them over, and cook them on the other side. You could also use small red torpedo onions; cut these in half with the skins on, brush with oil, and season. Grill them cut side down. If they're not done by the time they're finished on the cut side, turn them over and let them cook on the other side until soft.

Grilled Onions with Cinnamon-Chili Butter

This seasoned butter was suggested by Elizabeth David. Though it may sound odd, the combination of onions with cinnamon is perfectly right. A pinch of cayenne pepper or ground New Mexican chili keeps it piquant and on the savory side. Grill the onions as suggested, and spread the following butter over them.

THE CINNAMON-CHILI BUTTER

½ cup unsalted butter
2½ teaspoons ground cinnamon
¼ teaspoon cayenne pepper or red chili
salt
½ teaspoon lemon juice

Work the butter with the cinnamon and cayenne. Add salt to taste and the lemon juice. Chill until ready to use; then let the butter come to room temperature before using it.

Grilled Onions with Rosemary Butter with Sage and Juniper

The sweetness of the onions sets off the rather strong, earthy tastes of the herbs and juniper. This is especially appealing as a winter dish and could be done on a grill set in a fireplace.

Grill the onions as suggested and spread rosemary butter with sage and juniper (page 311) over them.

Sweet Bell Peppers

Bell peppers that have been roasted over coals until the skins are blackened form the basis of that extremely delicious and useful condiment—roasted peppers. It's usually easier to do this over a gas flame in the kitchen, so the directions for roasting, peeling, and marinating peppers are given in another section, on page 329. However, if you're grilling and have a chance to roast a few peppers in this fashion, the results will be very much worth the effort. Just grill them until they're charred all over; then set them in a bowl covered with a plate to steam them and follow the directions from there.

Otherwise, peppers can be grilled and served as a side dish: Slice red or yellow

peppers in half lengthwise and cut away the membranes and seeds. Make a couple of slashes in the curved ends of the peppers; then gently press on them to open up the peppers and make them as flat as possible. Brush both sides of the peppers with light olive oil and season with salt. Grill the peppers over the coals until they have softened and are nicely marked. Cut them into large pieces and serve them alone, with lemon wedges or balsamic vinegar.

Tomatoes

Tomatoes are rather too delicate and unwieldy to grill for serving, but they are delicious to cook with and require little fussing. Using grilled tomatoes in place of fresh can completely transform a soup or sauce, giving it a sweet, smoky edge that is unexpected and delicious.

Wash firm, ripe tomatoes and put them, whole, on the grill over a low fire. Turn them occasionally until they are soft and lightly charred all over the surface. Purée them in a food processor or blender, with the skins, and use the purée in place of fresh tomatoes.

Zucchini

Zucchini tastes good with all the seasonings that go with eggplant—garlic mayonnaise (page 314), herb sauces and butters of all kinds, and walnut and pine nut sauces (pages 322 and 324).

Really small garden zucchini need only be sliced in half, scored, brushed lightly with oil, and grilled slowly. Salt, freshly ground pepper, and lemon juice are perfectly delicious with such tender little squash.

Larger zucchini can be cut in half or into slabs about ½ inch thick, brushed with oil, and grilled. Unlike eggplant, the flesh won't melt into a purée—it stays intact even when soft.

Zucchini can also be sliced into rounds and skewered to cook *en brochette*.

Grilled zucchini is wonderful on a piece of sourdough bread with a spoonful of salsa verde (page 317) for a quick bite to tide people over while the rest of dinner is cooking.

Try it also with the lemon caper butter (page 185), used for baked or steamed zucchini.

Grilled Vegetable Packages

This is a wonderful way to treat tender vegetables, especially those from the garden. Choose a variety—green beans, little potatoes, different kinds of summer squash, quartered peppers, new carrots, or tiny garlic cloves. Set them on a piece of heavy foil, include a few branches of herbs if you have them, and salt them lightly. Wrap up the foil and set the package right on the coals for about 20 minutes. The moisture in the vegetables will make enough steam to cook them. Unwrap the package, inhale the steam, and serve. Butter isn't even necessary.

Any of these vegetables can also be cooked singly in packages of their own. Freshly dug potatoes are heavenly cooked this way.

Grilled Garlic

Remove the outer papery husk from garlic heads and set them in foil with a little virgin olive oil and a sprig of rosemary or thyme. Wrap well and set directly on the coals to bake for about 30 minutes. Turn the package occasionally so that the heat is evenly absorbed. When done, the cloves of garlic should be very soft inside. Eat it just like this or squeeze the warm purée over bread or potatoes and season with freshly ground pepper to taste and extra-virgin olive oil.

Down to Earth

Rice, Potatoes, and Beans

These are the solid, earthy cupboard foods that are always on hand, the farinaceous foods, the starches. They are filling, they can be made in quantity, and they are inexpensive. Like soups and stews, they keep well and their flavors often improve with time. They tend to be very comforting foods too—soft, bland until seasoned, easy to eat.

Rice, like pasta, can be cooked quickly. Rice dishes are often perfect for late-night suppers—easy to put together, filling but light. Leftovers are great in scrambled eggs, too. Beans require the forethought of soaking and a long cooking time, but the resulting rich and flavorful broth gives body to other dishes, especially soups and stews. Many bean dishes improve as they sit in the refrigerator, so it's worth making enough to have for a while or even to freeze, especially if you've taken the time to cook your own beans. Canned beans can also be used, although their broth is usually a little too salty.

Potatoes are one of the most versatile vegetables; they can be simply roasted, boiled, or steamed and then seasoned with any of the herb butters and they will be delicious. Or they can be treated in more complicated ways—thinly sliced, layered in skillets, baked in clay, fried with herbs and cheese, or combined with other vegetables. When fresh and new, they require little if any seasoning to be utterly delicious, but all potatoes readily absorb the flavors of oil, butter, and herbs and are well enhanced by these aromatic additions.

Most of these dishes reflect the solid and filling nature of the main ingredients and will make a substantial one-bowl supper. With a salad or cooked vegetable alongside, a piece of cheese, and some fruit, a plate of rice or a bowl of beans can be extended into a fully respectable meal.

Cumin Rice with Eggplant and Peppers

A rich mixture of rice, summer vegetables, and spices—cumin, ginger, and turmeric. This dish is started on the stove and finished in the oven, baked in a large, beautiful casserole. It can stand as a filling, main-course dish, enriched if you like with mild cheese, diced and stirred into the dish just before serving. Or it can be served with an accompaniment of yogurt cheese (page 28) alongside.

Makes 4 servings as a main course or 6 to 8 servings as a side dish

1½ cups brown rice
2 tablespoons vegetable oil
1 tablespoon butter
1 10- to 12-ounce eggplant, cut in ½-inch cubes
1 medium-sized onion, cut into ¼-inch squares
salt
1 small green bell pepper, cut into ½-inch squares
1 small red or yellow pepper or a mixture, cut into ½-inch squares
2 medium-sized tomatoes, peeled, seeded, and cut into large pieces,
    or 1 15-ounce can tomatoes, drained and cut into large pieces
4 teaspoons ground cumin
½ teaspoon turmeric
¼ teaspoon ground ginger
¼ teaspoon ground cinnamon
½ teaspoon freshly ground pepper
¼ cup chopped parsley or cilantro
3 cups water
1 cup (about 3 ounces) diced provolone, Monterey Jack, or
    Muenster cheese (optional)

Rinse the rice, cover it with water, and set it aside to soak while you prepare the rest of the vegetables.

Preheat the oven to 375°F.

Warm the oil and butter in a large skillet. Add the eggplant and onion, salt them lightly, and rapidly sauté them to distribute the oil. Cook over medium heat until the eggplant is soft but not mushy, about 5 minutes. Add the peppers, tomatoes, spices (including the pepper), parsley, and more salt to taste. Stir carefully, combining everything well. Drain the rice and add it to the pan along with 3 cups water. Turn up the heat to bring the water to a boil, then transfer everything to a baking dish, such as a large, earthenware gratin dish. Lay a piece of parchment over the top, cover with foil, and bake until the rice is done, about 45 minutes. Toss the diced cheese, if you're using it, into the rice and serve.

Yellow Squash and Rice Tian

A few thoughtful words of Elizabeth David's inspired this summer rice dish. It's pleasing, light, and full of the singular flavor of squash, which emerges when it's allowed to cook beyond the tender-crisp stage.

Crookneck squash is grated and cooked, the rice is boiled, and the two are combined and covered with a light béchamel sauce. Although it might be tempting to add cheese to make a more substantial dish, the delicate flavors of the rice and squash would be hidden. If you want more substance, add something else to your meal instead.

This *tian* is very nice served with grilled vegetables or a summer soup, a salad, and a fresh ricotta or herbed cheese.

Makes 4 servings

THE BÉCHAMEL

> *1½ cups milk*
> *2 tablespoons butter*
> *1 tablespoon flour*
> *½ small onion, finely chopped*
> *1 bay leaf*
> *1 small marjoram branch or a pinch of dried*
> *salt*
> *a few gratings of nutmeg*
> *freshly ground pepper*

Warm the milk in a small pan and make the roux: Melt the butter in a saucepan over low heat, stir in the flour, and cook for 2 or 3 minutes, stirring constantly. Whisk in the heated milk; then add the onion, herbs, and salt to taste. Cook slowly, stirring occasionally, for 25 minutes while you cook the squash and the rice. Season with a little nutmeg and pepper to taste. Remove the bay leaf before using the sauce in the *tian*.

THE RICE AND SQUASH

1 cup long- or short-grain white or brown rice
salt
1 pound crookneck zucchini, or patty pan squash, approximately
2 tablespoons butter or olive oil
1 teaspoon chopped marjoram or ½ teaspoon dried

Bring plenty of water to a boil and add salt to taste and the rice. Give it a stir, lower the heat, and cook at a slow boil until the rice is done but still has a little bite—about 15 minutes for white rice, 40 for brown. Pour the rice into a colander, rinse briefly, and set aside to drain.

While the rice is cooking, prepare the squash. Grate it on the large holes of a hand grater or in a food processor. Melt the butter in a wide skillet, add the squash, salt it lightly, and cook it slowly for 10 to 15 minutes, stirring occasionally. The squash should release moisture as it cooks, but if the pan seems dry and the squash in danger of sticking, add a little water to the pan. Don't let the squash brown.

Preheat the oven to 375°F and rub a gratin dish or *tian* with a little butter or oil. Add the rice and the squash and toss them together with half of the béchamel sauce. Even out the mixture and pour the rest of the sauce over the top. Bake until the top begins to color, about 25 minutes.

Rice with Fennel and Fontina Cheese

This dish can be made in the time it takes to cook the rice. The rice is boiled and then tossed with the sauce and cubes of Fontina cheese, which melt and draw the grains together into fragrant clusters. The sauce is made with leeks and fennel, simmered in white wine until tender. Although the pale colors of the dish make it look delicate, it is full of big tastes and makes a satisfying main dish for a meal. Either white or brown rice can be used, but if you choose brown rice, allow an additional 20 minutes of cooking time.

I would follow this dish with some sweet, juicy pears to eat out of hand and some freshly cracked almonds or walnuts.

Makes 4 servings

> salt
> 1½ *cups brown or white rice such as Arborio, Carolina, or short-grain rice*
> 2 *medium-sized fennel bulbs*
> 1 *large or 2 medium-sized leeks, white parts only*
> 3 to 4 *tablespoons olive oil, butter, or a mixture*
> ½ *teaspoon fennel seeds*
> 2 *tablespoons finely chopped fennel greens*
> 1 *tablespoon finely chopped parsley*
> *freshly ground pepper*
> ½ *cup dry white wine or water*
> 1 *cup water*
> 2 *tablespoons pine nuts*
> 3 *ounces Fontina cheese, cut into small cubes, approximately 1 cup*
> *freshly grated Parmesan cheese*

Bring a large pot of water to boil for the rice. When it comes to a boil, add salt to taste and pour in the rice. Give it a stir, lower the heat, and cook the rice at a gentle boil while you make the sauce. White rice will cook in 15 to 18 minutes; brown rice in 35 to 40.

Pull off the outer leaves of the fennel if they look tough or scarred. Quarter the bulbs, remove the cores if they are tough, and chop them into ¼-inch squares. Quarter the leeks lengthwise and chop them into pieces about the same size as the fennel. Rinse them well.

Warm the olive oil in a sauté pan and add the fennel, leeks, fennel seeds, and half the fresh herbs. Season with salt and pepper, then pour in the wine. Simmer until the wine is completely reduced; then pour in the water and continue cooking until the vegetables are tender and most of the liquid has cooked away, about 20 minutes. While the vegetables are cooking, toast the pine nuts in a dry pan until they are golden and set them aside.

When the rice is cooked, pour it through a strainer. Put it into a warm bowl and add the cheese, the vegetables, most of the remaining herbs, and the pine nuts; toss together. Season with pepper and garnish with the rest of the herbs and the Parmesan cheese.

Suggestions: For a soupier, wetter rice, pour in 1 cup of the rice cooking water or heated light cream and toss it with the vegetables and herbs.

Try this dish with other cheeses, such as Taleggio, mozzarella, provolone, Monterey Jack, or a mild goat cheese. They all have slightly different characteristics, and all of them would go well with the fennel.

Rice with Spinach, Herbs, and Cheese

This recipe makes a soothing, simple, and reasonable supper. Sautéed Tomatoes with Vinegar (page 184) would make a lively, easy accompaniment.

This is the kind of dish that can be varied easily. Including eggs makes it a more substantial, one-dish meal. Different kinds of rice have different flavors and textures; try using white or brown basmati, for example. Other greens—watercress, mustard or turnip greens, chard, or more exotically, rocket (arugula), hyssop, or borage leaves (blanched first)—mixed with the spinach add interest and complexity. Provolone is a good cheese for its strength of flavor and texture, but rich, buttery Fontina is also delicious, as are mozzarella and even a low-fat ricotta cheese.

Makes 3 to 4 servings as a main dish

> *1 cup long- or short-grain white or brown rice*
> *salt*
> *1 1-pound bunch of spinach*
> *a dozen sorrel leaves, if available*
> *1 tablespoon olive oil or butter*
> *1 medium-sized yellow onion, finely diced*
> *1 garlic clove, minced*
> *1 teaspoon chopped or two pinches of dried thyme leaves*
> *¼ cup finely chopped parsley*
> *pinch of red pepper flakes*
> *¼ pound provolone cheese, grated, approximately 1⅓ cups*
> *3 eggs, beaten (optional)*
> *1 teaspoon coarsely ground black pepper*
> *additional virgin olive oil*

Bring a pot of water to boil, add salt to taste and the rice and cook at a slow boil until the rice is tender but still a little undercooked—about 15 minutes for white rice, 30 minutes for brown. When it is done, drain, rinse briefly with cool water, shake off the excess water, and put the rice in a mixing bowl.

Remove the stems from the spinach and wash the leaves in several changes of water to get rid of the sand. Cook the spinach and sorrel in a large skillet with the water that clings to the leaves just long enough to wilt them; then set the greens in a strainer. When cool enough to handle, chop the spinach and sorrel roughly without wringing them dry—the juice will keep the rice moist while baking.

Heat the oil or butter in a small skillet, add the onion, and cook over low heat

for about 5 minutes or until softened. Toward the end of the cooking, add the garlic and thyme. Preheat the oven to 350°F.

Combine all the ingredients together and season with salt to taste and the pepper. Lightly film a baking dish with oil, add the rice mixture, and, if you like, drizzle additional oil over the top. Cover lightly with foil and bake until heated through and the cheese is melted, about 25 minutes. Remove the cover and cook for another 5 minutes.

Rice with Black Pepper Sauce

This makes a good late-night dinner when you recognize pangs of hunger at ten o'clock and realize you've forgotten to eat. Although it's not a risotto, it's particularly good made with Arborio rice; the short, round grains are substantial and well textured. While the rice is cooking, prepare the rest of the ingredients—this dish can be made in about 20 minutes.

Makes 2 servings

> 1 cup Arborio or short-grain white rice
> salt
> ⅓ cup chopped parsley
> 1 teaspoon chopped thyme leaves or several pinches of dried
> 2 sage leaves, chopped, or a pinch of dried
> 1 large garlic clove, finely chopped
> 1 to 2 teaspoons coarsely ground black pepper
> ½ cup grated mixed Fontina and mozzarella cheese or provolone alone
> 2 tablespoons butter
> 1 tablespoon olive oil

Bring a large pot of water to a boil and add the rice and salt to taste. Boil until the rice is done, from 12 to 15 minutes, depending on the type of rice used. Pound the parsley, thyme, sage, garlic, and pepper in a mortar to release their oils and aromas or chop them together on a board. When the rice is done, pour it into a colander, shake off the excess water, and toss it in a bowl with the cheese.

Heat the butter and oil in a small skillet, stir in the herbs and garlic, and as soon as the butter foams, pour it over the rice, toss, and serve.

Green Rice

Rice cooked with a mixture of scallions, spinach, and herbs emerges flecked with green and with the taste of the different herbs mingled into one. Serve it with plenty of pepper and freshly grated cheese. Leftover rice is great mixed into scrambled eggs. If the fresh herbs—marjoram, dill, and cilantro—aren't available, make the rice with just the scallions, parsley, and spinach.

Makes 4 servings

> 1 bunch of scallions, including a few inches of the greens, finely chopped
> 2 or 3 handfuls of spinach leaves (stems removed), finely chopped
> ½ cup finely chopped parsley
> 2 tablespoons finely chopped marjoram
> 1 tablespoon finely chopped dill
> 2 tablespoons finely chopped cilantro
> 1 tablespoon olive oil
> 2 tablespoons butter
> salt
> 1 cup long- or short-grain white rice
> 1¾ cups water
> freshly ground pepper
> freshly grated Romano or Parmesan cheese

Wash and cut everything as suggested. Heat the olive oil and half the butter in a heavy saucepan; add the scallions, spinach, herbs, and salt to taste and cook over medium heat for a few minutes, stirring frequently. Add the rice and cook several more minutes, until the grains of rice begin to turn clear and golden. Add the water, bring it to a boil, turn the heat to low, cover the pan, and cook until the water has been absorbed, about 20 minutes. Add the remaining butter and lightly stir it into the rice with a fork. Turn the rice into a serving dish, grind pepper over the surface, and dust with a grating of cheese.

Pan-Fried Potatoes with Cheese, Rosemary, and Sage

An herbaceous treatment of golden pan-fried potatoes, especially wonderful for those who love these two strong herbs, rosemary and sage. The cheese melts over the potatoes and holds them together in fragrant little bundles. If you've planned to have cheese elsewhere in your meal or it just seems excessive, you can leave it out and still have some very good potatoes.

Makes 4 to 6 servings

> 5 ounces Fontina or Taleggio cheese
> 1½ to 2 pounds large, smooth-skinned red potatoes
> salt
> ½ teaspoon peppercorns, or more to taste
> 6 fresh sage leaves, roughly chopped, or ½ teaspoon dried
> 1½ teaspoons roughly chopped fresh rosemary, or ½ teaspoon dried
> 3 to 4 tablespoons olive oil or a mixture of olive oil and
>   clarified butter (page 415)

Cut the cheese into small cubes and let them warm to room temperature while the rest of the dish is prepared. Wash the potatoes, even off the ends, and slice them lengthwise about ½ inch thick. Slice each slab into thirds and each resulting stick into pieces to end up with cubes. Discard the odd-shaped small pieces, which are likely to burn later on.

Bring a pot of water to a boil, add salt to taste and the potatoes, and cook until they are just barely done, about 8 minutes. Pour them into a strainer, rinse them quickly in cool water, and set them on a towel to dry. Grind the peppercorns in a mortar, keeping them coarse. If you're using dried herbs, smash them with the peppercorns.

Heat the oil in a wide skillet (preferably cast iron). When it's hot, lower the heat to medium and add the potatoes. Let them sit for several minutes until they begin to form a crust on the bottom; then begin shaking the pan every few minutes so that the potatoes will turn and color on all sides. When they are nicely browned, add the herbs and the pepper. Quickly toss the cubes of cheese among the potatoes and serve right away.

Skillet Potatoes and Onions

These potatoes and onions can be varied endlessly with herbs and cheeses. With a salad, they make a simple and satisfying meal.

The wonderful flavor and succulence of the finished dish is out of proportion to the minor effort it requires to put this together. Thinly sliced potatoes and onions are layered in a heavy cast-iron pan and cooked very slowly on top of the stove. As steam rises, it cooks the potatoes so that the bottom layer is crisp and the rest of the potatoes are moist and tender. If you like, you can invert the cake on a plate, slide it back into the pan, and brown the second side as well.

I like to include herbs—marjoram, bay leaf, basil, sage, or thyme—or bits of herb butter if I have some left over. The heat brings out their perfumes, which are absorbed by the potatoes. Cheese can also be included—Gruyère, Fontina, Swiss, a milder cheese such as Bel Paese, or a sharper cheese, like goat cheese. When using cheese, make sure the bottom layer of potatoes is completely solid. If the cheese melts through to the bottom of the pan, it will stick and burn.

Makes 3 or 4 servings as a main dish

> *2 pounds red potatoes, scrubbed but not peeled*
> *2 to 4 tablespoons olive oil or clarified butter (page 415)*
> *1 large or 2 medium-sized yellow onions, thinly sliced into rounds*
> *2 tablespoons fresh herbs such as marjoram, basil, thyme, or sage*
> *   or several bay leaves or 2 teaspoons dried*
> *salt*
> *freshly ground pepper*
> *3 to 4 ounces (about 1 cup) grated cheese (optional)*

Slice the potatoes very thinly, either by hand or in a food processor.

Pour enough oil or clarified butter into a 10-inch cast-iron skillet or other heavy skillet with a nonstick surface to cover the bottom generously. Then make a solid layer of overlapping potatoes. Follow with onions, a sprinkling of herbs, and season with salt and pepper. Add a layer of cheese, if you're using it. Repeat this layering, ending with a layer of potatoes.

Cover the pan tightly with foil. Place it over low heat and cook for 40 minutes; then remove the foil and check the potatoes on top by poking them with a knife. They should be tender. Gently slide a spatula under the potatoes to loosen them. Put a plate over the pan, grasp it firmly on 2 sides, and flip the whole thing over. The cake will fall out onto the plate. If any of the potatoes are stuck in the pan, loosen them individually and place them where they should go. To brown the second side, add a little more oil or butter to the pan and slide the cake back in.

Cook, loosely covered, for another 15 minutes or until the potatoes on the bottom are browned; then slide them out. Serve right away.

If you have any problem with the potatoes sticking, just toss them together, garnish with herbs and pepper, and serve right in the pan. They will look rather rustic, but that's entirely appropriate, and they will taste wonderful.

Skillet Potatoes with Sage and Taleggio Cheese

This one is made with Taleggio, a creamy Italian cheese that melts beautifully and has a marvelous, delicate flavor. It isn't always easy to find, especially outside of large cities. If you can't find it where you live, substitute Fontina (preferably Italian) or a mixture of Fontina and Bel Paese. The flavors of the clarified butter and sage are perfect with both the cheese and the potatoes.

Makes 3 to 4 servings as a main dish

> ¼ cup clarified butter (page 415)
> 12 fresh sage leaves or 1 teaspoon dried
> 2 pounds red potatoes, scrubbed and thinly sliced
> salt
> freshly ground pepper
> 6 ounces Taleggio cheese, thinly sliced

Heat half the butter in the skillet with 3 of the sage leaves, left whole. Roughly chop or tear the rest of the leaves. Cover the bottom of the skillet thoroughly with 2 overlapping layers of potatoes. Season with salt and pepper to taste and cover with a portion of the cheese. Continue layering the potatoes and cheese, seasoning each layer with salt and pepper. Finish with a layer of potatoes.

Tightly cover the pan with foil. Set over low heat and cook for about 40 minutes or until the potatoes are tender when pierced with a knife. Loosen the bottom layer with a spatula, invert the cake onto a plate, and add the rest of the butter to the pan. Slide the cake back in and continue cooking until the bottom layer is lightly browned, another 15 minutes or so. Turn out of the pan and serve.

Skillet Potatoes with Goat Cheese and Thyme

In this variation, use 5 to 6 ounces fresh goat cheese, omit the sage, and use 1 teaspoon fresh thyme leaves *or* ¼ teaspoon dried and 1 teaspoon fresh rosemary leaves (or ½ teaspoon dried) roughly chopped. Follow the directions above, scattering the herbs over the potatoes along with the salt and pepper.

Grated Potato and Artichoke Cake

This cake requires some special effort, but it's a wonderful dish, crispy on the outside, with contrasting textures of potatoes and artichokes on the inside. A big salad or a dish of cooked escarole would make a fine accompaniment, or serve it with a simple steamed vegetable, like green beans, and a mound of fresh ricotta cheese garnished with pepper and fresh parsley.

Makes 1 9-inch cake, serving 2

1¼ pounds red potatoes
2 large artichokes
1 lemon
2 to 3 teaspoons olive oil
1 garlic clove, sliced
salt
freshly ground pepper
1 tablespoon chopped marjoram or ½ teaspoon dried
1 tablespoon chopped parsley
¼ cup clarified butter (page 415) or oil for frying

Peel the potatoes; then grate them coarsely on the large holes of a hand grater or use the shredding attachment on a food processor. Put the potatoes in a large bowl of cold water. Rinse them several times until the water is no longer cloudy; then dry the potatoes in a salad spinner, wrap them in a towel, and refrigerate them until needed. They will keep fine, without discoloring, even overnight.

Trim the artichokes. Break off the tough outer leaves and cut off the top two thirds of the remaining greens. Trim away the broken stubs on the outside and pare away the remaining leaves. As you work, rub the artichokes with lemon to keep them from browning. Scoop out the choke with a spoon; then slice the hearts crosswise into pieces a little less than ¼ inch thick. Put them into a bowl with water to cover and the juice of the lemon.

Heat the olive oil in a skillet with the garlic. Drain the artichokes. When the garlic has colored, remove it and add the artichokes. Season with salt and pepper and add the marjoram and parsley. Sauté briskly for about a minute; then lower the heat and add enough of the acidulated water to barely cover. Simmer until the artichokes are tender and the water has evaporated.

Warm 3 tablespoons of the butter or oil in a cast-iron or nonstick skillet. Make a layer with half the potatoes and season with salt and pepper. Lay the artichokes

over them; then cover with the remaining potatoes and season. Gently even the cake, gathering any stray potatoes from the edges, and press them gently down with a spatula. Cook over medium heat until the bottom is crisp and golden, about 15 minutes.

Loosen the cake around the edges. Lay a plate over the pan, grasp both plate and pan firmly with both hands, and flip it over. Add the remaining butter or oil to the pan, let it melt, and swirl it around the bottom of the pan. Slip the cake back in and cook the second side until golden, about 10 minutes. Slide the finished cake onto a cutting board, cut it into quarters, and serve.

Potatoes Baked in Clay with Garlic and Herbs

These potatoes emerge tasting as if they've been cooked over a wood fire. They take little or no oil and are clothed with the scent of the herbs and garlic. Although potatoes sound like wintry fare, they in fact are freshest and most delicate in the summer, and the same is true for garlic. Try them in the summer, especially if you live where the evenings are cool.

Makes 4 servings

> 6 to 8 small (about 1¼ pounds) white or red potatoes
> 2 to 3 teaspoons olive oil
> ½ teaspoon chopped rosemary, or several pinches of dried
> several thyme branches or 2 pinches of dried
> 1 bay leaf
> salt
> 1 head of garlic, the cloves separated but unpeeled

Soak both halves of the clay pot for 15 minutes; then empty them. Preheat the oven to 350°F. Wash the potatoes. If the potatoes are different sizes, cut them into pieces about the same size and toss them with the oil, herbs, and salt. Put them in the clay pot with the garlic, cover, and bake until the potatoes and garlic are tender, about an hour. Eat the potatoes with freshly ground pepper and the softened garlic spread over each bite.

Potatoes and Pasta with Herb Paste

The strong herb mixture in this dish is pounded into a rough paste with pepper-corns, juniper, and salt. This seasoning was taught to me by a friend from Abruzzi. She spread it under the skin of a turkey leg or breast before roasting, but it's also wonderful on potatoes and pasta.

The pasta and potatoes cook separately and are then combined with the herbs and butter. The herb mixture can be prepared while the pasta and potatoes are cooking. The rosemary and sage should be fresh, but if they're not available, use them dried and double the amount of parsley.

Makes 4 to 6 servings

> 1 pound White Rose or red potatoes
> salt
> ½ pound orecchiette (little ears) or other small pasta shapes
> 2 teaspoons rosemary leaves or 1 teaspoon dried
> 12 fresh sage leaves or 1 teaspoon dried
> 2 tablespoons marjoram leaves
> ¼ cup parsley leaves
> 3 large garlic cloves
> 15 peppercorns
> 5 juniper berries
> 2 tablespoons olive oil
> ⅓ cup unsalted butter

Peel the potatoes and cut them into bite-sized pieces. Bring a pot of water to a boil, add salt to taste and the potatoes, and boil until tender, about 10 minutes. Or, if you prefer, steam the potatoes.

Bring a second pot of water to boil; add salt to taste and the pasta. Cook until it is *al dente*; then drain the pasta.

While the potatoes and pasta are cooking, make the herb paste. Roughly chop the herbs and garlic; then put them in a mortar with the peppercorns, juniper, and ½ teaspoon coarse salt. Pound everything together to form a paste. This can also be done in a small food processor, or the ingredients can just be chopped on a board by hand until everything is fine. Put the herb-garlic mixture in a bowl with the olive oil and the butter. When the potatoes and pasta are done, drain them, add them to the herbs, and toss them together.

■ If any of the seasoning is left over, try it in scrambled eggs—unusual but delicious.

Broiled Potatoes

This method is especially nice when used on new potatoes or creamy-fleshed potatoes like yellow Finnish or Rose Firs. If they really are fresh, they will be quite a treat, and you should allow, as with fresh corn, several small potatoes per person. To enjoy the flavor of freshly dug potatoes, use simply unsalted butter, salt, and pepper. Herb butters, however, are also quite good with potatoes.

Makes 4 servings

> *12 freshly dug Finnish, Rose Firs, or red new potatoes*
> *unsalted butter*
> *salt*
> *coarsely cracked pepper*

Slice the potatoes in half lengthwise and steam them until the flesh is tender. Preheat the broiler. Set them in a baking dish, cut side up. Make a few slashes in the surface of each potato and spread with butter. Set the dish under the broiler until the surface is bubbly and golden; then serve the potatoes with salt and coarsely cracked pepper to taste.

Flageolet Bean and Artichoke Gratin

Flageolets are small, pale green beans with a delicate flavor. One can buy them here, imported from France, but they aren't difficult to grow. When allowed to mature and then harvested from the pods and cooked while plump with moisture, they make an exquisite treat. If they are not available where you live, use small white navy or lima beans in their place.

In this gratin they are combined with braised artichokes and leeks, layered with soft, creamy goat cheese, lightly covered with bread crumbs, and seasoned with rosemary. As the beans heat in the oven, the cheese softens and the bread crumbs crisp and brown. With its varied flavors and textures, this gratin is filling and satisfying as a main dish. With a parsley salad (page 54) and cold quince compote (page 361) it would make a fine fall or winter supper.

The recipe can easily be halved or doubled.

Makes 4 to 6 servings

> *1 cup dried* flageolet *beans or small white navy beans*
> *1 bay leaf*
> *salt*
> *2 to 3 large leeks, white parts only, chopped (about 2 cups)*
> *2 to 3 large artichokes*
> *2 lemons*
> *3 to 5 tablespoons olive oil*
> *3 garlic cloves, finely chopped or pounded*
> *1 teaspoon chopped rosemary leaves, or several pinches of dried*
> *1 cup water*
> *freshly ground pepper*
> *5 ounces soft goat cheese*
> *3 cups fresh bread crumbs*

Soak the beans for 6 hours or overnight; then drain, put them in a pot, and cover them generously with fresh cold water. Bring to a boil, boil vigorously for several minutes, and lower the heat. Add the bay leaf and simmer for 30 minutes. Add salt to taste and continue cooking until the beans are tender but still hold their shape, another 30 to 60 minutes. Keep an eye on the water to make sure the beans are amply covered.

While the beans are cooking, prepare the vegetables. Quarter the leeks length-wise and chop them into pieces about ⅓ inch wide; rinse them well. Trim the artichokes: Break off the tough outer leaves; then slice off two thirds of the top part of the leaves. Trim the base. Cut them into quarters, take out the choke with a paring knife, and slice the quarters. Rub a little lemon on the pieces as you work so they don't discolor; put the finished pieces in water to cover mixed with the lemon juice.

Warm 2 tablespoons of the olive oil in a sauté pan. Add the leeks, artichokes, garlic, and rosemary. Cook for 3 or 4 minutes, turning the pieces so that all are coated with oil. Season with salt and add the water. Press a piece of parchment paper directly onto the vegetables to keep them from discoloring and cook over medium-low heat until the vegetables are tender and the water is reduced. (Should the water evaporate before the vegetables are finished cooking, add more in small amounts until they are done.) Taste and season with salt and pepper. Preheat the oven to 400°F.

When the beans are cooked, drain them, saving the cooking liquid, and mix them with the vegetables. Put them into a roomy gratin dish and add enough bean liquor just to cover. Crumble the cheese over the beans. Toss the bread crumbs with the remaining olive oil until they are moist; then pat them over the top. Bake until the beans are hot and the crust browned, about 25 minutes. Let settle for a few minutes before serving.

Suggestion: Expanding on the vegetable side of the dish, you could also braise, along with leeks and artichokes, strips of savoy cabbage, peas and fava beans, spinach, or fennel bulbs.

Stewed Lentils with Celery Root and Walnut Oil

Lentils aren't a particularly showy food, but they have an earthy, reliable taste that's good to return to every now and then. Celery root, or celeriac, is seasonal during the same months one would be inclined to cook lentils, and the two go well together. Pressed in the fall, even the walnut oil is somewhat seasonal. Its heavy fragrance and high viscosity also seem best enjoyed in the colder months of the year.

Makes 4 servings

1¼ cup lentils
1 tablespoon olive oil
¼ cup finely diced onion
⅓ cup finely diced carrot
¼ cup finely diced celery
1 bay leaf
1 garlic clove, minced
1 tablespoon chopped parsley
½ small celery root, peeled and cut into small cubes
salt
1 quart water

To Finish:

1 tablespoon walnut oil, or more to taste
1 tablespoon finely chopped parsley
1 teaspoon sherry vinegar or red wine vinegar
plenty of coarsely ground pepper

Rinse the lentils, drain them, and set them aside. Heat the olive oil in a soup pot; then add the onion, half the carrots, the celery, bay leaf, and garlic. Fry lightly over medium heat, taking care not to brown the garlic, for 4 to 5 minutes; then add the drained lentils, parsley, celery root, and season with salt. Add the water and bring it to a boil; then simmer until the lentils are tender, about 35 minutes. Add the rest of the carrots during the last 10 minutes of cooking.

If there is a lot of excess water left, drain it off and save it to use in a soup or sauce. Return the lentils to the heat and add the walnut oil, parsley, and vinegar. Check the seasonings and finish with plenty of coarsely ground pepper.

■ For those who haven't used celery root before, its gnarled, dirt-encrusted appearance may look rather daunting. It's not hard to deal with, though. First rinse it off; then peel it as you would an orange: slice off the top and bottom and then cut down the sides with a sawing motion, getting just under the skin. Thinly slice it; then cut the slices into strips, and the strips into cubes. Celery root will brown when exposed to the air, so if it's to be held for more than 5 or 10 minutes, put it in some water acidulated with lemon juice until needed. If you're using just part of the root, cut off what you need and leave the rest with its skin on and wrap it tightly in plastic.

Lentils in Red Wine

Cooking lentils in wine transforms their taste, making them rich and a little tangy. They can be served alongside other foods or as a simple main dish, with thin slices of grilled or toasted bread, a crisp, refreshing salad, or a simply cooked vegetable. Brown lentils are most commonly available, but the tiny slate-green ones from France, which hold their shape so beautifully, would make this rustic dish nearly elegant.

Makes 2 or 3 servings as a main dish or 4 servings as a side dish

1 cup lentils
1 tablespoon butter
1 tablespoon olive oil
1 small onion, finely diced
2 garlic cloves, chopped or sliced
2 bay leaves
pinch each of dried thyme and dried marjoram
¼ cup chopped parsley
1 teaspoon sun-dried tomato purée (page 326) or tomato paste
2 cups hearty red wine, such as Beaujolais, gamay, or red "jug" wine
1½ cups water
salt
red wine vinegar or sherry vinegar
1 to 2 tablespoons additional butter
freshly ground pepper
grilled bread (optional)

Rinse the lentils well, cover them with hot water, and set them aside while you prepare everything else.

Warm the butter and olive oil in a wide skillet or sauté pan and add the onion, garlic, bay leaves, thyme, marjoram, and half the parsley. Cook over medium heat, stirring occasionally, until the onions have begun to color. Stir in the to-mato purée; then add the wine. Bring to a boil and cook for 1 minute. Drain the lentils and add them to the wine with the water, and lightly salt. Return to a boil; then lower the heat, cover the pan, and simmer until the lentils are tender, about 40 minutes.

When the lentils are done, taste for salt, add a dash of vinegar to sharpen the flavors, and stir in the additional butter. Pepper generously, garnish with the re-maining parsley, and serve with or without the bread.

Anasazi Beans with Juniper

Anasazi beans are pretty, mottled purple and white beans. They are an ancient bean, grown and eaten by the Anasazi Indians in the past and now being cultivated in Colorado. They can be found in natural foods stores. If you can't find them, pinto beans are good cooked the same way.

This bean dish is truly simple and very satisfying. Often when I'm riding on the desert, my horse sidles into the shade of a juniper tree and lets me grab a small handful of the blue berries as we pass. There are always a few in my jacket pocket, handy when I want to cook these beans. One of my favorite meals is this dish with Wild Green Salad (page 44) and Piñon Bread (page 32). It is utterly basic and satisfying in the way that complicated food often isn't.

Makes 4 servings

> 2 cups dried Anasazi or pinto beans
> 10 coriander seeds
> 8 juniper berries
> 1 small onion
> 1 tablespoon vegetable oil
> 1 teaspoon ground red chili (optional)
> 1 teaspoon dried Mexican or Greek oregano
> 2½ quarts water
> salt

Sort through the beans, rinse them well, cover them with cold water, and set them aside for 6 hours or overnight.

Bruise the seeds and berries in a mortar and chop the onion into small squares.

Warm the oil in a wide-bottomed soup pot; add the onions, coriander seeds, juniper berries, chili, and oregano. Cook together over medium heat for 3 or 4 minutes, stirring occasionally. Drain the beans and add them to the pot along with the fresh water. Bring to a boil; then lower the heat and simmer for 40 minutes. Add salt to taste and continue cooking until the beans are as tender as you like them—probably another 30 minutes or so. When done, check the seasoning. Serve the beans in a bowl with the broth.

Suggestion: There are lots of tasty additions you can use—cilantro, mint, scallions, spoonfuls of thick Mexican cream, cheese, and so forth—but try the beans plain first. They should have a wonderful clean, uncluttered taste that can be quite refreshing.

Cannellini Beans with Cabbage and Cumin Seeds

It's hard to imagine a more humble combination than beans and cabbage. This simplest of dishes is based on an ancient Italian soup called *jota*. If it's available, use the crinkly-leafed savoy cabbage; it has a more delicate flavor and texture.

This makes a modest but nourishing stew that would be nicely complemented by a special salad, like the Salad of Roasted and Pickled Vegetables (page 76) or something simpler but clean and robust, like Parsley Salad (page 54).

Makes 4 to 6 servings

> 1½ cups dried cannellini (white kidney) or lima beans,
>   soaked 6 hours or overnight
> 1 bay leaf
> 2 fresh sage leaves or a pinch of dried
> 3 to 4 tablespoons olive oil
> salt
> 1 small head (about 1 pound) of savoy or green cabbage
> 1 tablespoon cumin seeds
> 3 garlic cloves, peeled and sliced
> chopped parsley
> freshly ground pepper
> freshly grated Asiago or Parmesan cheese

Drain the soaked beans and cover them generously with fresh cold water. Boil vigorously for 5 minutes, skim off the foam that rises to the surface. Lower the heat and add the bay leaf, sage, and 1 tablespoon of the oil. Simmer for 30 minutes; then add salt to taste. Continue cooking until the beans are tender, 1 hour or more, depending on the type and age of the bean. Make sure there's enough water. There should be a few cups of broth left once the beans are cooked.

Cut the cabbage into wedges about 2 inches wide, leaving most of the core so that the leaves will remain joined. When the beans are nearly tender, remove 1 cup of the water and put it in a wide skillet. Add the cabbage wedges, cumin seeds, and salt lightly. Cook until the color begins to brighten and the leaves start to soften, about 5 to 8 minutes. Turn the cabbage over several times. The cabbage should be tender but not overcooked.

While the cabbage is cooking, heat the rest of the oil in a small pan with the garlic. When the garlic has browned, remove the cloves and set the oil aside. Stir in the parsley.

Combine the beans and cabbage and 1 cup of the bean broth. Pour the oil and parsley over the dish, toss gently together, and season with plenty of pepper. Grate cheese over the top or pass it separately.

Red Bean and Rice "Soup"

In the end there is very little broth, yet this dish is "soupy" enough to serve in a bowl. This soup requires an hour and a half on the stove to cook, but not your presence. It can be served right from the pot or turned into a casserole, dotted with butter and Parmesan cheese, and baked. With the deep red beans, strips of carrot, and red from the tomato, the colors are dark and earthy, especially when presented in an earthenware dish. This is a good fall or winter dish. One recipe makes enough to feed a family or last for a few days.

Makes 6 to 8 servings

> *1 cup brown or short-grain white rice*
> *1 cup kidney beans, soaked 6 hours or overnight*
> *2 tablespoons olive oil*
> *2 garlic cloves, finely chopped*
> *1 small onion, finely diced*
> *2 large celery stalks, finely diced*
> *1 large carrot, grated*
> *¼ teaspoon dried thyme*
> *½ teaspoon dried basil*
> *1 bay leaf*
> *salt*
> *1 15-ounce can tomatoes, chopped, the juice reserved*
> *1 tablespoon sun-dried tomato purée (page 326), or tomato paste*
> *2 tablespoons butter or olive oil*
> *3 tablespoons finely chopped parsley*
> *freshly ground pepper*
> *freshly grated Romano or Parmesan cheese*

If you're using brown rice, cover it with water and set it aside to soak while the beans are cooking. Drain it before adding it to the beans.

Warm the olive oil in a large soup pot; add the garlic, onion, celery, carrot, herbs, and lightly salt. Stir together and cook over medium heat until the onions begin to soften, about 5 minutes. Add the chopped tomatoes and the tomato purée. Measure the liquid from the tomatoes and add enough water to make 2½ quarts. Drain the beans and add them to the pot; bring to a boil, lower the heat, and simmer for 40 minutes. Season to taste with salt. When the beans are tender but still a little firm, add the rice and continue cooking until the rice is done—15 to 20 minutes for white rice and about 35 for brown.

Pour the "soup" into a serving dish and stir in the butter or oil, the parsley, and a generous amount of pepper. Pass the cheese and a small grater.

Lima Beans with Olives and Peppers

Several notions garnered from Greek cookbooks are combined in this recipe. Although this type of dish is usually served as an accompaniment to meat dishes, it is substantial and flavorful enough to stand on its own as a light one-dish meal.

Dried limas are called for here, but you could use about 3 cups of fresh or frozen beans. If this is to be a main dish, ladle it into soup plates with some of the sauce. Or serve it chilled, as a salad, with a wedge of lemon.

Makes 4 servings as a main course, 6 servings as a side dish

> 1¼ cups dried lima beans, soaked 6 hours or overnight
> 2 tablespoons olive oil
> 1 onion, finely diced
> 2 garlic cloves, sliced
> 2 carrots, peeled, quartered lengthwise, and chopped
> 1 celery stalk, chopped into ¼-inch squares
> several celery leaves, chopped
> 1 bay leaf
> 5 tablespoons chopped parsley
> 2 tablespoons chopped dill or 2 teaspoons dried
> several thyme branches or a pinch of dried
> salt
> 2 yellow bell peppers, or 1 red and 1 yellow pepper,
>   roasted (page 329) and cut into squares
> 12 Greek olives, pits removed, cut into large pieces
> extra-virgin olive oil, to finish the dish

Drain the beans and cover them with fresh cold water. Bring them to a boil, boil rapidly for several minutes; then skim off any foam that rises to the surface. Lower the heat and cook the beans slowly until they are tender but still a little on the firm side, about an hour.

When the beans are ready, warm the olive oil in a roomy skillet or sauté pan; add the onion, garlic, carrot, celery, celery leaves, bay leaf, all but a little of the parsley and dill, and the thyme. Cook briskly for 1 or 2 minutes, stirring everything about; then add the beans, enough of their cooking liquid to cover them, and salt to taste. Simmer everything together over medium-low heat until the beans are tender and the liquid is mostly reduced. Stir in the peppers and the olives, let them stew with everything else for a few minutes, and serve the beans garnished with the remaining fresh herbs and finish with a spoonful of olive oil drizzled over all.

White Beans with Escarole and Tomato

Plump *cannellini* (white kidney) beans make a fine foil for the strong, sharp flavor of escarole or its cousin, curly endive. If the beans have already been cooked or you're using canned beans, this dish can be put together in just a few minutes and be ready to eat. Serve it laced with a fine-flavored olive oil and plenty of coarsely ground pepper and pass a piece of Parmigiano-Reggiano with a grater. The beans can be a side dish or a one-bowl meal.

This dish provides a good illustration of how the same ingredients can be assembled in various ways. If there is leftover bean broth, you can add it and have an excellent soup. A splash of vinegar over the same dish, served tepid or slightly chilled, would make a refreshing salad. The same beans could be put in a gratin dish, covered with bread crumbs, laced with olive oil, and baked. Food is flexible.

Makes 4 to 6 servings

> 1¼ *cups dried* cannellini *beans, soaked 6 hours or overnight,*
>   *or 2 15-ounce cans white kidney beans*
> *salt*
> *1 head of escarole or curly endive*
> *1 tablespoon olive oil*
> *¼ teaspoon red pepper flakes*
> *2 large garlic cloves, finely chopped*
> *1 large ripe tomato, halved, seeded, and chopped*
>   *or 1 cup chopped drained canned tomatoes*
> *extra-virgin olive oil, to finish the dish*
> *coarsely ground pepper*
> *freshly grated Parmigiano-Reggiano*

Drain the beans, and cover them generously with water. Bring the water to a boil, lower the heat, and cook gently for 30 minutes. Add salt to taste and continue cooking until the beans are tender but still hold their shape, another 30 minutes or longer, depending on the beans. Save the broth. If you're using canned beans, drain them and set the liquid aside, unless it's very salty. Wash the greens, discard the really tough or ragged outer leaves, and chop the rest into small pieces.

Heat the oil with the red pepper flakes, then add the greens with the water clinging to their leaves, the garlic, and salt lightly. Cook until the greens have wilted; then add the beans and simmer until the greens are cooked and the beans are hot. Add a little of the bean broth to the pan to moisten everything and make a little sauce. Just before serving, add the chopped tomato and cook until the tomato is warmed, another few minutes. Serve with the extra-virgin oil laced over the top, plenty of pepper, and a dusting of cheese.

Chick-Pea and Tomato Pilaf

Each grain of rice and each round pea remain separate in this pilaf. It's a clean, light, and pretty dish, the pink-tinted rice flecked with green. A juicy eggplant stew, a summer vegetable *tian*, or any juicy vegetable mélange would be a happy accompaniment.

If you've cooked the chick-peas, you can use the liquid in the pilaf. If they're canned, drain the liquid and use water in its place.

A pot with a tight-fitting lid to keep in the steam is essential for a pilaf to come out light, with separate, well-cooked grains of rice.

Makes 4 servings

> *1 cup long-grain white rice*
> *2 to 4 tablespoons butter*
> *1 bay leaf*
> *1 garlic clove, thinly sliced*
> *3 thyme branches or a pinch of dried*
> *2 large tomatoes, peeled, seeded, and finely chopped, or 1 15-ounce*
>   *can tomatoes, drained and finely chopped*
> *1½ cups cooked chick-peas or 1 15-ounce can chick-peas, rinsed*
> *salt*
> *freshly ground pepper*
> *2 cups water, vegetable stock, or bean broth*
> *chopped parsley for garnish*

Rinse the rice well, cover it with hot water from the tap, and set it aside. Melt the butter in a heavy soup pot or large saucepan with the bay leaf, garlic, and thyme. Add the tomatoes and cook over medium heat, stirring frequently and breaking them up with a wooden spoon; then add the chick-peas and continue cooking until most of the tomatoes have cooked down into a thick sauce, about 20 minutes.

Drain the rice. Add 2 cups liquid to the tomatoes and chick-peas and season with salt and pepper. Bring to a boil, add the rice, and give it a quick stir; then cover and cook over medium-high heat for 5 minutes. Lower the heat and cook until the moisture has been absorbed, about 2 minutes more, though possibly longer, depending on the rice. Once the liquid has been absorbed, turn off the heat and lay a clean folded cloth over the rice. Return the lid and let the pot stand undisturbed for 30 minutes. Gently loosen the rice with a fork and shake it into a heated serving dish. Garnish with the parsley and serve.

Millet Pilaf with Saffron Peppers

Millet makes a lovely golden pilaf with a pleasant nutty flavor and textural surprises. Unlike other grains, individual millet seeds do not end up completely separate, nor do they cook absolutely evenly. What you'll end up with is a fluffy pilaf
that is also a little crunchy. Millet is also a thirsty grain with an enormous capac-
ity to absorb liquids. A juicy stew—one made with eggplants and tomatoes,
chick-peas, or plump white beans—would be just the thing to serve alongside.

This pilaf is seasoned with marjoram, basil, and a hint of saffron from the peppers. Toasting the millet seeds in butter gives the millet a nutty flavor and keeps it
moist and succulent. The saffron peppers can be made days or weeks in advance.

Makes 4 servings

> *3 to 4 tablespoons butter or sunflower seed oil*
> *1 cup millet*
> *1 small onion, finely chopped*
> *1 bay leaf*
> *¼ teaspoon turmeric*
> *2 teaspoons chopped marjoram or ½ teaspoon dried*
> *1 tablespoon chopped basil or 1 teaspoon dried*
> *1 tablespoon chopped parsley*
> *salt*
> *2 cups water*
> *½ cup roasted peppers with saffron and basil (page
>   330), diced into small squares*
> *1 tablespoon chopped herbs for garnish*
> *freshly ground pepper*

Melt half the butter in a skillet, add the millet, and roast, stirring often, over medium heat. When the grains have started to color (and possibly pop), after about
4 minutes, remove them from the heat and set them aside.

Melt the rest of the butter in a heavy saucepan fitted with a lid, add the onion
and herbs, and cook slowly until the onions are soft, about 5 minutes. Season
lightly with salt. Add the millet, stir to combine, and pour in the water. Bring to
a boil, cover, and adjust the heat to very low or set the pot on a Flame-Tamer.
Cook for 35 minutes; then add the roasted peppers and gently combine them
with the millet, using a fork. Return the lid to the pot and continue cooking for
5 to 10 minutes or until the millet is sufficiently done. (If it isn't quite done but
the water has been absorbed, add 2 or 3 tablespoons water, cover, and continue
to cook for 5 minutes.) Loosen the grains and gently heap the millet into a serving dish. Garnish with the herbs and freshly ground pepper to taste.

Falafel with Walnut Sauce and Garnishes

Falafel, the tasty Middle Eastern mixture of chick-peas, yellow peas, wheat, and herbs, is made into a thick batter, shaped into cakes, and fried. You could make this wholesome, delicious food from scratch, but it is widely available in health food stores, and the quality is excellent. The mix is useful to have around; it needs only to be combined with water and then fried lightly in olive oil.

Here's a suggestion for a lunch or dinner plate, a kind of ploughman's lunch, made with falafel mix.

Makes 4 servings

> *1½ cups falafel mix*
> *1 cup plus 2 tablespoons water*
> *safflower, canola oil, or olive oil*
> *walnut or pine nut sauce (pages 322 to 324)*

SUGGESTED GARNISHES

> *sliced cucumbers*
> *sliced tomato*
> *olives*
> *feta cheese*
> *pita bread*
> *baked or broiled eggplant (page 215)*
> *roasted peppers (page 329) or strips of raw pepper*

Stir the falafel mixture and the water together; then let it stand for 10 minutes. When the moisture has been absorbed, shape 8 patties.

Heat enough oil to generously cover the bottom of a cast-iron or nonstick pan. When it is hot enough to sizzle a drop of water, add the patties. Cook them on both sides until crisp and golden. Serve the patties on a plate with the walnut or pine nut sauce and any of the garnishes.

Morning Foods for Day and Night

Morning foods are comforting, gentle foods. Simple eggs, baked goods, warm cereals, and soft, soothing cheese dishes are foods we often associate with breakfast and morning, which is, for many people, the fragile time of day. There are also breakfast foods that are far more dynamic and sturdy, such as green chili omelets, hash, biscuits and gravy, and that sort of thing, but generally they're for a bit later, when the day has begun to roll and you've already had coffee.

Probably because breakfast *is* soothing and familiar, it is taken at any hour. Many people I know take a certain pleasure in eating pancakes and eggs for supper—certainly my university days included innumerable midnight breakfasts at pancake houses with friends, and long road trips always include breakfast at odd hours. For some families a pancake and egg supper on Sunday night, at the close of the weekend, is a tradition. Brunch is a concept intent on confusing conventions regarding what's eaten when. Teenagers I know don't seem to mind eating muffins or cold cereal just before dinner—or in place of it. Conversely, some of us like eating leftover pasta or vegetable dishes for breakfast, cereal and yogurt for lunch, then a more conventional dinner. Food boundaries are really very flexible.

Early-morning breakfast is the one meal that people tend to be most particular about. Daily breakfast routines don't demand the change and variation we seem to want at lunch or dinner, and when it comes to eggs, people know exactly what they want. One person may be terrified of an uncooked white in a scrambled egg, while another may shudder if it's solidified. The one perfect way to boil an egg or make an omelet is the only way we'll eat it, and that's that.

So this chapter doesn't literally address itself to the first thing you eat in the morning but rather to those foods that are particularly suitable for breakfast no matter the time of day. It also acknowledges Sunday, holiday, or company breakfasts with recipes for breakfast breads—both quick breads and yeasted ones—pancakes, and simple pastries. The egg dishes all make a perfect, fast meal for breakfast, lunch, or dinner. Hot cereals are one of the most satisfying, wholesome, warming-to-body-and-soul foods there are, and there are recipes for some new ones. Then there are a few items that sidle over to brunches, luncheons, and suppers—a delicate cottage cheese pie, and cheese ramekins.

Omelet with Croutons

Instead of having the usual piece of toast alongside eggs, try tucking these crispy fried croutons inside the creamy eggs. The contrasting textures come together in one mouthful. The croutons can also be dried in the oven rather than fried if you prefer to avoid the extra butter. Use a firm, homemade white or whole grain bread.

Makes 1 serving

> *2 to 3 teaspoons butter or light olive oil*
> *1 slice bread, cut into small cubes*
> *2 eggs, beaten*
> *salt*
> *freshly ground pepper*
> *additional butter for the pan*

Melt the butter in a small frying pan, add the bread cubes, and toss them in the butter. Turn them constantly until they are browned and crisp on all sides. Set them aside.

Season the beaten eggs with salt and pepper. Melt additional butter in the pan, add the eggs, and cook them over medium heat. Bring the outer edges of egg into the middle of the pan with a fork and tilt the pan so that fresh wet egg takes its place. When the eggs are as set as you like, scatter the croutons over the top, fold the omelet in thirds, and serve.

Fresh Herb Omelet

Fresh herbs—whether a single branch of marjoram leaves or a handful of mixed herbs—always improve eggs. Parsley and chervil, chives, tarragon, small amounts of lovage, plenty of marjoram, thyme, and torn basil leaves are all good herbs to mix with eggs, though not necessarily all at the same time. Try them in different combinations. It's always safe to include parsley, chervil, and chives and then vary the accents by including one strong, assertive herb, such as lovage or tarragon.

Makes 1 or 2 servings

> *2 tablespoons chopped mixed herbs*
> *2 eggs*
> *2 tablespoons water*
> *salt*
> *freshly ground pepper*
> *2 to 3 teaspoons butter*

Combine the herbs with the eggs and water and lightly beat them together. Season the mixture with salt and pepper. Melt the butter in an omelet pan. When it's hot, add the eggs and, as soon as they begin to set around the edges, gently pull the cooked edges into the middle of the pan, tilting the pan as you do so to allow fresh wet egg to cover the exposed surface. As soon as the eggs are set, fold the omelet into thirds and serve.

■ A little bunch of fresh watercress on the side would make a strong, lively garnish for this omelet.

Sorrel Omelet

Sorrel is an herb that goes perfectly with eggs. Lemony and tart, it adds considerable liveliness to a food that is naturally dense. I like to add a spoonful of warm cream to the omelet, which slightly softens the acidity of the sorrel and seeps into the eggs.

Makes 1 or 2 servings

15 sorrel leaves, stems removed
2 to 3 teaspoons butter
2 eggs
2 tablespoons water
salt
freshly ground pepper
1 to 2 tablespoons cream (optional)

Cut the sorrel leaves into strips, melt half the butter in an omelet pan, and cook the leaves until they have wilted and turned a gray-green color, a minute or 2.

Lightly beat the eggs with the water, season with salt and pepper, and stir in the sorrel. Melt the remaining butter in the omelet pan and, when it is hot, add the eggs. As the edges cook, pull them into the middle of the pan with a fork, tilting the pan as you do so that uncooked egg will flow into its place.

When the eggs are cooked, fold the omelet into thirds and turn it out onto a plate. Return the pan to the heat and add the cream. Bring it to a boil and let it reduce to thicken slightly. Make a slice down the center of the omelet, pour in the cream, and serve.

Squash Blossom Omelet

In the markets of Mexico and Italy one can find enormous golden bouquets of squash blossoms. They are tempting to buy for their beauty alone, but they're also wonderful to cook with, lending not only their color but a delicate squash flavor to eggs, soups, and quesadillas. They can sometimes be found in Italian and Mexican markets in the United States and often at farmers' markets. If you grow your own zucchini or pumpkins, you can start harvesting the blossoms once you've had your fill of squash. If possible, use mostly male flowers so that your vegetable harvest will continue. (The male flowers are attached to stems; the female flowers are attached to their small fruits.)

This omelet is big, flat, and thin so that the yellow petals can be seen and tasted throughout. Serve it with toast or warm tortillas.

Makes 2 to 3 servings

6 to 8 squash blossoms
2 to 3 large basil leaves or 4 parsley branches
3 or 4 eggs
2 tablespoons water
salt
freshly ground pepper
grated Monterey Jack cheese or crumbled Mexican white cheese, queso fresco
2 to 3 teaspoons butter
1 large scallion, thinly sliced

Preheat the broiler. Remove the stems from the blossoms and break off the center parts and discard them. Snip the petals into strips about ½ inch wide. Cut the basil leaves into narrow strips or chop the parsley.

Beat the eggs with the water, season with salt and pepper, and stir in the cheese. Heat half the butter in a 10-inch nonstick pan and add the squash blossoms, basil, and scallion. Cook over a medium heat for several minutes; then stir the mixture into the eggs. Add the remaining butter to the pan and, when it is hot, pour in the eggs. Shake the pan back and forth to loosen the bottom and gently distribute the blossoms with a fork. Cook until the eggs are golden brown on the bottom, then slide the pan under the broiler and lightly brown the top.

Feta Cheese Omelet

The sharp, salty tang of feta cheese really perks up eggs, and oregano or marjoram is an ideal herb to use with both feta and eggs. This makes a handsome flat omelet, finished under the broiler so that the cheese browns lightly. This is a good egg dish for lunch or supper.

Makes 1 or 2 servings

> 1 ounce feta cheese
> 2 eggs
> 2 tablespoons water
> 2 teaspoons chopped oregano or marjoram or ½ teaspoon dried
> 1 to 2 teaspoons olive oil
> freshly ground pepper

Preheat the broiler. Taste the cheese; if it's very salty, rinse it in cold running water. Lightly beat the eggs and water with half the fresh herbs. If you're using dried herbs, crumble them between your fingers into the eggs.

Warm the olive oil in an omelet pan and, when it is hot, pour in the eggs. Shake the pan back and forth a few times to loosen the bottom, then work your way around the pan, raising the cooked egg at the edge of the pan and allowing the uncooked egg to flow underneath onto the pan. After going around the pan once or twice, crumble the feta over the top and continue cooking until the eggs are nearly set on top.

To finish the omelet, set the pan under the broiler and lightly brown the cheese. Scatter the remaining herbs over the top, pepper generously, and serve.

Onion Omelet with Vinegar and Walnuts

If I had to name favorites, this is the omelet I'd choose. I love the sweet, delicate bite of the onions and the lively finish of butter and vinegar, reduced at the last minute to syrupy froth. A teaspoon or so of walnut oil mixed with the onions gives them a rich, nutty flavor, as do the walnuts themselves. This makes a good fall meal, served with an escarole salad and a piece of Gruyère cheese. With such a substantial filling, this omelet works best cooked in a large nonstick pan and finished under the broiler rather than folded.

Makes 2 or 3 servings

> *⅓ cup walnut pieces*
> *a few drops of walnut oil*
> *salt*
> *freshly ground pepper*
> *3 (about ¾ pound) medium-sized onions*
> *2 teaspoons olive oil*
> *1 teaspoon walnut oil*
> *1 tablespoon sherry vinegar*
> *4 or 5 eggs*
> *1 tablespoon chopped parsley*
> *2 teaspoons butter for the pan*
> *1 tablespoon butter*
> *1 tablespoon additional sherry vinegar*

Preheat the oven to 375°F. Toss the walnuts in a few drops of walnut oil, season with a pinch of salt and pepper, and roast on a cookie sheet until they are lightly browned and smell toasty, about 7 minutes. Remove the nuts and turn the oven up to broil.

Slice the onions a little wider than ¼ inch. Warm the olive and peanut oils in a 10-inch skillet and, when hot, add the onions and salt them lightly. Stir immediately to coat the pieces with the oil; then cook over fairly high heat for about 10 minutes, stirring occasionally. Lower the heat, add 1 tablespoon of vinegar, and let it reduce, which it will do in seconds; then remove it from the heat. Season to taste with plenty of pepper.

Break the eggs into a bowl and beat them lightly with a fork to combine them. Season with salt and pepper and stir in the parsley and the cooked onions. Using the same pan, heat the butter and pour in the eggs. Slide the pan back and forth to loosen the bottom, add the walnuts, then cook over medium-low heat until the eggs are set and nicely colored on the bottom. Set the pan under the broiler to finish cooking the top.

Slide the omelet onto a serving plate and return the pan to the stove. Raise the heat and add 1 tablespoon of butter. When it has melted and begun to foam, add the additional tablespoon of vinegar. Slide the pan back and forth and cook briskly until the vinegar is slightly reduced and well combined with the butter, just a few seconds. Pour the vinegar over the eggs and serve.

Green Tomato Omelet

Every fruiting tomato plant has green tomatoes on it, and in late summer or fall, depending on the generosity of your climate, there is always that moment when you realize the remaining tomatoes in the garden aren't going to ripen. You can use green tomatoes in chutneys or in mock apple pies, fry them in cornmeal, or cook them with eggs. Many people consider green tomatoes a delicacy. They're firm, almost crisp, and have a nice acidity that cuts the richness of other foods. Here they're first fried just a little to keep in the juices; then they're covered with the beaten eggs.

Makes 4 to 6 servings

> *1 pound firm green tomatoes, approximately*
> *cornmeal or flour*
> *olive oil or butter for the pan*
> *6 eggs*
> *3 tablespoons chopped scallions*
> *a few basil leaves, torn or finely sliced*
> *salt*
> *freshly ground pepper*

Slice the tomatoes into rounds a little less than ½ inch thick and dredge them in the cornmeal or flour. Heat enough oil in a 10-inch nonstick pan to cover the surface lightly and fry the tomatoes briefly on each side, until they are lightly colored. Don't let them get soft.

Lightly beat the eggs with the scallions and basil and season them with salt and pepper. Pour them over the tomatoes. Let the eggs sit for about a minute, then give the pan a shake to loosen the bottom. Cook over medium-low heat until the eggs are nicely colored on the bottom, then slide the omelet out onto a large plate. Place the pan over it, invert, and return it to the heat to cook the other side. Turn the omelet out onto a serving plate and serve, hot or tepid, cut into wedges.

Artichoke and Parsley Frittata

This Italian-style omelet can be cooked either at the last minute and served warm or, to make it easier on the cook, ahead of time and served at room temperature. The artichokes, which have a meaty flavor and texture, are first fried in olive oil with pepper and parsley and then cooked with the eggs. This would make a good dish for a late-morning breakfast or for a picnic, with a pile of pickled red onion rings on the side.

Use a nonstick frying pan or an omelet pan that is well seasoned, to keep the eggs from sticking.

Makes 1 frittata, serving 4 to 6

> *3 large artichokes*
> *juice of 1 large lemon*
> *3 to 5 tablespoons olive oil*
> *1 large garlic clove, sliced*
> *salt*
> *15 peppercorns, coarsely ground in a mortar*
> *½ cup finely chopped parsley*
> *6 to 8 eggs, lightly beaten*
> *½ cup coarsely grated Romano cheese*

Break off the hard outer leaves of the artichokes; then cut off the top two thirds of the greens. Trim the outsides, cut the artichokes into quarters, and immediately put them in a bowl with cold water to cover and the lemon juice. Remove the choke from each piece with a knife; then thinly slice each quarter into 3 or 4 pieces and return them to the water. Just before cooking, remove the pieces from the water and blot them dry with a towel.

Heat 2 or 3 tablespoons of the olive oil in an 8-inch frying pan with the garlic. When the garlic colors, remove it and then add the drained artichokes. Give the pan a shake right away to coat the pieces with oil, then season with salt and pepper and add about 2 tablespoons of the parsley. Sauté until the artichokes are browned and thoroughly cooked.

Beat the eggs, season them lightly with salt, and add the rest of the parsley, the cheese, and the cooked artichokes. Wipe out the pan, add enough of the remaining oil just to coat the bottom, and pour in the eggs. Give the pan a shake to loosen the eggs, then lower the heat. Cook, covered, until the bottom is golden. Slide the frittata onto a plate, then turn it back into the pan, with the opposite side down, and continue to cook until it is also nicely colored. Serve the frittata warm or at room temperature, sliced into wedges.

Scrambled Eggs and Corn in Tortillas

Wrapped in a hot tortilla with some grated cheese, given a few hard splashes of Smoked Chili Salsa (page 320), these eggs make a fast and zesty meal. The safflower stamens, sometimes erroneously sold as saffron, can usually be found in the Mexican section of supermarkets. They give a nice color to the eggs, but if you can't find them, just leave them out.

Makes 1 serving

> 2 to 3 teaspoons butter, safflower oil, or sunflower oil
> 2 scallions, including some of the firm green parts, chopped
> 5 cilantro sprigs, chopped
> 1 ear of corn or ⅓ cup frozen corn, defrosted
> a healthy pinch or 2 of safflower stamens
> 2 eggs, lightly beaten
> 2 tablespoons water
> salt
> 1 large flour or 2 small corn tortillas
> grated Monterey Jack or Muenster cheese
> smoked chili salsa (page 320)

Melt the butter in an 8-inch pan and add the scallions, cilantro, corn, and safflower stamens. Cook for a minute or so, or until the corn is tender. Beat the eggs with the water and salt, pour them into the pan, and scramble them gently with a fork. Warm the tortillas in a dry cast-iron or nonstick pan. Transfer the tortillas to a plate and ladle the eggs over them. Sprinkle the cheese and as much salsa as you like over the eggs.

Variations: In lieu of salsa, mince half of a seeded jalapeño pepper and stir it into the eggs. Or use roasted sichuan pepper salt (page 330) to flavor the eggs—it tastes wonderful with eggs, corn, and chili.

Cottage Cheese and Cheese Pie

If you're handy with crusts or have one on hand in the freezer, this can be put together very quickly. The filling is made with dry-curd cottage cheese bound with eggs and enriched with mild cheese—Monterey Jack, Muenster, a mild cheddar, or something richer. If you're making your own crust, include a portion of whole wheat flour; the nutty flavor goes especially well with the cheese.

The simplicity of this pie makes it a soothing morning dish to serve with strawberry preserves or an accompaniment of fresh fruit. Later in the day it would be good with something full of color and bite, such as the Asparagus with Peanut Oil, Shallots, and Parsley (page 175), one of the seasonal vegetable stews or grilled vegetables.

Makes 4 to 6 servings as a main course or 8 servings as an appetizer

> *1 unbaked 9-inch pie shell (recipe follows)*
> *1½ cups grated mild cheese such as Muenster, Monterey Jack,*
>   *or Bel Paese or 1 cup grated cheese and ½ cup ricotta*
> *2 cups dry-curd cottage cheese*
> *3 eggs*
> *½ cup milk*
> *¼ teaspoon salt*
> *1 tablespoon flour*
> *several gratings of nutmeg*
> *freshly ground pepper*
> *dash of paprika*

If you're using the pie crust recipe below, prepare it and set it in the freezer until the dough is firm, about 10 minutes. Preheat the oven to 400°F.

Put the crust directly from the freezer into the oven on the lowest rack and bake for 10 minutes or until the crust is set. Check it after about 5 minutes; if the crust has swollen, deflate it by poking it with the tip of a knife. Remove the crust from the oven and scatter some of the grated cheese lightly over the bottom.

Put the cottage cheese and the ricotta, if you're using it, in a food processor with the eggs and work until smooth. Add the milk, salt, and flour and process for another 10 seconds or so. Stir in the remaining grated cheese and season to taste with the nutmeg and pepper.

Pour the filling into the shell and shake a little paprika over the top. Set the pie in the middle of the oven, lower the heat to 375°F, and bake until the custard is set, a knife inserted in the center comes out clean, and the top is nicely colored— about 35 minutes. Let the pie rest for 10 minutes before serving it.

WHOLE WHEAT PIE CRUST

Your crust will come out flakier if you make it by hand rather than in a food processor. With the food processor it's too easy to overmix the shortening and the flour; if you do use one, be sure to use just very short pulses to work the fat into the flour and then add the water by hand.

½ cup whole wheat pastry flour
1 cup unbleached white flour
½ teaspoon salt
¼ cup butter
¼ cup shortening
3 to 4 tablespoons cold water

Combine the flours and salt in a bowl. Cut in the butter and shortening with 2 knives or work it lightly between your fingertips until it resembles a coarse meal. Sprinkle half the water over the mixture and mix it in lightly with a fork. Keep adding water slowly just until the pastry will hold together when pressed gently with your hands. Gather it into a ball.

Dust the counter with flour and gently flatten the ball into a disk. Keep it round by patting it around the edges and dust the top lightly with flour. Start rolling it out from the center, turning the dough as you go and lifting it from the counter to make sure it's not sticking. If it is, add a little more flour to the surface. Roll it into a circle about 2 inches larger than the pan. Fold it into quarters, lift it into the pan, and unfold it. Settle it into the pan, making sure it fully covers the bottom, but don't stretch it. Trim off the uneven pieces of dough and then crimp the edge, making an attractive rim. Set the finished crust in the freezer to harden. If you're not going to use it right away, cover it securely with foil.

Cheese Ramekins

Cheese ramekins have the light and airy charm of soufflés but are slightly sturdier, holding their cloud of air for at least a few minutes. They are quick to put together and have the irresistible fragrance of melting cheese.

The flavor of these ramekins comes from the singular characteristics of the cheese you use. Gruyère and Fontina cheeses are sweet and nutty. Cheddar is less elusive but has a strong, familiar taste that goes wonderfully with tomatoes. Goat cheese is subtle and fragrant, wonderful with thyme. I've found many times that people who think they don't like goat cheese love it when it's baked like this.

Although the word *ramekin* refers to the small porcelain baking dish as well as to what's baked inside it, one need not be limited to a particular container. The same batter bakes beautifully in shallow dishes—and cooks more quickly. You could also use a prebaked tart shell as the container and bake the soufflé as a large, beautiful tart. Use 6 ½-cup ramekins or soufflé dishes, a baking dish measuring about 8 by 10 inches, or a 10-inch prebaked tart shell.

Makes 4 generous or 6 modest servings

THE BASIC RECIPE

butter for the baking dishes
2 to 3 tablespoons freshly grated Parmesan cheese
1⅓ cups milk or water
½ small onion, cut into large pieces
1 bay leaf
½ teaspoon chopped thyme leaves or pinch of dried
1 parsley branch
½ teaspoon salt
5 eggs
5 ounces (about 1½ cups) cheese such as Gruyère,
*   Fontina, cheddar, or goat cheese*
¼ cup butter
5 tablespoons unbleached white flour

Preheat the oven to 400°F. Generously butter the ramekins or baking dish and shake the grated Parmesan against the sides to coat them. Slowly heat the milk or water in a saucepan with the onion, bay leaf, thyme, parsley, and salt. While the milk is heating and steeping, separate the eggs, beat the whites into firm peaks, and grate or crumble the cheese.

When the milk boils, turn off the heat and let the milk stand for at least 15 minutes for the flavors to develop; then pour it through a strainer and return it to the pan. Add the butter and heat until the butter is melted. Remove the pan from the burner and dump in the flour all at once. Whisk it vigorously, return the pan to the burner, lower the heat, and stir until the mixture is thick and smooth.

Remove the pan from the burner and add the egg yolks one at a time, beating well until each is completely incorporated; then stir in the cheese. Don't worry about getting it to melt thoroughly.

Check the egg whites, beating them again if they've started to liquefy in the bottom of the bowl. Stir a quarter of them into the mixture to lighten it. Then fold in the rest. Take care not to deflate the whites; little chunks of whites are fine.

Divide the batter among the ramekins or pour it into the baking dish or prebaked pie shell. Bake in the oven until puffed and browned—about 20 minutes for the ramekins, flat baking dishes, or pie shell; 5 or 10 minutes longer for a single large soufflé dish. Serve the ramekins the moment they are done.

Creamy Rice

White rice with milk is one of the most soothing, comforting foods I know. It can consist of just a bowl of dinner rice with milk poured over it or this luxurious version, in which rice is cooked slowly in milk. When done, it is thick and creamy, like a rice pudding, and naturally sweet from the sugars in the milk. Serve it with additional milk, a pat of butter, and a sprinkling of brown sugar if desired.

Makes 4 servings

> *1 cup short-grain white rice*
> *2 cups water*
> *salt*
> *¼ teaspoon ground cinnamon*
> *a few gratings of nutmeg*
> *3 cups milk*

Bring the rice and 1 cup of the water to a boil in a saucepan. Simmer until the water is absorbed, then add the second cup of water, a pinch of salt, the spices, and the milk. Bring to a boil, then cook over very low heat, stirring occasionally, until the milk is absorbed, about 45 minutes. Serve right away.

■ If left to cool, the rice will become completely firm. To reheat it, just thin it with a cup or so of water and reheat it in a pan. Eventually it will break apart and become creamy and smooth.

Couscous for Breakfast

Couscous has the familiar, comforting taste of cream of wheat, but more texture, for those who like a little more challenge in the morning. Diced prunes go wonderfully with couscous, and so would dates and raisins. Cook the couscous in milk or water; the milk will give it a richer, creamier texture.

Naturally, before going to work no one would go through the elaborate process of steaming couscous, so use the instant variety. You stir it into the milk or water, turn off the heat, and by the time you've showered, it's done. Serve it with a little brown sugar, milk, and a pat of butter if desired.

Makes 2 servings

> 2 cups milk or water or a mixture
> salt
> ¼ teaspoon ground cinnamon
> 1 cup instant couscous
> 6 prunes, cut into quarters

Bring the milk or water to a boil in a saucepan. Add a pinch of salt and the cinnamon. Pour in the couscous, lower the heat, add the prunes, and stir for 30 seconds. Turn off the heat, cover the pot, and let it stand for 7 or 8 minutes, until the liquid is absorbed.

Wild Rice Cereal with Currants or Raisins

A mixture of wild and white rice cooked with raisins makes an unusual and hearty morning cereal. The currants may make it sweet enough, but if not, add a sprinkling of brown sugar and pour milk or cream over all.

Makes 4 servings

> ⅓ *cup wild rice*
> ⅓ *cup short-grain white rice*
> *2 tablespoons dried currants or raisins*
> ¼ *teaspoon salt*
> *1 quart water*

Rinse both rices well and put them in a saucepan with the rest of the ingredients. Bring to a boil, then cover partially and simmer until the wild rice is tender, about 40 minutes.

This will make a fairly dry rice, one without much extra liquid. If you prefer it to be wetter, just add more water or even milk while it's cooking.

Cornmeal Cereal with Vanilla

A sweet and different way to eat cornmeal for breakfast. It's how my dad used to make it, and it's as nice now as when I was a kid.

Makes 4 cups

> *1 quart water*
> *1 cup fine yellow cornmeal*
> *salt*
> *2 teaspoons vanilla extract*

Bring 3 cups of the water to a boil in a heavy saucepan and mix the fourth cup with the cornmeal to make a slurry to help prevent lumps from forming. Once the water has come to a boil, whisk the slurry into the water. Add salt to taste and the vanilla and cook over very low heat or in a double boiler, stirring occasionally, until the cereal is amply thickened and cooked—about 5 minutes for a finely ground cornmeal; longer if the cornmeal is a rougher grind. Serve the cereal with brown sugar and milk.

Blue Corn Mush

I first ate blue corn at the Hopi Cultural Center on Second Mesa more than 10 years ago, a few years before it was "discovered." It was cooked like cornmeal mush, molded in a bread pan, and then sliced and fried. It was delicious, with a clear corn flavor and that odd purple-blue color. Now that it's made its way into the larger culture, there are many sophisticated recipes for blue cornmeal, but I still like this one for its utter simplicity. It's good just the way they served it at the cultural center, with eggs and bacon, but it can also be enjoyed with butter and syrup or served alongside a dish of Squash, Pepper, and Hominy Stew, (page 122).

Makes 6 servings

> 1 quart water
> salt
> 1½ cups blue cornmeal
> butter or cooking oil for frying

Bring the water to a boil in a saucepan, add salt to taste, and whisk in the cornmeal. Lower the heat and stir the cornmeal for 10 minutes or until it tastes done. The coarser the meal, the longer it will take. Pour the cooked cereal onto a cookie sheet or into a bread pan and set it aside to cool for an hour or so or until firm. Once it has cooled, slice it into pieces for frying. Fry the slices in butter or oil in a nonstick pan until lightly crisped on both sides. If this is to be eaten as a savory, sprinkle a little red chili or paprika on top just before serving.

Pecan-Oat Muffins

Aside from its healthful virtues, whatever they may be, I find oat bran a pleasure to cook with. It has a mild, nutty taste and contributes texture and flavor to baked goods without taking over the way wheat bran tends to. These muffins can be made Sunday-morning special by adding the streusel topping.

It doesn't take much sugar to obscure the natural sweetness of grains. The amount in this recipe is sufficient to my taste, but those who like a sweeter muffin can add more, as much as ½ cup.

Makes 12 muffins

> 1½ cups buttermilk
> 1 cup oat bran
> 2 eggs
> ¼ cup light brown sugar
> ½ teaspoon vanilla extract
> 3 tablespoons canola oil or melted butter
> ⅓ cup oat flour or whole wheat pastry flour
> ¾ cup whole wheat pastry or unbleached white flour
> ¼ cup finely chopped walnuts or pecans
> 1 teaspoon baking soda
> ½ teaspoon salt

Preheat the oven to 375°F. Mix the buttermilk and the oat bran together and set aside while you assemble the rest of the ingredients.

In another bowl, lightly beat the eggs with the brown sugar, vanilla, and oil or melted butter. Mix the flours, nuts, baking soda, and salt together. Combine the buttermilk-bran mixture with the eggs, then stir in the dry ingredients lightly with a fork. Don't overmix the batter.

Make the streusel topping. Lightly grease the muffin tins or line them with paper. Fill them half full, scatter the streusel over the top, and bake the muffins in the center of the oven until risen and lightly browned on top, about 25 minutes.

STREUSEL TOPPING

> 2 tablespoons butter
> 3 tablespoons chopped pecans
> ¼ cup light brown sugar
> ½ teaspoon freshly grated nutmeg or ground cinnamon
> ⅓ cup unbleached white flour

Mix everything together with your fingertips until crumbs are formed.

Cottage Cheese and Currant Pancakes

Plumped currants or raisins fleck these tender pancakes like little morsels of sugar. Serve the pancakes with powdered sugar and a wedge of lemon, plus extra sour cream if desired.

Makes 20 3-inch pancakes

> 1 cup dried currants or raisins
> 1 cup cottage cheese, dry-curd if possible
> 1 cup sour cream or ricotta cream cheese (page 353)
> 5 large eggs
> 1 teaspoon vanilla extract
> 1 teaspoon grated lemon zest
> several gratings of nutmeg
> 1 tablespoon sugar
> 1 cup unbleached white flour
> 1½ teaspoons baking powder
> ¼ teaspoon salt
> butter for frying

Unless the currants or raisins are soft, cover them with very hot water and set them aside to plump up while you make the batter.

Whisk the cottage cheese and sour cream together; then beat in the eggs one at a time. Stir in the vanilla, lemon zest, nutmeg, and sugar; then add the flour, baking powder, and salt. Stir gently to combine without overmixing.

Melt a tablespoon of butter in a wide frying pan and, when it's hot, drop in the batter by spoonfuls. Cook over medium heat until browned on the bottom; then flip once and cook until lightly colored on the other side.

Popped Millet Griddle Cakes or Waffles

These griddle cakes are really a delight—high and golden, with the satisfying taste of corn and the unexpected crunchy bite of popped millet. The millet is toasted in a skillet until the little grains begin to pop. You can hear them pop more easily than you can see them, though if you look closely, they look like miniature popcorn. These cakes are wonderful served with sorghum, honey, or molasses, and a luxurious dollop of sour cream or the Mexican cream, *natas*.

Makes approximately 12 3-inch pancakes

> ½ cup whole millet
> 1 cup unbleached white flour
> ½ cup corn flour or stone-ground cornmeal
> ½ teaspoon baking soda
> 1 teaspoon baking powder
> ¼ teaspoon salt
> 1 tablespoon sugar
> 2 large eggs
> 1½ cups buttermilk
> 1 teaspoon vanilla extract
> 2 tablespoons vegetable oil or melted butter
> butter for the pan

Cover the millet with hot water and set it aside while you assemble the rest of the ingredients.

Put the dry ingredients in a bowl and mix them together. Beat the eggs in another bowl and stir in the buttermilk, vanilla, and oil. Pour the liquids into the dry ingredients and gently whisk them together until well combined.

Strain the millet and put it in a wide skillet over medium heat. The water will steam, softening the grains; then the millet will dry and begin to toast. Gently shake the pan back and forth, as if you're making popcorn. When it begins to pop and smell toasty, stir it into the batter.

Melt a small piece of butter in a nonstick skillet. When the pan is hot, add about ¼ cup of batter, cook over medium heat until holes begin to appear on the surface, then gently turn the pancake over and cook on the other side. For lighter pancakes, resist any temptation to pat them down with a spatula or turn them more than once.

To make waffles, separate the eggs and beat the whites until they form soft but firm peaks. Stir a third of them into the batter to lighten it, then fold in the rest. The batter will make 6 waffles.

Wild Rice and Ricotta Fritters

Not too sweet and very light, these small fritters have the pleasing chewy texture and nutty taste of wild rice. Brown basmati or other brown rice would also have plenty of character and be delicious treated the same way. Serve these fritters with honey or syrup, a squeeze of lemon juice, a dollop of sour cream, or whatever you fancy. These cakes are very moist.

Makes 8 3-inch fritters

> *1 cup ricotta cheese*
> *3 egg yolks*
> *½ teaspoon salt*
> *1 to 2 tablespoons sugar*
> *¼ cup melted butter*
> *1 tablespoon grated lemon zest*
> *¼ cup whole wheat pastry flour*
> *3 egg whites*
> *1½ cups cooked wild rice*

Beat the ricotta with the egg yolks, salt, and sugar until smooth; then stir in the melted butter, lemon zest, and flour. Beat the egg whites until they hold soft peaks; then fold them into the batter. Gently fold in the rice.

Heat a griddle or large skillet; then lower the heat. Drop the batter into small cakes and smooth them out with the back of the spoon to make circles. Cook until browned on the bottom; then flip and cook the other side.

Whole Wheat Buttermilk Biscuits

Buttermilk biscuits aren't so unusual—you can find a recipe nearly anywhere—but when made with good flour they are very special. I was reminded of this when given a gift of several pounds of flour made from wheat grown and ground by a farmer in Kansas. Coarsely textured and sweet-smelling, it made the most satisfying biscuits you can imagine, and I treasured this flour as much as expensive vials of saffron. Its good flavor, nutty and complex, derived from the fact that it included the bran and the germ and was fresh. Your local natural foods store may be a source of good flour, or you may be inspired to grind your own. These biscuits feel nourishing. They make a good breakfast or, with a salad or soup, complete a light meal. Bake these on a cookie sheet or directly on a baking stone.

Makes approximately 12 biscuits

> 2 cups whole wheat flour or 1 cup each whole
>   wheat and unbleached white flour
> ½ teaspoon salt
> 2 teaspoons baking powder
> ½ teaspoon baking soda
> 1 teaspoon sugar
> ½ cup butter
> ⅔ cup buttermilk

Preheat the oven to 400°F. If you're using a baking stone, put it in the oven to warm. Combine the dry ingredients in a bowl and toss them together with your hands to make sure any lumps of soda are broken up. (A sifter will be useless as the bran will get separated.) Cut in the butter using 2 knives, a pastry cutter, or your fingers. Work it until it is well dispersed among the dry ingredients; then pour in the buttermilk and lightly stir together with a fork.

Dust your board or counter with flour and turn out the dough. Knead just enough to bring it together, about a dozen times, then roll or pat it into a circle or rectangle about ½ inch thick. Cut out round biscuits or cut the dough into rectangles. Gather together the scraps to make an additional biscuit or 2.

Place the biscuits directly on the baking stone or a cookie sheet and bake until risen, firm, and lightly browned—about 15 minutes.

Scottish Oat Scones

These scones have a fine, delicate crumb and a good, wholesome flavor. Oat flour can be found in health food stores and increasingly in supermarkets. The cream is partly responsible for the tender crumb, but if if it's not in your diet plan, use milk in its place.

More often than not, when I go to put something in the oven, I find I've left my baking stone there from earlier bread baking. Rather than pull it out hot and try to find a place for it, I use it, and I've found that it works quite well for practically everything, especially scones and biscuits.

Makes 8 triangular scones

> 1 cup unbleached white or whole wheat pastry flour
> ½ cup oat flour
> ½ cup rolled oats
> ½ teaspoon salt
> 1 teaspoon baking powder
> 1 tablespoon light brown sugar
> ¼ cup butter
> 1 egg
> ½ cup cream or milk
> ¼ teaspoon vanilla extract
> 1 tablespoon additional cream or milk for glaze
> 1 tablespoon additional sugar for glaze

Preheat the oven to 375°F. If you're using a baking stone, put it in the oven at the same time so that it can heat through. Mix all the dry ingredients together in a mixing bowl; then cut in the butter until it is well dispersed and the dough is the texture of coarse cornmeal. Lightly beat together the egg, cream, and vanilla. Pour them into the dry ingredients and stir quickly and lightly with a fork to bring the dough together. Turn it out onto a floured board and gently knead it for about a half-minute; then roll or pat the dough into a circle about ½ inch thick.

Mix an additional tablespoon each of cream and sugar together and brush the mixture over the top of the dough. Cut the circle into eighths and bake the scones directly on the baking stone or a cookie sheet until puffed and browned on top, about 25 minutes. Serve them warm, sliced down the middle, with butter and marmalade, jam, or honey.

Buttermilk Skillet Corn Bread

Many corn breads are dry and crumbly, but this one is moist and tender, with a very thin band of custard just under the surface. Made with milk, it's a good everyday corn bread. But my friend Marion Cunningham makes a version with cream poured over the top that is really luscious!

You can make this bread with white, yellow, or blue cornmeal—all are good. What's important is to use a meal that includes the germ—it's healthier and has a lot more flavor than overrefined meals. Whole cornmeal, which is usually stone-ground, can be found in health food stores. Baking the bread in a skillet, while not essential, looks wonderful, and the thick iron walls help to make a good crust on the sides.

This is a savory bread, good to serve alongside bean and chili stews. Sometimes when I'm making this for breakfast, I double the sugar and include a teaspoon of vanilla extract for a sweeter morning bread.

Though this makes eight servings, everyone will take seconds; so plan on serving only four.

Makes 8 servings

> 1⅓ *cups stone-ground cornmeal*
> ⅓ *cup whole wheat pastry or unbleached white flour*
> 1 *teaspoon baking soda*
> ½ *teaspoon salt*
> 2 *tablespoons sugar*
> 1 *cup buttermilk*
> 2 *cups milk or 1 cup milk and 1 cup cream*
> 3 *eggs, slightly beaten*
> 2 *tablespoons butter*

Preheat the oven to 350°F. Combine the cornmeal, flour, soda, salt, and sugar in a bowl and mix them together with a spoon. In another bowl, whisk together the buttermilk, 1 cup of the regular milk, and the eggs. Melt the butter in the skillet, spread it around the sides with a brush, and then pour the excess into the wet ingredients.

Combine the wet and dry ingredients and lightly stir them together with a fork. Pour the batter into the skillet, pour the remaining milk (or cream) over the top, and bake until the corn bread is lightly browned on the surface and springs back when touched, about 45 minutes. Serve warm with honey and butter.

Pear Coffee Cake

Two flavors that always go beautifully with pears are almond and cardamom, and this sour cream coffee cake has both. The pears are cut into small pieces and worked right into the batter. Warm from the oven, this makes a pretty luxurious start to any Sunday morning.

Makes 1 9-by-13-inch coffee cake serving 6 to 8

> ½ cup butter
> ¾ cup sugar
> 2 eggs
> 1 teaspoon vanilla extract
> ½ teaspoon almond extract
> ½ teaspoon freshly ground cardamom or ¾ teaspoon powdered
> 2 cups unbleached white flour
> 1 teaspoon baking powder
> ¼ teaspoon baking soda
> ¼ teaspoon salt
> ½ cup sour cream
> 1 large Bartlett or Comice pear, peeled and cut into ½-inch pieces

Preheat the oven to 375°F and lightly grease a 9-by-13-inch baking pan. Make the topping below.

Cream the butter with the sugar until lightly colored, then beat in the eggs one at a time. Stir in the vanilla, almond, and cardamom. Sift the dry ingredients together and add them to the butter mixture, alternating with the sour cream, taking care not to overmix the batter. Stir in the pears. Spread the thick batter in the pan and cover with the topping. Bake until the top is golden brown all over, about 40 minutes. Cut the cake into pieces and serve it warm.

THE TOPPING

> 2 tablespoons butter
> 2 tablespoons almond paste
> ½ cup brown sugar
> ½ cup finely chopped walnuts
> ½ teaspoon ground cardamom

Work everything together with your fingers or in a food processor to make a crumbly paste.

Cheese Stöllen (A Quick Bread)

A friend gave me this recipe, and I've changed it only by adding plenty of pistachio nuts for their uplifting color and taste. Ample and impressive with its fine aroma and delicate, rich crumb, this is a wonderful quick bread to have in your repertoire. If you use candied fruits that you've prepared yourself, it will be even better; candied grapefruit is especially good. I find this stöllen comes out as well when made in a mixer as when made by hand, which speeds the process. It can easily be mixed and baked the morning you plan to serve it, and leftover bread makes delicious toast.

You can either bake this stöllen in a bread pan or, with the addition of a little more flour, you can shape it into the traditional folded crescent and bake it on a baking stone or cookie sheet. If you have leftover batter due to a too-small bread pan, bake the extra in little ramekins or a miniature loaf pan.

Makes 1 large loaf serving 6 to 8

> ½ cup butter, at room temperature
> ½ cup sugar
> 1 tablespoon grated lemon zest
> 1 teaspoon grated orange zest
> 1 teaspoon almond extract
> 1 large egg
> 2 egg yolks
> 1 cup ricotta cheese
> 1 cup plain yogurt or low-fat cottage cheese
>
> ½ cup golden raisins
> ½ cup black raisins
> ¾ cup chopped candied grapefruit peels (page 396), or a
>   mixture of different citrus peels
> ⅓ cup pine nuts, walnuts, or almonds
> ¼ cup peeled and roughly chopped unsalted pistachio nuts
>
> 3 cups unbleached white flour
> 2 teaspoons baking powder
> ½ teaspoon baking soda
> ½ teaspoon salt
>
> powdered sugar
> lemon juice (optional)

Preheat the oven to 350°F. Butter and flour a large bread pan. By hand or in a mixer, cream the butter with the sugar until it is light and fluffy. Add the zest, almond extract, and the egg and egg yolks, one at a time. When well mixed, add the ricotta cheese and the yogurt or cottage cheese and continue mixing until well incorporated.

Combine the fruits and nuts in a bowl. In another bowl, sift together the dry ingredients. With the mixer running, add half the fruits; then gradually add half the flour. When it is mixed in, add the rest of the fruit; then, again gradually, add the remaining flour. Continue mixing until everything is well combined, but don't overwork. The batter will be quite dense. If you're mixing by hand, you might prefer to flour a counter, turn out the dough, and knead it as if it were a yeast dough.

Turn the dough into the prepared pan or baking sheet and bake for 1 hour and 15 minutes. Although it may look done sooner, it's a moist dough with the addition of the cheeses and needs the full baking time to be actually cooked. Dust the stöllen with powdered sugar or drizzle a simple icing of powdered sugar mixed with lemon juice over the top.

Cardamom Holiday Bread

When I first discovered cardamom, I used it in everything, but I think I liked it best—and still do—in this bread. The sweetened dough, studded with raisins, is rich and tender with butter and eggs. The woven surface is varnished golden, covered with pine nuts or almonds and little squares of sugar. It's just the thing to have on Christmas morning or with tea in the afternoon. Leftover cardamom bread makes superlative bread puddings and French toast; it's worth keeping that in mind and making the full amount.

This is a lovely dough to knead by hand. It's soft and silky to the touch with fragrant whispers of cardamom coming toward you with every push.

Makes 3 1-pound loaves or 2 braided wreaths

> *1½ cups milk*
> *½ cup butter*
> *1½ teaspoons freshly ground cardamom*
> *½ cup sugar*
> *1 teaspoon salt*
> *grated zest of 1 lemon*
> *1 ¼-ounce package active dry yeast*
> *1 cup golden raisins*
> *3 eggs*
> *6 cups or more unbleached white flour*
> *¼ cup pine nuts or slivered almonds, approximately*
> *sugar squares or crystal sugar, if available*

Heat the milk with the butter, cardamom, sugar, salt, and lemon zest. Stir occasionally until the butter is melted and the sugar is dissolved. When the milk has cooled to lukewarm, stir in the yeast and let the mixture stand for 10 minutes or until the yeast is nice and foamy.

While the milk is cooling, cover the raisins with warm water, let them stand until the yeast is finished proofing, and then pour off the water and gently squeeze out any excess.

Lightly beat the eggs together with a fork, set aside a few spoonfuls for the glaze, and add the remainder to the milk and yeast mixture along with the raisins. Next begin adding the flour, whisking it in to make a smooth batter until it becomes too thick; then change to a wooden spoon and continue adding flour until

it is again too thick, at which point you can turn the dough out onto a floured surface and begin kneading. Work in more flour as is necessary to keep it from sticking. Knead for at least 7 minutes, until the dough is smooth and shiny; then set it aside in a bowl that has been lightly filmed with butter or a flavorless oil. Rub a little of the butter or oil over the top; then cover with a damp towel or plastic wrap and set it aside in a warm place to rise until doubled in bulk. When the dough has risen, turn it out onto the counter.

To make braids, divide the dough for each bread into 3 equal pieces; then roll each piece into a long rope, about ½ inch thick. Braid the ropes tightly together, crossing them first in the middle and then working out from both ends. Leave the braid long and straight, bend it to make a circle, or curve it gently into a horseshoe shape, drawing the ends up toward the middle together, like a pretzel. Set the breads on a cookie sheet.

To make loaves, butter 3 bread pans. Divide the dough into 3 pieces and press each piece into a rectangle roughly the length of the pan. Roll it up, pinch the seam together, and place the dough seam side down in the pan.

Brush the reserved beaten egg over the surface, press in the pine nuts or almond slivers, and sprinkle the surface with the sugar squares. Loosely cover the breads and set them aside again to rise until about doubled in bulk, about 45 minutes.

While the breads are rising, preheat the oven to 350°F. Just before putting them in the oven, look at the breads and see if the dough has expanded so that some areas are now unglazed and unsugared. Brush some more glaze on these areas and cover them with a sprinkling of sugar and more pine nuts. Bake the breads until they are a deep golden brown on top, about 40 minutes. Allow them to cool on cooling racks.

Finishing Touches

Sauces, Salsas, and Condiments

These pantry items are the intensely flavored condiments that can bring an ordinary dish to life and make its personality sparkle. A smoky-flavored salsa to enhance a black bean soup, a pungent olive sauce to toss with pasta or spread on toast, the sweet-tart bite of a chutney to complement the hot flavors of a curry, Chinese pepper salt to sprinkle over eggs—these are the small items that transform and complete other foods. They are the vibrant dash of color in a more subtle landscape.

These flavored butters, sauces, salsas, pastes, and fruit preserves can be made at the last minute, but they all keep well, for at least a week, and many will keep more or less indefinitely. Once you have them on hand, you'll have the power of a quick-change artist. Having an array of condiments in your pantry will allow you to put together a number of unusual and tasty foods quickly and easily or to finish a dish with a flourish.

Herb Butters

Butters infused with the flavors and scents of herbs do a great deal for whatever they touch—simple steamed vegetables, grilled vegetables, and more neutral-tasting foods like pasta, potatoes, rice dishes, and beans. They can also be spread on bread or toast, and a spoonful can finish a simple soup or flavor an omelet.

Herb butters are particularly useful to have on hand. Because they are so aromatic, they extend the effectiveness of their rich medium—butter—and smaller quantities are needed. They can be made in quantity, rolled into cylinders, and frozen; then you can cut off pieces as needed. When they're sliced into rounds, they reveal beautiful markings, especially when herb blossoms have been included.

An herb butter gains its character with the single taste of one herb like lovage, dill, basil, or rosemary or a mixture of compatible herbs—parsley or chervil mixed with chives, tarragon, and thyme. Wonderful butters can also be made with dried, powdered herbs and spices; for example, the Spicy Moroccan Butter.

When you're making herb butters, start with unsalted butter for the best results. Two or 3 tablespoons of chopped herbs should be enough for ¼ pound of butter, depending on their strength. A very assertive herb like rosemary should be used in smaller quantities than a more delicate one, like chervil. Some fine lemon zest and a few drops of lemon juice give a sharp note that supports the flavors of the herbs. Finely diced shallots and pepper can also be included. Endless combinations are possible. Try what captures your fancy.

Here are some butters that I use often.

Butter with Fines Herbes and Garlic

A classic herb butter with a mixture of familiar herbs—excellent with all vegetables and stirred into soups.

Makes ½ cup

½ cup unsalted butter, at room temperature
3 tablespoons finely chopped mixed fresh parsley,
*   chervil, tarragon, chives, and oregano*
1 teaspoon lemon juice
1 large shallot, finely diced
1 garlic clove, minced to a purée
freshly ground pepper

Work the herbs into the butter and gradually add the lemon juice. Stir in the shallot, garlic, and pepper.

Lovage Butter

The wild celerylike taste of lovage comes through clearly in this green-flecked butter. Lovage is delicious with anything made with potatoes and makes an interesting variation on the baked-potato-with-butter theme. It's also good in a sandwich of tomatoes and cucumbers or simply spread on whole wheat bread.

Makes ½ cup

½ cup unsalted butter, at room temperature
3 tablespoons chopped lovage leaves and small shoots
1 shallot, finely diced
a few pinches of grated lemon zest
lemon juice
freshly ground pepper

Cream the butter until soft and light; then work in the lovage and shallot. Stir in the lemon zest, a few drops of lemon juice, and pepper to taste.

Rosemary Butter with Sage and Juniper

These herbs lend a robust taste to the butter that's especially appropriate for winter. It's excellent with roast potatoes. This is a strong infusion of tastes; a little will go a long way.

Makes ½ cup

> *½ cup unsalted butter, at room temperature*
> *1 tablespoon finely chopped rosemary leaves*
> *2 teaspoons finely chopped sage leaves*
> *12 juniper berries, pounded*
> *freshly ground pepper*
> *1 or 2 garlic cloves, pounded until smooth (optional)*

Cream the butter until soft; then stir in the rest of the ingredients. Add the garlic if you wish.

Blossom Butter

Herb blossoms mixed with the fragrant leaves make a beautiful butter that is also very good. Stir this into something plain, like pasta or white beans or rice, where the colors will be as noticeable as the taste.

Makes ½ cup

> *½ cup unsalted butter, at room temperature*
> *2 to 3 tablespoons finely sliced or chopped mixed fresh basil,*
> *   particularly opal basil, marjoram or oregano, chives, and thyme*
> *2 tablespoons chives, basil, sage, rosemary, borage, thyme,*
> *   or calendula blossoms, cut into large pieces*
> *several pinches of freshly ground white pepper*

Cream the butter with the herbs and the cut blossoms until well mixed. Wrap well and let stand until needed or freeze. This butter looks particularly beautiful when rolled into a cylinder and then sliced. All the flecks of color are streaked throughout.

Nasturtium Butter

The chopped blossoms—particularly a harvest of yellow, orange, and scarlet nasturtiums—look quite extraordinary in this butter, but they also make it taste nice and peppery, like watercress. It's excellent stirred into soups where the lift of something a little spicy is just what's needed. It also makes an unusual spread for biscuits or bread.

Makes ½ cup

½ cup unsalted butter, at room temperature
2 handfuls of nasturtium blossoms
2 tablespoons finely chopped tender nasturtium or watercress leaves
2 teaspoons snipped chives

Pound or cream the butter until it is soft. Check the blossoms to make sure there are no bugs; then remove the petals from their calyxes. Slice them thinly, then chop them using just a few, clean strokes so as not to bruise them. Stir the nasturtium or watercress leaves and chives into the butter; then gently stir in the nasturtium blossoms.

Mustard Butter with Parsley

Mustard butter goes especially well with members of the cabbage family and is also very tasty tossed with fresh noodles and chives.

Makes ½ cup

½ cup unsalted butter, at room temperature
1 teaspoon grated lemon zest
lemon juice
2 to 3 teaspoons Dijon mustard
2 tablespoons finely chopped parsley
1 tablespoon snipped chives
1 shallot, finely diced
coarsely ground pepper

Cream the butter with the lemon zest, a few drops of juice, the mustard, parsley, and chives. Taste and add more mustard if you like it stronger. Stir in the shallot and season with coarsely ground black pepper.

Spicy Moroccan Butter

This recipe for a fragrant, spicy butter is inspired by one in Paula Wolfert's book *Couscous and Other Good Food from Morocco* that caught my eye. It was given as a seasoning for grilled chicken, and I thought a similar blend would also be wonderful with vegetables, such as Baked Winter Squash (page 227), to stir into rice or couscous, or to sandwich in between layers of bread dough, as in Stuffed Pan Breads (page 29). Even a spoonful stirred into a soup or spread over toasted bread can brighten the most ordinary food.

Makes ½ cup

½ bunch of scallions, white parts only, chopped
1 to 2 garlic cloves, roughly chopped
1 tablespoon sweet paprika
1 tablespoon ground cumin
½ teaspoon coriander seeds
¼ to ½ teaspoon New Mexican ground chili or cayenne pepper
2 tablespoons chopped parsley
1 teaspoon chopped mint leaves
1 to 2 tablespoons chopped cilantro
½ teaspoon salt
½ cup unsalted butter, at room temperature

Pound the herbs, scallions, garlic, spices, herbs, and salt in a mortar to form a smooth paste. Work in the butter until well blended. Taste and add more chili, if desired. To store, roll the butter into cylinders in plastic wrap and freeze until needed.

Garlic Mayonnaise or Aïoli

There is nothing timid about the presence of garlic here. This unctuous, Proven-çale sauce is wonderful with endless numbers of foods—with cooked vegetable mélanges such as ratatouille or the other summer vegetable *tians*, with grilled vegetables as well as simply blanched ones (fennel, eggplant, green beans, pota-toes, and zucchini to name just a few); it makes a beautiful coating for hot white beans and chick-peas; it can be spread on grilled bread and covered with grilled vegetables or fresh tomatoes, stirred into soups, and melted into pasta.

Makes 1 cup

> *4 to 8 garlic cloves*
> *coarse salt, if available, or fine*
> *1 egg yolk, at room temperature*
> *¾ cup light olive or peanut oil*
> *juice of 1 lemon*
> *good-quality extra-virgin olive oil*
> *hot water*

Pound the garlic with a couple of pinches of coarse salt until it has thoroughly broken down into a smooth purée. Add the yolk and whisk until thick and slightly sticky; then begin adding the light oil, at first drop by drop, until the sauce begins to thicken, and then in a thin, steady stream, whisking constantly. When the oil has been incorporated, stir in the lemon juice; then whisk in several tablespoons of the heavier oil, to taste.

Add hot water by the tablespoon to thin the sauce. It should be thick but pour-able, not a dense, quivering mass. Taste and season, as needed, with more salt and lemon juice. Cover and refrigerate until ready to use.

Alternatively, once the garlic has been pounded, the mayonnaise can be made in a blender or food processor. The method is the same, but use a whole egg in-stead of just the yolk.

Mustard Cream Vinaigrette

This lively sauce goes especially well with chick-peas and white beans and with grilled foods, particularly fennel and leeks.

Makes approximately ½ cup

> 1 large garlic clove
> salt
> 1 teaspoon Dijon mustard, or to taste
> 1 tablespoon sherry vinegar
> 5 tablespoons olive oil
> 2 tablespoons sour cream, crème fraîche, or cream
> 1 shallot, finely diced, or 2 tablespoons snipped chives
> freshly ground pepper

Pound the garlic in a mortar with ¼ teaspoon salt until it has completely broken down into a smooth purée; then work in the mustard to form a paste. While stirring with the pestle or a whisk, add the vinegar, then the oil, and finally the cream. Whisk vigorously until the sauce is smooth and emulsified. Stir in the shallot or chives and season with salt and pepper to taste.

■ If the sauce sits for a long time, it may separate. If that happens, just stir to bring it together again.

Olive Sauce

This sauce is similar to olive paste (page 22), but the flavors are more complex and the texture is rougher, better for tossing with pasta or vegetables. Cooking the sauce deepens and intensifies the flavors. Refrigerated, it should keep more or less indefinitely.

Makes approximately ¾ cup

> 2 tablespoons olive oil
> ¼ medium-sized onion, finely chopped
> 2 tablespoons roughly chopped pine nuts
> 1 garlic clove, minced
> ½ teaspoon herbes de Provence
> 1 tablespoon chopped parsley
> ¼ pound olives, stoned and chopped (about ⅔ cup)
> 2 sun-dried tomatoes, chopped, or 1 teaspoon sun-
>   dried tomato purée (page 326)
> ¼ cup red wine
> red wine vinegar

Warm the olive oil in a sauté pan and add the onion, pine nuts, garlic, and herbs. Cook for 3 to 4 minutes or until the onions begin to soften; then add the olives, tomato, and wine. Simmer slowly for 5 to 6 minutes; then add vinegar to taste.

Salsa Verde

The term salsa verde covers a wide variety of sauces, all based on a blending of green herbs and oil seasoned with a little onion, garlic, perhaps capers, maybe the yolk of a hard-cooked egg or ground nuts for thickness, and always vinegar or lemon juice to make the whole combination sparkle. Parsley is usually the main herb with other herbs used as accents. If possible, use the flat-leaf Italian parsley, which has better flavor than the curly variety.

Salsa verde is one of those very useful sauces to have in the refrigerator, and if the vinegar or lemon juice is added just before you use it, the color and taste will be bright and fresh. It is delicious tossed with warm pasta, warm white beans, or potatoes; served with hard-cooked eggs; used to season a mayonnaise; or spread on bread to be savored alone or covered with thin slices of cheese or tomatoes. A little stirred into a soup or simple vegetable stew will finish the dish with a bright flourish.

This sauce will keep for about a week, though the fresher the better.

Makes approximately 1 cup

> *1 cup finely chopped Italian or curly parsley*
> *2 garlic cloves, very finely minced*
> *1 to 2 tablespoons capers, rinsed and chopped*
> *³/₄ cup olive oil*
> *¼ cup red wine vinegar, Champagne vinegar or lemon juice, or to taste*
> *salt*

Combine the parsley, garlic, capers, and olive oil in a bowl and stir in vinegar or lemon juice to taste. Season with salt.

Suggestions: Include a small portion of other fresh herbs with the parsley, such as chervil, basil, dill, fennel greens (and the crushed seeds), lovage, salad burnet, marjoram, thyme, blanched and chopped watercress, or rocket (arugula).

If you're using lemon for the acid, include some of the zest in the sauce.

To soften the flavor and thicken the sauce, include the yolk of a hard-cooked egg, first mashed with the garlic and capers. For the same reason, include the soft crumbs of a slice of white bread or ¼ cup finely chopped walnuts. If you're using walnuts, add a little walnut oil to the sauce to bring out their flavor.

Cilantro Salsa

If you like chilies and cilantro, you may find yourself using this lively salsa on everything—over pasta, atop pizza, in eggs, on sandwiches, stirred into soups, spread over grilled vegetables, drizzled over couscous or rice, and so forth. If you combine everything but wait to add the lime juice or vinegar until just before using the salsa, you can keep it, refrigerated, for several days. Vary the flavors, if you like, by including other spices, such as ground cumin and paprika.

Makes approximately ½ cup

> *2 cups cilantro leaves and some stems*
> *1 or 2 jalapeño peppers, seeds and veins removed*
> *grated zest and juice of 2 limes*
> *2 garlic cloves*
> *5 tablespoons olive oil*
> *salt*
> *additional lime juice or white wine vinegar*

Wash and dry the cilantro. Roughly chop the cilantro and jalapeños; then put them in a blender or food processor with the lime zest, juice, and garlic. Blend or process until well chopped, gradually adding the olive oil as you do so. Season with salt and add additional lime juice or vinegar to taste.

Tomatillo-Avocado Salsa

Both pleasantly tart and creamy-textured, this versatile sauce can be used with many different foods—with potatoes, in scrambled eggs, and in quesadillas; as a sauce for enchiladas or a garnish for avocados; as a dip for cubes of jicama and cucumbers, tossed with corn. To make a sauce with no fat, leave out the avocado. It won't be quite so thick, but it will still have plenty of satisfying flavors.

Cooking the onion, garlic, and green chilies with the tomatillos makes the overall taste softer than if the same ingredients were raw, but there is still the lively acid quality of the tomatillo plus the warmth of the chili. If you crave the harsher heat of raw jalapeño and garlic, cook only half the chili and garlic and add the rest after the sauce has been puréed.

This salsa is very simple to make, and it keeps well, refrigerated.

Makes 2 cups

> 8 tomatillos, husked
> 1 medium-sized white or yellow onion, thickly sliced
> 2 jalapeño peppers, halved, seeds removed
> 4 garlic cloves, peeled
> 1 large bunch (1 cup) of cilantro leaves
> 1 medium-sized avocado, peeled and pit removed
> lime juice or white wine vinegar
> salt

Bring several cups of water to boil in a small saucepan; add the tomatillos, onions, jalapeños, and garlic and lower the heat to a simmer. Cook gently until the tomatillos have turned a dull shade of green, about 12 to 15 minutes. Transfer the vegetables to a food processor or blender. Add the cilantro and avocado and process or blend until everything is broken up and well combined. If it's too thick, add enough of the cooking water to thin it to the desired consistency. Remove to a bowl and season to taste with lime juice or vinegar and salt.

Suggestions: Add sour cream, crème fraîche, or the thick Mexican cream called *natas*, and use the sauce in the same ways as suggested above.

Smoked Chili Salsa

This sauce is based on a bottled Mexican sauce I like very much but that is almost impossible to find. The brand name, Búfalo, is illustrated with a picture of the charging body of a red buffalo, which is about how it feels in your mouth. *Chipotle* chilies, which are dried and smoked jalapeños, make it hot and smoky-tasting. It's great splashed on quesadillas and enlivens soups, beans, and eggs.

Canned *chipotle* chilies aren't so hard to find (they can be found in Latin and Mexican markets), and they serve as the base for this sauce. One little canful makes about 2 cups of hot sauce, enough to last some people forever and others a few short weeks. The recipe can easily be reduced.

Makes 2 cups

> 1 7-ounce can chipotle *chilies in* adobo *sauce*
> 2 cups boiling water
> 3 tablespoons tomato paste
> 1 tablespoon strong red wine or balsamic vinegar, or more to taste
> 2 tablespoons brown sugar

Blend the chilies and water together in a food processor or blender until smooth. Add the other ingredients and blend again. Taste and adjust the flavorings as desired.

Aromatic White Sauce

This herb-scented béchamel sauce is what I use in place of cream. Though thickened with flour, it is just the texture of cream, and when cooked the full length of time, it shouldn't have a floury taste. When you're making a recipe that calls for this sauce, begin with it so that the herbal flavors have a chance to infuse.

Makes 2 cups

> *2 cups milk*
> *¼ small onion, sliced or chopped*
> *1 bay leaf*
> *5 peppercorns, bruised*
> *several thyme branches or a pinch of dried*
> *4 parsley branches*
> *1 tablespoon butter*
> *1 tablespoon flour*
> *salt*
> *freshly grated nutmeg*

Slowly heat the milk in a saucepan with the onion, bay leaf, peppercorns, thyme, and parsley. While it is heating, make the roux in another pan: Melt the butter, stir in the flour, and cook over medium heat for about 1 minute. Whisk in the warm milk, herbs and all. Add a pinch of salt and set the sauce over low heat or on a Flame-Tamer and cook for 25 minutes, stirring occasionally. When the sauce is done, taste for salt and season to taste with freshly grated nutmeg. Strain before using.

Suggestion: Season the milk with other herbs, those that best enhance the dish you're cooking. Either add them at the beginning and cook them with the sauce or using them as a seasoning, finely chopped, added at the end.

Walnut Sauce with Fennel Seeds

This ivory-colored sauce has the consistency of thick cream and a delicate flavor. A spoonful of walnut oil accentuates the taste of the nuts. The sauce can be left simply as is or embellished with any of the seasonings suggested below.

Walnut sauce goes wonderfully with beans and grilled vegetables and can also be used as a dip for raw vegetables. I like to use it as the sauce in a pita sandwich or serve it over falafel.

This sauce will keep for a week or more in the refrigerator. The underlying taste of the fennel seeds will increase with time. When made with freshly shelled walnuts, it is really exquisite.

Makes approximately 1½ cups

> 1 cup walnut meats
> 1 small garlic clove
> ¼ cup fresh bread crumbs
> 1½ cups boiling water, approximately
> 2 to 3 teaspoons walnut or olive oil
> ¼ teaspoon fennel seeds, crushed
> salt
> freshly ground pepper

Put the walnuts, garlic, and bread in a food processor and process briefly until everything is the texture of fine crumbs. With the motor running, gradually pour in about 1 cup of the water. Stop and scrape down the sides; then add the rest of the water. Check the consistency, and if you want it thinner, add more water until it is as thin as you want. Stir in the oil and fennel seeds and season to taste with salt and pepper. If you're not going to use it right away, cover and refrigerate the sauce.

Variations: To finish this sauce in different ways, add any of the following:
- chopped parsley
- chopped cilantro
- chopped mint leaves
- plain yogurt
- cayenne pepper
- ground cumin
- lemon juice

Here is a particular variation that I like. The yogurt and lemon give it a snappier feel.

Walnut Sauce with Yogurt and Mint

walnut sauce (above)
2 tablespoons plain yogurt
1 tablespoon chopped mint leaves
1 scallion, finely chopped
cayenne pepper or paprika
lemon juice, to taste
additional mint leaves and paprika for garnish

Combine all the ingredients except the garnishes. Cover and refrigerate for an hour before using so that the flavors can develop. Serve garnished with a dusting of paprika and mint leaves.

■ It is truly a labor of love to do so, but if you cover the walnuts with boiling water, let them sit for a minute or so, and then peel off the skins before making the sauce, the result will be a more delicate-tasting sauce. I have done this for a friend who, like many people, has an unpleasant reaction to walnuts. Removing the skins seems to help, but it is very time-consuming. Another alternative is to make the pine nut sauce on the following page which is quite similar in taste and texture to this one.

Pine Nut Sauce

If you have pine nuts in your freezer, you can make this sauce on the spur of the moment. It can also be seasoned with the herbs and spices for the walnut sauce (page 322), but when it's simply seasoned, as in this recipe, the subtle pine nut flavor can be better appreciated.

Pine nut sauce is delicious on warm beans, especially white beans and chickpeas, and with grilled vegetables. It can be used wherever walnut sauce is called for. It will keep for a week or more in the refrigerator.

Makes approximately 1 cup

> *½ cup soft bread crumbs*
> *½ cup pine nuts*
> *1 sliver of garlic*
> *¾ cup boiling water*
> *salt*
> *extra-virgin olive oil*
> *lemon juice*
> *1 scant tablespoon finely chopped parsley*
> *freshly ground pepper*

Put the bread, pine nuts, and garlic in the work bowl of a food processor and process until everything is finely chopped. With the motor running, gradually pour in the water and continue to process until the mixture is smooth. Transfer the sauce to a bowl and season it to taste with salt, olive oil, and lemon juice. Stir in the parsley, leaving a little to sprinkle over the top, and finish with a grinding of pepper.

Red Chili Paste

This seasoning is based on *harissa*, the Moroccan chili paste. Using different kinds of chili will give the sauce different flavors. New Mexican chili gives the warmest, richest flavor, in my opinion.

Use this paste to flavor a sauce for couscous (page 131) or to stir into other sauces and soups where a little extra punch is needed. If your palate has high heat tolerance, you can spread it on toasted bread or tortillas and then add cheese or avocado. Stir a little into a salad dressing or scrambled eggs; work a spoonful into some butter and use it on grilled corn or onions. This paste is versatile, and it keeps more or less indefinitely.

Makes approximately ⅓ cup

> 2 garlic cloves
> 1 teaspoon coriander seeds
> ½ teaspoon cumin seeds
> ¼ cup New Mexican or other ground red chili
> ¼ cup water, approximately
> salt
> light olive oil or sunflower seed oil

Pound the garlic and spices in a mortar until they are fairly well pulverized; then add the chili and stir in enough water to make a thick paste. Season with a pinch of salt; then pack the paste into a small jar, cover it with a thin layer of oil, and store it in the refrigerator.

Suggestion: If you're using whole dried chilies, such as *ancho* or *pasilla* chilies, use 1 ounce in place of the ground chili. Remove the stems, seeds, and veins, add just enough boiling water to cover, and soak for an hour. Once the chili is soft, purée it in a blender with the soaking liquid; then add it to the garlic paste.

Sun-Dried Tomato Purée

Dried tomatoes that haven't been packed in oil are hard and leathery but very concentrated, with faintly smoky overtones. They're usually a lot less expensive than the oil-packed imports. One way to use them is to make them into a thick purée and use it to season soups and stews or to spread thinly over toast or pizza crusts.

There are no added seasonings or sugar—just the intense flavor of the tomatoes. Pack the purée into a clean jar, cover it with olive oil, and store it in the refrigerator. It will keep several months.

One ounce will make nearly a cup of paste, which is a lot since it's so concentrated, but it's harder to make smaller amounts unless you have one of the mini–food processor attachments for your blender.

Makes approximately ½ cup

> *1 ounce (about ¾ cup) sun-dried tomatoes*
> *1 cup water*
> *1 to 2 teaspoons olive oil*

Put the tomatoes and water in a small, heavy saucepan and bring to a boil. Lower the heat and simmer gently for 15 minutes. Transfer the tomatoes and their liquid to a food processor. Process for several minutes, until the sauce is fairly smooth and the skins are broken up. If necessary, add more water to loosen the mass and make it easier to purée. Transfer the purée to a clean jar, film the top with the oil, and cover it tightly. Store it in the refrigerator.

Fast Tomato Sauce

Cherry tomatoes are frequently sweeter and more flavorful than the standard varieties, which don't really come into their own until late summer. They can provide an excellent little sauce, as long as they're sweet, during many months of the year. A food mill is helpful here although not absolutely necessary.

This is not a slow-simmering type of sauce but one that is made quickly and seasoned lightly, keeping the tomato flavor fresh and lively. Dried herbs won't work in this sauce. Use it with pasta, in soups, on pizzas, or wherever you want a fresh accent.

Makes approximately 1 cup

> 1 generous pint basket of cherry tomatoes
> ¼ cup water
> sugar
> 1 to 2 teaspoons unsalted butter or olive oil
> salt
> freshly ground pepper
> fresh herbs—such as basil, marjoram, tarragon, lovage, or dill, optional

Wash the tomatoes well and remove their stems. Put them in a wide saucepan with the water, cover, and cook over fairly high heat for 2 to 3 minutes. Remove the lid and lower the heat. When the tomatoes begin to split, help them along by breaking them up with a wooden spoon. Add a little water, as needed, to keep the mixture loose. Don't let it reduce to a thick mass, or the sugars will burn and give the sauce a scorched taste.

When the tomatoes have all burst open and released their seeds and pulp, pass them through a food mill or work them through a sieve using the back of a spoon or a rubber scraper. Taste the sauce; if it is too tart, stir in a little sugar to taste. For a thicker sauce, continue cooking it, slowly, stirring frequently. Season the sauce with butter or olive oil and salt and pepper to taste. Stir in fresh herbs, the leaves whole or finely chopped, if desired.

Tomato Sauce with Rosemary

This is a sauce to put away for a drab day in January when the preserved taste of summer provides needed encouragement. Although I often use canned tomatoes for cooking, nothing is better than real garden tomatoes, and the rosemary makes an interesting change from the more usual basil or oregano. This sauce can be used wherever tomato sauce is called for, but I especially like it spread over pizza dough and baked with nuggets of Gorgonzola cheese.

Sometimes the ugliest tomatoes have the best flavors. I recall the tomatoes I used in this sauce one summer well because they were small and misshapen, and the skins were marked with rough patches. They didn't look promising, but I was grateful to receive them and even happier to cook with them. The rough skins and odd shapes didn't matter in the long run, but the big, sweet flavor inside did.

The tomatoes that are most intensely sweet and concentrated seem to be those that ripen at the very end of the season, sometimes after the foliage has been killed by the first frost. Inside they are practically jam. They make a wonderful base for soups using onions and wild mushrooms.

Makes 1 quart

> *6 pounds ripe, sweet tomatoes*
> *2 to 3 tablespoons olive oil*
> *1 small red onion, thinly sliced*
> *salt*
> *1 small rosemary branch, the leaves removed and chopped*

Wash the tomatoes well; then cut them into sixths or, if they are large, into eighths. Warm the olive oil in a large, flat stainless-steel or nonstick pan; add the tomatoes, onion, salt to taste, and rosemary. Cook over gentle heat until the skins are wrinkled and have really cooked away from the flesh, about 30 minutes. The tomatoes should be melting into a purée. Pass them through a food mill. Check the consistency; if you wish a thicker sauce, return it to the pan and cook over medium-low heat until it is the thickness you like. Add salt to taste and process in jars, according to canning directions, or freeze.

Suggestion: If rosemary isn't your favorite herb, use a bay leaf, some thyme branches, basil, or marjoram in its place.

Roasted Peppers

It's very useful to have roasted peppers on hand—they can be used in so many ways. They can be cut into wide strips and used as a little hors d'oeuvre or salad, garnished with olives, herbs, a splash of vinegar, or thin slices of Fontina cheese. Cut into thin strips, they can fill a sandwich, garnish a pizza, or become part of a composed salad. Diced into squares, they can be tossed with pasta or cooked with rice or millet, as in Millet Pilaf with Saffron Peppers (page 273).

If you're grilling, take advantage of the coals to roast the peppers. Once roasted, they can be put into a covered dish to steam and then finished at your leisure. Otherwise use your burner, broiler, or a hot oven. For best results, choose peppers that have flat, even surfaces.

The peppers will keep for one or two weeks when covered and refrigerated.
Makes approximately 2 cups

> 2 large red or yellow bell peppers with thick flesh
> extra-virgin olive oil
> 1 or 2 garlic cloves, thinly sliced
> salt
> freshly ground pepper
> red wine vinegar or balsamic vinegar

To roast the peppers over a gas burner, set them directly in the flame. Turn them every few minutes so that the entire surface is exposed to the flame and the skin is eventually charred all over. Set the finished peppers in a bowl, cover it with a plate, and allow it to stand for at least 10 minutes to steam.

Carefully scrape away the charred peel with a knife. Save any of the syrupy juices that collect in the bottom of the bowl. Cut open the pepper, scrape out the seeds, cut the flesh into strips, and add them to the bowl with the juices. Toss with the olive oil, add the garlic, and season lightly with salt, pepper, and vinegar, to taste. Store in a covered jar in the refrigerator.

To roast peppers in an electric oven, set them on the top rack, right under the heat, turn them frequently until they are completely charred, then treat as above.

Another way to roast peppers in the oven is to cut them in half, brush them with light oil on both sides and set them, cut side down, on a cookie sheet, in a hot oven (400°F). After ten minutes or so the skins will be wrinkled and loose. Set the pepper halves in a covered bowl to steam then treat as above or use them to cook with. Since they haven't been charred, they won't have that smoky flavor, but they will be softened by the cooking and the skins will be easy to remove.

Roasted Peppers with Saffron and Basil

Roast the peppers as described above and cut them into strips. Warm 1 tablespoon of olive oil, add a pinch of saffron threads, and let stand until cooled. Pour it over the peppers, add several torn fresh basil leaves, and toss together. The saffron flavor will continue to deepen as the peppers sit.

Roasted Sichuan Pepper Salt

This is a variation on a condiment that's frequently mentioned in Chinese cookbooks. Barbara Tropp, the chef-proprietor of China Moon Cafe in San Francisco, taught it to me years ago, and I pass along her advice to use it with corn and eggs—it's wonderful and "right" with both. For example, use it on corn-on-the-cob or in Scrambled Eggs and Corn in Tortillas (page 285). A pinch or two is also good in the dressings for Asian Cobb Salad (page 50) and Nappa Cabbage Salad (page 48).

This keeps well if stored in a tightly covered jar, so you can make it in large quantities if you use it often, or just enough for several occasions, as below.

Makes 1/4 cup

> 2 tablespoons Sichuan peppercorns
> 1 teaspoon black peppercorns
> 1/4 cup coarse sea salt or kosher salt

Put the 2 peppers and the salt in a cast-iron skillet or wok and toast over medium heat until the peppers are fragrant and the salt has begun to turn off-white, 4 to 5 minutes. Stir constantly so that nothing burns.

Pound in a mortar or process in a small food processor until the peppercorns are well broken up. It's impossible to get a perfectly even consistency, so sift the salt through a fine-meshed strainer and discard the husks that remain. When cool, store it in a tightly covered jar.

Pepper and Onion Confit

This stew of succulent sweet peppers and onions could easily prove to be one of the most useful items in a summer pantry. It can be eaten by itself as a vegetable, but it also easily finds its way into other dishes—pastas, omelets, or tarts or on bread or pizza dough. Cold, tossed with capers and sprinkled with balsamic vinegar and garnished with some fresh basil leaves, it makes a refreshing little appetizer or salad on a hot evening.

All summer herbs taste wonderful with peppers, but different herbs—marjoram, basil, dill, or cumin—will lead the dish in different directions. Including some mild hot peppers with the sweet bells will give the dish a livelier edge.

Slicing everything very thinly will make a *confit* that's easy to use in eggs or on a pizza. Slicing everything into wide strips will make a dish that has more heft and bite and therefore works better on its own. Experiment with what you like, but it's a good idea to slice everything about the same width.

The confit will keep for several weeks, refrigerated.

Makes approximately 2 cups

> *1 pound red and yellow bell peppers, approximately*
> *2 tablespoons olive oil*
> *1 small red onion, quartered and sliced crosswise*
> *salt*
> *2 tablespoons tomato paste diluted with 1 cup water*
> *2 tablespoons chopped basil or marjoram*
> *2 tablespoons balsamic vinegar, or to taste*
> *freshly ground pepper*
> *additional herbs for garnish*

Cut the tops off the peppers, open them up, remove the seeds and veins, and slice them thinly, keeping the pieces 3 inches long or less. Heat the oil in a sauté pan, add the onion, and sauté briskly for a minute or so, searing the onions; then add the peppers and continue cooking over fairly high heat for a few minutes or until the onions have begun to soften. Season with salt and add the diluted tomato paste and herbs. Lower the heat and simmer slowly until the peppers are soft and the liquid has evaporated, about 20 minutes, depending on how thick the peppers are. Should the water evaporate, add more in small increments, until the peppers are as soft as you like. Once they are cooked, add the vinegar and reduce to a syrup. Season with salt and pepper to taste and garnish with fresh herbs.

Pickled Red Onion Rings

This recipe appeared in *The Greens Cookbook*, but because I find these beautiful pink onions so constantly useful as an ingredient and a garnish, I am including the recipe again. The onions lose their harshness and bite and are infused with pink within 15 minutes or so. They'll keep for weeks, refrigerated. With their beautiful color and sweet-tart bite, they enliven everything they're combined with—salads of all kinds, but especially beans, sandwiches, cold pasta or rice dishes, and eggs. It's also great just to have a big bowlful to serve alongside whatever else is on the table.

Pouring the boiling water over the onions softens them and hastens the curing process. You can omit this step if you prefer a crisper onion, but it will take several hours for the color to infuse.

Makes 2 cups

> *1 pound firm red onions*
> *1 quart boiling water, approximately*
> *1 cup white wine vinegar*
> *1 cup cold water*
> *1 tablespoon sugar*
> *several pinches of salt*
> *2 bay leaves*
> *10 peppercorns, lightly crushed*
> *marjoram or thyme branches, or a few pinches of dried*

Thinly slice the onions into rounds. This will be much easier with onions that are spherical rather than disk-shaped, as red onions are sometimes. Separate the rounds and put them in a colander. Pour the boiling water over them, then put the onions in a bowl with the rest of the ingredients. Cover and keep refrigerated. The color will begin to infuse in about 15 minutes.

Rhubarb Chutney

Hot, tart, and sweet, this is a condiment to serve with curries or with crackers and cream cheese. When finished, the color is sullen and dark, punctuated with black currants, but when you're putting the ingredients together, it's a springtime landscape with pieces of pink rhubarb brightened with green flecks of chili and black currants. The vinegar takes all that away, but it's the taste that counts ultimately, and this chutney will not disappoint.

Makes approximately 1 cup

> 1 pound rhubarb
> 2 teaspoons coarsely grated fresh ginger
> 2 garlic cloves
> 1 or 2 jalapeño peppers, seeds and veins removed
> 1 teaspoon paprika
> 1 tablespoon black mustard seeds
> ¼ cup dried currants
> 1 cup light brown sugar
> 1½ cups white wine vinegar

Wash the rhubarb and slice it into pieces ¼ inch thick. If the stalks are wide, first cut them into halves or thirds lengthwise. Finely chop the grated ginger with the garlic and jalapeños. Place all the ingredients in a non-corroding pan, bring to a boil, lower the heat, and simmer until the rhubarb is broken down and is the texture of a jam, about 30 minutes. Stored refrigerated in a glass jar, this chutney will keep several months.

Spiced Peaches in Syrup

From Ancient Roman times onwards, meats have been paired with fruits cooked with sweeteners and sharpened with vinegar. A book on Roman cuisine gives a recipe for Cornish hens with a peach sauce in which the peaches are sweetened with honey, cooked with an astonishing assortment of herbs as well as a truffle, and the whole finally finished with vinegar. Spicy, tart, and fruity flavors are lively and refreshing not only with meats but also with vegetables, particularly those cooked with hot and spicy seasonings, like curries.

These peaches are also good as a sweet, served on toast or alongside ricotta or cream cheese. To that end, I use much less vinegar than is customary. Basil leaves are another departure from tradition and one that seems quite appropriate—particularly the aromatic anise and cinnamon basils.

Makes approximately 2 cups

> 1½ *pounds firm but ripe peaches (slightly underripe*
>   *peaches are okay)*
> 1 *cup sugar*
> ½ *cup water*
> 4 *cloves*
> 5 *peppercorns*
> 1 2-inch *piece of cinnamon stick*
> 4 or 5 *small basil leaves (anise, cinnamon, or Italian basil)*

Bring a pot of water to a boil and immerse the peaches for about 30 seconds, to loosen the skins. Slip off the skins and slice the peaches into thirds or quarters.

Combine the sugar, water, and spices, bring to a boil, and stir to dissolve the sugar; then lower the heat and add the peaches. Simmer for 10 minutes, occasionally turning the peaches over with care. Remove the pan from the heat and set aside. Press a piece of plastic wrap directly over the fruit to keep their color from turning. Arrange each piece so that the part that was near the pit is covered with syrup. Let stand in a cool place overnight.

The next day, check the peaches. If they are still hard, return them to the stove and simmer until they are tender but still firm; then carefully transfer the peaches to a clean jar. Return the syrup to the stove, bring it to a boil with the basil, and cook until fine bubbles appear over the surface. Pour the syrup and spices over the fruit and cover tightly.

If you are planning to treat these as preserves, follow the instructions for whatever canning method you plan to use. Once a jar has been opened, keep it in the refrigerator.

Two Fig Preserves

More than any other fruit I can think of, figs hold in their sweetness the dry, sunny heat of the lands where they're grown. And where the trees haven't been overirrigated or where the heat isn't merely mild, the flesh of a ripe fig, shot through with myriad tiny seeds, is dense and intensely sweet, already like jam. If you have the opportunity, open a truly ripe fig and spread it over a slab of bread and cream cheese as if it were jam. Figs are fresh and available only two brief times of the year, however, so a jar of preserves helps to brighten a cheerless month when the sun doesn't shine.

Figs go well with savory tastes one might not expect of other fruits. Lavender, thyme, anise, fennel, and bay all balance and harmonize with the dense, sweet fruit. And on the other end of the spectrum, lemon, rose, cardamom, and ginger offer sharper, brighter, fruitier contrasts. Classically fresh figs and raspberries come together in summer desserts, but they combine well in a jam too. My father used to make a delicious fig jam with slices of lemon; the tart lemon perfectly cuts the dense sweetness of the fruit.

Peeling figs makes a jam with more even color and consistency, but when I want something a little rougher or have less time, I just leave the skins on and chop everything first.

There are many varieties of figs, but the black missions are what I'm used to cooking with and are probably the easiest to get. If I had an abundance of the rose-colored Adriatics or pale kadotas, I would certainly experiment with them as well.

Fig Jam with Cardamom and Rose Water

A fig grower in Fresno, California, told me that his family makes its fig conserves flavored with cardamom and rose water. If you really like the perfumed flavor of roses, you can bring it up by stirring in ½ cup of Greek rose jam. This is very aromatic.

Makes 2 cups

2 pounds (about 3 baskets) figs
1½ cups sugar
⅓ cup rose water
1 teaspoon finely ground cardamom seeds

Remove those skins that come off easily and leave the rest on. Chop the figs roughly; then stir in the sugar, half the rose water, and the cardamom. Cover and allow to sit overnight. If it's very hot and the figs are overripe, put them in the refrigerator to keep them from turning.

The next day, put them in a stainless-steel or other non-corroding saucepan and slowly bring to a boil. Lower the heat and cook slowly for about 1½ hours. As the jam begins to cook, check the bottom of the pot and make sure that all the sugar is broken up and dissolved; then stir occasionally as it cooks. When it has thickened, remove from the heat and add the rest of the rose water. Turn into sterilized canning jars; then immerse in a boiling water bath for 15 minutes.

Fig Jam with Lavender and Thyme

This recipe is unusual and delicious with the herbal overtones of lavender and thyme. Lavender honey, if it's available, would be the ideal choice here.

Makes 2 cups

> *2 pounds (about 3 baskets) figs*
> *4 thyme branches*
> *1 teaspoon dried lavender flowers*
> *½ cup honey, preferably lavender*
> *¼ cup shelled walnuts, chopped into quarters*

Remove the hard stems from the figs, rinse off the dust, and then chop them into small pieces, leaving the skins on. Put them in a heavy non-corroding saucepan with the thyme, the lavender blossoms, plucked first from the stems, and the honey. Gradually heat; then simmer until the jam is thickened, well flavored, and the pieces are broken down. Stir in the walnuts, cook another 5 minutes, and put into a sterilized jar. Either keep refrigerated or process according to whatever canning method you're using.

Lemon Suck

This is an old family recipe that was used in tea, both to sweeten it and to provide the lemon flavor. The candied walnuts, as well as the lemons, are delicious to suck on after the tea is drunk; hence the name. This conserve can also be used like a marmalade, although it's a little thin. English muffins or crumpets will catch the syrup. It can also be used as a garnish for lemon desserts or rice puddings.

Since you'll be eating the skins, use unsprayed fruits if possible.

Makes 1 quart

1 dozen (about 2 pounds) lemons, washed
3 cups sugar
1½ cups water
¼ cup shelled walnuts

Wash the lemons well and slice them thinly into rounds. Combine the sugar and water in a heavy pan and bring it to a boil. Stir to dissolve the sugar; then lower the heat and add the lemon slices. Cook over low heat until the lemons are golden-colored and starting to become transparent near the skin, after about 1 hour. Add the walnuts and cook for another 5 minutes. Pour into sterilized jars and process in a water bath according to the directions if you're planning to store the conserve. Otherwise, pour into clean jars and keep in the refrigerator.

▪ The family recipe says to leave the seeds in because you waste a lot of the juice, the lemon, and your time trying to take them out. Instead, just skim off those that come loose while they're cooking and ignore the rest.

Quince Threads

Because I'm so fascinated with quinces, I often ask people if they have any family recipes. This one comes up often—a quince marmalade made with strips, or threads, of quinces. The fruits are coarsely shredded and then cooked slowly in a syrup until they have turned clear and rose-pink. Large shreds look best. The grating attachment for the food processor does a good job, and cutting the quinces by hand into even julienne strips makes a really stunning finished marmalade, though it takes a good deal more time to prepare. To get the right-size shred on a hand grater, grate the whole, unpeeled fruit on the largest hole, digging in hard, and turning your wrist as you go to make firm, strong pieces. (If they're merely lightly grated, the quinces will cook into a mush.)

As well as being good to eat on toast, this marmalade can be used in filled cookies or tarts, such as Prune and Quince Tart in Walnut Pastry (page 370).

Makes 5 cups

> *1½ pounds (about 4 good-sized) quinces*
> *4 cups sugar*
> *2 quarts water*
> *grated zest of 1 lemon or orange*
> *lemon juice*

Choose fruits that are as golden and aromatic as possible. Rub the fuzz, if any, off the skins; then grate them coarsely, using any of the methods described above. If you're using a food processor, quarter the quinces first and cut away the cores. Don't worry about the grated quinces discoloring.

Bring the sugar and water to a boil, boil vigorously for a minute or so, and add the quinces. Allow the syrup to return to a boil; then stir frequently, pushing the fruits into the liquid until they are saturated enough to stay below the syrup. Add the lemon or orange zest, lower the heat, and cook slowly until the threads have turned a dark rosy pink, about 1½ hours.

Leave the preserve to sit out overnight. The next day, add lemon juice to taste. Bring the preserve back to a boil; then cook over low heat until most of the syrup is gone and the jam is uniform in texture and fairly wet.

Sterilize canning jars and fill them with the marmalade. Attach the lids and then process according to the instructions you're using.

Suggestions: Cook the quinces with 2 or 3 rose geranium leaves, 4 cloves, and a 2-inch cinnamon stick for a spicier, more aromatic preserve. After it has cooked, flavor it with rose or orange flower water.

Spiced Quince and Cranberry Compote

Quinces have their origins in Asia, but they traveled with the Romans to more northern climes. In this recipe they are combined with another northern fruit, the cranberry. Quinces are not always easy to find, but like many old fruits and vegetables, they are more available in markets than they used to be. In the past the quince was a favored tree, appreciated for its small, compact size, its luxurious blossoms in early spring, and the dense, long-keeping, fragrant fruits. They can often be spied in old orchards and gardens. Since most people don't know what to do with the fruits, they leave them on the trees, where they ripen to a rich golden-yellow and remain hanging on the branches long after the leaves have fallen.

Quinces appear in markets at the end of the summer and can be found throughout the winter, the same time that cranberries appear. This mildly spicy compote offers another way to present cranberries at a holiday or other large meal. It benefits by being made a few days in advance and is a good keeper, lasting at least a week. The quinces turn pink as they cook and are very beautiful mixed with the red berries.

Makes approximately 3 pints

> *5 or 6 medium-sized (about 3 pounds) quinces*
> *1½ quarts water*
> *2½ cups sugar*
> *12 cloves*
> *18 allspice berries*
> *1 3-inch piece of stick cinnamon*
> *2 packages fresh cranberries*
> *balsamic vinegar*

Choose fragrant quinces, the deepest yellow color you can find. Cut each one into quarters; then cut each quarter into slices about ½ inch thick. Cut out the cores and slice off the peels. If you are unfamiliar with quinces, you will find they have an odd, chalky texture that is a little difficult to work with. It helps to have a good, sharp knife and to hold each piece firmly as you work. When all the fruit have been cored and peeled, cut each piece into small chunky pieces or slices about ⅓ inch thick.

Combine the water, sugar, and spices in a saucepan, bring to a boil, stir to dissolve the sugar, and add the quinces. Lower the heat, cover the pan, and cook slowly until the quinces have turned a deep pink color. You don't need to worry about overcooking the fruit, for it will hold its texture well; it may take about 2 hours for the color to really deepen. If they're cooked slowly, there should still be quite a bit of liquid in the pan when the fruit is done.

Sort through the cranberries, remove those that are not in good shape, and rinse the rest. Add them to the pan. If the whole mixture seems too dry, add a little more water or some cranberry juice. Raise the heat a little and cook the cranberries until many of them have begun to pop open, about 12 to 15 minutes. Use a rubber scraper to mix them gently with the quinces. When done, set aside in the refrigerator to cool, then stir in vinegar to taste, starting with a couple of teaspoons. Keep refrigerated until needed and serve chilled or at room temperature. This is a nice sweet-tart relish that goes very well with winter vegetables as well as turkey, chicken, and pork.

■ I enjoy seeing the black cloves and allspice berries mixed in with the red fruits, but there's always a good chance of biting right into a whole spice. If this is not something you or your guests might enjoy, wrap the spices first in a piece of cheesecloth; then remove them after the fruits are cooked.

Suggestions: Pomegranate seeds might be used as a fresh garnish, or the tart juice of the pomegranate used in place of the vinegar. Fresh ginger could also be included, finely chopped and added to the water with the other spices.

Desserts

Fresh Fruits

Cream Cheeses for Fruit

Desserts and Pastries

Well-grown fruit, cultivated for taste and perfume rather than its commercial viability, is truly the ideal dessert—sweet with its own sugars, refreshing and light. There is nothing more beautiful than a still life of fruit with its varied colors and dusting of bloom that shows the fruit is both fresh and unhandled. When it tastes as good as it looks, it is truly exquisite. An excellent piece of fruit can stand entirely on its own or be accompanied by a fresh, delicate cheese; at the beginning of this chapter are suggestions for some particularly appealing seasonal combinations of fruits and fresh cheeses. The work that goes into creating extraordinary fruit is done by the farmer or the gardener. Our main task is the effort of procurement, which is not so easy these days; the usual array of supermarket fruit offers little that resembles the original, even though it looks pretty. Farmers' markets, U-Picks, and your own garden will be the best sources and worth seeking out. Organically grown fruits, in my experience, have consistently better flavor.

Since a well-grown fruit is as rare as a true tomato, what most of us have to work with are slightly green, hard fruits that only approximate the real thing. They are better cooked, so these fruits send us to the stove—making cobblers, cakes, crisps, pies, and tarts. Naturally the calories increase with our efforts, but there's no doubt that baked fruit desserts are wonderfully delicious. They're classics, and they make the best of an imperfect situation. When made with really fine fruit, they are extraordinary. On the lighter side, these fruits can also be rendered into syrups for sherbets and ices, omitting the crusts and crumbles.

Then there are those extravagant desserts that have little or nothing to do with fruit but focus on the richness and intensity of nuts, chocolate, and creams. In spite of our quest for the healthful and lean, many of us still love these sweets—cakes, tarts and cookies, custards and puddings—perhaps taken in smaller portions or less often, but taken, nonetheless, as the sweet finish to a meal or a treat with coffee or tea.

A Spring Compote

Peel blood oranges and navel oranges, slice them into rounds, and arrange them on a platter. Cover with strawberries, quartered or halved, and ollalieberries, if available. Squeeze a little fresh orange juice over all and sugar lightly.

A Fruit Basket for Early Summer

Arrange a mound of apricots in a basket and intersperse cherries among them, along with some perfect strawberries, washed and dried, and paper cones of blackberries and raspberries.

White Peaches

There are several varieties of white peach, but the Babcock is best known in this country. This small peach is very fragile and bruises easily. The flesh is creamy white with a pale greenish tint, and the peaches are full of sweet juice. The scent is best—an exotic mingling of peach with background notes of raspberries and roses—like the Playboy floribunda rose. Once, in Rome, I served white peaches for dessert. A thirteen-year-old girl struggled dubiously with her fruit knife, then took a bite and exclaimed to everyone, "This is like eating a flower!" It was, too. These make an exquisite dessert. Serve a basket of peaches with fruit knives to accompany. Or slice them into dishes, sugar lightly, and serve.

A Fruit Plate for the End of Summer

White peaches, fresh figs, raspberries, muscat and Concord grapes, newly harvested walnuts, Bartlett pears—arrange them on a platter or in a basket. If you're serving just a few people, make a dessert plate for each person with perfect pieces

of fruit—a few slices of peach and pear, different varieties of figs, halved so that their glistening seeds show, a little mound of berries, clusters of grapes, 1 or 2 walnuts, cracked but still in their shells. Slice the pears last so they won't discolor.

Melons

All the summer melons—Persians, casabas, Cranshaws, canaries, honeydews, cantaloupes, watermelons—are perfumed and very refreshing, filled with sweet juice. They make a perfect finish to a meal of spicy foods. Although chilling usually diminishes taste, in the case of melons it seems to improve them, as long as they're not too cold. Serve a single variety or several together, in slices, with wedges of lemon and lime and a dish of salt for those who like it. Some people like to grind a little fresh pepper over melons.

A compote of diced red watermelon with blackberries garnished wth mint leaves makes an especially dramatic dessert. Another nice combination is cantaloupe or, if you can find them, the small Charentais melons, halved, their cavities filled with wild strawberries or raspberries. Sweet muscat wines lightly sprinkled over Charentais and Cranshaw melons are particularly good. Ginger is also a natural complement to melon. Use it fresh to flavor a syrup or serve a plate of candied ginger along with the melons.

Frozen Persimmons

Take a perfectly ripe Hachiya persimmon (this is the large variety that must be completely soft before being eaten) and freeze it until firm but not hard. Stand it on its base and cut it into 4 sections without going through the base. Gently open the sections, like the petals of a flower, sprinkle with kirsch, and serve. You will have a persimmon sherbet.

A Bowl of Berries

In a beautiful glass bowl, layer a mixture of berries—blackberries, raspberries of different colors, blueberries, ollalieberries, sliced strawberries, or whole wild strawberries. As you go, sprinkle them lightly with vanilla sugar (page 407) and a few of drops of kirsch. Serve right away or cover and refrigerate for an hour to draw out the juices and mingle the flavors. Serve just like this or with a pitcher of Rose Geranium Pouring Custard (page 355).

Blackberries with Brown Sugar

Layer blackberries with light brown sugar, cover, and set them aside to macerate for an hour. Serve in bowls with a plate of cookies or serve with cream, *crème fraîche*, or Rose Geranium Pouring Custard (page 355).

Nectarines and Raspberries

Ripe nectarines are fragrant and firm but not hard. Wash and dry them, but leave on the soft, beautiful skins. Slice them into a bowl, add a handful of raspberries here and there as you go, and sprinkle with a little superfine sugar or vanilla sugar (page 407). Squeeze a few drops of lemon juice over the top. The effect should be a glorious mixture of color and fresh, pure tastes. Wild strawberries would also be very good with nectarines and raspberries.

Figs and Raspberries

Allow 2 or 3 figs per person. Wipe the dust off them, set them on their bottoms, and quarter them, from the top, cutting just down to the base. Press gently against the base to open the figs like the petals of a flower. Tumble raspberries into the centers, spilling over onto the plate. Sugar very lightly.

Pears with Gorgonzola Cheese and Walnuts

Choose a buttery-fleshed pear, such as a Bartlett or Comice. It should be firm, but not hard, and very fragrant. Wash, but leave on the skin. Cut into quarters and slice away the core. Arrange on a dessert plate with a piece of fine Gorgonzola and several cracked walnuts. Serve with fruit knives so that people can cut away the skins. Or serve a bowl of golden- and red-skinned pears, a large piece of cheese, and a basket of walnuts and let all help themselves.

Apples with Cheddar Cheese

We take apples for granted since they are stored all year long, but a new fall apple, especially a freshly picked one, is marvelous—crisp and juicy, sweet or a little tart, depending on the variety. Many old varieties are now being grown, and they offer quite exciting tastes and flavors, even flesh that is softly tinged with pink. Still, my favorite is the Gravenstein, with its crisp, juicy bite and streaked skin. A basket of apples, a piece of sharp cheddar cheese, and a bowlful of walnuts make a delightful dessert, starting in June with the Gravensteins and lasting through the fall with other varieties.

Asian Pears or Pear Apples

These beautiful round Asian fruits are crisp like a new apple and juicy like a pear, a most refreshing combination. Slice them crosswise into thin rounds, exposing the flowerlike stenciling of the seeds inside. They can be held in the hand and nibbled to the core.

A bowl of Asian pears seems to express perfectly the muted colors of fall—soft to bright greens, golden browns and russet, all speckled and flecked with pinpoint markings. Although they are now being grown here, they are still rare enough to be fairly costly. Served in rounds, however, a single pear can go a long way.

Oranges

Oranges make the perfect ending to a winter meal with their clean, bright flavor and juicy flesh. To make them easy to handle at the table, slice off a piece from both ends and then score the skin down to the flesh. Each person can easily peel his or her own orange. Navel and blood oranges are both wonderful. For a more formal arrangement, peel the oranges and slice them into rounds. Arrange them on a platter, sugar lightly, and garnish with pomegranate seeds. Squeeze a little of the pomegranate juice over the top for its deep red color. This platter is especially beautiful when made with blood oranges.

A Winter Fruit Platter

Compose a platter of citrus fruits—tangerines, clementines, blood oranges, and the diminutive kumquats—clusters of black grapes, pomegranates, cut into halves or quarters to expose the garnet-colored seeds inside, red-skinned pears, a persimmon, and fresh black dates.

Pineapple with Honey and Kirsch

Peel a pineapple: First remove the top; then stand it firmly on its bottom and cut deeply enough down the sides with a sharp knife to remove the eyes. Or, go over the trimmed pineapple with a carrot peeler and use the end to cut away the eyes. Remove the core and slice the pineapple into rounds. Since the skins will have a bit of flesh attached to them, squeeze them over the slices to extract the juice. Drizzle a little honey over the pineapple, sprinkle with kirsch, and garnish with chopped unsalted pistachio nuts.

If the pineapple is truly ripe and very sweet, omit the honey.

A Tropical Compote

Slice a pineapple as described above and lay the rounds in a bowl. Peel several kiwifruit and intersperse them among the pineapple. Slice a few red bananas and add them as well. Halve three passion fruit, scoop out their flesh, and force it through a strainer. Sweeten it with a little sugar and pour it over the fruit. Cover and chill before serving.

Papaya with Lime

Peel a papaya, cut it in half, and scoop out the seeds. Serve it like a melon—in halves, with a thick wedge of lime—or neatly slice it into pieces, toss in a bowl with lime juice, and serve.

Fruit with cream is a timeless combination. Whatever the particulars, the essence of fruit and cream seems to be found in the contrast of flavors and textures—the sweet, moist fruits paired with delicate, smoothly textured cream. Of course thick fresh cream is always delicious poured over fruit, but so are lighter cheeses made with cream cheese and cream, yogurt, or ricotta. Some fruits that are especially good served with a mound of sweet cheese are fresh berries, fresh figs, baked dried apricots, poached pears, and dried fruits, like dates and figs.

Below are some suggestions for creamy cheeses to serve with fruit. They take hardly any time to assemble but benefit by being left to drain overnight before being unmolded. If time is short, they can be made and served in a bowl with the fruit alongside.

Coeur à la Crème

This classic French dessert offers a beautiful pairing of cream cheese and fruit. When I was cooking at Greens, I often served this to parties celebrating a wedding or an anniversary. The white, heart-shaped cheese, surrounded by berries and washed with cream, has an innocence and charm that are timeless.

The cheese can be made a day or two in advance, and the recipe can be multiplied virtually without end. It's a great dessert to have on a buffet table.

The heart-shaped molds, made of metal, porcelain, or straw, can be found in specialty food stores. Lacking these special molds, use a fine sieve or basket to mold the cheese.

Makes about 1 pound, serving 10 to 12

> 1 pound cream cheese
> 1 cup cream
> 2 tablespoons vanilla sugar (page 407)
> 2 egg whites
> 3 pints strawberries or mixed berries
> kirsch
> additional cream and vanilla sugar

Combine the cream cheese, cream, and vanilla sugar in a bowl and beat with a mixer until smooth. Whisk the egg whites or beat them with an electric beater until they form stiff peaks; then fold them into the cream cheese mixture. Add kirsch to taste.

Line a heart-shaped mold, basket, or sieve with 2 layers of dampened cheese-

cloth. Add the cheese, folding the ends of the cloth over the top. Place the mold in a dish, cover with plastic wrap, and refrigerate for several hours or overnight.

When ready to serve, peel back the cheesecloth and turn the cheese out onto a plate; then pull off the cloth. Surround the cheese with lightly sugared berries, pour the additional cream over the cheese, letting it drip over the sides, and sprinkle with vanilla sugar.

Coeur à la Crème with Blackberries and Rose Geranium Leaves

Makes 10 to 12 servings

coeur à la crème (above)
rose water
3 to 4 rose geranium leaves, plus additional leaves for garnish
3 pints blackberries
sugar
cream
vanilla sugar (page 407)

Make the cheese mixture and stir in rose water to taste. Lay the rose geranium leaves on the bottom of the mold, over the cheesecloth; then pour in the cream cheese mixture. Let stand overnight; then unmold onto a platter. Remove the leaves or let them remain, as you wish.

Toss the blackberries with sugar to taste. Scatter them around the cheese and garnish with additional geranium leaves. Pour cream over the top, sprinkle with vanilla sugar, and serve.

Spiced Cream Cheese

Cream cheese has an affinity for spices as well as for fruits. This spiced cream cheese, a variation on the coeur à la crème can be served, in place of butter, with toast and muffins. It's also delicious with fresh fruits—berries, peaches and nectarines, and Comice pears—or poached dried fruits. The mantle of additional cream and sprinkling of sugar can be included or not, as you wish.

Make the recipe on page 351, adding about ½ teaspoon each freshly grated nutmeg and ground cinnamon, a few pinches of ground cloves, or ¼ teaspoon ground cardamom mixed into the cheese to taste. If you like the refreshing taste of citrus, include some finely grated zest of lemon or orange as well.

Ricotta Cream Cheese

This is a low-fat version of the coeur à la crème recipe. The texture is creamy and smooth even though made with ricotta and cottage cheese. Serve it mounded in a bowl with fresh berries or alongside poached or baked fruits. Or use it as a breakfast cheese, spread on toast with jam or preserved fruits.

Dry-curd cottage cheese will make a firm-textured cheese that is ideal for molding. Ordinary cottage cheese will be looser and come out more like very thick pouring cream. You could thin it even further with yogurt or sour cream and use it as a sauce over fresh fruit or pancakes. Ricotta has more body, but the texture is a little grainy, so it's best to use no more than half ricotta. You needn't hold yourself to the amounts given below—they are really just a point of departure for your own variations and preferences.

Makes 1 cup

> ½ *cup ricotta cheese*
> ½ *cup cottage cheese*
> 1 *tablespoon buttermilk, sour cream, or plain yogurt*
> 1 *tablespoon sugar or honey, or to taste*
> *kirsch*
> *grated zest of* ½ *lemon*

Combine the ricotta, cottage cheese, buttermilk, and sugar in a food processor and work until the mixture is perfectly smooth, about 1 minute. Scrape down the sides and process for another few seconds. Flavor with the kirsch and lemon zest, pile into a bowl, and serve.

For a sturdier cheese, line a strainer with a piece of rinsed cheesecloth and pour the cheese into it. Twist the ends and then tie them over the handle of a wooden spoon and let the cheese hang over a bowl in the refrigerator for several hours or overnight. After it has drained, scrape the cheese off the cloth into a bowl and whisk it together to even out the consistency.

Ricotta Cheese

Occasionally it's a pleasure to make your own ricotta cheese. The procedure isn't particularly complicated, nor does it demand much time. The resulting cheese will be soft and creamy, with a fresh, mild flavor. It's perfect to serve as a sweet with honey and fresh figs or as a savory with a spoonful of olive oil and plenty of coarsely ground pepper. It also makes a delicate sauce for pasta (see page 163).

In addition to the pleasure the finished dish affords, making ricotta cheese is fascinating—the transformation from milk to cheese brought about by the simple additions of acid and heat always seems miraculous. Traditionally ricotta is made with whey, a by-product from cheese making, but since that's not usually available, this recipe uses milk. The same cheese is also called curd cheese or quark. Either whole milk or low-fat (2%) milk can be used. Whole milk yields a richer, creamier cheese.

This cheese will stay sweet and fresh for five to seven days.

Makes approximately 1 pint

> ½ *gallon milk*
> 3 *tablespoons freshly squeezed lemon juice, Champagne vinegar*
>   *or white wine vinegar*
> *salt*

Combine the milk and acid in a heavy pot and turn the heat to very low. Gradually bring the temperature to 180°F. (At 7,000 feet, I bring it to 172°F.) It takes about 30 minutes. What you will notice is a ring of very fine bubbles around the edge of the pan. There will be some movement below the surface of the milk, which will be covered by a fine skin.

When it reaches the desired temperature, turn off the heat, cover the pan, and leave it in a warm spot—an oven that has been heated briefly or has the pilot light on is perfect—for 6 hours.

Line a sieve or a basket with a double thickness of cheesecloth or a coarse, porous towel, rinsed first in cold water, and set it over a bowl. Ladle the curds into the sieve and season them with salt, roughly a half-teaspoonful. (The whey, which will drain into the bowl, can be used for baking.) Refrigerate overnight or until the cheese is well drained. For a thicker, firm cheese, tie the ends of the cheesecloth over a wooden spoon balanced over a bowl and let it hang until all the whey has drained out.

Fold back the top layers of the cheesecloth or toweling and turn the cheese carefully out onto a plate. The imprint of the cloth will be left on the cheese.

Honey Cream

Thick and unctuous with a smooth, silky texture, this cream can be made in just a few minutes. It's wonderful with fresh figs, poached pears, sliced peaches and nectarines, slices of ripe pineapple, blackberries, and raspberries. The special flavor of the honey you choose will come through. Thyme blossom honey from

Greece and French lavender honey are both exquisite, especially with figs. I'm sure that Aristotle was reflecting on thyme blossom honey when he said that honey is "dew distilled from the stars and the rainbow."

Makes approximately 3 cups, serving 10

> 1 egg
> ¼ cup Greek thyme or French lavender honey
> 1 cup whipping cream
> pinch of freshly ground white pepper

Beat the egg and honey together with an electric mixer until the mixture is pale, thick, and sticky. Add the cream and continue beating until the cream has thickened and has a satiny sheen. Add the pepper. Refrigerate until needed.

Fresh Figs with Ricotta and Honey

Fresh figs, a mound of homemade ricotta cheese drizzled with a special honey—the Greek honey made from thyme blossoms or lavender honey—and a few fresh almonds or milky-fleshed walnuts make a simple and perfect September dessert.

A beautiful plate can be made using a variety of figs—Calmyras, Kadotas, the purple-black Missions, and Adriatic figs with their brilliant rose-colored flesh and pale green skins. Whatever the variety, the important thing is that they be ripe and sweet.

Put nicely shaped spoonfuls of ricotta on each plate. Peel the figs, slice them into halves or rounds, and arrange them on the plate. If the skins are very thin, slice the figs without peeling them. Add a few cracked nuts and drizzle the honey over the ricotta.

Rose Geranium Pouring Custard

A rose-flavored cream is perfect, in my mind at least, with all berries of the rose family, especially blackberries and raspberries, whether they're fresh or frozen into sherbets. This is also lovely poured over Lemon-Rose Sherbet (page 363) or used as the custard base for *oeufs à la neige* (the whites can be used for the meringues). Garnishes of slivered rose petals, both fresh and candied, are pretty and perfect with all these desserts.

Though from a different plant altogether, rose geranium leaves are extremely effective for making a rose-scented infusion. You could also use masses of unsprayed petals, but the geranium leaves are easier to come by for most people— the plants can be found in nurseries along with other scented geraniums. In addition to their pleasing fragrance, they have a beautiful, delicate leaf form. If no rose-scented plants are available, flavor the custard to taste with rose water.

Makes a little more than 2 cups

> 2 cups milk
> 5 rose geranium leaves
> 3 egg yolks
> ⅓ cup sugar
> rose water (optional)

Heat the milk in a saucepan with the geranium leaves. Bring it just to a boil; then turn off the heat and let the milk cool, with the leaves, for about 20 minutes.

Have ready a strainer set over a bowl. Beat the egg yolks and sugar together; whisk in about ½ cup of the milk to warm them and then add the rest. (Try not to make too many bubbles, or it will be difficult to tell, later, when the custard is cooked.) Return the mixture to the pan and cook over low heat, stirring constantly with a wooden spoon. One with a flat, rather than curved, bottom works best for this. As the mixture heats, check the back of the spoon to see if the custard is thickening. As soon as it has thickened enough to coat the spoon, pour the entire mixture through the strainer. Don't let it come to a boil, or the yolks will curdle.

Cover and refrigerate until cooled. Taste the cream; if it needs more rose flavor, add rose water to taste.

Suggestion: Mash 1 cup blackberries, work them through a sieve, and stir the juice into the cream. Serve the cream with a bowl of lightly sugared berries or with a slice of cake, such as Dorée's Extravagant Almond Cake (page 374). The berries will lend both their flavor and their delicate color.

Plum and Nectarine Crisp

People with plum trees experience an annual dismay, as well as pleasure, when the fruits finally appear. The trees bear heavily for a few weeks, or many weeks if one has several varieties, the yard is covered with falling fruit, and the owner is overwhelmed. My mother has a plum tree, and she once arranged to get rid of a few fruits by baking a plum crisp for me on the eve of a long car trip to the Southwest. The next morning I enjoyed a sunrise breakfast at Mono Lake—the plum crisp with a pot of espresso brewed over a fire, a memorable meal, shared with a chipmunk family.

Plums make a wonderful, juicy crisp, but the skins are always tart, especially when baked, so I mix them with a few nectarines to soften their effect and serve the crisp with sweetened whipped cream flavored with orange flower water.

The nice thing about a plum crisp is that it works both with tree-ripened fruit and the hard fruits encountered in supermarkets. If the plums you're using are ripe and juicy, add a few teaspoons of tapioca or flour to the fruit before baking to thicken the juices.

Makes 6 servings

THE FRUIT

1½ pounds purple plums such as Santa Rosas
½ pound nectarines
½ cup light brown sugar
⅛ teaspoon ground cloves
1 teaspoon ground cinnamon
1 teaspoon grated orange zest
1 teaspoon tapioca or flour (if fruit is very juicy)

Preheat the oven to 375°F. Wash the fruit, cut it into sixths, and toss it with the sugar, spices, zest, and tapioca if you're using it. Let it sit while you make the topping below. Put the fruit into a glass pie plate or gratin dish, cover with the topping below, and bake until the top is lightly browned, about 30 minutes. Serve it warm from the oven or at room temperature with vanilla ice cream or softly whipped cream, sweetened to taste with sugar and flavored with orange flower water.

THE TOPPING

¾ cup unbleached white flour
½ cup sugar
¼ cup unsalted butter
⅛ teaspoon salt
1 teaspoon ground cinnamon

Combine the ingredients in a bowl and work them together with your fingers to form a dry but even-textured meal. Press it lightly over the fruit.

Dried Apricots Baked with Vanilla

When dried apricots are baked with vanilla and sugar, they emerge from the oven plump, succulent, and firm. Ginger is perhaps more often paired with apricots, but vanilla is very good, too; although not sweet itself, it emphasizes that aspect of the fruit. These apricots are delicious served chilled, with a mound of Ricotta Cream Cheese (page 353) or Coeur à la Crème (page 351); they can also be used in place of fresh apricots, in Apricot Upside-Down Cake (page 373), rolled inside a crêpe, or served alongside a piece of almond cake.

A cupful of dried apricots, about ½ pound, equals approximately 25 small apricots. Plan to serve 4 or 5 apiece. These apricots will keep for at least a week.
Makes 6 servings:

1 cup dried apricots
1 cup warm water
a 1-inch piece of vanilla bean, sliced in half lengthwise
1 tablespoon sugar

Preheat the oven to 350°F. Cover the apricots with the warm water and let them stand for 15 minutes if they are already plump and soft, 30 minutes if they are hard to begin with. Drain, but reserve the water.

Put the water and vanilla bean in a baking dish—an 8-inch pie plate is just right. Scrape out the seeds of the vanilla bean with the tip of a knife and break them up in the water. Add the apricots, sprinkle them with the sugar, cover with foil, and bake until the water is nearly absorbed, about 1 hour. Turn each of the apricots over in the syrup; then cover and refrigerate. Serve chilled.

Baked Apricots with Buttered Bread Crumbs

If you're longing for the kind of tree-ripened apricot you tasted in California or France but have only underripe fruit available, this recipe offers an approxima-tion. Baking greatly improves the slightly green fruit we find in our markets, al-most ripening it in the oven. But include some ripe apricots as well if you can. Their flavor is incomparable, and they break down to make a little sauce for the dish.

When I first made this recipe, I didn't use the bread crumbs but, following the advice of Elizabeth David, set the apricots in a pan over a piece of vanilla bean, added a little water, sprinkled them with sugar, and baked them. The apricots tasted wonderful, but they collapsed completely and looked rather unappealing. The covering of bread crumbs helps protect them and makes a fragile, buttery crust. It's a little like eating warm fresh jam with toast. The simpler version, though, uses no butter. The cooked fruits are delicious served chilled with Ri-cotta Cream Cheese (page 353).

Makes 4 modest servings

> 1½ *pounds fresh apricots*
> 4 *to 5 tablespoons vanilla sugar (page 407) or*
>   *plain sugar plus a 2-inch vanilla bean*
> 2 *tablespoons water*
> 2 *cups fresh bread crumbs made from white bread*
> ¼ *cup melted unsalted butter*

Preheat the oven to 350°F. Wash the apricots, slice them in half, discard the pits, and toss them with the sugar. Put the water in the bottom of a glass pie plate or baking dish. If you're using the vanilla bean, slice it in half lengthwise and lay it in the water; then set the apricots on top. Toss the bread crumbs and melted but-ter together; then spread them over the apricots. Bake until the bread crumbs are just lightly browned and the fruit tender, about 25 minutes. Let the dessert settle and cool before serving it warm with a pitcher of cream or a bowlful of lightly whipped cream sweetened with sugar and a drop of vanilla.

Poached Peaches with Raspberries

I once saw a rose at an exposition that was streaked pale yellow and pink, the color of a sunrise. Named Playboy, its scent was a most unforgettable blending of perfumes, hinting of wild strawberries, raspberries, and rose, with a subtle spicy note of lemon. This summer compote aspires to the memory of that rose.

Poaching fruit in syrup is a good technique to use with fruit that is slightly underripe or low in sugar. A sweet ripe peach, dripping with its own ample syrup, is hard to improve on, but less fortunate fruits can use some help. The syrup also prevents the fruit from browning. This compote tastes best chilled, so make it ahead of time.

White peaches are the most delicate and fragile; they would be perfect for this compote and best of all combined with the unusual red-fleshed Indian peaches. However, other varieties are more likely to be available.

Makes 6 servings

> *1 pint red raspberries or a mixture of different kinds of raspberries*
> *a handful or 2 of wild strawberries, if available*
> *4 peaches*
> *⅔ cup water*
> *¼ cup sugar*
> *a small piece of lemon peel*
> *kirsch or rose water to taste*

Mash ½ cup of the raspberries; then force them through a sieve. There should be about 2 tablespoons of purée.

Bring a small pan of water to a boil, immerse the peaches for about 10 seconds, and then plunge them into a bowl of cold water to stop the cooking. Carefully peel them and cut them into wedges about ¾ inch thick.

Combine the water, sugar, and lemon peel in a saucepan and bring to a boil. When the sugar is dissolved, lower the heat, add the sliced peaches, and gently cook—about 5 minutes if underripe; 2 or 3 minutes if ripe. When they're cooked, ladle them into a serving bowl.

Bring the syrup back to a boil and boil energetically for a minute; then pour through a strainer into another bowl. Stir in the raspberry purée and flavor with the kirsch or rose water. Pour the hot syrup over the peaches and add the raspberries and wild strawberries, if you're using them. Gently push them into the syrup so that they are coated at least once; then cover and refrigerate until cold. Serve them ladled onto a plate or into dessert bowls with a candied rose petal and possibly a thin slice of almond cake (page 374).

Quince Compote

Sliced quince are simmered in a light syrup flavored with cardamom, cloves, and vanilla until they turn pink. Serve this compote chilled, either alone or mixed with other fall and winter fruits, such as poached pears, fresh figs, and raspberries, or with vanilla or clove-flavored ice cream. The quince slices can also be used in cooked desserts, such as the Prune and Quince Tart in Walnut Pastry (page 370) or alongside meat dishes where traditionally apples might be served. Once cooked, they will keep for a month or longer, refrigerated.

Makes approximately 1 quart serving 4 to 6

> 1½ quarts water
> 2 pounds ripe quinces
> ¾ cup sugar
> ½ vanilla bean, split lengthwise
> 1 2-inch cinnamon stick
> 5 cloves
> ⅛ teaspoon cardamom seeds
> 2 wide strips of orange peel

Put the water in a pan to heat. Rinse the quinces and wash off any fuzz that might be left on their skin. Using a good, sharp knife, quarter the quinces; then carefully cut out the core, taking care not to snap each piece in 2 as you do so. (If the quinces are very large, it might be easier to work with smaller sections.) Slice each quarter into 2 or 3 pieces, each about ½ inch thick, then cut away the peels. As you work, put the cores and peels in the heating water—eventually they will impart both flavor and body to the water. Once the water boils, lower the heat and simmer, covered, with the peels and the cores, for 30 minutes; then strain. (Don't worry about the peeled quinces discoloring; they turn an even rosy pink as they cook.)

Combine the sugar, spices, orange peel, and strained liquid in a non-corroding pan. Bring to a boil, stir to dissolve the sugar, and add the quinces. Cut out a disk of parchment paper and place it directly on the surface to prevent any exposed slices from drying out. Lower the heat and simmer until the quinces have turned pink and are slightly translucent and firm to the touch, about 2½ hours. When done, transfer them to a bowl and chill.

Rhubarb Blood Orange Compote

The deep reds and golds of the fruit punctuated with the black currants always remind me of stained glass—clear and luminescent. The flavor has clarity too—the naturally tart fruits sweetened with syrup, brightened with orange peel, and perfumed with rose water. This is a lovely dessert for winter or early spring, served with a Walnut Nugget Cookie (page 379) or alongside a slice of cake.

If blood oranges aren't available, use navels instead.

Makes 4 to 6 servings

> *1 pound rhubarb*
> *2½ cups water*
> *1½ cups sugar*
> *3 cloves*
> *1 tablespoon dried currants*
> *3 strips orange zest, cut into narrow slivers*
> *3 to 4 blood oranges*
> *1 navel orange*
> *1 teaspoon rose water, or to taste*
> *6 kumquats, if available*

Wash the rhubarb, trim the ends, and cut each stalk into pieces about an inch long. If the stalks are field-grown and uneven in width, cut the wider ones length-wise to make all the pieces more or less the same size.

Bring the water to a boil with the sugar and cloves. When the sugar is dissolved, add the rhubarb and lower the heat. Simmer gently until the pieces are just tender when pierced with a fork—about 8 to 10 minutes, depending on the size. Carefully lift them out with a slotted spoon and put them in a roomy bowl. Add the currants and the slivered orange peel to the syrup, bring to a boil, and reduce until a little over a cup is left, about 10 minutes. Fine bubbles will appear over the surface when it's ready.

While the syrup is reducing, peel the oranges: Cut a piece off both ends, stand them on a cutting board, and slice away the peel, removing all the white membrane as you do so. Thinly slice them into rounds and put them in the bowl with the rhubarb. If you don't need to economize on blood oranges, squeeze a whole one into the syrup to give it a rosy color.

When the syrup has reduced, add the rose water to taste. Pour the syrup over the fruit. Slice the kumquats, if you're using them, and add them to the compote. Cover and refrigerate. Serve well chilled.

Lemon-Rose Sherbet

The lemon-rose combination comes from an old collection of American recipes. Traditionally the crushed petals of old-fashioned fragrant roses would supply the rose flavoring, but I find rose geranium leaves just as effective and easier to come by. Rose water can also be used, lacking either of the plants.

Both the sweet Meyer lemons and the more acidic Eurekas make excellent sherbets. Meyers, available mainly in California and in specialty stores, are perfumed, sweet, and complex. The Eureka type of lemon, which is what we usually find in supermarkets, has a sharp, clean scent and flavor. Serve this sherbet alone or with plump blackberries, wild strawberries or raspberries, and a candied rose petal finely chopped and sprinkled on top.

Makes approximately 1½ quarts

> 6 rose geranium leaves or 2 teaspoons rose water, or to taste
> 2 cups half-and-half
> 2 cups milk
> grated zest of 3 lemons
> 1 cup freshly squeezed lemon juice
> 1 cup sugar, or more to taste
> pinch of salt
> very small pinch of ground cloves
> rose geranium flowers or fresh or candied rose petals for garnish

Bruise the leaves lightly with your fingers; then put them in a saucepan with the half-and-half. Slowly bring to a boil; then remove from the heat and set aside to cool and steep.

Combine the grated zest, lemon juice, sugar, salt, and cloves in a bowl and stir to combine. Pour the steeped half-and-half through a strainer into this mixture, add the milk, and stir to dissolve the sugar. (The milk will curdle, but once frozen, the ice will be smooth.) If you're using rose water, stir it into the mixture. Taste the mixture and add more sugar or rose water if needed.

Freeze in an ice cream maker according to the manufacturer's instructions. Be sure to scrape the lemon zest off the dasher and fold it into the sherbet. Pack it into a container, cover tightly, and freeze.

Garnish the sherbet with rose geranium flowers or fine slivers of fresh or candied rose petals.

Wild Blackberry Sherbet

Blackberries seem to grow by country roadsides everywhere. Irrigated only by chance rains, the fruits are often small, but their flavor is concentrated and full, which is why some water is used in making the syrup. It's worth the scratches to make this at least once a season. Being partial to the combination of blackberries with roses (members of the same botanical family), I serve this either with a confetti of rose petals or a pouring custard flavored with the fragrant leaves of the rose geranium (page 355).

Makes approximately 1 quart

> *6 cups blackberries*
> *⅔ to 1 cup sugar*
> *⅔ cup water*
> *pinch of salt*
> *freshly squeezed lemon juice*

Mash the berries into a coarse purée using a potato masher (a blender or food processor breaks up the seeds too much); then work the purée through a sieve or fine-meshed food mill, forcing out as much juice as possible. You should have approximately 3 cups. Taste the purée; if it is quite tart, use the larger amount of sugar in the next step.

Combine the sugar and water in a saucepan and bring to a boil. Stir; as soon as the sugar is completely dissolved, remove it from the heat. The sugar is dissolved when you can rub a drop of syrup between your thumb and finger and it doesn't feel gritty. Transfer the syrup to a bowl and cool over ice or in the refrigerator.

When cool, combine the syrup and the purée and add a pinch of salt and lemon juice to taste. Freeze it in an ice cream maker according to the manufacturer's instructions; then pack it into a covered container and store it in the freezer.

Concord Grape (or Slipskin) Pie

This unusual pie is from New England and upstate New York, where the Concord grape was originally developed and most are grown. It's a pie that deserves to be better known, and with the new interest in old foods, perhaps it will be. Concord grapes are roundly sweet, like a dead-ripe blackberry, and in fact, this pie does remind me of berry pies. The grapes are usually "slipped" or squeezed from their skins, which are a little tough. It was a favorite in our family when we had a dairy farm in upstate New York. After moving to California, my father planted Concords, continuing the tradition, and every summer my mother made a few of these luscious pies. Recipes for Concord grape pie can be found in old Shaker cookbooks and in an early edition of *Joy of Cooking*.

While most Concord grapes are grown in the East and shipped around the country, they are also grown in the Midwest and California. I have seen bottles of the juice, but not the grapes, at farmers' markets. The growers tell me that their customers don't like seeds in grapes, so the entire harvest is made into juice—a shame, because seeds or not, they are delicious, both as eating grapes and as pie grapes.

This is a good pie for children to help with since all the grapes must be "slipped" or squeezed from their skins, a job kids seem to like. It may also remind you of Halloween nights when a bowl of skinned grapes, felt in the dark, passed for a bowlful of eyes!

Makes 1 double-crust 9-inch pie

> *1 recipe pie crust (recipe follows)*
> *2½ pounds Concord grapes*
> *½ to ¾ cup sugar*
> *3 tablespoons unbleached white flour*
> *grated zest and juice of 1 lemon*

Prepare the pie crust according to the recipe below. Use half the dough to line a 9-inch pie plate and roll out the other half for the top. Set both in the refrigerator while you make the filling.

Wash the grapes carefully, as you will be using the skins as well as the pulp. Slip the grapes out of their skins by squeezing them into a saucepan. Set the skins aside in a bowl. Heat the grapes at a slow boil until they turn whitish and the seeds start to loosen, about 3 minutes. Then pass them through a food mill to separate the seeds, working directly into the bowl with the skins. Stir the pulp and

the skins together and add ½ cup of sugar, the flour, and the lemon zest. Taste the mixture; if it is too tart, add the remaining sugar. Squeeze in lemon juice to taste and let the mixture cool for about 15 minutes. Preheat the oven to 400°F.

Pour the cooled filling into the lined pie tin and cover with the second crust. Brush a light film of water where the 2 crusts meet; then press them firmly together, fluting the edges in a decorative fashion. For a golden, glazed crust, brush some beaten egg yolk over the top. You can use the tip of a knife to etch a decorative design into the dough or fashion some grapes and grape leaves out of dough scraps and fasten them to the top with a little water. Cut a hole in the top for a vent. Set the pie on a cookie sheet and place it on the lowest shelf of the oven. Bake for 10 minutes; then lower the heat to 350°F and bake for another 35 minutes. Remove the pie when the crust is nicely browned and let it cool before serving. Serve it alone or with thick cream or vanilla ice cream. For some people, leftover grape pie makes a perfect breakfast.

Suggestions: A Shaker recipe I've seen includes a mixture of butter and sugar (a few tablespoons of each) dabbed over the crust before the filling is added. When baked, the little dabs become soft pockets of sweetness. Add these if you wish, but you may find the pie is already sweet enough as it is.

To make a deep-dish pie, use about 3 pounds of grapes. Or if grapes are expensive or in short supply, modify the recipe to make a tart or a more shallow pie. A lattice crust also makes a beautiful top, allowing the deep purple filling to show, but if you choose a lattice style, don't fill the crust clear to the top. The filling is juicy and will boil over unless held by the second crust.

PIE CRUST

> *2 cups unbleached white flour*
> *⅜ teaspoon salt*
> *6 tablespoons unsalted butter*
> *6 tablespoons vegetable shortening*
> *3 tablespoons cold water*
> *egg yolk*
> *milk or cream*
> *sugar*

Combine the flour and the salt; then add the butter and shortening and work them into the flour using a wire pastry blender, 2 knives, or your fingers. Work until the fat is roughly dispersed throughout the flour.

Dribble in the water, lightly lifting the flour mixture with a fork as you do so; then gather the whole together in your hands and form it into a ball, working it

as little as possible. If crumbs remain on the bottom of the ball, add enough water to gather them together. Separate the dough into 2 parts, one slightly larger than the other, and shape them into round, flat disks. If you are going to use them later, wrap them in plastic and refrigerate until needed.

Flour your work surface, roll out the larger piece about 2 inches larger than the pie plate and about ⅛ inch thick, and fit it into the pie plate. Trim the edge and set it in the refrigerator. Roll out the second piece just before setting it over the filling.

To make a lattice crust, roll out the second piece, also ⅛ inch thick, and cut it into strips. Some people find it easier to make the lattice on a piece of wax paper and then slide it onto the filled pie, and others are as comfortable constructing the lattice right on the pie. Do whichever you like. Trim the ends, press them into the edge of the crust, first sealing the 2 pieces with a little water, and flute the edge attractively.

To give the crust a nice color and sheen, mix an egg yolk with a little milk or cream and sugar and brush it over the top.

Pecan-Coffee Tart

I hadn't really thought of Mexico in connection with pecans until I traveled there one winter and saw huge sacks of them in the markets and wonderful pecan brittles—as big as pies—at candy stands. The vision inspired me to think about them in combination with other Mexican tastes—*piloncillo*, the dense cones of unrefined brown sugar one sees in Mexican markets, and the spices, especially the clove, pepper, and cinnamon triad that appears in Mexican recipes, both sweet and savory. *Piloncillo* has a rougher and more complex taste than our brown sugar; it goes well with these spices and coffee. (Many supermarkets feature a rack with Mexican herbs and spices, including *piloncillo*, but if you can't find it, use dark brown sugar mixed with molasses.)

This recipe makes a large, shallow tart with just a single layer of pecans, each one placed with the curved side facing up. It is a handsome and somewhat lighter variation on the traditional holiday pecan pie. Make it in a 10-inch tart pan, preferably with a removable rim, and serve it on a large, handsome platter.

Makes 1 10-inch tart, serving 10 to 12

> 1 recipe tart dough (recipe follows)
> 8 peppercorns
> 4 cloves
> 1 2-inch cinnamon stick
> 4½ ounces piloncillo or ¾ cup dark brown
>   sugar and 2 tablespoons molasses
> ½ cup corn syrup
> ⅓ cup brewed espresso or other strong coffee
> 6 tablespoons unsalted butter
> 1 large egg
> 2 large egg yolks
> 3 tablespoons half-and-half or cream
> pinch of salt
> ½ teaspoon vanilla extract
> 1 tablespoon unbleached white flour
> 2 cups pecan halves

Begin by making the tart shell below. This can be done well in advance and the shell kept frozen, wrapped in foil.

Bruise the peppercorns and cloves, crushing them a little with a pestle; then

combine them with the cinnamon, sugar, syrup, and coffee in a saucepan. Bring to a boil; then simmer for about 10 minutes or longer, if necessary, to dissolve the *piloncillo*, if you're using it. You can help it along by breaking it up with a spoon. When the sugar is dissolved and cooked, pour it through a strainer into a bowl; then add the butter and stir until melted.

Beat the egg and egg yolks together, warm them with some of the sugar mixture, and then stir them back into the mixture. Add the rest of the ingredients except the pecans.

Preheat the oven to 325°F. Roast the pecans on a cookie sheet until they begin to smell toasty, about 5 minutes. Set them on the prebaked tart shell, placing them so that the rounded sides are all facing up for an especially pretty tart. Carefully pour the syrup around the nuts and bake the tart for 35 minutes or until set.

TART DOUGH

1 cup plus 2 tablespoons unbleached white flour
4 teaspoons sugar
⅛ teaspoon salt
9 tablespoons unsalted butter
4 teaspoons water
½ teaspoon vanilla extract

Mix the flour, sugar, and salt together; then cut in the butter with a wire pastry blender, a food processor, 2 knives, or your fingers until it is the texture of cornmeal. Add the water and vanilla and continue to work it until the dough is a smooth and uniform texture and can be shaped into a ball.

Line a 10-inch tart pan with a removable bottom by pressing the dough over the bottom and then up the sides. The sides should be about a quarter inch thick, even with the top of the pan, slightly thinner toward the base. You may need to fiddle with it for a while to get it right, but the extra handling won't effect the dough, which is short and tender.

Set the finished shell in the freezer to harden. Preheat the oven to 400°F. Prebake the frozen shell in the middle of the oven until it is lightly but evenly browned, about 12 minutes. Check during the baking. If the bottom is swelling anywhere, prick the swellings with the tip of a knife to deflate them.

Prune and Quince Tart in Walnut Pastry

This rich fruit tart is perfect for the cold months of the year. The filling includes prunes, golden raisins, poached quinces or quince jam. The colors of the fruits— black, golden, and deep pink—are as luscious as their flavors. A sweet walnut pastry completely encases the pie and is dusted white with powdered sugar.

If you've already made the Quince Compote or Quince Threads, it's relatively easy to put this together. And if you haven't any quinces, use a commercially prepared quince jam and omit the poached fruit. This is a fairly sturdy dessert that can be made early in the day and served in the evening without the crust getting soft. It's good the second day, too.

Tea is often used as a poaching liquid for prunes. Dark teas—orange pekoe, Darjeeling, Earl Grey—all taste quite good with the fruit.

Serve the tart with a spoonful of cold crème fraîche or sour cream.

Makes 1 9-inch tart, serving 8 to 10

THE WALNUT PASTRY

1½ cups unbleached white flour
⅓ cup sugar
¾ cup finely ground walnuts
pinch of salt
½ cup unsalted butter
1 egg
¼ teaspoon vanilla extract

Toss the flour, sugar, walnuts and salt together in a bowl; then cut in the butter, using a wire pastry blender, your fingers, or a food processor. Work the butter until it is dispersed throughout the dry ingredients.

Beat the egg with the vanilla and pour it over the dough. Lightly work it into the dough, using a fork or your fingers; then turn it out onto the counter and knead briefly to bring it together. Divide the dough into 2 more-or-less equal pieces, flatten them into round disks, wrap, and refrigerate or freeze until needed.

THE FRUIT FILLING

2 cups pitted prunes
4 cups dark tea
1 cup golden raisins
1 cup quince compote (page 361), drained, or ⅓ cup quince
*   threads (page 339) or quince jam*
⅓ cup sugar
2 tablespoons Armagnac or brandy
2 teaspoons orange flower water, or to taste
1 teaspoon grated orange zest
additional ½ cup quince threads or quince jam
powdered sugar
crème fraîche or sour cream

Cut the prunes into thirds or quarters. Add them to the tea and cook gently in a saucepan until they are soft, anywhere from 10 to 20 minutes, depending on how hard they were to begin with. When they have softened, put them into a colander to drain, but save the tea. When drained, transfer the prunes to a bowl.

Add the raisins to the hot tea and let them stand until they plump up, about 5 minutes. Drain and add them to the prunes. Add the poached quince, if using, or the quince threads or jam. Sprinkle in the sugar, Armagnac, orange flower water and orange zest and gently mix everything together; then set it aside to cool while you form the pastry.

Forming the tart: Preheat the oven to 375°F. Use a 9-inch tart pan with a removable rim so that it can be unmolded. (Or use a 9-inch pie plate, but plan to serve the pie in it.) Line it with a piece of parchment or wax paper the same size as the bottom to prevent the sugars in the crust from caramelizing and sticking to the pan.

On a lightly floured surface or between 2 pieces of plastic wrap, roll out one of the disks of dough, a little larger than the pan, then set it in the pan. If it tears anywhere, patch it by pressing the dough together. Make sure the sides are about ¼ inch thick.

Spread a thin layer of the additional quince threads over the bottom, then add the cooled fruit and even out the surface. If you really like the taste of quince, dab a few extra spoonfuls of jam here and there over the tart.

Roll out the second circle of dough and lay it over the pie. Pinch the sides together, cut a star pattern or X in the center, and chill until the dough is firm, about 10 minutes. Set the chilled tart on a baking sheet in the center of the oven and bake until the crust is lightly browned over the surface, about 50 minutes. If the edges darken before the top, cover them loosely with strips of foil.

When the tart is done, remove it from the oven, and holding it firmly, gently lift the bottom slightly up and away from the side, working your way around the circumference to cool the outside of the crust. (This will harden the sugars so that they won't stick later.) Twice around should be enough. Return the tart to its pan and set it on a cooling rack until you're ready to serve it. Remove it from the pan, set it on a serving plate, and dust the surface with powdered sugar.

Serve with a bowl of sour cream or crème fraîche, beaten until smooth and silky.

Apricot Upside-Down Cake

This classic cake is made with fresh apricots and cherries. A little nugget of almond paste is slipped into the hollow of each apricot for a burst of unexpected flavor. Upside-down cakes always bake perfectly in a cast-iron skillet.

This cake is good at any temperature, but it's really wonderful when still a little warm, served with whipped cream or ice cream—or nothing at all.

Makes 1 10-inch cake serving 6 to 8

> 2 tablespoons almond paste
> 10 apricots, halved
> ¾ cup unsalted butter
> ¾ cup light brown sugar
> 10 Bing cherries, pitted and halved
> ½ cup plus 2 tablespoons sugar
> 3 eggs
> 1 teaspoon vanilla extract
> ½ teaspoon almond extract
> 1¼ cups unbleached white flour
> 1 teaspoon baking powder
> ½ teaspoon baking soda
> ¼ teaspoon salt
> ½ cup buttermilk or sour cream

Put a little almond paste in the cavity of each apricot half. Melt ¼ cup of the butter with the brown sugar in a 10-inch cast-iron skillet. When the sugar has melted, turn off the heat. Spread the mixture evenly around the bottom of the pan; then place the apricots, stuffed side up, in a ring around the edge of the pan. Use the smaller halves to fill in the center and place the cherries decoratively in the gaps. Preheat the oven to 375°F.

Cream the remaining butter with the sugar until light-colored and fluffy. Beat in the eggs one at a time. Add the vanilla and almond extracts. Sift the flour, baking powder, soda, and salt together and stir them into the batter, alternating with the buttermilk or sour cream. Combine everything in as few strokes as possible so that you don't overmix the batter. Distribute the batter over the fruit and bake the cake in the middle of the oven until the cake has risen and a toothpick or cake tester inserted in the center comes out clean, about 40 minutes.

Let the cake rest for a few minutes; then set a serving platter over the pan, grasp it firmly with both hands, and carefully flip the whole thing over. Everything should fall neatly onto the plate. If any of the fruit sticks to the pan, just remove it gently and lay it on the cake where it belongs.

Dorée's Extravagant Almond Cake

My friend Dorée and I both love almond cakes more than any other. This is her recipe for a handsome, rich cake filled with the flavor of almond. She uses almond paste both blended into the batter and broken up into pieces that are stirred in just before baking, leaving pure pockets of almond throughout the cake. Almond *aficionados* will want it both ways, but it's perfectly delicious without the final addition.

This recipe is very easy to make and is also very easy to cut in half, making a smaller 1-pound cake.

Serve the almond cake with coffee, tea, or a dessert wine. Berries, peaches, and nectarines, sliced and sugared, are also delicious served alongside, with or without a spoonful of *crème Anglaise*. In fall and winter I like to serve this cake with the Preserved Figs with Star Anise and Bay (page 404) or Quince Compote (page 361).

Commercial almond paste usually comes in 8-ounce cans. You can also make your own with the recipe on page 394. If you're planning to use it in both ways, you'll need a whole pound.

Makes 1 large bundt cake, serving 12 to 16

> unsalted butter and flour for the cake pan
> ½ pound almond paste
> 1¼ cups sugar
> 1 cup unsalted butter, at room temperature
> 5 eggs
> 1 cup sour cream
> 2 teaspoons vanilla extract
> 1 teaspoon almond extract
> 3 cups unbleached white flour
> 1½ teaspoons baking powder
> 1 teaspoon baking soda
> ¼ teaspoon salt
> ½ pound additional almond paste (optional)
> powdered sugar

Preheat the oven to 325°F. Butter and flour a bundt pan or a 9-inch springform pan. Combine the ½ pound almond paste and the sugar in a food processor and work until well blended. Add the butter and continue to process until blended; then add the eggs, one at a time, the sour cream, and the flavorings. Transfer the mixture to a mixing bowl.

Sift the flour with the baking powder, soda, and salt. Add it to the batter a third at a time, gently stirring in each cupful. For the extravagant touch, break another ½ pound—or less—almond paste into pieces and fold them into the batter. Turn the batter into the baking pan and bake the cake in the middle of the oven until the cake is golden on top and springy to the touch, about 1 hour.

Remove the cake from the oven and let it stand to cool slightly; then turn it out onto a serving plate. When cool, dust it with sifted powdered sugar. This cake will keep well, wrapped tightly, for several days.

Quince Almond Cake

Grate a quince on the large holes of a grater and stir it into the batter. The shreds are thin enough to cook during the time it takes the cake to bake, and they will flavor the cake with their unique perfume.

Orange-Currant-Walnut Cake

Food writers everywhere, myself included, are continually warning their readers about the bitterness of the white membrane that lies just under the colored peel of the orange. Here, however, a whole orange is used with no ill effects—probably because there are so many other ingredients—so proceed without second thoughts.

This cake is based on an old recipe that originally required a meat grinder or hand mill for the grinding. A food processor works quite well in its place.

A warm syrup is poured over the finished cake, ensuring its moistness. Dense with ground nuts and currants, this is a good winter cake and a simpler alternative to more complicated fruitcakes.

Makes 1 9-inch round cake serving 8 to 10

THE CAKE

> 1 cup dried currants
> 1 navel orange, preferably organic
> ¾ cup shelled walnuts
> ½ cup unsalted butter
> ¾ cup sugar
> ½ teaspoon vanilla extract
> 3 eggs
> 2½ cups unbleached white flour
> 1 teaspoon baking soda
> ½ teaspoon salt
> 1 cup buttermilk
> butter and flour for the cake pan

Cover the currants with hot tap water and set them aside to soak until they are plumped and soft—about 10 minutes, but longer if they are as hard as pebbles. Once they have softened, squeeze out the water and set aside a quarter of them.

Wash the orange well, cut it roughly into chunks, and put it in a food processor with the walnuts and three quarters of the currants. Process until you have a paste that is flecked with currants and small pieces of nuts; there should be a little texture to the paste. Set aside. (If you're using a hand mill, force the oranges through, mixing them with the walnuts and currants.)

In another bowl, cream the butter with the sugar until it is light and well combined; then stir in the vanilla. Add the eggs one at a time and beat until smooth. Sift the flour with the soda and salt; then gradually stir it into the butter mixture, a third at a time, alternating with the buttermilk. Stir in the orange-currant-walnut paste and the reserved whole currants.

Preheat the oven to 325°F. Line a 9-inch round baking pan with parchment or wax paper and butter and flour the sides. Turn the batter into the pan and rap the pan a few times on the counter to settle the batter. Bake the cake in the center of the oven until the top is browned and springs back to the touch, about 50 minutes.

Remove the cake from the oven and set it on a rack, still in the pan, to cool while you make the syrup below. When the syrup is done, turn the cake out of the pan and brush half the syrup over the bottom, letting it soak in as you do so. Then turn the cake onto the serving platter you're going to use, top side up, and paint the remaining syrup over the surface. Brush a little around the sides to make them shine. (For a fancier cake, you could press finely chopped walnuts onto the sides.)

THE SYRUP

2 tablespoons unsalted butter
2 tablespoons orange blossom honey
2 tablespoons light brown or white sugar
2 teaspoons grated orange zest
1 teaspoon orange flower water (optional)

Melt the butter in a small saucepan with the honey, sugar, and orange zest. Cook for several minutes over medium-high heat until the sugar is dissolved; then stir in the orange flower water, if you're using it.

Chocolate Cake with Candied Fruits

This is one of those moist, dense, rich chocolate cakes that stop just short of being fudgey. Its smooth texture is broken with pieces of fruit—raisins soaked in brandy, candied grapefruit or orange peel, or cherries preserved in syrup. The final touch is a simple dusting of powdered sugar. This cake looks especially attractive baked in a 7½-inch fluted cake pan with a removable bottom. There will be an extra ½ cup or so of batter—bake it in a small buttered ramekin to make a special little cake for someone.

Makes 1 8-inch round cake, serving 6 to 8

> *butter and flour for the cake pan*
> *5 ounces semisweet chocolate*
> *½ cup unsalted butter*
> *¼ cup brewed espresso or strong coffee*
> *3 large eggs, at room temperature*
> *⅔ cup sugar*
> *½ teaspoon vanilla extract*
> *½ cup ground walnuts or pecans*
> *½ cup sifted unbleached white flour*
> *½ cup raisins, soaked in 2 tablespoons brandy for 20 minutes,*
> *   or ½ cup candied orange (page 397)*
> *   or grapefruit peel, cut into small pieces,*
> *   or ½ cup cherries preserved in syrup, pits removed*
> *powdered sugar*

Preheat the oven to 350°F. Butter and flour an 8-inch round cake pan or springform pan. If you're using a regular cake pan, line the bottom with a piece of parchment or wax paper. If you're using a pan with fluted sides, melt the butter and brush it into each indentation.

Break the chocolate and butter into small pieces and put them in a heavy saucepan or double boiler with the coffee. Heat slowly until the butter and chocolate have melted. Stir occasionally, but make sure the mixture stays just warm and doesn't get too hot. While the chocolate is melting, combine the eggs and sugar with an electric mixer and beat at high speed until thick, foamy, and pale yellow, about 7 minutes. Add the vanilla. Then gradually beat in the melted chocolate. Fold in the ground nuts and flour; then add the dried fruit.

Pour the batter into the prepared pan and bake it in the center of the oven until the cake is firm at the edges and springs back when touched in the center, about 40 minutes. Remove from the oven and allow to cool in the pan. When ready to serve, turn the cake out onto a serving plate and dust it with powdered sugar.

Walnut Nugget Cookies

Delicate, dry, and sweet, these simple cookies seem to disappear in the mouth. Walnut oil accentuates the flavor of the nuts. These cookies make a perfect accompaniment to fall fruits and compotes, especially Fresh Figs with Ricotta and Honey (page 355).

The dough is shaped into logs about ½ inch square and then cut into pieces a little less than ½ inch thick. They end up irregularly shaped, like little nuggets. The dough needs to harden in the refrigerator before baking. It can be shaped into logs and frozen until needed. If frozen, it should be allowed to warm up for 10 or 15 minutes before being baked. It will require a little more baking time than fresh dough.

Makes about 40 cookies

> 1 cup walnut meats
> ½ cup unsalted butter, at room temperature
> 1 tablespoon walnut oil
> ¼ cup sugar
> ¼ cup light brown sugar
> pinch of salt
> 1 teaspoon vanilla extract
> 1¼ cups unbleached white flour
> vanilla sugar or powdered vanilla sugar (page 407)

Chop the nuts until they resemble coarse sand, either by hand or in a food processor. Watch them carefully if you're using a food processor as they can quickly turn to nut butter. Cream the butter and oil together; then gradually add the sugars and the salt. When well combined, add the vanilla and then the walnuts. Finally work in the flour, bit by bit.

Divide the dough into 2 or 3 pieces and roughly shape each piece into a log. Wrap the logs in plastic wrap and then shape the dough with your hands to make a square log about ½ inch across each side. Refrigerate until hardened, about 30 minutes, or freeze.

Preheat the oven to 350°F. Cut the logs into squares and set them on a lightly greased baking sheet. Bake until they are lightly browned on top, about 15 minutes. Very carefully remove them with a spatula to a cooling rack. When warm they are very fragile, but as they cool they will become firm. Dust them with vanilla sugar or powdered sugar and store them in a covered container.

Persimmon Bars with Lemon Glaze

This recipe makes a tender cakelike bar filled with currants and drizzled with a tart-sweet lemon glaze. I have always loved the sight of persimmons hanging on the trees after the leaves have fallen—bright orange against the autumn sky— which is sometimes bright blue and sometimes gray. Filled with spice and the color of pumpkin pie, these bars are a truly autumnal cookie. This recipe comes from Helen Potter, a friend and the historian of Sutter Creek, California.

For persimmons, use the large Hachiya variety. These are the juicy ones; they should be dead-ripe and as soft as jam.

Makes about 32 bars

> *butter and flour for the pan*
> *1 cup dried currants*
> *1¾ cups unbleached white flour*
> *1 teaspoon ground cinnamon*
> *1 teaspoon freshly grated nutmeg*
> *¼ teaspoon ground cloves*
> *1 cup persimmon pulp (about 2 dead-ripe persimmons)*
> *1 teaspoon baking soda*
> *¼ teaspoon salt*
> *1½ teaspoons lemon juice*
> *1 egg*
> *1 cup sugar*
> *½ cup melted unsalted butter or neutral-tasting oil*
> *1 cup chopped walnuts or pecans*

Preheat the oven to 350°F. Grease and flour a 10- by 14-inch baking pan. If the currants are dry and hard, cover them with warm water and set them aside while you assemble the other ingredients.

Combine the flour with the cinnamon, nutmeg, and cloves in a bowl. In another bowl, beat the pulp until it is smooth; then stir in the soda, salt, lemon juice, egg, and sugar. Pour in the melted butter or oil.

Gently stir the dry ingredients, a third at a time, into the wet. Make sure they are blended, but do not overmix. Drain the currants if they've been soaking, squeeze them dry, and stir them in along with the nuts.

Spread the batter over the pan and bake until firm and lightly browned on top, 20 to 25 minutes. Remove the pan from the oven and let the bars cool in the pan while you make the lemon glaze below. Dribble the glaze from the ends of a fork over the top, then cut into pieces. These are soft, moist cookies and will keep well stored in an airtight tin.

THE LEMON GLAZE

juice of 1 lemon, approximately
1 cup powdered sugar

Stir enough juice into the sugar to make it the texture of thick cream.

Chocolate-Chestnut Log

This fudgelike log takes only a few minutes to assemble and a few hours in the refrigerator to set. It will keep easily for a week and would be just the thing for a large holiday party. Set on a platter and decorated with candied fruits and evergreens, it looks very festive. The canned chestnut purée can be found in specialty food stores.

Makes 12 servings

> *5 ounces semisweet chocolate*
> *¾ cup unsalted butter*
> *1 1-pound can chestnut purée*
> *1 tablespoon dark rum*
> *1 cup walnut meats*
> *walnut halves for garnish*
> *1 cup whipping cream*
> *½ teaspoon vanilla extract*

Combine the chocolate and butter in a heavy saucepan and melt slowly over low heat. Stir occasionally to make sure it's not sticking and to break up the chocolate. Alternatively, melt the butter and chocolate in a double boiler.

Put the chestnut purée in a bowl. When the chocolate has melted, add it to the purée along with the rum. Whisk until the mixture is smooth and shiny; then stir in the walnuts. Cover and refrigerate until cool and firm, about 1½ hours.

Put a large piece of plastic wrap on the counter. Scrape the cool chestnut mixture onto it and shape it roughly into a log about 8 to 10 inches long. Fold the plastic tightly over the log; then shape it with your hands. Transfer to a flat plate and return it to the refrigerator until hardened, another 2 hours or so.

To serve, peel away the plastic wrap and set the log on a serving dish. Garnish it with the walnut halves. Whip the cream until it holds soft peaks and stir in the vanilla. Slice the log and serve each piece with a spoonful of cream on the side.

Elli's Rusks

The Finnish version of *biscotti*, rusks are also "twice-baked" cookies, good for dunking into coffee or wine and good keepers. A Finnish friend taught me about rusks when I was in college. At the time they seemed odd and exotic—dry and not too sweet—but delicious. Now we have a market flooded with all kinds of *biscotti*. How fashions in food change!

Try these with different kinds of nuts—almonds, walnuts, hazelnuts, and pine nuts—or a mixture of your favorite nuts.

Makes about 50 3-inch cookies

> ½ cup unsalted butter, at room temperature
> ½ cup sugar
> ½ cup light brown sugar
> 2 eggs
> 1 teaspoon vanilla extract
> ½ cup sour cream
> 3 cups unbleached white flour
> ½ teaspoon salt
> ½ teaspoon baking soda
> 1 cup whole wheat pastry flour
> ½ cup finely chopped almonds or walnuts
> ¼ cup roughly chopped almonds or walnuts

Preheat the oven to 325°F. Beat the butter until soft; then gradually add the sugars and beat until light. Beat in the eggs one at a time; then add the vanilla and sour cream and beat until the mixture is smooth.

Sift the white flour, salt, and baking soda together; then work it into the butter and egg mixture a little at a time along with the whole wheat flour and the nuts. When it becomes too stiff to work with a spoon, stop and use your hand to mix in the remaining flour.

Roll the dough into logs about 1 inch across, lay them on a cookie sheet, and bake them in the middle of the oven until they are golden all over, about 40 minutes. Remove them from the oven and lower the temperature to 300°F. Slice the

cooked logs diagonally about ½ inch thick or slightly less for a more delicate cookie. Place the slices, cut side down, on the cookie sheets and return them to the oven. Bake them until browned on both sides, about 15 minutes or so. Transfer them to a rack to cool. Store the rusks in a covered tin.

Suggestions: Different varieties of nuts, such as pine nuts or hazelnuts, can be used in these cookies in place of almonds. If using pine nuts, chop half of them and leave the rest whole. If using hazelnuts, roast them first in a 350°F oven until they begin to smell toasty, about 7 or 8 minutes; then remove them. When they're cool, rub them together in a towel to loosen the skins. Chop the hazelnuts into large pieces before using them.

Raisin Squares and a Dozen Diamond Cookies

Raisin squares are a treat my grandmother always made for her family in California for the winter holidays. Two moist layers of raisins cooked with lemon are sandwiched between thin layers of pastry. The pastry on top should be thin and crisp, generously dusted with sugar and cinnamon. They go wonderfully with a pot of Earl Grey tea.

Every time I make raisin squares, I cut back the amount of dough so that there will be plenty of raisins in proportion to the pastry. However, there is always dough left over. Instead of trying to get it exactly right, I just roll out the scraps and cut them into diamond shapes, dust them with cinnamon and sugar, and bake them as little cookies. They are just rich enough and not too sweet.

Originally the raisins were ground in a meat grinder, but a food processor works perfectly. This filling is delicious; you could also use it to make a raisin pie with a lattice crust or individual tartlets.

Makes about 36 squares

THE FILLING

1 pound raisins
grated zest of 1 lemon
3 to 4 tablespoons sugar
1 cup boiling water
juice of 1 lemon
1 tablespoon flour
¼ cup dried currants

Rinse the raisins; then put them in a food processor with the lemon zest and sugar. Start the machine, pour in the boiling water, and process until you have a coarse purée that still has some texture. Transfer the purée to a saucepan and add the lemon juice, flour, and currants. Cook, stirring frequently, over medium heat until the mixture has thickened a little, about 5 minutes. Set aside to cool.

THE DOUGH

½ cup unsalted butter
½ cup sugar
1 teaspoon vanilla extract
2 eggs
2 cups unbleached white flour
1 teaspoon baking powder
¼ teaspoon salt
3 tablespoons milk or sour cream
1 tablespoon sugar
2 teaspoons ground cinnamon

Cream the butter with the ½ cup sugar until light and well mixed; then beat in the vanilla, 1 whole egg, and the yolk of the second egg. (Reserve the white.) Beat until smooth.

Sift the flour, baking powder, and salt together; then gradually stir it into the butter mixture, adding ½ cup at a time, alternating with the milk or sour cream. When you get to the last cup, the dough will be too stiff to work easily with a spoon, so work in the flour with your fingers until the dough feels fairly dry and not too sticky. Turn it out onto the counter and knead in the rest of the flour. When it has all been incorporated and the dough feels smooth, slip it into a plastic bag and set it in the refrigerator for at least 15 minutes.

When you're ready to form the squares, preheat the oven to 350°F. Divide the dough into 3 equal parts. Roll each piece into a thin sheet large enough to cover the bottom of a 9- by 12-inch pan. Set the pan on the dough and trim away the excess so that it will fit more or less exactly. Fold it in half as you would a pie crust, lift it into the pan, and unfold.

Spread half the raisin filling over the pastry; then cover it with a second pastry layer. Spread over the rest of the filling and cover it with the third piece of dough. Beat the reserved egg white with a fork and brush it over the top layer of the pastry. Combine the tablespoon of sugar and the cinnamon and sprinkle it over the top.

Bake until the top is crisp and lightly browned, about 40 minutes. Allow it to cool; then cut it into squares, keeping them on the small side since the filling is concentrated and intensely flavored.

The Diamond Cookies: Gather together all the dough scraps and briefly knead them. Roll the dough into a rectangle, cut it into strips, and then cut the strips into diamonds. Place them on a cookie sheet, brush them with egg white (or melted butter), sprinkle them with cinnamon and sugar, and bake until lightly browned, about 12 minutes.

Cardamom-Orange Oeufs à la Neige

Oeufs à la neige, or "snow eggs," are tender poached meringues floating on a perfumed custard. It's an old-fashioned dessert but really one of the best. Though light and airy, the meringue has texture, like biting into hundreds of little channels and pockets of air held together by the thinnest membranes—not unlike snow—and the spoonful of custard is by contrast creamy, cold, and unctuous. *Oeufs à la neige* make the perfect finish to many meals, but especially those pungent ones with lots of spices and hot flavors.

These meringues are quite a bit easier to handle than baked ones. The whites are whipped with sugar until stiff and glossy and then simply poached in water. The custard can be made one or two days before it's needed, and the meringues one or two hours before serving time.

The custard is also good served with fruit—such as sliced oranges, ripe red bananas, fresh pineapple and mangoes.

Makes 4 to 6 servings

THE CUSTARD

> 2 cups milk
> ¼ cup sugar
> 1 teaspoon freshly ground cardamom
> 3 large egg yolks
> 1 teaspoon grated orange zest
> 1 tablespoon orange flower water

Heat the milk with the sugar and half the cardamom in a saucepan over low heat. While it is heating, gently whisk the yolks together in a bowl. Have a strainer ready and a wooden spoon with a flat bottom.

When the milk has nearly reached a boil, stir a little of it into the yolks to warm them; then gradually add the rest of the milk. (Avoid making too many bubbles and foam, or it will be hard to tell in the next step when the custard is done.)

Return the combined milk and yolks to the saucepan and scrape out the bowl. Set the bowl near the pan and put the strainer on top. Heat the custard over medium heat and stir constantly with the wooden spoon, scraping over the bottom of the pan while you do so. Periodically check the back of the spoon to see if the

custard is beginning to thicken. When it clearly clings to the spoon and you notice little lumps of cooked fragments of egg white, pour it through the strainer into the bowl. Don't let it boil, or the yolks will cook.

Stir in the orange zest and the orange flower water. Add enough of the remaining cardamom to replace any left behind in the strainer. Cover and set the custard in the refrigerator to cool.

THE MERINGUES

3 egg whites, at room temperature
¼ teaspoon cream of tartar
5 tablespoons sugar
8 unsalted pistachio nuts, shelled, peeled, and chopped
freshly grated nutmeg or ground cinnamon

Make sure the egg whites are at room temperature. If not, warm them by swirling them over a burner. Beat them with the cream of tartar until they form stiff peaks. Beating more slowly, gradually add the sugar.

Heat a wide pot or pan of water until it is just below a simmer. Scoop up a large spoonful of meringue, push it off with a finger or a second spoon, and slide it into the water. Cook for 3 minutes; then carefully turn it and cook for another 3 minutes. Don't let the water boil, or the meringue will be very tough. Set the cooked meringues on a clean towel.

To serve, pour the chilled custard into a serving bowl and set the meringues on top. Garnish with the chopped pistachio nuts and a delicate dusting of nutmeg or cinnamon.

Violet Custard

This romantic floral custard is scented with an infusion of violet petals, round husky coriander seeds, pieces of cinnamon bark, and blood orange or lemon zest. If you want the flavor of violets, one thing is certain: *handfuls* of violets are needed. Even a hundred violets make only 5 tablespoons of petals, just enough to impart their perfume. But violets spread energetically throughout a garden, so the possibility of harvesting a hundred blossoms is not at all preposterous.

When first removed from the oven, the petals will appear washed out and gray, but as the custards cool, the color comes back. Working with handfuls of violets—with their heady fragrance and piercing color—is a sensual experience.

Orange or lemon blossoms also delight with their fragrance and can be used along with or in place of violets. And if all this sounds silly, forget the flowers— you'll still have a delicately scented, creamy dessert.

Makes 6 servings

> *100 or more fragrant violets*
> *10 coriander seeds*
> *1 1-inch piece of cinnamon stick*
> *1 wide strip of orange or lemon peel*
> *1 cup milk*
> *1½ cups half-and-half*
> *6 tablespoons sugar*
> *2 egg yolks*
> *2 whole eggs*

Pluck the petals from the base of the flowers or cut them off with a knife. Put all but a few tablespoons of the violet petals in a pan along with the coriander seeds, cinnamon, and lemon peel. Add the milk, half-and-half, and sugar and heat to just below a simmer. Set aside to steep, covered, in the refrigerator for at least an hour but preferably overnight. (If you keep the infusion overnight, rewarm the milk when you make the custard.)

Combine the yolks and whole eggs in a bowl, beat them well with a fork, and add the warmed milk mixture. Pour the mixture through a strainer and then into custard cups. Distribute the remaining violet petals over the custards.

Preheat the oven to 325°F. Bring a kettle of water to heat. Set the custards in a baking pan with sides that are higher than the cups. Pour in the hot water to within ½ inch of the top. Cover tightly with foil and bake in the center of the oven until the custards are set on the outside but still a little loose in the center when you give them a shake, about 25 minutes. Serve just slightly chilled.

Rice and Coconut Milk Pudding

Most people have rice on hand, and with a can or two of coconut milk in the cupboard as well, you can make this dessert on the spur of the moment. It is wonderful chilled and served with fruit—honeydew, pineapple, or bananas—but best are slices of ripe, sweet mangoes.

Coconut rice puddings are made in South America and in Asia. This simple pudding is based on a traditional Thai dessert made with steamed glutinous rice. It is wonderfully dense and delicious, but the sticky rice isn't readily available and requires soaking overnight. In its place, use any kind of white rice. Basmati is the most fragrant, and its delicate flavor is lovely with the coconut, but a short-grain rice will give the pudding more body.

Makes 4 to 6 servings

> 1 cup white rice, preferably basmati or short-grain
> 2 cups water
> salt
> 3 cups milk or a mixture of milk and coconut milk
> ¼ cup sugar
> 1 can coconut milk (not piña colada mix)
> 1 mango or other tropical fruit, such as banana or melon, sliced
>   or cut into small cubes, or 1 passion fruit
> 8 unsalted pistachio nuts, shelled, peeled, and chopped

Rinse the rice well. If you're using basmati rice, cover it with cold water and soak it for 30 minutes after rinsing; then drain. Handle it carefully as the grains are fragile. Combine the rice and water in a pan, bring to a boil, lower the heat, and simmer gently until the water has been absorbed. Add a pinch or 2 of salt, the milk, and the sugar. Bring to a boil, lower the heat, and simmer slowly, stirring occasionally, for 45 minutes. Stir in the coconut milk and set the mixture aside to cool. Gently fold the fruit into the pudding, or squeeze the passion fruit over the pudding. Garnish the pudding with the pistachio nuts and serve it warm or chilled.

Suggestion: Omit the fresh fruit and cook the rice with a small piece of sliced, fresh ginger, a piece of cinnamon stick, and a few cloves. Serve it dusted with cinnamon.

Lemon Pudding Cake with Crystal Sugar

A thin batter separates while baking, yielding a tender crumbed cake sitting on a lemon pudding. It's an old-fashioned recipe, but one that never grows old, at least for me. I've tried it with tangerines and oranges for variation, but lemon is best. Sweet Meyer lemons are even better. The decorative crystal sugar—little clear squares of sugar that will hold their shape through baking—are like sequins on a dress; they add a festive touch. *And* they crunch in your teeth—not at all what you would expect from a soft pudding cake. (The sugar can sometimes be found in the baking section of supermarkets or in specialty stores. Bakeries will often sell it, if asked.)

This pudding cake can be served alone or with a drift of whipped cream. It's also very nice garnished with a cluster of red currants or served with raspberries or blueberries.

Makes 4 to 6 servings

> 3 tablespoons unsalted butter
> ¾ cup sugar
> grated zest of 2 lemons
> 4 eggs, separated
> ⅓ cup freshly squeezed lemon juice (juice of 1 or 2 lemons)
> 3 tablespoons unbleached white flour
> 1 cup milk or light cream
> a few gratings of nutmeg
> ⅛ teaspoon salt
> 1 tablespoon crystal sugar squares, if available

Preheat the oven to 350°F. Heat a kettle of water for the water bath.

Cream the butter with the sugar; then stir in the lemon zest and the yolks, one at a time, beating until smooth. Stir in the lemon juice; then add the flour, milk or light cream, and nutmeg.

Beat the egg whites with the salt until they form soft peaks; then fold them into the batter. Pour the batter into a 6-cup baking dish or into individual ramekins. Set in a large pan and add enough of the hot water to come halfway up the sides. Bake for 15 minutes; then carefully pull out the pan and sprinkle the crystal sugar over the top. Return the pan to the oven until the cake is lightly browned and set, about 10 more minutes for individual ramekins and 35 more minutes for a single cake. Cool and serve either tepid or chilled.

Sweetmeats

The Final Flourish

Plump fresh dates filled with rose almond paste, candied fruit peels dipped in chocolate or dusted with sugar, disks of scented nut pastes tucked between walnut halves and netted with caramel, or a simple fig stuffed with a roasted almond—these are a few of the jewellike confections that can be crafted from simple ingredients. Based on whole nuts, nut pastes scented and colored with floral extracts, and dried fruits, sweetmeats were undoubtedly some of the first desserts. Adding chocolate and sugar elaborates what is basically a simple treat—nuts preserved in their shells and fruits dried in the sun.

Winter is the time for sweetmeats, when fresh fruits are somewhat limited except for those expensive items imported from the ends of the earth. There are, however, many citrus fruits available, from the tiny kumquat to the enormous, puffy pomelo—all their peels can be converted to candies. Many of the fruits that were fresh a few short months ago—peaches, figs, apricots, apples, cherries, prunes—have been dried, and their flesh should be succulent and moist. We don't usually think of dates as having a season, but over a hundred varieties, varying in color from pale gold to black, are grown in southern California; they begin to mature in November and continue through January. Fresh dates are luscious and soft. The sugars have not yet hardened, and their plump flesh melts on the tongue.

Sweetmeats are a pleasure to make. Almond paste, the basis of many of these treats, can be made weeks before you plan to use it. Although candied peels are particularly succulent when fresh, they will keep for months. And some of the other sweetmeats, though most tender and moist when really fresh, will last for weeks if tightly wrapped.

Toasting and chopping nuts, melting chocolate, and making caramel are the work of a moment. Once you have a number of parts made, you can quickly put together a plate of assorted sweetmeats to serve at the end of a meal or to take somewhere as a gift, each sweetmeat tucked into its own paper case and set in a box. Each is a gem to offer.

Serve these sweets at the end of a meal, with fresh fruit or with cheese, in place of dessert, or serve them later in the evening after dessert, with a glass of port.

Basic Ingredients for Sweetmeats

Here is a list of elements to have on hand for making a variety of sweetmeats. Recipes are given for those starred, and specific suggestions follow.

almond paste*
black dates
medjool dates
pitted prunes
dried apricots
whole almonds
unsalted pistachio nuts
whole walnuts and walnut halves
candied citrus peel*
orange flower water
rose water
food colorings or vegetables for coloring
candied violets and roses*
light corn syrup
superfine granulated sugar
crystal sugar
candied ginger
semisweet chocolate
paper candy cases

Almond Paste

This confection is the basis for many sweetmeats. It can be colored and flavored with rose, orange, and pistachio and used to stuff dates and prunes or embraced with matching halves of walnuts. You can buy it in the baking section of most supermarkets and then tint and color it yourself, but it is a fraction of the cost to make it yourself—and yours will be much fresher.

A modern facsimile of this ancient hand-pounded confection can be made swiftly in a food processor. It's good to make it at least a week in advance so that the flavor of the almonds can ripen fully. It will keep for six months, refrigerated, so you can make it well before the holiday season becomes hectic.

There are many varieties of almonds, and they differ in shape, size, and taste. Unfortunately there are not so many varieties to choose from in a typical market, but the mission almond, grown in California, can occasionally be found. Missions are small; there are usually two almonds with hard, pointed tips in a shell, tightly curved against each other. They are a little harder to peel than other almonds, but their flavor is clearly and pronouncedly almond, closer to the virtually unobtainable bitter almond that is traditionally used in almond paste and marzipan, and they smell wonderful when they are being ground.

Makes approximately 1 pound

> 2 cups whole almonds, preferably Mission
> 1 cup sugar
> ½ cup water
> 2 tablespoons light corn syrup
> a few drops of almond extract

Cover the almonds with boiling water and let them stand for at least a minute. Slip off the skins with your fingers. If they are very stubborn, cover them again with boiling water or let them soak and remove them just a few at a time to work on.

Combine the sugar, water, and corn syrup in a pan and cook, without stirring, until the temperature is 235°F. Then stir in the almond extract.

While the syrup is heating, preheat the oven to 250°F. Put the peeled almonds on a cookie sheet and leave them just long enough to dry out and warm up, about 8 to 10 minutes. Then, while they're still warm, grind them in a food processor until the texture is fine and smooth. If necessary, add 1 or 2 tablespoons of water to loosen the mixture and make it easier to process.

With the food processor going, gradually pour in the syrup in a slow, steady stream. Process until the paste is uniform. Remove it from the work bowl, wrap it well in plastic wrap, and refrigerate it until needed. To make it soft and easy to work with, put it in a warm place, such as on top of the stove while the oven is on, or heat it in a double boiler or a steamer set over simmering water.

Orange Almond Paste

1 recipe almond paste (opposite)
grated zest of 4 large oranges, or more to taste
2 teaspoons orange flower water, or to taste
1 drop orange food coloring, or more

Knead the almond paste with the rest of the ingredients or mix them in the food processor. Make any other additions, such as more orange flower water or coloring, gradually and carefully. The flavors will deepen as the paste ripens.

Rose Almond Paste

1 recipe almond paste (opposite)
a few drops of beet juice or red food coloring
1 to 2 teaspoons rose water, or to taste

Knead the almond paste with a few drops of beet juice or food coloring until it is as pink as you wish. Then work in rose water to taste.

Pistachio-Almond Paste

In the almond paste recipe on the opposite page, replace ½ cup of the almonds with ½ cup unsalted pistachio nuts. Put the pistachios in a preheated 350°F oven for about 10 minutes to dry and loosen the skins; then remove the skins with a paring knife or your fingers. They should come right off. Work the pistachio nuts with the almonds in the food processor. If you wish to end up with a uniform pale green color, add either some concentrated spinach juice, a drop or 2 of green food coloring, or about a tablespoon of powdered Japanese green tea, *matcha* (a wonderful suggestion from Rose Levy Beranbaum's *The Cake Bible*).

Candied Grapefruit Peels

Grapefruit peels are so thick that they yield big, plump, soft candies. They can be dusted with sugar and served as sweetmeats after dinner or left plain and used in baking, such as the Cheese Stöllen on page 302. Ruby or white grapefruit will yield pink or pale yellow candies respectively. Use organically grown fruit in order to be certain the skins aren't dyed or coated with pesticides.

3 grapefruits, preferably organic
2½ cups sugar
1¼ cups water
2 tablespoons light corn syrup
additional superfine sugar for coating

Either score the grapefruits into quarters and carefully pull off the peels or cut them in half, juice the fruits, and cut the halves in half again. Put the peels in a pot, cover with cold water, and bring to a boil. Simmer for 25 minutes; then remove the peels and let cool until they are easy to handle. Using a teaspoon, hold the peels firmly and gently scrape away as much of the white pith as possible. Cut the cleaned rinds into narrow strips with a knife or scissors.

Combine the sugar, water, and corn syrup in a 2-quart non-corroding saucepan, stir, and bring to a boil. When the syrup is clear, add the peels, lower the heat, and cook slowly until they are translucent, about an hour.

Set a cake rack over a baking sheet. Remove the peels, a few at a time, and spread them out on the rack. If you're using them for cooking, allow them to stand until they have dried; then put them in a plastic container or jar, cover, and keep refrigerated until needed.

If you wish to use the peels for a sweetmeat, take a clean plate and cover it generously with sugar. Let the peels drain for a minute on the rack; then lightly toss them in the sugar (chopsticks work perfectly for this). Set them on a clean rack. It will be necessary to do this in several batches. If you're reusing the sugar, pass it through a sieve first to get rid of the lumps formed by the drops of syrup.

Allow the sugared peels to sit until they have dried some, an hour or so, then carefully package them in a tin or plastic container and store. They will keep for several weeks on a cupboard shelf or several months refrigerated.

Candied Orange or Lemon Peel

Use 5 or 6 thick-skinned oranges or 6 large lemons and treat them as above. Being thinner, they may take less time to cook than the grapefruit. Again, avoid using fruit that has been dyed and sprayed.

Chocolate-Covered Candied Fruit Peels

The combination of citrus and chocolate is sublime and timeless.

Rather than coating the finished rinds in sugar, let them drain on a rack until they are fairly dry and not too sticky; then dip them in melted bittersweet or semisweet chocolate. They can be kept in the refrigerator and then brought to room temperature before being served.

Enough to cover approximately 2 cups candied peels

> *5 ounces semisweet chocolate, chopped into small pieces*
> *2 teaspoons unsalted butter*

Put the chocolate and butter in the top of a double boiler or in a heavy saucepan and gradually melt over low heat. Stir to combine the butter and chocolate. Dip each piece of fruit into the chocolate; then set it on a piece of parchment or foil to cool. Chopsticks, a pair of forks, or fingers will all work. If it's warm in the kitchen, set the chocolates in a cool place, like a porch or near an open window, or the refrigerator to set.

Each piece can be coated entirely or just in part, leaving one end uncovered to serve as a kind of handle.

Suggestions: If you have little drops or shards of caramel on hand, you can set them in the chocolate when it is almost completely set for a sparkly garnish. (If you're using caramel, the sweetmeats should be served the same day they're made as the caramel will absorb moisture and soften.) Finely chopped pistachio nuts sprinkled over the moist chocolate make a pretty garnish, particularly when part of the fruit is left unglazed.

Candied ginger and squares of almond paste are also delicious with a chocolate coating.

Caramel Syrup for Threads and Dots

You can use this syrup to make a smooth, glassy covering over nuts, or by waving it from the ends of a fork you can encase a confection with golden threads. If you let it drip onto a piece of marble or parchment paper, you'll get little golden disks or dots that can be fastened onto almond paste or chocolate-dipped citrus peels. Caramel will soften with exposure to moist air, so it's necessary to store these baubles in an airtight container.

If you're planning to make confections frequently over several days, you can reuse extra caramel by reheating it in a double boiler. Store extra caramel in a cool place until needed.

Makes enough caramel for approximately a dozen almond confections

> *½ cup sugar*
> *2 tablespoons water*
> *2 tablespoons light corn syrup*

Use a small, heavy saucepan with a light-colored interior so that you can see what's happening. Pour the sugar into the pan, dribble the water over the top, and let it sit for a few minutes to seep into the sugar. Pour in the corn syrup and gently heat over low heat, swirling the pan to mix the ingredients and dissolve the sugar. Cook until the syrup is a warm golden color, at 350°F; then set the pan in a bowl of cold water and ice cubes to stop the cooking. If you can't tell what color it is in the pan, spoon a drop onto a white plate.

At first the caramel will be very thin, but as it cools it will become thicker. While it is thin, use it for dipping nuts so that the coating will be very light. As it cools to about 240°F and becomes more viscous, use it for making threads or dots.

To make threads, dip a fork into the caramel and wave it back and forth. The caramel will form long, brittle threads that will cool in the air. You can let the threads form over a piece of parchment paper and use them as a garnish or wave the caramel directly over a confection to make a net. These threads are fragile and sharp, so handle the finished sweetmeats carefully.

Candied Flowers

It's not difficult to candy blossoms, and they will have much more taste and be even prettier than those you can buy. They can be used whole to garnish cakes and ice creams, or finely chopped and sprinkled over various desserts or sweetmeats. Rose petals and violets are most commonly seen in sugared form, but there's no reason you couldn't try coating other edible blooms with sugar, such as orange or lemon blossoms, borage, lilacs, and jasmine, to name but a few. Not all flowers are edible, so be certain that the ones you are contemplating using are.

Also be sure to use blossoms that haven't been sprayed with chemicals. Choose the most aromatic flowers you can find. Wild violets or rambling lawn violets often have intense perfume, as do certain kinds of old roses and wild roses. The flowers should be free of insects and dry before you candy them.

To candy blossoms, you'll need a pastry or watercolor brush and a cookie sheet. One egg white will cover lots and lots of flowers.

> *fresh blossoms*
> *1 egg white*
> *superfine sugar*

Beat the egg white with a few drops of water until it is well broken up and a fine froth coats the top. Sprinkle sugar in a thick layer over a flat dish or cookie sheet.

Dip a pastry or watercolor brush into the froth and carefully paint the blossoms. Sprinkle them with the sugar so that they are evenly but lightly coated. If you use too much sugar, it will be hard to see the petals.

Set the sugared blossoms into the dish or pan of sugar. Place the blossoms face down so that the petals will dry spread out rather than stuck together. Sprinkle more sugar over any thin spots. Set aside to dry for several hours; then store in an airtight container.

The color will fade fairly quickly, so if you're making candied petals for their color, it is best to do so the day you're planning to use them. Otherwise the candies can be stored, and although the color will fade, the sugar will be infused with the scent of the blossoms.

Medjool Dates with Orange Almond Paste

Medjools, the largest of the blond dates, make a big, plump mouthful.

Carefully slit open the dates and remove the pits. Roll a marble of orange almond paste (page 395) between your palms, shape it into a lozenge, and insert it into the date. Close the sides neatly around the paste, leaving a wide ribbon exposed. Take a few pieces of candied orange peel (page 397) and chop into small pieces. Sprinkle them over the orange almond paste along with finely chopped pistachio nuts. A few hardened drops of caramel sprinkled on top will give the confection a glittery effect.

Black Dates with Rose Almond Paste

Large, luscious, and dramatic-looking, black dates set off all colors well, but the combination of pink almond paste and a dusting of green against the shiny black is especially pretty.

Carefully slit the dates lengthwise and remove the pits. Roll a piece of rose almond paste (page 395) between your palms to give it a lozenge shape and insert it into the date. Bring the edges of the date neatly against the paste. To strengthen the rose flavor, brush a little rose water over the surface. Gently press the paste into a mound of finely chopped unsalted pistachio nuts or decorate with a single bright green piece.

Date-Almond Confections

Although its dark appearance suggests something that's healthy but a little dull, this confection is quite luscious. It can be made in moments in the food processor, and the finished sweetmeat will keep for several weeks if well wrapped and refrigerated.

Makes about 30 pieces

> *⅔ cup shelled blanched or unpeeled almonds*
> *½ pound black, Medjool or a mixture of different kinds of dates*
> *½ cup shelled unsalted pistachio nuts*
> *3 ounces almond paste (page 394)*
> *1 tablespoon orange flower water*

Preheat the oven to 325°F. Put the almonds on a cookie sheet and bake until they smell toasty, about 7 minutes. Remove and let cool for a few minutes.

If the dates are at all hard or dry, set them in a steamer over boiling water until they're softened, 3 to 5 minutes. Let them cool for a few minutes; then remove the pits.

Peel the pistachio nuts and chop half of them coarsely. Slice the others in half.

Put the dates and almond paste in the food processor and process until a roughly textured paste is formed. Add the almonds and orange flower water and process again until the almonds are roughly chopped.

Turn the paste out onto a counter and divide it into 2 pieces. Knead each piece with the chopped pistachio nuts; then set each piece on a piece of plastic wrap and shape it into a square log with sides about an inch wide. Peel back the plastic and garnish the sides with the halved pistachio nuts; then rewrap tightly and store in the refrigerator until needed. To serve, cut into ½-inch pieces and place in paper cases.

Almond and Walnut Confections
with Caramel Threads

This is a very pretty confection with smooth disks of colored almond paste bracketed by perfect walnut halves, the whole thing netted in threads of caramel. The caramel will soften when exposed to the moisture in the air, so keep these in an airtight container until just before serving.

> *almond paste (page 394)*
> *walnut halves, 2 for each confection*
> *finely chopped peeled pistachio nuts*
> *caramel syrup (page 398)*

Use any flavor of almond paste or a mixture of flavors and colors. Roll a large marble of paste between your hands to make a smooth ball; then press it gently to make a flat disk. Embrace the disk with 2 walnut halves. Roll the sides in the finely chopped pistachio nuts.

Dip one side of each confection into the hot caramel syrup to cover the nut lightly; then set it on a piece of parchment or wax paper to cool. When the caramel is cool, dip the other side into the caramel to cover the nut; then cool. Chopsticks, if you are comfortable with them, make an ideal tool for this operation. It may be necessary to keep moving the pan on and off the heat to keep the caramel soft without overcooking it.

After all the nuts have been dipped, dip a fork into the hot caramel and wave it back and forth over the tops of each one so that it is crisscrossed with delicate threads. Experiment over a piece of paper until you get the hang of it. It may be necessary to let the caramel cool just a little for the threads to form. Carefully set each confection in a paper case and store them in an airtight container.

Suggestion: For a fancy, colorful addition, chop some candied violet or rose petals (page 399) very finely and press them, along with the pistachio nuts, into the sides of the almond paste disks.

Prunes Stuffed with Walnuts, Chocolate, and Orange Peel

People are always surprised by the combination of prunes with chocolate, but the two have a natural affinity for each other. Orange also goes beautifully with both, and the three together make a tasty bite. These prune confections can be assembled in moments from ingredients you might already have on hand.

I remember being served prunes with orange zest once and thinking, for some odd reason, that the little bits of orange, which were showing just ever so slightly, were carrots. I was so busy wondering why someone would put carrots with prunes that I wasn't prepared for the burst of fresh, bittersweet orange peel that finally came, and it was a wonderful surprise!

It's best to use unsprayed, undyed oranges.

> *large pitted prunes*
> *bittersweet chocolate*
> *walnut quarters*
> *fine strands of fresh orange zest (preferably*
> *   organic), removed with a citrus zester*
> *superfine sugar (optional)*

If the prunes aren't pitted, steam them over hot water until they are soft; then remove the pits. Insert a nugget of chocolate and a piece or 2 of walnut into each prune. Gently stuff a few strands of orange zest inside, leaving some showing or not, as you like. Sprinkle superfine sugar over the prunes if you want to give them a frosted look. Put them in paper cases.

Suggestions: Use tangerine peel or thin slices of kumquats in place of the oranges. Though similar to the orange, their flavors will seem vaguely mysterious mixed with the prunes and chocolate.

Make a mixture of chopped toasted hazelnuts, grated chocolate, and fine lemon zest. Stuff it into the prunes and roll the prunes in fine sugar.

Instead of prunes, try both mixtures of chocolate and nuts with dried figs, particularly black mission figs.

Dried Figs with Almonds

Blanch as many almonds as you have dried figs. Cover them with boiling water for a minute or as long as it takes to loosen the skins; then drain the almonds and slip off the skins. Toast the almonds—or walnuts or pine nuts—in a moderate oven until they are lightly colored and crisp. Cut a slit in a dried fig, insert a roasted almond, and then cover it tightly with the flesh of the fig.

Preserved Figs with Star Anise and Bay

Here the figs are halved, with the skins left on. They make a succulent dessert served with a spoonful of fresh ricotta cheese (page 353) or a mild goat cheese. I also like to serve a few alongside a slice of almond cake (page 374). They look beautiful in their jars, the loose seeds falling into scalloped rows.

Makes 1 quart

> 3 pounds figs
> 1 lemon
> 2½ cups sugar
> ¾ cup water
> 6 whole star anise
> 1 bay leaf

Cut off the tough stems of the figs; then halve them and put them in a non-corroding bowl. Remove several wide strips of lemon zest with a carrot peeler; then slice them into thin slivers.

Bring the sugar and water to a boil with the lemon zest, anise, and bay and boil slowly for 5 minutes, stirring at first to dissolve the sugar. Then pour the syrup over the figs, squeeze over the lemon juice, and leave them to stand overnight, covered, in a cool place.

The next day, transfer the figs to a wide saucepan. Gently bring them to a boil and cook slowly for the better part of 2 hours. Occasionally check the figs and give them a stir so that they are all submerged, taking care not to break them. Prepare canning jars in boiling water to sterilize them; then ladle in the figs, add the tops, and process according to the method you're using.

Dried Fruit and Sesame Sweetmeats

An ancient Roman recipe inspired this concoction of dried fruits and roasted sesame seeds perfumed with orange flower water and spiced with fennel and cinnamon. The original used only figs for fruit and included quite a bit of cumin. The cumin is quite interesting but jarring to our modern sensibilities regarding sweets, so I've left it out of this version, but you might give it a try.

The paste can be shaped into logs and sliced or rolled into balls, which are easier to form. Since the fruit is a little sticky, it helps to coat the balls with something easier to handle—roasted sesame seeds or powdered sugar.

Makes 24 1-inch sweetmeats

> 1 pound mixed dried fruits such as figs, black or golden raisins, and dates
> ⅓ cup toasted sesame seeds
> ½ cup walnut meats
> grated zest and juice of 1 orange
> ½ teaspoon ground cinnamon, or to taste
> ½ to 1 teaspoon fennel seeds
> orange flower water, to taste
> 1 to 2 tablespoons brandy (optional)
> additional toasted sesame seeds or sugar or powdered sugar

If the fruits are hard, steam them over hot water for several minutes or until they're soft. Remove the stems from the figs and the pits from the dates. Put the fruit in a food processor with the sesame seeds, walnuts, orange zest and juice, cinnamon, and fennel seeds. Process until you have a rough paste; then add the orange flower water and brandy, if you're using it. Taste and add more cinnamon or fennel seeds as desired.

Break the paste into even pieces and shape them into balls about an inch across; then roll them in the sesame seeds or dust with sugar. Store them on a plate covered tightly with plastic until ready to serve; then set each one in a paper cup.

Candied Kumquats

I've always thought of kumquats as the backward fruit. When I was a child, my father made me eat one, insisting that I begin with the skin. Thinking it was a trick, I did so but only with reluctance. Actually it *was* a trick, but a nice one, for it's the skin of the kumquat that's sweet and the fruit inside that's sour.

These beautiful little egg-shaped citrus fruits are a perfect size to candy. As with the citrus peels, they are parboiled and then cooked slowly in syrup, allowed to cool, and then set on a rack to drain. They can be dusted with superfine sugar, if desired, and set in paper cases. They do have small seeds, which can be removed when the kumquats are sliced.

Makes approximately 2 cups

> *1 pound firm but ripe kumquats, preferably organic*
> *3½ cups sugar*
> *2 cups water*
> *superfine sugar, if desired*

Wash the kumquats well, put them in a pan, cover them with cold water, and bring to a boil. Simmer the fruits for about 10 minutes; then drain.

Combine the sugar and water in a heavy, non-corroding saucepan, bring to a boil, and stir to dissolve the sugar. Add the parboiled kumquats; then lower the heat and cook slowly until the fruits begin to look translucent, about 20 minutes, or longer if they are large. Once they are beginning to look clear, turn off the heat and allow them to cool in the syrup. Set a rack over a cookie sheet and remove the cooled fruits to it. Allow the syrup to drain off and the fruits to dry, several hours or overnight. Dust or roll the dried fruits in superfine sugar, if desired, and set them in paper cases. Store in an airtight tin.

■ Save the syrup to sweeten juices for compotes, to add to tea, or to spoon over ice cream.

Kumquats with Cloves

This touch is for people who love cloves. Add 3 cloves to the kumquats while they are cooking; then insert a clove into each one. The flavor will permeate the fruit, but the cloves can easily be withdrawn before the kumquats are eaten.

Kumquats in Syrup

If you prefer, rather than letting the kumquats dry, pack them in a clean jar in their syrup and store them in the refrigerator. They should keep indefinitely. They can be used in fruit compotes, either whole, if they are small, or sliced. Or work them into sweet breads, like the stöllen on page 302, or slice them and serve them over ice cream or stir them into rice puddings.

Vanilla Sugar

After vanilla beans have been used to flavor a custard or pudding, a lot of flavor remains. Recycle them in vanilla sugar. Wipe the beans with a towel and set them on a plate to dry overnight. If they still have their seeds, scrape them with the point of a knife into a jar of granulated or powdered sugar. Rub the little clumps of seeds between your fingers to break them up and disperse them among the grains of sugar. Plunge the pods into the jar and cover it tightly.

In a few days their aroma will have penetrated the sugar. Keep adding beans as they become available. The sugar is especially nice to sprinkle over fresh and baked fruits or on top of a sweet cream cheese, like Coeur à la Crème. Powdered vanilla sugar can be used to dust over cookies and cakes.

Appendix

My Kitchen—The Pots and Pans

For most of my life my kitchen has been a community or restaurant kitchen, but in the past few years a personal kitchen has begun to take shape. It has moved from one tiny apartment to another and finally a house. Although my present kitchen is at last spacious, with room for a work table in the middle, a wicker rocker in the corner for a visiting friend, and a sunny room for eating off to the side, it holds relatively little cooking equipment. My preference is to have fewer things and to use them over and over, rather than to have a large number of pots and pans. (The one exception is a stack of stainless-steel mixing bowls.) You don't really need a lot of equipment unless you're cooking a variety of specialized dishes that require particular types of pots and pans or you like having them just because they're beautiful or inspiring.

For me the basics are three sizes of frying pans, two sizes of saucepans, a large pot for pasta, a strainer, 10 or so mixing bowls of different sizes, and the usual battery of wooden spoons, rubber scrapers, whisks, and tongs. For electric gadgets I have a blender, a food processor, and, just this year, a Kitchen-Aid mixer. My favorite pieces of equipment are mortars and pestles and earthenware dishes for baking. In addition to these there are some other pieces of standard equipment, like strainers and colanders, a glass juicer, a food mill, tart pans, a baking stone . . . I don't have a microwave oven, although I know that many people find them useful, even indispensable. What I like about the process of cooking is to be able to see, smell, and touch the food. I like the marriage of flavors that comes from long simmering or baking in the oven, the warmth of the kitchen, the aromas of food cooking—and for me that's well accomplished by the stove and the oven. Those who do use microwave ovens will, I'm sure, be able to adapt my recipes.

Although none of my equipment is particularly unusual or hard to find, there are a few things that make a real difference in how I cook and the pleasure I take in cooking. Here are some particularly useful ones.

FOOD MILL

This old-fashioned tool seems to work best for puréeing soups, sauces, and purées, especially those containing potatoes. The texture can be regulated by the choice of screen, and the relatively gentle action of an arm turning the handle prevents potatoes from getting gummy. A food mill is also very useful for screening out tough bits, like tomato skins or apple cores, when making sauces.

GRATIN DISHES AND TIANS

Gratin dishes are among the most frequently used items in my kitchen, both the porcelain kind and the oval, red-glazed earthenware dishes called *tians*. Food cooks well and always looks beautiful in them. I use them for both savory vegetable dishes and fruit desserts. They have a homey, comfortable look and are always a pleasure to bring to the table.

A large oval dish, 14 by 10 inches, will hold eight to ten servings; a smaller one, about 8 by 10 inches, will accommodate four servings, and for crowds, use a large round glazed dish about 12 inches across.

Another ceramic baking dish I use with great regularity is a small one measuring just 6 by 9 inches. This is a perfect size for one or two people—the food cooks well and looks plentiful rather than skimpy.

KNIVES

You don't really need a lot of knives. The most important thing about knives is to keep them sharp! A sharp knife makes everything in the kitchen go much more easily, while a dull knife is frustrating to work with and makes cooking unnecessarily onerous and difficult. Learn to use a sharpening stone or some other tool that you like or take your knives to be sharpened on a regular basis.

What you do need are a few different kinds of knives: a good paring knife, a 10-inch cook's knife, a serrated knife, and a 6-inch cook's knife.

Good, heavy, double-forged stainless-steel knives are well made and will last virtually forever. I used to use these exclusively; then I realized that they were too heavy for me, particularly the large cook's knife. I switched to a lighter knife that probably won't last a lifetime, but it feels much better in my hand and will not cost much to replace. A heavy knife is useful for difficult tasks, like halving a hard winter squash or huge blocks of cheese. A Chinese cleaver is also good for these jobs.

Another knife I like using is a light, stainless-steel Japanese knife with a rectangular blade. These are very inexpensive knives, and if you do a lot of chopping and slicing, you might want to try one. They are held in such a way that they feel and move like an extension of your hand; they move with your hand rather than pivoting in it, which allows for very quick movements and fast work.

A 6-inch cook's knife can be used both like a paring knife and like a cook's knife. It's small enough to hold in the hand and peel a potato and just large enough that you can switch its position and slice the potato. It is both too big and too small for certain jobs, but it does a lot of different things well and is versatile.

A good, strong paring knife is a very worthwhile investment. Get one with a blade that can hold a sharp edge. The problem with paring knives is that, like scissors and socks, they disappear, so you may need more than one. It's a good idea to have several inexpensive paring knives around for helpers and older children.

A long serrated knife is great for slicing bread, but it's also the perfect knife to use on tomatoes and artichokes. Save the edge on your cook's knife and use a bread knife instead.

MORTAR AND PESTLE

Next to my knives, the mortar and pestle is my most essential kitchen tool, one I use almost every day. My favorite one is old and large, made of olive wood, a gift from a friend in Provence. It is a treasured companion in the kitchen. Given the easy availability of food processors and blenders, a mortar and pestle might seem like a hopelessly old-fashioned tool, clung to for sentimental reasons. But in many cases I prefer it to the food processor for the way the pounding releases the perfume of garlic, peppercorns, herbs, and spices. Garlic pounded to a paste has a sweeter taste to me than processed garlic. Somehow the effect of smashing is different from the metallic slicing and chopping of the food processor, although there are also occasions when I happily prefer the machine. I like standing over a mortar, watching what's happening as I work and inhaling the aromas. Often I find it easier to reach for and clean up, too. And if I'm making a sauce, such as garlic mayonnaise or *aïoli*, I just serve it directly from the mortar instead of transferring it to another dish.

It's a good idea to have at least two mortars and pestles if you enjoy using them. I use my large wooden one for garlic and herbs, *aïoli*, *pesto*, and other sauces. It's heavy enough to sit firmly on the counter while I'm making a sauce, and it is forever seasoned with garlic. A large marble mortar would be good for the same things, and it's heavy enough so that you don't have to chase it across the counter while whisking together a mayonnaise.

I use a smaller porcelain mortar only for spices, such as cardamom, cloves, coriander, and allspice. I use it for quantities that are too small to work successfully in an electric spice mill. I always try to keep the sweet spices separate from the herbs and more pungent spices since their oils linger and flavor the mortar.

PASTA SCOOP

This large, oval strainer works very well for scooping up pasta from a pot of boiling water. Its shape captures and holds the pasta, and the absence of hooks on the edge makes it possible to get right down to the bottom of the pot and slide the strainer up the side.

PIZZA STONE AND PEEL

This large ceramic stone and wooden paddle, or peel, are sold ostensibly for making pizzas. I didn't include pizza recipes in this book (there is a whole chapter on pizza in *The Greens Cookbook*), but I use a stone constantly; in fact, it's always in my oven. It's great for baking breadstuffs that don't require a pan—round or braided breads, rolls, biscuits, scones. The peel is needed to transfer large loaves to the stone since moving them with your hands will usually destroy their shapes. I also set baking dishes and cake pans directly on the stone with no ill effects.

TONGS

Spring-loaded kitchen tongs are wonderfully useful. Like an extension of your hand, they can be used just as skillfully to pick things up, turn them over and around, and even reach for things in high places. An 11-inch pair is easiest to handle in the kitchen, but a 14-inch pair is ideal for charcoal grilling, especially if you like to cook over a large grill; the tongs allow you to work out of the direct range of smoke and intense heat. Tongs can be found in restaurant supply houses.

PANS

My large, nonstick skillet is the pan I use to cook almost everything in. It measures 12 inches across the top, 10 on the bottom. It has enough room to hold entire dishes, and its nonstick surface requires very little oil and is easy to clean. It's what I refer to throughout the book as a "large skillet" or a wide pan. I also like to use a 10-inch cast-iron frying pan, especially for potato cakes and corn breads, and a stainless-steel sauté pan for browning onions and making quick sautés. Although you don't need a special pan to make omelets and crêpes, crêpe pans are useful to have for their shape is suited exactly for the task. Also, the more you use them, the better tempered they become.

A small, heavy saucepan is perfect for small jobs such as blanching tomatoes, reducing sauces, and making syrups. One with a light-colored bottom, such as a tin-lined copper or enamel pan, allows you to check the color of the contents.

The Pantry

My pantry is rather simple, stocked with basic foods to work from and tasty condiments like olive paste, chutneys, preserved figs, and chili paste—things to use at a moment's notice for a quick bite or as a seasoning for soups or pastas. I have a wide variety of oils—11 in my refrigerator at this moment—and vinegars, a selection of olives, herbs and spices, always a large hunk of good Parmesan cheese. A varied supply of pasta, rice, and grains is on hand and there's always a variety of flours in the refrigerator. A few canned and frozen items that I have found quite useful at times are chick-peas and white beans, peas, and artichoke hearts. A cross section of my freezer would reveal frozen logs of herb butters, tins of nuts, bags of roasted green chilies, some frozen breads and perhaps a pie shell or cookie dough.

Here are some basic ingredients I use frequently and some exotic ones I use more rarely. They are the elements I feel make a difference to the quality and the ease of my cooking, and I refer to them throughout the book.

BUTTER

Butter has its own unique flavor and properties in cooking. Often its particular taste is what gives a dish its special character or charm, especially desserts but also savory dishes calling for clarified or browned butter.

There are four basic forms of butter, all of which are used in this book.

Unsalted or Sweet Butter: Since salt acts as a preservative and stabilizer, unsalted butter, also called sweet butter, is more fragile and easily absorbs the tastes and odors of other foods. Try to buy it frozen and keep it in the freezer until needed. Its taste is sweet and delicate, and it's particularly nice to use in pastries and essential for herb butters. Look for butter graded AA.

Salted Butter: This category also includes lightly salted butter. Salt is added to butter to prevent the growth of microorganisms and to keep it from turning rancid. Because of the salt it has a stronger flavor than sweet butter. Salted butter usually contains more water. I use it generally in cooking except where the delicate taste of sweet butter is preferred.

Clarified Butter: When butter is melted, the milk solids separate and can be removed. This process accentuates the "buttery" taste and renders it suitable for frying since there are no longer any milk solids to burn. Because the taste is more concentrated, clarified butter can be mixed with a neutral oil, so you can use less saturated fat while keeping the buttery taste.

To Clarify Butter: Slowly melt the butter in a heavy saucepan over low heat. Skim off the foam that rises to the surface and discard it. Let the melted butter stand for several minutes to settle; then carefully pour off the liquid, leaving behind the sediment of milk particles. To be sure of a thorough separation, pour the butter through cheesecloth or a paper coffee filter. Transfer it to a jar with a lid. Although clarified butter can be kept at room temperature, I usually store it in the refrigerator. It will keep more or less indefinitely and is useful to have on hand, particularly if you enjoy making curries and Moroccan dishes.

Brown Butter: If clarified butter is allowed to stay longer over the heat, it will eventually turn golden brown and take on a sweet, nutty aroma. Its flavor is wonderful with many vegetables and makes a nice change from the usual bath of melted butter.

To Brown Butter: Clarify the butter as described above; then return it to the pan and continue to heat it. More foam will rise to the surface, and the butter will begin to sound as if it's frying. Skim off the foam so that you can see the butter. When it turns golden brown, remove it from the heat and decant right away; it will continue to darken if it sits in the pan. Store it in a tightly covered jar. Refrigerated, it will keep more or less indefinitely.

CANNED CHICK-PEAS AND WHITE BEANS

The advantage of cooking your own legumes is that the broth is so useful in cooking, whereas the liquid that surrounds canned peas and beans is usually too salty to use. However, cooking your own requires forethought and planning, and sometimes we come home with neither and just want to eat. At such a moment canned beans can be a real help. Canned chick-peas can quickly be made into *hummus* or tossed into pasta, for an easy nutritious meal. The white beans can be combined with vegetables in a salad or cooked with greens for a warm side-dish, to give just a few examples. This is good emergency food.

CHEESES

Fontina: Italian Fontina is a semi-hard cheese from the Valle d'Aosta. Its taste is both sweet and nutty and its texture creamy and soft when left at room temperature. It's a fine cheese to place on the table at the end of a meal. The true Italian Fontina is expensive and not readily available outside of large cities. Danish Fontina is easier to find, although it is not such a fine cheese. It melts well when cooked and can be used in place of the Italian cheese when necessary.

Gorgonzola: A creamy-textured, mild (unless overripe) blue-veined Italian Gorgonzola has lots of character. Those who like blue-veined cheeses will undoubtedly enjoy this one. When combined with warm foods, like pasta, it melts and becomes intensely fragrant. It is also a good table cheese, wonderful with pears and walnuts. I usually use *dolcelatte*, a particularly sweet and mild Gorgonzola—like 'sweet milk,' as the Italian words suggest.

Parmesan and Parmigiano-Reggiano: Parmesan cheese is a hard, aged cow's milk cheese that always gives a special finish to pasta dishes and, often, soups. Although usually grated, it can also be sliced very thinly and served over grilled bread or vegetables. The term *Parmesan cheese* covers a wide range of cheeses made in that particular style; Parmigiano-Reggiano is the true Parmesan cheese from Parma. Its name is always stenciled in brown on the rind. It is aged at least two years, and its excellence is usually reflected in its high cost. I like to use it where its fine quality will be noticed and appreciated. Other times I use cheese sold as Parmesan or other hard cheeses, like Asiago, Romano and aged dry Monterey Jack. The flavors all differ in sharpness and depth and lend different qualities to the dishes they garnish. Buy these cheeses in hunks and grate them yourself.

CHIPOTLE CHILIES

These are jalapeño peppers that have been dried and smoked. They can be found in Mexican markets in 7-ounce cans, usually packed in a mild red *adobo* sauce. They are very hot, and just a little will convey both their heat and a delicious smoky flavor. They can be puréed and used just a spoonful at a time, made into a hot salsa or used right out of the can, roughly chopped. They are especially good with beans.

CREAM

Types of cream are referred to by different names in various parts of the country. Rather than attempting to accommodate each regional difference, I have limited myself to the use of the words "half-and-half" for light cream, and "cream" for heavy cream, including whipping cream. If you live where creams are distinguished by the amount of butterfat and labeled accordingly, you will be familiar with their properties in cooking and be able to choose accordingly what will work best for your taste. If you're planning to whip cream, you should use "heavy" or "whipping" cream; light cream will not whip.

FLOWERS

Flowers add beauty, scent, and flavor to food, and their bright, luminous colors are uplifting to the spirit. The practice of cooking with flowers is both old and new; it's been done since ancient times in many cultures and has recently been rediscovered.

Some flowers, like squash, cucumber, and pumpkin flowers, are meant to be cooked, literally stewed in butter or oil, mixed with eggs, used in quesadillas, and so forth. Others are candied—notably violet and rose petals, but also lilacs, orange and lemon blossoms, and acacia blooms. Their scents are preserved and absorbed by the sugar, and they can be used whole, as candied garnishes, or chopped and sprinkled over desserts.

Some flowers, such as nasturtiums, borage flowers, and any of the herbs when they're in bloom, have more peppery, herbal flavors and are wonderful used in salads.

Although flowers can be eaten, they aren't necessarily effective when placed whole on a plate. Is the diner supposed to dig into them with a knife and fork, ignore them, or what? Eating a whole flower often feels a little odd—they're soft and either slippery or furry. Unless they are very tiny blooms, flowers are most effective when they're slivered or cut into small pieces. That way their flavor still pervades, but the oddity of the texture doesn't overwhelm. When cutting flowers, treat them gently and cut them as cleanly as possible. Use a pair of scissors and snip them or use a sharp knife. Flower petals bruise easily, so use very deliberate moves when you cut; don't chop them as if they were parsley.

To prepare flowers, shake them several times to get rid of any little insects that might be inside. Then remove the stem, the base of the flower, and, if the flowers are large, the stamen and sepal. Small blossoms, like thyme flowers and rosemary blossoms, can simply be used whole. Flowers will keep for several days if kept in zip-lock bags and refrigerated.

Many flowers are edible, but some are not. Flowers that have been sprayed with insecticides, herbicides and fungicides should not be eaten—that includes flowers from the florist. Flowers growing by roadsides where they are likely to be covered with exhaust fumes shouldn't be eaten either. (This is also true for wild mushrooms and wild greens.) And some flowers shouldn't be eaten because they are poisonous. A few of the more common poisonous flowers are azalea and rhododendron, daffodil and narcissus, foxglove, hyacinth, iris, sweet pea, hydrangea, lupine, oleander, delphinium and larkspur, and plants of the nightshade family. Undoubtedly there are more dangerous plants than these, but there are so many safe ones, why not concentrate on them? Here are some that are especially pretty or tasty:

Hyssop and anise hyssop
Borage
Rosemary
Thyme
Various sages
Lavender
Red, golden, and culinary oregano
Scented geraniums
Chive, onion, and garlic blossoms
Cilantro (coriander)
Citrus flowers

Mustard blossoms or the flowers of any brassica
Nasturtium
Johnny-jump-ups, pansies and violets
Scarlet runner beans and other bean flowers (but not sweet peas)
Squash, cucumber, and pumpkin blossoms
Daylilies
Roses
Jamaica (hibiscus)
Calendulas
Sunflowers

GROUND RED CHILI

Chili powder is usually a blend of chilies, spices, herbs and garlic. Ground red chili, on the other hand, is just that—red chilies that have been finely ground. The flavor is more singular and very pure. You can make your own by grinding different varieties of dried chilies, but in many places it's possible to buy ground New Mexican chili, which is what I like to use. It's very fragrant and sweet, as well as hot. My favorite is from Chimayo. It comes in different degrees of hotness; mild is quite sufficient for most people. Look for it in natural foods stores, specialty stores, or through growers in New Mexico.

HERBS

Fresh herbs, more than any other single element in cooking, give life and sparkle to food. They can transform an ordinary dish into something special. And for me, one of the great pleasures of cooking is handling the aromatic leaves and blossoms of these plants and inhaling their perfumes.

Herbs are handsome, vigorous garden plants, tolerant of conditions that are often devastating to ornamentals: they suffer drought and love heat. Even in the adverse high altitudes of northern Arizona, I have managed to grow some herbs—different varieties of basil, dill, marjoram, chives, parsley, rosemary, sage, lovage, nasturtiums, tarragon, and thyme. Even though my harvest is small, it doesn't take vast quantities to make a difference; a little dill and parsley in a salad, a few basil leaves tossed with tomatoes, a small branch of lovage in a soup—all go a long way toward lifting a dish out of the mundane.

In addition to the pleasure of using fresh herbs from the garden, growing your own allows you to dry the excess harvest and use it throughout the winter months. Your own herbs will have a great deal more vitality and flavor than most commercially dried herbs; you'll be surprised. If you haven't a garden, try growing a few favorites on a sunny windowsill. Transplant the herbs into larger pots and let them mature a bit before snipping them; if you keep them in the little 2- or 4-inch containers they're sold in, they'll be used up in no time.

Herbs should be of particular interest to people whose diets are severely restricted. The strong aromatic flavors of herbs will help a great deal in giving life to food where fat and salt are missing.

Here are some herbs I enjoy and use throughout this book that may be unfamiliar.

Italian parsley: Also called flat-leaf parsley, this variety has much more flavor than the common curly-leaf parsley. The flavor is sweet, strong, and delicious. It is delightful to eat as a salad green, either in a parsley salad or torn up and tossed with lettuce. The large, flat leaves are a dark, glossy green. Although you don't always see it in stores, your grocer can get it if you ask. Plants and seeds can also be purchased. It is vigorous in the garden.

Lovage: This handsome perennial with large celerylike leaves is one of my favorite herbs. It has a wild taste, reminiscent of celery and parsley, and it is delicious with potatoes, tomatoes, corn, tossed into salads, or eaten in a sandwich. It takes just a few of the strong-tasting leaves to be effective. One plant should provide enough for everyone you know.

Scented Basils: Intensely spicy and aromatic, cinnamon basil is one of my favorites. Its perfume is very complex, an exotic mingling of mint, basil, clove, and cinnamon tones. It makes a harmonious addition to curries and Mexican dishes—in fact, I have seen this herb in Mexican markets.

Other scented basils include lemon, anise, and basil. They carry the flavors or color suggested by their names—hints of lemon and anise. Anise basil is also called Thai basil and is used in Thai cooking. The perfume of opal basil is closer to Italian basil, perhaps a little spicier, and the leaves are a beautiful deep plum or opal color. All of these basils make beautiful additions to vegetables and salads.

Rocket (Arugula): This pungent green is nutty and warm. As it matures it gets hotter. It makes a lively addition to salads and combines especially well with beets and hard-cooked eggs. It can also be cooked, included in soups or stewed and tossed with pasta. It's one of the easiest and most rewarding plants to grow, particularly for a beginner; it germinates in three days and shoots right up. Where the weather is hot, it's likely to bolt and flower within weeks. The crucifer-shaped flowers are creamy colored with violet or blood-red veins and they are lovely to use in salads as a garnish. Rocket is so easy to grow, you can just continually seed the bed to have a constant crop of tender young plants to replace the older ones, which are too hot for most tastes.

Sorrel: This perennial plant yields tender leaves that have a faint lemony taste and the sharp acid bite of lemon. Large volumes of leaves will cook down into a small, creamy purée. Although it may not look like much, even a little can brighten soups and sauces. Sorrel lends a shining note to salad greens and similarly brightens potato and egg dishes. Once it's in the ground, it's an easy plant to tend to. Although sorrel leaves can now be bought in supermarkets, they don't hold up well in their plastic bags and are often spoiled by the time they're sold. Better to find a plant or two and put them in the shady corner of your garden.

Rosemary: This hearty herb with its dark green, needle-like leaves is very assertive. Many people find the taste too strong, but when used judiciously, it can add a great deal to a dish, especially to mild-tasting foods like beans and potatoes. I often chop it finely and pound it with garlic and pepper to make a paste before adding it to a dish. Or a piece of a branch can be put in whole, then fished out when the flavor is strong enough. A few branches thrown on the coals will make a wonderful aromatic smoke for grilled foods, and the violet colored blossoms are lovely tossed in salads.

Sage: Like rosemary, the velvety grey-green sage leaves can be overpowering. They can also be delicious. The flavor of sage is frequently associated with the taste of stuffings and game; when used with beans, and potatoes, the association can often be evoked. A few leaves can deliciously flavor clarified butter or olive oil. I like sage in combination with rosemary and garlic. There are many different varieties of sage, but culinary sage is the one to use. If you're using dried sage, try to avoid the powdered variety and use whole leaves instead. Powdered sage always seems to have an unpleasant, musty taste.

Marjoram and Oregano: These two culinary herbs, which are closely related, are often associated with each other and sometimes given interchangeably in ingredient lists. Sometimes I use one in place of the other, depending on what's available. Fresh marjoram is sweet, mild, and as aromatic and summery as basil. Fresh oregano is much stronger and somewhat more harsh. Oregano is usually used dried; Greek and Mexican varieties are especially strong and aromatic. Marjoram is used dried or fresh, but it's best when fresh.

Thyme: Thyme is a constant herbal companion; it seems to go everywhere. It has an anchoring effect in a dish, bringing assorted flavors down to earth. A few branches plucked from the plant are always good added to the onion base of a dish. When in flower, the tiny pink blossoms make a beautiful garnish for plates of olives, peppers, and cheeses. Lemon thyme has a fresh, lemony scent and sounds a bright, uplifting note in salads.

OILS

I use many different oils for their flavors and their cooking properties. Oils are very important for conveying the tastes of herbs and spices to food, and they also have marvelous flavors and fragrances of their own. The better the quality of the oil you use, the more effective it will be and the less you will need. It is worthwhile to get to know different kinds of oils and use the best, particularly if you are concerned about fats but enjoy the taste of oil.

Olive Oil: This is the oil of the Mediterranean and the one used most often in this book. There is enormous diversity among olive oils, having to do with the country and region of origin, the type of olive and the process of manufacture. Extra-virgin olive oils (oils from the first pressings) from Greece, Spain, and southern Italy have big, strong flavors; Californian and Mexican olive oils are also aromatic but tend to be hot in the back of the throat. These oils are less costly than the fine, perfumed extra-virgin oils from Tuscany and Provence, but the olive flavor is full and pronounced. Your elegant, expensive estate-bottled extra-virgin olive oils are best used for finishing a dish—drizzling over pasta or soup or bathing a bowlful of garden beans—for the delicate balance of flavors is altered when these oils are heated directly over fire.

Until recently the words extra-virgin were hardly ever seen on a label. Instead the percentage of acidity was given. Now there's a proliferation of inexpensive oils all claiming to be extra-virgin—the same bottles I've always bought in the past with no such claim. Whether they really are, or whether their acidity has been chemically lowered, I don't know. It's hard to believe there's enough true extra-virgin olive oil to go around and at such low cost—and in fact, the quality varies greatly. When I call for olive oil, I mean your less expensive extra-virgin olive oil—a fragrant, everyday olive oil that you can cook with or use in a salad dressing, as opposed to a very costly finishing oil.

When choosing olive oil, look for oils that are full of aroma and flavor, with rich color ranging from green to gold and a taste you like. It's hard to recommend particular brands. New brands seem to be proliferating and it should be remembered that the quality of olive oil, like wine, varies from year to year. When I want the flavor of olives in a dish, I tend to use the Greek, Spanish, and Portuguese virgin olive oils. They are affordable and generally good. Extra-virgin oil from Tuscany or Provence is the oil I reserve for finishing a dish. Delicatessens, Greek or Italian markets, and specialty food shops are good places to look for different kinds of oils. Among the nationally distributed supermarket oils, Goya, Pompeian, Berio, and Bertolli are useful brands.

Pure olive oil, which is the most refined of the types of olive oils, has none of the character of oils from the first pressings, but it's useful when you want to use a neutral tasting oil, for a mayonnaise or to soften a slightly harsher but flavorful oil. It is referred to as "light" olive oil throughout the book.

Peanut Oil: The less refined the oil, the more obvious the presence, body, and character of the source. Roasted peanut oil bursts with the exquisite aroma of freshly roasted peanuts. It is clear, pure, and strong. It is good used both as a seasoning and to cook with. It gives extraordinary presence to Asian-inspired sauces and dressings. Although we tend to associate the flavor of peanut oil with Asian cuisine, it's equally delicious with Western seasonings. Tossed on green beans or asparagus with parsley and basil, it's sublime.

Roasted peanut oils, such as Lion and Globe, can be found in Chinese markets. According to Bruce Cost in his book *Asian Ingredients,* the most fragrant Chinese peanut oil comes in a red and gold gallon can with no English whatsoever on it except for the words "NET 2910 G." An excellent American peanut oil is manufactured by Loriva. It is absolutely delicious and comes in bottles that are much easier to handle than gallon cans.

Refined peanut oils, though practically without aroma, have their usefulness, too. Their neutrality makes them a good choice for mayonnaise or sautéing where a neutral flavor is desired, and their high smoke point makes them the oil to use for deep frying. Panther and Planters are both good cooking oils.

Walnut and Hazelnut Oils: Sniffing a freshly opened can of nut oil is quite a delight; it's as if a whole walnut or hazelnut orchardful of nuts is compressed in the can, waiting to be released. Nut oils are intensely fragrant and are intended to be used as a seasoning, not as cooking oils. They are highly unstable, tending quickly toward rancidity, and should be kept in the refrigerator once opened. They are expensive but generally go a long way.

Because of their soft, round flavors, walnut and hazelnut oils are especially suited to bitter greens—chicory, radicchio, curly endive, Belgian endive, and wild greens. They also go well with fruits, and the combination of pears or apples with greens, cracked nuts, and nut oils makes a wonderfully balanced dish. They can also be used to flavor a fresh herb cheese or a sweet, like walnut cookies. Walnut oil drizzled over a cooked dish adds an unusual finishing note.

The French nut oils are excellent—rich and full of flavor. With the exception of one American brand, Loriva's walnut and roasted hazelnut oils, our nut oils tend to be over-refined, thin, and pale, with only a memory of the original perfume. A good nut oil should be highly aromatic, have a rich amber hue, and have a rich feel in the mouth. One that looks light in the bottle probably won't have much taste.

Sesame Oil: Roasting sesame seeds before pressing them gives Asian sesame oil its dark color and intense fragrance. Rich and viscous, it is used principally as a flavoring, added to foods after they are cooked or used, often in combination with peanut oil, in sauces, marinades, and dressings. When exposed to high heat, the volatile flavor disintegrates and is lost. Dark sesame oils can be found in Japanese and Chinese markets or the Chinese section of most supermarkets.

Loriva makes a highly aromatic roasted sesame oil that has a lighter body and color than the Asian but all the warmth and flavor. It is delicious tossed with steamed or blanched vegetables. More highly processed sesame oils, with correspondingly little fragrance and body, can often be found in health food stores, but they are rather expensive and have little distinction.

Mustard Oil: Mustard oil is used in Indian cooking. It is highly aromatic, with an amber-golden hue. The oil explodes in the mouth with the bite of mustard and the hot tones of horseradish. In India it is favored for pickling and used for deep frying. I like to use it in salad dressings; its pungency enlivens food much the way adding a little minced chili to a dish brings all the flavors up and makes them sing. Mustard oil can be found in stores carrying Indian foods. Look for it in small bottles; a little goes a long way.

Canola and Safflower Oils: Both of these oils are ideal for cooking when the flavor of the oil should be as unobtrusive as possible. Canola oil, also called rapeseed oil, has long been favored in Europe because of its high smoke point, and it's becoming popular here because it's high in monounsaturates and Omega-3. Its flavor is neutral and non-interfering.

Safflower oil, when mechanically pressed at low temperatures, can have a subtle, warm, nutty taste. But usually it is very bland, which makes it a good, all-purpose oil that can be used in desserts as well as savory dishes. It is also a rich source of polyunsaturates.

Neutrality of flavor doesn't necessarily imply lack of character or quality. There is still the "feel" of the oil in the mouth. A good oil should be light in the mouth, roll unctuously over the tongue, and then disappear, leaving the mouth feeling clean. Inferior oils have an unpleasant, greasy feel that coats the mouth. All purpose vegetable oils generally have little taste and little character. Given all the other choices in oils, there's really no reason to use them.

SAFFLOWER STAMENS

Also called "false saffron," these look very much like extralong saffron threads. Cellophane packets of safflowers can be found in Mexican and Latin groceries. They cost a fraction of the price of true saffron and offer just a fraction of the flavor, but they lend a warm color to dishes and suggest some of the peculiar flower-pollen quality of saffron.

SAFFRON THREADS

Saffron, the stigma of a particular crocus flower, has a powerful, rich flavor that is unusual and captivating. It's not really like any other spice; it has the musky scent of pollen, and once the dried stigmas have been soaked in warm water, the penetrating aroma is released. The color is as pleasing as its taste—a rich, warm gold that stains everything it touches. Saffron is truly the touch of Midas.

Saffron is the most expensive spice in the world; fortunately just a few threads can be very effective in flavoring and coloring a soup, a rice dish, or pasta. It is also sold in powdered form, but I think there's more flavor in the threads; you can always powder them yourself by rubbing them between your fingers.

SALT

I prefer to use coarse and fine sea salt; its flavor is more complex and a little stronger than refined table salt. What kind and how much salt to use is a matter of personal preference and sometimes health concerns, so I have not included many precise salt measurements, except for baked goods. What is important is to use salt in each step of a dish—the sautéed vegetables, the sauce, the boiling water. Although you may feel like you're constantly adding salt, in the end you won't need to use so much, and each part of a dish will be sufficiently seasoned. The total effect will be quite different from that produced by simply adding a lot of salt at the end.

SICHUAN PEPPERCORNS

These are not true peppercorns, but the dried berries of another plant altogether. Reddish brown and flowerlike in appearance, they have a sweet, spicy flavor and a floral aroma. In the mouth they have a slightly numbing effect. Sichuan peppercorns can be found in Chinese markets, usually in small plastic or cellophane packages. If stored in a tightly closed jar, they will retain their potency more or less indefinitely.

SILKEN-FIRM TOFU

This tofu has a soft, silky texture, like *flan*. It is fragile and best used cut into cubes and included in a salad or served with a sauce. It is now sold in vacuum-packed boxes. The shelf life is long, and the need to pack the tofu in water is eliminated, making it possible to use the tofu right from the box without having to drain it and press out the water first.

UNSALTED PISTACHIO NUTS

These are the pistachio nuts to use in cooking since they haven't been salted. I usually find them in health food stores, at farmers' markets, and at fruit stands. They come either roasted or unroasted and both are delicious. The nuts are covered with a papery husk that can be removed fairly easily with a paring knife, especially when they're fresh. Underneath the husks the nuts are bright green on the outside, usually paler inside. They make a beautiful garnish for salads and desserts and are lovely included in sweet breads and cakes.

Special Dishes for Entertaining

These are some dishes that are particularly nice for special occasions with friends or family. A few, but not all of them, take a little extra time and effort. Almost all of the "Quick Bites" would make fine appetizers for a party.

Stuffed Pan Breads
Olive Bread
Cheese Bread
Saffron Crêpes

Cheese Stöllen
Cardamom Holiday Bread

Refined Green Salad with Herbs and Vegetables
Endive, Lemon Balm, and Violet Salad
Avocado and Papaya Salad with Mango Vinaigrette
Cucumber Mousse with Mustard Oil Vinaigrette
Celebration Salad with Blossom Confetti

Asparagus and Pea Velouté
Fennel Soup with Watercress Purée
Chestnut and Lentil Soup
Spring Vegetable Stew
Couscous with Winter Vegetables
Stewed Artichokes with Olives and Moroccan Spices

Saffron Butterflies with Basil and Peas
Capellini with Lemon and Basil
Pasta Soufflé with Mushroom Filling
Macaroni and Cheese
Wonton Ravioli

Artichokes and Peas with Sage
Garden Peas, New Onions, and Basil
Potato and Kale Gratin
Baked Endive with Gorgonzola Cream

Cheese Ramekins
Cheese Puffs (Gougère)

Grated Potato and Artichoke Cake
Skillet Potatoes with Sage and Taleggio Cheese

Food for Crowds

These recipes are good for crowds because they multiply easily, hold well and look good on a buffet table. The gratins and tians are especially easy to multiply and they look beautiful in their baking dishes.

Eggplant Spread with Yogurt and Herbs
White Cheese with Feta and Walnuts

Wild Rice and Asparagus Salad
Quinoa Salad with Dried Fruits and Pine Nuts
Celery-Apple Salad with Walnuts and Currants
Tomato Aspic with Saffron Cream

Cold Tomato Soup with Avocado and Lime
Winter Squash Soup with Cinnamon, Cloves, and Mint
Black Bean Soup for a Crowd
Squash, Pepper, and Hominy Stew
Mushrooms Flagstaff

Macaroni and Cheese
Cold Noodles with Peanut Sauce
Baked Rigatoni with Eggplant and Garlic Sauce

Potato and Kale Gratin
Baked Winter Squash with Spicy Moroccan Butter
Artichokes with Cilantro Salsa and Cumin
Roasted Onions with Sage

Anasazi Beans with Juniper
Red Bean and Rice "Soup"
White Beans with Escarole and Tomato
Cumin Rice with Eggplant and Peppers

Cheese Stöllen
Pear Coffee Cake
Cardamom Holiday Bread
Piñon Bread
Cheese Bread

Coeur à la Crème
Dorée's Extravagant Almond Cake

Dishes with Little or No Fat

Most of the dishes in this book use comparatively little oil or butter, and usually alternative or optional amounts are suggested, while other recipes make use of traditional amounts of butter and cream. Here are some dishes that are particularly low in fat.

Sabzee—Green Herb Sandwich
Eggplant Spread with Yogurt and Herbs
Yogurt Cheese

Oranges with Pickled Onions and Pomegranates
Quinoa Salad with Dried Fruits and Pine Nuts
Potato Salad with Tomatillo Sauce
Tomato Aspic with Saffron Cream

Barley-Buttermilk Soup
Cold Tomato Soup with Avocado and Lime
Sorrel-Lentil Soup
Bean, Corn, and Barley Soup
Black Bean Soup

Shredded Zucchini with Yogurt Sauce
Blanched Winter Vegetables with Thyme
Potato and Garlic Purée
Winter Vegetable Purée

Shells with Spinach and Chick-Peas
Wonton Ravioli
Fettuccine with Mushrooms and Dried Tomatoes

Asparagus with Peanut Oil, Shallots, and Parsley
Red Cabbage Braised in Wine
Artichokes, Dried Mushrooms and Potatoes, Baked in Clay

Anasazi Beans with Juniper
Potatoes Baked in Clay with Garlic and Herbs

Tomatillo-Avocado Salsa
Fast Tomato Sauce
Roasted Peppers
Pickled Red Onion Rings

Grilled Vegetables, when served with lemon or vinegar

Fresh Fruit Desserts
Ricotta Cream Cheese

Sources

Here are some mail-order sources for a number of ingredients I have suggested using that may not be available where you live.

DATES

Great Date in the Morning
PO Box 31
Coachella, CA 92236
619-398-6171
Many different kinds of fresh, organic dates, including black dates. Catalog available.

FLOURS (ORGANIC, STONE GROUND, WHOLE GRAIN)

Great Valley Mills
687 Mill Rd.
Telford, PA 18969
Catalog available upon written request; more than 20 different flours.

Walnut Acres
Penns Creek, PA 17862
717-847-0601
Flours, cereals, grains, good peanut butter, and other items. Catalog available.

NUTS AND DRIED FRUITS

Torn Ranch
1122 4th St.
San Rafael, CA 94941
Many dried fruits and nuts. Price list available.

Timber Crest Farms
4701 Dry Creek Rd.
Healdsburg, CA 95448
707-433-8251
Dried fruits and nuts. Price list available.

Reza Oghabian
8017 Stutz Ct.
Sacramento, CA 95828
916-689-5343
Pistachio nuts, unsalted and unroasted as well as shelled and dry roasted pistachio nuts flavored with garlic, chili, etc; pistachio butter; almonds. Write or call for price list.

OLIVES

Adams Ranch Gourmet Olives & Olive Oil
Bob Bente
P.O. Box 821
Meadow Vista, CA 95722
916-878-2143
Many varieties and styles of cured olives and California olive oil. Write or call for price list.

Peloponnese Products
Aegean Trader
PO Box 1015
Point Reyes Station, CA 94956
A variety of Greek olives, oils, and oregano.

SEED COMPANIES FOR HERBS AND VEGETABLES

Nichols Garden Nursery
1190 North Pacific Highway
Albany, OR 97321
Catalog available.

Shepherd's Garden Seeds
7389 W. Zayante Rd.
Felton, CA 95018
Catalog available.

SPECIALTY STORES FOR A VARIETY OF PRODUCTS

G. B. Ratto, International Grocers
821 Washington St.
Oakland, CA 94607
800-228-3515 in Calif.; 800-325-3483 outside Calif.
A wide variety of ethnic foods, including olive and walnut oils, vinegars, pistachio nuts and pine nuts, chestnut spread, parchment paper, vanilla beans, Loriva oil products, etc. Catalog available.

Dean & Deluca
560 Broadway
New York, NY 10012
212-431-1691
Wide variety of specialty products on the East Coast, including oils, dried mushrooms, orange flower and rose water, French lentils, dried fennel.

Williams-Sonoma
PO Box 7456
San Francisco, CA 94120-7456
Specialty food items and kitchen equipment. Stores throughout the country. Catalog available.

NEW MEXICAN PRODUCTS

M & S Produce
PO Box 220
Alcalde, NM 87511
505-852-4368
Ground corn flour, posole, New Mexican chili. Price list available.

CHINESE PRODUCTS

There are Chinese markets throughout the country, and many supermarkets carry a limited selection of Chinese noodles and sesame oils. It's probably possible to find the few Chinese ingredients I've suggested near where you live, but here's one store that has a catalog, does ship and is, according to Chinese cookbook author Barbara Tropp, very reliable:

The Chinese Grocer
209 Post St. at Grant Ave.
San Francisco, CA 94108
415-982-0125 or 800-227-3320

Bibliography

Al Buona Cucina. *Formaggi Cotti e Crudi*. Roma: Curcio Periodici S.P.A. (date unknown).

Barry, Naomi, and Bellini, Beppe. *Firenze in Padella*. Bologna: Poligrafici Consoline & Co., 1969.

Brennan, Georgeanne, et al. *The New American Vegetable Cookbook*. Berkeley: Aris Books, 1985.

Cosman, Madeleine P. *Fabulous Feasts: Medieval Cookery and Ceremony*. New York: George Braziller, 1976.

Cost, Bruce. *Bruce Cost's Asian Ingredients: Buying and Cooking the Staple Foods of China, Japan and Southeast Asia*. New York: Morrow, 1988.

David, Elizabeth. *An Omelette and a Glass of Wine*. New York: Viking, 1985.

———. *Spices, Salts and Aromatics in the English Kitchen*. London: Penguin Books, 1970.

Eren, Neşet. *The Art of Turkish Cooking*. New York: Doubleday, 1969.

Escudier, Jean-Noel, and Fuller, Peta J. *The Wonderful Food of Provence*. Boston: Houghton Mifflin Company, 1968.

The Fannie Farmer Cook Book. Revised by Marion Cunningham. New York: Alfred A. Knopf, 1982.

Field, Carol. *The Italian Baker*. New York: Harper and Row, 1985.

Gray, Patience. *Honey from a Weed: Fasting and Feasting in Tuscany, California, the Cyclades, and Apulia*. New York: Harper and Row, 1987.

Grigson, Jane. *Jane Grigson's Fruit Book*. New York: Atheneum, 1982.

———. *Jane Grigson's Vegetable Book*. New York: Atheneum, 1979.

Jaffrey, Madhur. *An Invitation to Indian Cooking*. New York: Random House, 1975.

Kavena, Juanita Tiger. *Hopi Cookery*. Tucson: University of Arizona Press, 1980.

Kennedy, Diana. *The Cuisines of Mexico*. New York: Harper and Row, 1972.

LaPlace, Viana, and Kleiman, Evan. *Cucina Fresca*. New York: Harper and Row, 1985.

Larkcom, Joy. *The Salad Garden: Salads from Seed to Table; A Complete, Illustrated, Year-Round Guide*. New York: Viking, 1984.

Levy, Faye. *Fresh from France: Vegetable Creations*. New York: E. P. Dutton, 1987.

Luard, Elisabeth. *The Old World Kitchen: The Rich Tradition of European Peasant Cooking*. New York: Bantam, 1987.

MacNicol, Mary. *Flower Cookery, The Art of Cooking with Flowers*. New York: Fleet Press Corporation, 1967.

Madison, Deborah, and Brown, Edward E. *The Greens Cookbook*. New York: Bantam, 1987.

McGee, Harold. *On Food and Cooking: The Science and Lore of the Kitchen*. New York: Charles Scribner's Sons, 1984.

Mondadori, Arnoldo, ed. *Feast of Italy*. New York: Thomas Y. Crowell, 1973.

Olney, Richard. *The Good Cook: Technique and Recipes*. Alexandria, Va.: Time-Life Books, 1979.

———. *Simple French Food*. New York: Atheneum, 1974.

Quintana, Patricia, and Orme, William A., Jr. *The Taste of Mexico*. New York: Stewart, Tabori & Chang, 1986.

Rattazzi, Llaria. *Tante Cose con Il Pane*. Milano: Fratelli Fabbri, 1978.

Ross, Janet, and Waterfield, Michael. *Leaves from Our Tuscan Kitchen*. New York: Vintage Books, 1975.

Sahni, Julie. *Classic Indian Cooking*. New York: William Morrow and Company, 1980.

Schneider, Elizabeth. *Uncommon Fruits and Vegetables: A Commonsense Guide*. New York: Harper and Row, 1986.

Seymour, John. *The Self-Sufficient Gardener: A Complete Guide to Growing and Preserving All Your Own Food*. New York: Dolphin Books, 1978.

Shere, Lindsey Remolif. *Chez Panisse Desserts*. New York: Random House, 1985.

Simon, Andre L. (director). *A Concise Encyclopaedia of Gastronomy, Section III, Vegetables*, Great Britain: Curwen Press, 1941.

Solomon, Jon, and Solomon, Julia. *Ancient Roman Feasts and Recipes: Adapted for Modern Cooking*. Miami, Fla.: E. A. Seemann Publishing, Inc. 1950.

Thomas, Anna. *The Vegetarian Epicure*. New York: Vintage Books, 1972.

Tropp, Barbara. *The Modern Art of Chinese Cooking*. New York: William Morrow and Company, 1982.

Wechsberg, Joseph. *Blue Trout and Black Truffles*. New York: Alfred A. Knopf, 1966.

Willan, Anne. *French Regional Cooking*. New York: William Morrow and Company, 1981.

Witty, Helen, and Colchie, Elizabeth Schneider. *Better than Store-Bought*. New York: Harper and Row, 1979.

Wolfert, Paula. *Couscous and Other Good Food from Morocco*. New York: Harper and Row, 1973.

———. *Paula Wolfert's World of Food: A Collection of Recipes from Her Kitchen, Travels and Friends*. New York: Harper and Row, 1988.

Wright, Jeni. *The Encyclopedia of Italian Cooking*. London: Octopus Books, 1981.

Yianilos, Theresa Karas. *The Complete Greek Cookbook*. New York: Funk and Wagnalls, 1970.

Zane, Eva. *Greek Cooking for the Gods*. San Francisco: 101 Productions, 1970.

Index

Metric Conversion Chart

CONVERSIONS OF OUNCES TO GRAMS

Ounces	Grams	Ounces	Grams
1 oz	30 g*	11 oz	300 g
2 oz	60 g	12 oz	340 g
3 oz	85 g	13 oz	370 g
4 oz	115 g	14 oz	400 g
5 oz	140 g	15 oz	425 g
6 oz	180 g	16 oz	450 g
7 oz	200 g	20 oz	570 g
8 oz	225 g	24 oz	680 g
9 oz	250 g	28 oz	790 g
10 oz	285 g	32 oz	900 g

*Approximate. To convert ounces to grams, multiply number of ounces by 28.35.

CONVERSIONS OF POUNDS TO GRAMS AND KILOGRAMS

Pounds	Grams; Kilograms	Pounds	Grams; Kilograms
1 lb	450 g*	5 lb	2¼ kg
1¼ lb	565 g	5½ lb	2½ kg
1½ lb	675 g	6 lb	2¾ kg
1¾ lb	800 g	6½ lb	3 kg
2 lb	900 g	7 lb	3¼ kg
2½ lb	1,125 g; 1¼ kg	7½ lb	3½ kg
3 lb	1,350 g	8 lb	3¾ kg
3½ lb	1,500 g; 1½ kg	9 lb	4 kg
4 lb	1,800 g	10 lb	4½ kg
4½ lb	2 kg		

*Approximate. To convert pounds into kilograms, multiply number of pounds by 453.6.

CONVERSIONS OF INCHES TO CENTIMETERS

Inches	Centimeters	Inches	Centimeters	Inches	Centimeters	Inches	Centimeters
¹⁄₁₆ in	¼ cm*	4¼ in	11½ cm	10 in	25 cm	21 in	53 cm
⅛ in	½ cm	5 in	13 cm	11 in	28 cm	22 in	56 cm
½ in	1½ cm	5½ in	14 cm	12 in	30 cm	23 in	58 cm
¾ in	2 cm	6 in	15 cm	13 in	33 cm	24 in	61 cm
1 in	2½ cm	6½ in	16½ cm	14 in	35 cm	25 in	63½ cm
1½ in	4 cm	7 in	18 cm	15 in	38 cm	30 in	76 cm
2 in	5 cm	7½ in	19 cm	16 in	41 cm	35 in	89 cm
2½ in	6½ cm	8 in	20 cm	17 in	43 cm	40 in	102 cm
3 in	8 cm	8½ in	21½ cm	18 in	46 cm	45 in	114 cm
3½ in	9 cm	9 in	23 cm	19 in	48 cm	50 in	127 cm
4 in	10 cm	9½ in	24 cm	20 in	51 cm		

*Approximate. To convert inches to centimeters, multiply number of inches by 2.54.

CONVERSIONS OF FAHRENHEIT TO CELSIUS

Fahrenheit	Celsius	Fahrenheit	Celsius
170°F	77°C*	375°F	190°C
180°F	82°C	400°F	205°C
190°F	88°C	425°F	220°C
200°F	95°C	450°F	230°C
225°F	110°C	475°F	245°C
250°F	120°C	500°F	260°C
300°F	150°C	525°F	275°C
325°F	165°C	550°F	290°C
350°F	180°C		

*Approximate. To convert Fahrenheit to Celsius, subtract 32, multiply by 5, then divide by 9.

CONVERSIONS OF QUARTS TO LITERS

Quarts	Liters	Quarts	Liters
1 qt	1 L*	8 qt	7½ L
1½ qt	1½ L	9 qt	8½ L
2 qt	2 L	10 qt	9½ L
2½ qt	2½ L		
3 qt	2¾ L		
4 qt	3¾ L		
5 qt	4¾ L		
6 qt	5½ L		
7 qt	6½ L		

*Approximate. To convert quarts to liters, multiply number of quarts by 0.95.